Empires of God

EMPIRES OF GOD

*Religious Encounters
in the Early Modern Atlantic*

Edited by

LINDA GREGERSON
and SUSAN JUSTER

PENN

UNIVERSITY OF PENNSYLVANIA PRESS

PHILADELPHIA

Copyright © 2011 University of Pennsylvania Press

Published by
University of Pennsylvania Press
Philadelphia, Pennsylvania 19104-4112
www.upenn.edu/pennpress

Printed in the United States of America on acid-free paper
2 4 6 8 10 9 7 5 3 1

Library of Congress Cataloging-in-Publication Data

Empires of God : religious encounters in the early modern
Atlantic / edited by Linda Gregerson and Susan Juster.
    p. cm.
Includes bibliographical references (p.   ) and index.
ISBN 978-0-8122-4289-8 (hardcover : alk. paper)
    1. America—Church history. 2. Great Britain—Colonies—
America—Religion. 3. France—Colonies—America—
Religion. 4. Spain—Colonies—America—Religion. I.
Gregerson, Linda. II. Juster, Susan.
    BR500.E46 2011
    277.3'06—dc22
                                    2010028882

To Carroll Smith-Rosenberg

CONTENTS

PART III. VIOLENT ENCOUNTERS

FINAL REFLECTIONS:

INTRODUCTION

Susan Juster and Linda Gregerson

The Bible was the foremost travel guide in modern European history. With its tales of the rise and fall of great empires devoted to rival gods, of religious seekers driven from their homes in search of elusive Promised Lands, of the marvelous and monstrous wonders lying just beyond the borders of the known world, the Old Testament provided a vivid template for the explorations and conquests of the great European Age of Discovery. Packed alongside the exquisite maps and navigational instruments that made overseas travel possible in the fifteenth and sixteenth centuries, Bibles were part and parcel of the Christian explorer's essential travel kit. And as vernacular Bibles proliferated during the course of the Reformation, the narratives of exploration and conquest expanded to include not only Latin and Hebrew but also English, Dutch, German, French, and—eventually—Natick, Mohawk, and other native American languages.

The intimate connection between religious and political narratives of discovery and resettlement in the early modern Atlantic world is the key insight that organizes this book.[1] Much like the armchair travel writers of the sixteenth and seventeenth centuries, we invite readers to explore New World encounters both familiar and strange, with spiritual narratives—many, though not all, derived from the Bible and the attendant devotional literature of western Christendom—fixed firmly in mind. It is no exaggeration to say that religious passions and conflicts drove much of the expansionist energy of post-Reformation Europe: they provided both a rationale and a practical mode of organizing the dispersal and resettlement of hundreds of thousands of people from the Old World to the New. Exhortations to conquer new peoples and lands in the name of God were the lingua franca of western imperialism. Tempting as it is to dismiss these missionary calls to empire as cynical and obfuscating, the scholarship of the past twenty years has established firmly the genuine spiritual aspirations that drove men like the mystically inclined Christopher Columbus to risk their lives and their fortunes to bring the gospel to the Americas. And in the thousands of religious refugees seeking asylum from the vicious wars of religion that tore the continent apart in the sixteenth and seventeenth centuries, these visionary explorers found a ready pool of migrants equally willing to risk life and limb for a chance to worship God in their own way. English Puritans and Quakers, French Huguenots, German Moravians, Scots-Irish Presbyterians—all constituted a significant fraction of the human cargo that was transported to New World colonies in ships bearing such names as *Hopewell*. Financed directly and indirectly by Europe's great powers, entangled as they invariably were in national drives for political and material dominance, imperial ventures in the New World were also foundationally shaped by the will to enlarge the international borders of competing Protestant and Catholic domains.

Religion was thus an ideological spur and recruiting ground for imperial aspirations. The link between religion and empire can be described in several ways: as a *causal* relationship (the story of how religion helped drive New World empires and how imperial ambition helped drive the expansionary or diasporic topography of religion), as an *oppositional* relationship (the story of how religious and imperial agendas undermined or compromised one another), as a *dialectical* relationship (the story of how religious and imperial aspirations mutually constituted one another), or as a more diffuse *affiliative* relationship (the story of how religious and imperial projects came to resemble one another in form and function). The ideological and commercial fervor of those agents of expansion (joint-stock companies, speculators, adventurers, missionaries, soldiers of fortune) who promoted the empire as a sure path to glory for God and King transformed imperialism from an accidental conjunction of historical forces into a rationalized blueprint for global supremacy. From their ad-hoc and often chaotic beginnings Atlantic empires took on the structures, ideologies, and moral imperatives of organized religion, functioning as a kind of parallel universe to the confessional apparatus of missions, pilgrimages, conversion narratives, and martyr tales erected in post-Reformation Europe. If empires often functioned as religions in the early modern era, religions created their own empires in turn. Western Christendom and Islam squared off in a contest for dominion over southeastern Europe, the Mediterranean, and North Africa following the reconquest of the Iberian peninsula in the fifteenth century. The presence of an aggressive, expansionist Ottoman Empire on the edges of eastern Europe set in motion much of the scramble for territories and resources that consumed the Christian powers in the sixteenth and seventeenth centuries. Muslim slaves were sold in American plantations, while captive Europeans toiled in the ports of the Barbary coast—a concrete example of how intertwined the Muslim and the Christian worlds were in the age of Atlantic empires.[2] While western Christianity is the focus of this volume, the shadow of rival imperial gods is apparent in several of the essays.

Whichever term comes first, and in whichever direction one draws the causal and affiliative links, religion and empire were the constitutive forces of nation building, economic expansion, and identity formation in the early modern era. A disciplinary divide lurks beneath the different approaches that have governed recent scholarship in the field: historians are much more comfortable arguing causality than are literary scholars, whereas the latter excel in uncovering the homologies that bind disparate phenomena together. One goal of this collection is to signal the disciplinary barriers that constrain truly interdisciplinary scholarship as well as the common analytical ground and investigative opportunities literary and historical studies can illuminate for one another. We have pursued this goal in part by means of juxtaposition (presenting literary and historical essays side by side under a common rubric) but also by asking our contributors to think explicitly and comparatively about the ways their own disciplinary training has shaped their approach to our subject. The theme of multidisciplinarity, in other words, runs through many of the essays as well as connecting the volume as a whole.

Another contribution of the volume is to bring scholars of the major New World empires together around a common set of questions. The comparative study of empire is thriving today in the academy, as historians and literary scholars ask (to cite just a few examples) how the experience of slavery differed in the Spanish and English colonies; how legal codes and jurisprudential assumptions about the relationship of law to society shaped colonial governance in New France and the British colonies; how the literature of discovery and conquest provided an intertextual frame of reference that guided stockholders and adventurers in their various Atlantic voyages; how gender roles, domestic arrangements, economic systems, and patterns of child rearing gave rise to distinct New World societies across the Atlantic littoral. With their command of multiple textual fields and their interest in tracing structures of meaning rather than originary moments, literary scholars have perhaps been more adventurous in pursuing a transnational vision of colonialism: certainly the work of Stephen Greenblatt, Anthony Pagden, and Tzvetan Todorov, among others, has been seminal for historians and literary scholars alike.[3] But historians of empire, such as J. H. Elliott, Robin Blackburn, and Hugh Thomas, have also in recent years provided a broad road map of comparative analysis around the themes of migration, slavery, and state formation upon which to build a sturdy comparative history of particular trends and developments.[4]

The authors gathered together here—literary scholars and historians who study the imperial ventures and sectarian dislocations of English-, French-, Spanish-, and German-speaking peoples—focus on the formative period of European exploration, conquest, and settlement in the Americas, from roughly 1500 to 1760. Emerging from their investigations of the dynamic expansion, fragmentation, and dispersal of religious communities and ideas in the sixteenth and seventeenth centuries are several interrelated themes: the material life of religious and cultural affiliation in Old and New World settings—its instantiation in texts and people; the linguistic and cultural practices of translation whereby Europeans and natives tried to make sense of one another's spiritual, domestic, and political systems; and the tension between theory and practice in the creative adaptation of Old World forms to New World realities. Binding all the essays together, regardless of disciplinary conventions or analytical orientation, is a firm commitment to historical inquiry. Each examination, each chosen facet of the interconnection between religion and empire, is firmly situated in time and space. Some of the essays focus on specific material objects (a book of martyr tales, a wood-splint basket, church buildings, and rosaries); others on individual lives (a French Jesuit, an Ursuline nun, and an anonymous Algonquian woman), individual texts (a German-language almanac, an English catechism for Indian converts), or local sites (Mexico City in the 1600s); yet others on key moments in the history of imperial practice and justification (a staged debate in the Spanish court of 1550). This interest in the particularistic has been, paradoxically, one of the unintended benefits of the Atlantic turn in early modern scholarship. The "Atlantic" has come to stand for a perspective that straddles the local and the global, bringing together on-the-ground investigations of the lived experiences of people and goods "on the move" with hemispheric considerations of the larger structural forces that constrained individual choice and collective action.[5]

Most broadly, the volume explores the power of religious narratives as templates for empire. Quite aside from its ideological and organizational prowess, religion provided a discursive map of opportunities and perils that guided the post-Reformation state and its various agents in their overseas endeavors. By "narratives" we mean more than the story lines found in the Christian canon, though these were obviously crucial sources of inspiration and guidance for New World migrants: we also mean the more elusive if no less potent schemas that framed the private and public quests for spiritual perfection of Reformation-era Christians. The core drama of Exodus fired the wanderlust of Europe's pilgrims, who liked to fashion themselves "New Israelites" in search of New Jerusalems, and elements of this narrative found their way into a remarkable array of personal and official accounts of missions to the Americas. New candidates for the role of Moses, from the conquistador Hernán Cortés to the Puritan divine John Cotton, stepped up to lead messianic expeditions; evil Pharaohs, mostly of Iberian or Hapsburg origin, harassed godly voyagers at every turn; wilderness wanderings, of varying duration and severity, afflicted the faithful on their voyage to the Promised Land.

The prophetic books provided another popular script for European empire builders. The great Iberian empires were preoccupied with the eschatological possibilities of their American colonies: that Spain in a single year had defeated the Moors of Granada and expelled the peninsula's long-established Jewish community famously inspired Christopher Columbus to launch his search for a northwest passage and prompted his patron Ferdinand to style himself the king of a revived Jerusalem.[6] Far to the north, Spain's confessional enemy, the Calvinist Dutch General States, consulted a local prophet before launching their own western design in the 1620s in defiance of the eschatological pretensions of the Hapsburgs. The millennial promise that the conversion of the Jews would usher in the Second Coming was translated by English and French missionaries into a mandate to convert the Indians of North America, the putative "lost tribe of Israel."[7] Biblical narratives of expulsion, salvation, and the apocalypse were thus deeply embedded in early modern imperial projects.

The literature of exploration and conquest, building upon this scriptural foundation, soon created its own enduring narratives, which functioned as a secular bible for European expansion. Specifically, tales of captivity and redemption, which circulated widely throughout the Atlantic, translated the scriptural drama of sin and salvation into a more expansive template that could be applied to diverse peoples and settings. Modeled on martyr tales— the emblematic Reformation story—the captivity narrative became the emblematic tale of empire in the sixteenth and seventeenth centuries.[8] Produced in many European languages and circulated widely throughout the Atlantic world, these captivity tales told the story of imperial aggression and conquest through the trials and tribulations of ordinary people caught up in webs of empire. Sailors, vagabonds, orphans, and the other social detritus of early modern capitalism, along with farm wives, ship captains, missionaries, and the occasional government official, found themselves forcibly exposed to new faiths and cultures in ways that sorely tested their personal convictions and confessional loyalties. Some converted, some escaped and lived to tell the tale, some became pawns of international politics and were ransomed or exchanged for fellow prisoners; many—perhaps most—died alone in a strange land. While the literature of captivity produced by the lucky few who made it home resembles a hodgepodge of literary genres from the picaresque to the sermonic, the theme of redemption—from slavery and sin—that runs through the entire corpus made these stories effective religious allegories of empire. The most famous of these texts in the Anglophone world (Mary Rowlandson's *The Sovereignty and Goodness of God*, 1682) posits the heroine as the personification of the Puritan "errand into the wilderness," whose triumph over her barbaric and heathen captors heralds the ultimate victory of reformed Christianity in the New World. For others, spiritual triumph came in the form of a heroic death at the hands of infidels—a form of colonial martyrdom at which the Catholic missionaries, especially the Jesuits, excelled.[9] Whether dead or alive, captives were living reminders that empire was a dangerous and violent enterprise.

The emphasis on narratives both formal and unwritten that threads through so many of the essays collected here builds on another key insight of literary critics: that the conquest of the Americas was as much a linguistic as a political or military venture, or rather, that language itself, like other technologies of settlement and expansion, is among the political instruments of empire. What scholars call the "literal advantage" of the European newcomers—the ability to think and act through the written word—proved a potent weapon for appropriating or occluding native cultures in the service of church and state.[10] The "literal advantage" meant not just that the European conquerors had the tools of scribal culture at their disposal (vital records, law codes, administrative rules and regulations, instruments of credit and exchange, property deeds, etc.), but more broadly that possession of native lands was accompanied by translational practices that forced indigenous beliefs and practices into strange, new, and profoundly alienating discursive forms. Acts of territorial *possession*, in other words, became through the strategic deployment of literacy simultaneous acts of linguistic and cultural *dispossession*—a kind of conquest by semiotics. Nothing illustrates this double-edged threat better than the *requerimiento,* the supreme ceremony of possession enacted by the Spanish conquistadors, in which a document confirming Spanish ownership of land was read aloud to peoples who could neither understand the words nor respond in kind with a written counter-narrative. Such mystification of alphabetic writing constituted a kind of power that was at once deeply cynical and profoundly distorting for the practice of history itself.[11] The very notion that a people "without writing" deserve to be destroyed was one of the most damning legacies of colonization, coexisting darkly alongside appeals to convert the natives through the saving power of the Word.

At its most basic, evangelization of the New World involved translating devotional texts and acts from one language, one cosmology, to another, an enterprise fraught with misreadings both deliberate and inadvertent. The Indian Library of the Puritan evangelist John Eliot (including an Algonquian-language Bible, the first vernacular Bible printed in the Americas) was a monumental achievement of literary translation, its ambition matched only by the magnitude of its inefficacy.[12] Eliot's Algonquian Bible (1663) was followed by the German emigrant Christoph Saur's German-language version in 1743. Protestant empires naturally promoted translation projects more vigorously than did their Catholic counterparts, but even within New Spain native-language devotional texts began to appear in the sixteenth century.[13] Beyond these literal translations of Christian texts, missionary outreach entailed a series of more intricate cultural translations that often cut to the heart of indigenous traditions and beliefs. Cultural anthropologists and historians have excavated a rich world of syncretic religious practices that blended Christian, Islamic, and indigenous spiritual elements into a captivating (sometimes toxic) brew. The concept of syncretism has come in for a fair amount of criticism recently[14] but retains, we would argue, real usefulness, provided we keep firmly in mind that the process was contestatory, partial, and, sometimes, subject to cynical manipulation. Translation went both ways: Catholic saints were incorporated into the pantheon of native American gods, while elements of indigenous ritual practice found their way into Christian devotionalism.[15]

As in any act of translation, much was lost or destroyed along the way. The role of violence in the colonial encounter is another major theme explored in the volume—violence both physical and hermeneutic. The "darker side of the Renaissance" (in Walter Mignolo's phrasing) encompasses the violence done in word and deed, or rather *through* word and deed, as Europe pursued its quest for knowledge and dominion over new territories and realms of experience.[16] The question posed by one provocative study of Indian warfare in colonial New England ("can literacy kill?") has been answered in the affirmative by literary scholars and historians impressed by the distinctly materialist theory of language espoused by early modern men and women.[17] Of course, disputes over words and texts had constituted the front lines of theological warfare since the beginning of the Reformation, but with the aggressive mapping of confessional hostilities onto the lands and peoples of the New World, the battle to root out false gods took a new and deadlier turn. By 1570 New Spain had its own Inquisition, and campaigns to extirpate idolatry were in full swing from Peru to Mexico.[18] Lacking the institutional power of a formal Inquisition, the efforts of British and French colonies to dismantle native "devil-worship" and replace it with true gospel order were perhaps less systematic but no less determined. The Bible, here as elsewhere, was both muse and how-to manual: for example, the Old Testament story of the destruction of the Amalekites became, in the hands of New World colonizers, a scriptural warrant for spiritual genocide. The fiery Boston minister Cotton Mather summoned Amalek to rally his fellow Puritans to a holy war against the Indians in 1698: "Turn not back till they are consumed," urged Mather. "Tho' they Cry; Let there be none to Save them; But beat them small as the Dust before the Wind."[19] The rhetoric of extermination usually exceeded the actual ability of colonial authorities to destroy native populations, at least outside of New Spain, but endlessly repeated, such prophecies of biblical vengeance became yet another weapon—maybe the most potent of all—in the arsenal of "violent evangelism."[20]

From hopeful tales of new beginnings to horrific stories of enemies vanquished, the narratives that guided European explorers and settlers on their journeys to the New World bespoke a world saturated with spiritual meaning. By harnessing the distinctive skills of literary critics and historians as they reexamine some of the critical texts and exemplary forms of cultural encounter in the early modern Atlantic world, this volume seeks to understand how spiritual narratives became templates for empire. In the spirit of multidisciplinary, comparative scholarship, we have organized the volume into three sections: Launching Imperial Projects, Colonial Accommodations, Violent Encounters, with final reflections on empire and its end. We begin with four essays that explore key originary moments in Iberian and English imperialism. In "The Polemics of Possession: Spain on America, Circa 1550," Rolena Adorno contributes a probing analysis of written and oral debates between royal chronicler Juan Ginés de Sepúlveda and Dominican friar Bartolomé de las Casas in mid-sixteenth-century Spain. The question of how to carry out Christianization, conquest, and the imposition of governance in foreign territories had been debated in the Spanish court since the days of Ferdinand and Isabella, whose New World claims had been underwritten by papal bulls of donation. Some six decades later, when the major conquests of the Aztec federation in Mexico and the Inca empire in the Andes had already occurred, Charles V called for a new, formal consideration of the rights to foreign conquest. When Sepúlveda and Las Casas accordingly convened in the university city of Valladolid, the burden of their debates was this: is it legitimate to make war on America's native populations in order to evangelize them? Underpinning this core debate were foundational issues of guardianship, dominion, "natural slavery," the legitimate uses of force, and the elusive distinctions between property and possession, imposition and consent.

In her chapter, Carla Gardina Pestana adopts a comparative historical approach to reexamine the geopolitical struggles between England, Spain, and Holland for control of the colonies of Jamaica and New Netherland, struggles that redrew the boundaries of confessional identity in the New World. Prompted by the recent wars of conquest and determined to justify territorial aggression in the language of "just war" theory, English apologists began to subsume both old and new enemies (Catholic Spain and Calvinist Holland) under a common rubric: that of the religious tyrant. The association of Roman Catholicism with cruelty, which had been given new life by the tales of Spanish depredations in the West Indies, was creatively reworked to encompass Dutch resistance to English claims of a common Calvinist heritage. Pestana shows how politicians and playwrights alike constructed an image of Dutch cruelty that mapped onto, and in the process transformed, old Reformation-era antinomies.

For Barbara Fuchs as well, the focus is on England's fraught and belated entry into New World empire, but she introduces the lens of national and confessional identity formation. Observing that England's understanding of its own place in the transatlantic world was deeply indebted to Spain, Fuchs argues that the deliberate use of religious difference to distinguish England's imperial project from that of its Spanish rivals vastly overstated the actual ideological divide. In an effort to recover the contemporary confusion of confessional and imperial identities, Fuchs turns not to official formulations of religious doctrine and state policy but to the texts in which speculative and documentary imagination mingle: to real and imaginary encounter narratives, travel literature, and national epic. A central example is the account, in Richard Hakluyt, of a young English boy abandoned in New Spain and forced to navigate his survival in a Catholic context. Crucially, Fuchs suggests that religious difference is often far more tactical and situated than we have tended to recognize.

Turning to the Bible commonwealths of Puritan New England, Linda Gregerson examines the devotional, epistemological, financial, and technological conundrums that underlay the monumental task of proselytizing among the Algonquian Indians. She examines a series of promotional pamphlets published in seventeenth-century London on behalf of the New England mission. At a time when metropolitan England was wracked by civil war, the establishment and collapse of a Commonwealth, and the abolition and restoration of monarchy, these pamphlets sought to encourage both material and psychic investment in a tiny, emergent population of coreligionists on the other side of the Atlantic. Of particular interest to Gregerson are those sections of the pamphlets that purport to document the spiritual progress of the "praying Indians" by transcribing the questions they have addressed to their missionary teacher. To a twenty-first-century reader, these questions seem to contain a devastating cultural and political critique of proselytizing Christianity itself. Gregerson asks, whose voices are we really hearing in these transcriptions and catechistical exchanges? And what can they tell us about the structure of faith and community?

Part II tells particular stories about colonial accommodations in specific settings. The essays gathered here look at the dynamics of loss, longing, and mimesis among the agents of empire, the fugitives from religious persecution, the missionaries, and their converts alike. Mobility was the common thread that bound together all actors in the early modern Atlantic world, a movement often figured in the literature of exploration as a reenactment of core domestic dramas—of youthful rejections and prodigal returns, for example, or of sexual repression and transgression.[21] The themes of alienation and domestication surface in many travelers' accounts of their journeys, as the familiar is repudiated and the exotic embraced and tamed.

The salient unit of analysis in Cornelius Conover's essay is the city or municipality. Examining municipal devotions in seventeenth-century Mexico City, Conover proposes a key revision to our understanding of the affective allegiance generated as the Catholic liturgy was adapted to New World settings. The local identity fostered by the canonization and liturgical incorporation of New World saints has habitually been understood as laying the foundation for autonomous political consciousness. But Conover discerns another pattern. Tracing the aggressive Spanish policy promoting canonization and liturgical recognition of holy figures from their far-flung territories, as well as the complex rivalry for metropolitan recognition among colonial municipalities, Conover argues that seventeenth-century liturgical transformations tended to reinforce rather than to loosen ties between colonial cities and the Spanish crown. Instead of identifying a smooth progression along a binary spectrum from colonial dependence to post-colonial autonomy, in other words, Conover describes a fascinating series of triangulations, where an appeal to the Spanish crown can remedy perceived neglect from Rome and competition with a fellow colonial state can be of more immediate importance than the longing for independence that modern scholars are prepared to find. For a time at least, Mexico City constituted itself as a religious "home" by collaborating on the shift from a Rome-dominated to a Spanish imperial religion.

Allan Greer's case study of the peripatetic Jesuit missionary Pierre Chaumonot focuses on the personal and representational costs of transatlantic relocation, as well as on the subliminal competition between class and religious identity that often lies beneath the surface of imperial boundary crossing. Before training for the priesthood in a Jesuit college near Rome, Chaumonot wandered the roads of France and Italy as a teenaged vagabond, having fled his peasant home when he was twelve. Serving as missionary to the native populations of Canada, he became the leading Jesuit authority on the Huron and several Iroquois languages. But shadowing this remarkable aptitude for motion and change was a durable longing for homely, or familial, shelter: the lay confraternities he founded were dedicated to the Holy Family; the shrine he built near Quebec was a replica of the cottage where Jesus was believed to have lived with his parents in Nazareth. The models to which Father Chaumonot turned at the far outposts of his New World mission were those that predated and improved upon his own domestic origins.

Revisiting the figure of the Christianized Indian as a symbol of colonial accommodation, Kristina Bross tracks through various sightings in the transatlantic literature on religion and empire the tantalizing story of an unnamed Algonquian woman converted to Christianity by the Puritan missionary John Eliot. Surfacing in a wide range of texts for a variety of polemical purposes, the Algonquian woman was transformed through these successive reiterations from a simple anecdote of Indian godliness into a transatlantic female prophet, foretelling the success of Cromwell's "Western Design" and the triumph of radical Protestantism more generally. Through a creative reading of the importance of basket weaving in Indian women's lives, Bross is able to recapture something of what this experience of semiotic mutation may have meant for the woman herself, who left few traces of her own voice in the literary archive. To missionaries like Eliot, basket weaving signified successful incorporation of native labor practices into a civilized economy; but, imbued as they were with spiritual meaning, baskets signified to their Algonquian makers continuity with native religious traditions rather than wholesale conversion to Christian ways.

In another take on the cultural encounter between Jesuit and Algonquian, Dominique Deslandres explores the imaginary realm generated by the clash of two visionary traditions. When the dream culture of French missionaries met the spirit visions of their native converts in the Canadian forests, the resulting sequence of misprisions and mistranslations, Deslandres argues, constituted a spiritual warfare as real and as consequential as the better-known military battles of the seventeenth century. Native dreams occupied a spectrum from the premonitory to the instrumental, and in their determination to discredit indigenous spiritual traditions the Jesuits abandoned their own commitment to a prophetic dream culture in order to insist that all native visions were diabolical in origin. They knew better, however, as Deslandres demonstrates, and in attacking native dreams the missionaries were attacking a vital part of their own spiritual heritage. As a result the dream cultures of both groups were transformed by the contest over authentic revelation waged in the mission fields of New France.

Turning from New France to the polyethnic provinces of British America, Bethany Wiggin focuses on a particularly fraught period for German migrants to North America, when the early Quakers and Pietists were confronted by an influx of newcomers from the established German Lutheran and German and Dutch Calvinist churches. Christoph Saur (1695–1755) was among the earlier wave of settlers, radically separatist in his convictions, profoundly suspicious of organized religion. In his annual almanac, the *Deutscher Calender*, Saur evolved a specifically text-based strategy for constituting the German immigrant community in a form that would protect the freedoms he so vitally treasured while transforming and incorporating the new arrivals. Appended to the almanac was an advice column, framed as a conversation between a *Neukommer* (new arrival) and an *Einwohner* (inhabitant). Aiming to make a strange world familiar and, crucially, a familiar world strange, the older inhabitant punctuates his practical advice with warnings against organized religion and other incitements to violence. "Home" was an elusive category, as many of these essays demonstrate, but one that retained considerable emotional and political purchase for Atlantic migrants as they made their way in the New World. And origins require perpetual reinvention.

Part III examines another kind of colonial accommodation—the impulse to destroy what is unfamiliar and to embrace the violence of renewal. Along with theological disputes, oppressive systems of labor, grandiose visions of dynastic and national hegemony, and the administrative machinery of the early modern state, violence was exported to the Americas in forms both recognizable and new. From a reinvigoration of the discredited concept of "holy war" in the service of the newly confessionalized state to the emergence of new literary forms devoted to chronicling the experience of heroic death during the wars of the Reformation, Europe's Christians lived in a state of heightened awareness that violence was sometimes sacred.

In "Reconfiguring Martyrdom in the Colonial Context," Katherine Ibbett offers a nuanced ethnobiographical reading of the physical and spiritual journey of the Ursuline nun Marie de l'Incarnation from the comforts of Paris to the wilderness of New France. Prepared to suffer and die for her faith, Marie confronted hardships less dire but more disconcerting than she had anticipated and found herself transposing inherited models of martyrdom onto a strange new template. To be sure, others had encountered this problem of transposition before: violent death at the hands of the Iroquois, for instance, left no place for the stalwart declaration of faith so important to Old World martyrologies. Marie's most daunting challenges, however, were not extraordinary violence at all but the quotidian "martyrdom" of grueling physical and mental labor, especially the labor of learning "barbarous" languages. Most interesting of all, perhaps, in the present case is that the complex recasting of exemplary martyrdom became the joint project of Marie de l'Incarnation herself and the son who edited her works in France and whom she had abandoned in order to pursue her vocation.

As a particularly vivid example of the power of things, in this case, the material book, to forge a communal religious identity through the shared acts of production, distribution, use, and misuse, Patrick Erben explores the Mennonite *Martyrs' Mirror* from its original compilation in Amsterdam in 1660 to its reappearance in colonial Pennsylvania one hundred years later. Confronting what it feared would be a new period of persecution, both direct violence from the French and Indian Wars and hostility from fellow colonists who saw Mennonite pacifism as a dangerous betrayal of common defense, the

Mennonite community sought to fortify itself with the example of a book. That example was tripartite: (1) its core compilations involved narratives of Old World co-religionists who had suffered and died for their faith; (2) its translators and printers added their own tribulations to those of the collected martyrs; and (3) the physical book endured a dramatic history of mutilations and confiscations, becoming itself a model for the "suffering body."

Iconoclastic violence in the Reformation era arose in the dense ecclesiastical landscape of old Europe: a landscape filled with stained glass and frescoed walls, with monastery and cathedral, rood screen and statuary. But even in the frontier environment of colonial North America, where the traditional targets of organized iconoclastic raids were absent, Susan Juster finds an enduring strain of iconoclastic fervor. In "Iconoclasm Without Icons?" Juster asks how traditions of sacred violence were transplanted from one historical and material context to another. Surveying assaults on churches, ecclesiastical paraphernalia, ensigns, and gravestones in British North America, as well as the pamphlets, sermons, and letters that rhetorically conflate the mutilation of human bodies with the mutilation of religious objects, she asks us to reconsider the traditions of affective and ideological investment in sacred objects and, more ambitiously, the nature of image making itself.

Finally, in an essay that serves as a coda to the volume as a whole, Paul Stevens reexamines the theoretical premises that underlie our common enterprise. His particular subject is the poet Edmund Spenser, sixteenth-century colonist, civil servant, and author of England's national epic. His larger subject is the entire question of ideological imperatives and the role they do or do not play in large-scale historical movements. While acknowledging the formidable contributions of such theorists of empire as David Armitage and Joseph Schumpeter, Stevens argues that our ability to understand and to gain critical leverage on the dynamics of imperial expansion suffers badly if we fail to incorporate the histories of cultural longing and cultural memory. In particular, Stevens argues, the doctrine of divine grace, a central tenet in Reformation Protestantism, played a powerful role in shaping English imperialism in its earliest, Atlantic, manifestations. The Protestant understanding of Christian grace, unbounded and universal, not only breathed new life into the evangelical imperatives of the primitive church, it also insulated the English against the incongruity of their own violence, enabling belief to overwhelm the cosmopolitan relativism that humanist education had tended to foster, or, as Stevens tellingly puts it, allowing belief to overwhelm irony. Tracing the lineage of Edmund Spenser in later moments of imperial crisis—the speeches

of Winston Churchill, the wartime poetry of T. S. Eliot, the pronounce-
ments of official Washington in the wake of September 11—Stevens explicitly
acknowledges our own revisionist moment and helps us contemplate the difficult question of what it means to think historically at all, whether in the
throes of imperial fantasy or the throes of post-colonial debunking. Fear of
cultural impermanence, he argues, has driven the English-speaking empires
of the West to embrace a synchronic ideal that radically forecloses our ability
to imagine a world in which plural ways of living can coexist. All the essays
in this volume are shadowed one way or another by the latter-day histories of
empire and religion: "Spenser and the End of the British Empire" makes that
shadowing explicit in a broad and nuanced cultural critique.

The field of Atlantic studies has in recent decades profoundly reshaped our
ability to address questions of how those paradigmatic structures of the early
modern era—the confessional state and the overseas empire—were mutually
constituted. The essays collected in this volume, their disciplinary and geographical range, their methodological overlap and divergence, are powerful
testament to the continuing vitality of the circum-Atlantic perspective, especially in the formative era of confessionalization, state building, and overseas
exploration.

PART I

Launching Imperial Projects

CHAPTER I

The Polemics of Possession

Spain on America, Circa 1550

Rolena Adorno

In Europe's early modern Atlantic world the association of religion and empire may be said to begin with Spain's conquests in the Americas, from Columbus's Caribbean landfall in the autumn of 1492, through and well beyond the defeat in the 1520s of the mainland empire of the Mexica in the Central Valley of Mexico and in the 1530s of that of the Incas in the Andes of South America. The wedding of cross and sword, harking back to the Roman emperor Constantine's campaigns after his conversion to Christianity, gained new life in Spain at the end of the fifteenth century. Yet in Castile, Constantine's motto as recorded in Eusebius's *Life of Constantine*, "In this sign [of the cross] shalt thou conquer," was hotly contested. Discussions and debates at the Castilian court raged throughout this period, into the 1560s (my endpoint here) and beyond. It can also be argued, however, that the Castilian pursuit of religious unity did not begin in October 1492, but rather in January of that year when the last Muslim kingdom was defeated at Granada or nearly three months later, in March, when the edict to expel the Jews from the kingdoms of Spain was promulgated. Spain's efforts to achieve religious unity beyond its borders thus began with its efforts to create homogeneity within. Yet Ferdinand and Isabel recognized that the patterns of disappropriation, exclusion, and destruction applied at home could not be taken for granted abroad.

Antonio de Nebrija's pathbreaking *Gramática de la lengua castellana* [Grammar of the Castilian Language] was published in Salamanca in the same year of 1492. It is thought to have appeared subsequent to Columbus's August 1492 embarkation in search of a western route to Asia. It is also popularly *mis*understood as presaging the discoveries and conquests in the Americas, which would have meant that the Salamanca Latinist was much more well-informed about uncharted waters to the west than Columbus (who died thinking he had arrived in Asia). In the prologue to his *Grammar*, Nebrija remarked that language was always the companion of empire and that language followed empire so closely that they originated, grew, prospered, and fell together. Although Nebrija's biological model of language had its origin in Lorenzo Valla's conception of language as an organic being, linked to the life and death of empires, Nebrija's point was that the persistence of empire would be assured and made eternal by the art of grammar, recording imperial deeds in the vernacular language, preserving them for posterity.[1]

In his utterances about the "laws the victor imposes on the vanquished" and his mention of "barbarous peoples and nations of strange languages," Nebrija had in mind the histories ("lives") of the ancient Hebrews, the Greeks, and the imperial Romans.[2] His tone was more Roman and bellicose than Castilian and evangelical, and his projected point of reference was Spanish military actions newly in course in Africa, not America.[3] Along with the January 1492 reconquest of Granada, the crown of Castile attempted to gain control over the north coast of Africa to protect Spain from invasion and to defend Naples and Sicily against attacks from the Turks. From 1490 through 1511, when the Spanish were vanquished on the Isle of Gelves (Djerba, Tunisia), Ferdinand and Isabel, and especially Ferdinand in his second regency after Isabel's death, successfully gained ground on Mediterranean shores, west to east, from Melilla to Tripoli.[4]

If in following the Roman model of language and empire Nebrija made his remarks about imperial and linguistic prowess in reference to the threatening south rather than the unknown west, his words came to ring true in the end for Spain's imperial experience in America. Language did indeed follow empire, and empire endured, in Spain's understanding of its own experience, through the art of grammar in the Castilian language, that is, in the vernacular's role in the evangelization of native peoples, the debates on the rights of conquest, and the writing of conquest history. Yet the polemical and theoretical positions expressed in the Spanish "language of empire" were—and still are—often oversimplified and misunderstood.

Especially from the eighteenth century onward interpretations of Spanish thought and actions put forth by learned Europeans frequently, sometimes inadvertently, contributed to the Black Legend of Spanish history. Popular notions resulting from this legend have dulled the edges of the understanding of sixteenth-century Spanish thought, reducing its complexity and obscuring its impact to a few neat but erroneous commonplaces. These shibboleths, which I address below, are, first, that the Spaniards thought, or argued, that the Amerindians were not human or fully human; second, that some, applying Aristotle's theory of natural slavery, considered that the Indians were, in their essential human character, permanently incapable of self-governance; third, that the Dominican theologian Fray Francisco de Vitoria is to be remembered as the Indians' theoretical champion; and, fourth, that Fray Bartolomé de las Casas's efforts and works can be dismissed by claiming him (erroneously) to be the author or principal promoter of African slavery in the New World.

My chief aim in the following pages is to examine the principles (philosophical, juridical, scriptural) on which the most well-known and influential sixteenth-century Castilian thinkers and polemicists—Juan Ginés de Sepúlveda, Francisco de Vitoria, and Bartolomé de las Casas—based their advocacy or rejection of Spanish conquest in the New World and the means of its colonization. If the wars of military conquest and subjugation were fought in the Indies, the wars of ideas fought at court in response to those events were no less intense. Rehearsing those wars of ideas here, my goal is to set forth the thinking that reflected on the first European theater of intercontinental military, civil, and ecclesiastical operations of the early modern Atlantic period for the value that it might have in picking up its resonances in other times and places, despite differences of religious creed and philosophical preferences. My title, "The Polemics of Possession," alludes to the warlike and disputational resonances of "polemics," while "possession," in English as well as in Spanish, refers to that concept of law relating to physical control and implying ownership, actual or merely asserted.[5]

The heart of the "polemics of possession" is found in the papal bulls of donation (*Inter Caetera, Dudum Siguidem*) granted to Ferdinand and Isabel as sovereigns of Castile and León by Pope Alexander VI in 1493.[6] These bulls ceded to the Catholic monarchs and their successors full sovereignty over lands already discovered, and any and all to be discovered, by Christopher Columbus. (Portuguese claims to the New World were recognized shortly thereafter in the Treaty of Tordesillas.) The bulls' mandate to preach the Christian gospel quickly brought the Castilian language into the service of New World evangelization. Yet the meaning of the bulls was disputed for many decades after their promulgation: were they intended only to authorize evangelization of the peoples in the newly found lands or also to impose a Christian state upon them? Arms and letters—the unlimited use of arms and the clamorous use of letters—thus quickly came together and often opposed one another in the advancement of Spain over lands and peoples in the Americas. When these debates began, the time-honored just causes for waging war against other nations, oriented exclusively to the kingdom's self-defense as a medieval legacy of Spain's recovery of its lands lost to the Muslims, were basically three: to repel an invading people; to punish those who would not make restitution of goods and properties unjustly taken; and to combat those who would impose their own religion on the Christian community.[7]

New theories of just war were generated by the new American circumstances. By the end of the final decade of the fifteenth century Isabel and Ferdinand had achieved a hard-won national integration through the union of the crowns of Castile and Aragon, the control of the aristocracy, and "the imposition of royal authority over the country at large." The imperial era inaugurated two decades later in 1519 by their grandson, Charles V of the Holy Roman Empire (crowned Charles I of Spain in 1516), established "an alien dynasty with an alien programme, which threatened to submerge Castile in the larger entity of a universal Empire."[8] In America, the captain-conqueror of Mexico, Hernán Cortés, likewise imagined an imperial order, one that would place New Spain, the kingdom he founded but was not permitted to rule, into a universal order presided over by Charles V.[9]

Thus, if empire arrived in Spain and its America with the Hapsburg dynasty, the theoretical relationships between religion and empire were hammered out along the way if not after the fact. When the discussion of the relationship between Spanish empire and Christian religion emerged, its focal point was a concrete one: the New World's native inhabitants and Spain's right to govern them (or not). This debate did not begin at the abstract, theoretical level but in response to particular sets of circumstances, some of which were real and confirmed and others merely asserted and believed, as in the case of the laws regarding the allegedly cannibalistic inhabitants of the Antilles.[10] Polemics followed practice, and those practices were as follows.

Three basic alternatives in the Spanish governance of the natives, based on their location and type of social organization, quickly took shape. The sedentary native groups (mostly agriculturalists) generally were placed in *encomienda* (grants of native labor and tribute to Spanish trustees) or other systems of forced labor. The less sedentary groups were forced to work as domestic servants and slaves. Native groups that could not be subdued were submitted to campaigns of dispersion or extermination.[11] Focused on the treatment of the Indians, the disputations regarding the relationship of empire and religion crystallized in relation to the encomienda system, which had its origins in Spain and became from the earliest days of the sixteenth century in the Spanish Caribbean the "chief means of private Spanish control over Indian peoples."[12]

The encomienda consigned groups of Indians to privileged Spanish colonists who were charged with supervising the Indians' Christian indoctrination; the grantees (*encomenderos*) in turn were entitled to receive labor and tribute in goods from the Indians inhabiting the assigned lands. An encomienda grant conferred no landed property or juridical jurisdiction: it "was a possession, not a property, and it was per se inalienable and non-inheritable. Save insofar as the terms of particular grants might allow."[13] Its use spread from the Antilles to the mainland, and it was imposed on the peoples of the former Mexica federation in Mexico and of the former Inca empire in the Andes, and in all Spanish possessions in the Americas subsequently. The Indians were regarded as juridically free, yet the legal distinctions between encomienda, slavery, and other forms of servitude did not render the differences clear, or meaningful, in practice.

Given the goals of the evangelization of the native peoples and the salvation of their souls, it should be obvious that from the earliest years of the Spanish presence in the Indies, starting with Columbus himself, theologians, jurists, and missionaries did not doubt the humanity of the Indians and never raised the question. That is, although the character of the Indians' customs and their capacity to govern themselves when in contact with other ("superior") peoples were debated (and this was, as we will see, the crux of the debate), no member of the Castilian elite denied the Indians' condition as true human beings.[14] Nevertheless, accusations against the Indians' reputed or observed conduct had an effect on the laws drawn up to govern them on at least three occasions: the licentiate Alonso de Zuazo's 1519 "cannibal" order, legitimizing the capture and enslavement of Caribbean Indians deemed to be practitioners of anthropophagy; the royal authorization for enslaving Indians in 1526; and the order of August 2, 1530, to prohibit Indian slavery, and its revocation (that is, the legal reinstitution of Indian slavery) on February 20, 1534.[15]

At the same time, the meaning of references to the "bestial" customs of the Indians, attributed by Bartolomé de las Casas (1484–1566) to those who scorned and mistreated them, forms part of a rhetorical strategy aimed at

shaming the encomenderos and proponents of Indian slavery and provoking them with a call to conscience by insisting that the ill treatment of the
Indians was equivalent to considering them as lacking in the dignity they
possessed as fellow human beings. The best example comes from Las Casas's
account of a sermon preached in Santo Domingo in 1511 by Antonio de Mon-
tesinos in which the Dominican friar harangues against the encomenderos as
follows: "By what authority have you made detestable wars on these peoples,
who were living tranquilly and peacefully on their lands, where you have consumed such an infinite number of them, with assaults and deaths never heard
of?... These Indians, are they not human beings? Do they not have rational
souls? Are you not obligated to love them as you love yourselves?"[16] Las Casas,
too, employed this persuasive strategy, emphasizing the Indians' dignity as
fellow human beings and the Spanish settlers' ill treatment of them.[17]

Essential to the Indies debates were the lectures delivered in 1537–39 by
the theologian and professor (catedrático) of the University of Salamanca,
the learned Dominican Fray Francisco de Vitoria (c. 1492–1546). The Spanish university of those years was an influential institution, and the Castilian
monarchs frequently called upon its most illustrious thinkers, such as Vitoria
and his colleagues Domingo de Soto and Melchior Cano, to offer counsel on
such matters as the justice of the wars of conquest and the appropriateness of
mass baptism of adults without previous instruction in Christian doctrine.
Pertinent here are not Vitoria's lectures in theology but his 1539 Relecciones,
which were oral dissertations in which points previously treated summarily in
formal lecture were given further elaboration. Their topic was the question of
the right to make war against the Indians of the Americas. Although Vitoria
himself left no written drafts of these relecciones, they are extant in versions
prepared by his disciples, colleagues, and first editors. In spite of the fact that
the last of these transcribed or recalled dissertations, Relectio de Indis, was not
printed until 1557, it "circulated widely in manuscript both inside and outside
the university of Salamanca and it has been cited as having a lasting impact
on every subsequent discussion" of Spain's role in Indies affairs.[18]

In his 1539 Relectio de Indis and in response to the question as to whether,
before the arrival of the Spanish, the Indians had been legitimate lords of
their domains and possessions, Vitoria answered in the affirmative. In true
academic fashion, however, he added one condition for conquest "that cannot
be affirmed with certainty but that merits debate and that seems, to some,
to be legitimate": "As Aristotle said, learnedly and with elegance, 'There are
those who are slaves by nature,' or, rather, there are those for whom 'it is bet-

ter to serve than to lead.' They are the ones who do not possess sufficient reason even to govern themselves, but only to follow the orders of their masters, and whose strength is more in the body than in the spirit. Truly, if there be peoples of such a nature, these barbarians are it above all others."[19] Vitoria's citation of Aristotle led him to argue that, while the natives of the New World had been rulers of their own lives and liberty before the arrival of the Spanish, it was incumbent upon them, when met by the Spanish, to submit to their rule. Thus the Amerindians' alleged incapacity for self-governance emerged as Vitoria's eighth possible (uncertain) title authorizing Castilian conquest in the Americas.[20] Nevertheless, in the last of his 1539 lectures, *De indis, sive de jure belli hispanorum in barbaros, relectio posterior* (On the Indians, or the right of the Spanish to make war against barbarians, final arguments), Vitoria concluded that the sole just cause for war against the Indians was to repel injuries received and that the offenses suffered at the hands of the Indians had to be very grave to justify making war against them.[21] In short, after many considerations, including his earlier appeal to the Aristotelian theory of natural slavery, Vitoria rejected all but the most basic, universal justification to wage war against another people: self-defense.

After this final pronouncement by Vitoria the emperor Charles V decided that the time had come for these professor-priests ("maestros religiosos") to keep silent on matters of state. On November 10, 1539, the emperor ordered that "such teachers and members of the Order" who had discussed these matters in sermons or in their university lessons should give sworn statements about their past actions, surrender any writings that they had produced on such matters, and refrain from lecturing or preaching or printing anything on those topics without the express permission of the court.[22] Unfortunately, despite Vitoria's final verdict that the only just cause to wage war against the Indians was self-defense, his earlier dissertations, especially his eighth doubtful ("natural slavery") title, cited above, were recorded, circulated, and thus prevailed in the perceptions of his peers and successors.

In the following decade of the 1540s the theorization offered by the translator of Aristotle and imperial chronicler Juan Ginés de Sepúlveda (1490–1573) unequivocally defended the legitimacy of the wars of conquest. Circa 1545 his *Demócrates segundo, o de las justas causas de la guerra contra los indios* (The second Democrates, or on the just causes of war against the Indians) was written in Latin in that favored Renaissance genre, the dialogue, at the request of the president of the Council of the Indies.[23] Sepúlveda's *Demócrates segundo* has been called "the most virulent and uncompromising argument for the inferiority of the American Indian ever written," with the acknowledgment that "Sepúlveda's reading of Aristotle turns out in the end to be not so very far from Vitoria's own."[24]

Sepúlveda's interpretation of the concept of natural slavery and its Indies application are clarified by Vitoria's earlier speculations on the subject. The principles are the same, the only difference being the degree of certainty they respectively expressed about their applicability: Vitoria equivocates and qualifies; Sepúlveda is certain. Sepúlveda, in fact, asserted that Vitoria would approve his arguments.[25] Las Casas replied that such an affinity could be explained only by certain erroneous conclusions drawn by the Salamanca theologian, conclusions that were occasioned by "false information" Vitoria must have received from others.[26] For both the professorial Vitoria and the war theorist Sepúlveda (he had written an earlier treatise on the compatibility of war and the Christian religion),[27] natural slavery consisted of a hierarchical relationship between those with the ability to rule and those who were better off being ruled by others.

Sepúlveda is best known for the four causes that, he argued in the *Demócrates segundo*, legitimated making war against the Indians: to impose guardianship, that is, both the right and the need to govern those who were judged to be unable to govern themselves, the "natural slaves" (*siervos a natura*); to do away with the crime of devouring human flesh; to punish those who committed crimes against innocent persons; and to subdue peoples before preaching to them the Christian gospel. Sepúlveda set forth as the first argument for the justification of the Spanish conquests in the Indies "the rude nature of those peoples": to explain his meaning Sepúlveda rehearsed the Aristotelian principle of the rule of the less perfect by the more perfect: the soul over the body, reason over passion, the husband over his wife, the adult over the child, the father over his son.[28] He argued, "Those whose natural condition is such that they should obey others, and if they refuse their dominion and there remains no other recourse, they may be subjugated by force of arms; such a war is considered just in the opinion of the most eminent philosophers" (19). To make his argument concrete with respect to the Indians, he gave the example of their cowardice in war and the rude character of their institutions (36–37).

Sepúlveda shared some, though not all, of Vitoria's earlier principles for making just war against the Indians. Vitoria admitted among his just titles to conquest in the Indies the "natural need" that some peoples had to be ruled by others who were more competent (his eighth, uncertain title), and he considered as a just title the right to evangelize the Indies' pagan inhabitants (his second legitimate title). Vitoria did not consider human sacrifice in and of itself a just cause for war (Sepúlveda's second just cause), but the need to protect the innocent from such practices did (Vitoria's fifth legitimate title). Sepúlveda takes this principle, the protection of the innocent, as his third just cause for war. Finally, both Vitoria and Sepúlveda argued in favor of natural slavery with regard to the right of superior persons, or peoples, to govern over their inferiors, and they proposed consequently the rule of a "natural" order. Here the difference between Sepúlveda's certainty and Vitoria's doubt is patent: the right to make war against, and rule, peoples of inferior (untrained) intellectual and social development and deportment is, as discussed above, Vitoria's eighth doubtful title; it is Sepúlveda's unequivocating first just cause.

Sepúlveda did not consider the Indians of America to be deficient in human reason. He characterized their barbarity not as innate but rather as a product of custom that with time and contact with Christians would improve: "It is more to the benefit of these Indians and more in consonance with natural reason that they be subjected to the rule of princes or nations more civilized (*vt humaniorum/más humanos*) and virtuous than they are, so that, given the example of their [masters'] virtue and prudence and the fulfillment of their laws, they can abandon their barbarity, embrace a more civilized life (*in vitam humaniorem/una vida más humana*), conduct themselves in a more moderate (*morigerada*) manner, and practice virtue" (22; see also 27, 38, 63).

When Sepúlveda speaks of the progress that had been made in bringing the Amerindians to the practice of European customs, the image of the half-human being that has been attributed to him begins to fall away. Sepúlveda insisted that the Amerindian peoples were "sheep of the Lord but of a different fold" (76). Thus he relied on scriptural authority, paraphrasing the words of Jesus in describing the situation of these groups before God. The biblical passage reads, "And there are other sheep I have that are not of this fold, and these I have to lead as well. They too will listen to my voice; and there will be only one flock, and one shepherd" (John 10:16, Jerusalem Bible). Sepúlveda stated that "it is not true, as you say, that there is nothing in common between us and the pagans. On the contrary, there exist many things in common, for they are, and are called, our companions and fellow human beings and sheep of the same Lord, although not of the same fold. For One alone is the God of all, generous (*rico*) to all who invoke Him, and He wants all to be saved and arrive at the knowledge of the Truth" (76).

With regard to the meaning of the term *humano* in relation to the Indians,

Sepúlveda was not referring to the condition of humanity as such, as "a group of individuals of the human species or race," nor to "human nature" as such, but rather to the constellation of virtues that accompanies the plenitude of the exercise of reason.[29] An influential, early seventeenth-century Castilian dictionary states it succinctly: "Human: the one who is peaceable, compassionate, benign, and gentle" [Humano: el que es apazible (sic), compassible, acariciador, benigno y manso].[30] This is the evaluative sense of *humanitas*, that is, the Renaissance notion of courtesy, kindness, gentleness, empathy for— and solidarity with—others of one's kind, in other words, the ideal human type.[31] For Sepúlveda what was natural or innate in the Indians was not the lack of reason or rational capacity, but rather the necessity for them to enter into a relationship of hierarchy, assuming the inferior rank upon coming into contact with a superior (meaning Christian) people.

Sepúlveda sets forth this concept emphatically in book two of the *Demó-crates segundo*. (The consideration of Sepulveda's thought has usually been limited to book one, while book two, devoted to the type of governance that should prevail over the Indians and containing his most subtle theorizing, has been ignored.) Here he makes analogous the royal rule of a city or nation and the domestic administration of a household. He conceptualized the rule that should apply to the Indians of the Americas as a cross between social relationships based on the imposition of law and force, on the one hand, and those based on the mutual recognition of a natural hierarchy, on the other.

Sepúlveda argues that just as the household is constituted by the family, including its sons and daughters, as well as its servants, who are free, and also its slaves, and just as the father of the family rules over them all, treating each according to his condition and station, so the king should rule: "An eminently good and just king who wants to imitate such [an ideal] paterfamilias, as is his obligation, should govern the Spaniards with a paternal rule and [treat] those barbarians like servants, who are free, with a certain tempered rule, in which he acts toward the Indians as both a master (*heril*) and a father/ king (*paternal, civil*), and treats them according to their [current] state and the demands of circumstances."[32] Sepúlveda here proposes a mixture of two types of servitude, deriving one from (Aristotelian) philosophy and the other from jurisprudence. The first of these, which is likened to the dominion of the soul over the body, is translated into the social relationship of natural slavery in which, according to Aristotle, "the relationship between the [natural] slave and his master is natural, they are friends";[33] the second, "paternal" or "civil" rule, analogous to the control of the mind or reason over the passions, implies the social relationship of civil slavery, in which rule relies on law, force, and reprimand.[34]

Sepúlveda concludes that this combination will have positive results: "In this manner, with the passage of time, when they have become more civilized and under our rule the probity of customs and the Christian religion have been reaffirmed in them, they should be given greater freedom and treated with greater liberality" (120). Sepúlveda's proposal is not quite a direct throwback to Aristotle's theory of natural slavery; it is, rather, a position that, while not questioning the right to rule the Indians, finds inadequate both the philosophical notion of natural slavery and the juridical institution of civil slavery in formulating that relationship.

Sepúlveda again insists that Indian civil slavery should be prohibited, and he condemns the abuses of the Indians by those who "torment and annihilate them with intolerable burdens or unjust slavery and with arduous and unbearable labors, as some reportedly have done with consummate greed and cruelty in certain islands" (124; see also 117, 121–23). He asserts further that the Indians cannot be deprived of their estates or properties on account of being natural slaves. In short, the essence of Sepúlveda's position is not the characterization of the Indians as such, but rather the hierarchical relationship that should prevail on their encounter with other (superior) peoples.

This understanding of hierarchy is the basic presupposition of Sepúlveda's thinking, and it is similar to Vitoria's initial exploratory reasoning on the same subject. For this reason Sepúlveda placed great confidence in Vitoria's implicit support for his position. In his 1550 *Apología* Sepúlveda quotes directly the favorable opinion of Fray Diego de Vitoria (the Salamanca professor's brother) regarding the *Demócrates segundo*, and he infers that it signifies Fray Francisco's approbation as well, because "this author"—Sepúlveda refers to Fray Diego—"would not have pronounced this judgment so freely and without vacillation against the common opinion of his own confreres [the Dominicans] if he had not felt confirmed by the authority of his brother Francisco, a most learned man, of noble and generous spirit, who was living only two days' distance from him."[35]

It has been argued that Sepúlveda's offensiveness, apart from his trespass into the domain of the theologians and their hold on moral theology, was the language in which he gave his ideas expression, creating "an image of a half-man creature" in which the rhetorical effect was to "thrust the Indian back again among the *similitudines hominis*," that is, into a subhuman state.[36] This interpretation has certainly been common in our day, but at the time, in my view, the more offensive and dangerous effect of Sepúlveda's ideas was to affirm with certainty principles elucidated some six years earlier and later rejected (but to no avail) by Vitoria. Sepúlveda, with Vitoria as background, was able to articulate a type of relationship that combined in the role of the overlord the attributes of both the master and the tutor and to argue on philosophical grounds the right of the Spanish conquests in the Indies that could not be justified, as Las Casas always argued, on the basis of the traditionally accepted theories of just war: self-defense against invasion, the restitution of goods taken, and the repulsion of efforts to impose on Christians another religion.

It was on the matter of slaves taken as booty in the defensive war of Christian Europe against the Ottoman Empire that Las Casas, like the rest of his generation, understood (wrongly) that the African captives taken by the Portuguese throughout the fifteenth century and sold into slavery in Europe were civil slaves, legally acquired according to the traditional, time-honored rights of war. It should be remembered that the Turkish enemy had already reached Vienna and taken over parts of Italy, while Muslim dynasties across northern Africa threatened Mediterranean commerce. (Nebrija had in mind this latter threat to Spain's security when in 1492 he envisioned how language would continue to be "the companion of empire.")

Upon studying the classic works of Portuguese maritime history in the 1550s, Las Casas discovered that Africans had not been captured and enslaved in the just war against Islam; they were instead being stolen from their homes where they lived securely and in peace.[37] He was deeply troubled: he had indeed recommended to King Charles in 1516 that in addition to Charles's Flemish agents, who monopolized the trade, Castilian settlers should be permitted to buy royal licenses for the purchase of African just-war slaves, both black and white (that is, fair-skinned Berbers), from the North African coast and that this limited increment of slaves should serve such specific purposes as mining.[38] Four decades later, upon learning the truth about Portuguese slaving (to which he now devoted several chapters in his *Historia de las Indias*), Las Casas acknowledged it and stated that he doubted that divine judgment would excuse him for his earlier error, in spite of his ignorance on the matter.[39]

In Las Casas's view ignorance of the false premises on which he had based his 1516 recommendation did not remove the onus of his personal responsibility, and he applied this stern criterion to others, including the Spanish monarchs he advised (from Ferdinand to Philip II), as strictly as to himself.

It should be recalled that the importation of black Africans as slaves to the Indies was under way for at least a decade and a half when Las Casas wrote his memorandum. Instead of being the "author" of New World black African slavery, Las Casas became one of the few Europeans in the sixteenth century to speak out against it.[40]

While Las Casas is commonly considered to be Thomistic in his thought, following the Aristotelian-Thomist school of neo-Scholastic philosophy, particularly regarding natural law, it is also true that Las Casas was a jurist, a canon lawyer. The canon-law scholar Kenneth J. Pennington some thirty years ago argued that "the basic premise in Las Casas's position on the rights of the Indians is that legitimate secular power does exist outside the church." The tenet identified by Pennington as being employed by Las Casas was the principle of *Quod omnes tangit debet ab omnibus approbari*—"what touches all must be approved by all." Developed to regulate the affairs of a bishopric, the principle was applied by Las Casas to governance in the Indies. As it would be dangerous to assign a prince or a bishop to an unwilling people, so too a foreign king should not be imposed on a free people; "consequently, Las Casas concluded, the pope could not give infidels a new king without their consent."[41]

Applying this definition of *dominium*, Las Casas was able to conceptualize the rights of the Indians to sovereignty in their own domains on the authority and logic of the law. Taking Pennington's initial insight much further, José Cárdenas Bunsen has recently demonstrated that canon-law principles systematically undergird and orient all of Las Casas's major works: the eight treatises he published in Seville in 1552–53, the *Historia de las Indias* (1527–61), and the *Apologética historia sumaria* (1560).[42] Examining these works against the corpus of canon law and its commentaries and in relation to civil law, Cárdenas has shown that Las Casas's training, disciplinary perspective, and Indies thought were profoundly juridical. Here a new Las Casas emerges: not only the preacher and polemicist, well known for his passionate moral outrage, but also the lawyer, coolly analytical and innovative in the legal arguments he presented before court and king. Under this light the differences between his thought and that of his peers gains significant clarity.

The fundamental disagreement between Las Casas and Sepúlveda, and the early, speculative Vitoria, is that the latter two used the model of the family, from the fifth chapter of the first book of Aristotle's *Politics*, to propose the relationship between the Spaniards and the Indians, understood as a single entity (two halves of a whole, we might say), while Las Casas argued on the basis of the law that they were different entities. Vitoria had insisted that Aristotle "meant to say that there exists in them [the barbarians] a natural necessity to be ruled and governed by others, this subjection to others being very much in their interest, just as children need to submit to the will of their parents, and the woman to her husband."[43] Sepúlveda wrote, "For the same reason a husband has dominion over his wife, the adult over the child, the father over his son, in a word, the superior and more perfect over the inferior and more imperfect." The crux (and weakness) of Sepúlveda's analogical argument is found in his explicit statement that this same criterion is valid for all humankind in its mutual relations.[44]

Las Casas's interpretation of the superior-inferior dichotomy, and his objection to Sepúlveda's view, was a simple but profound one:

> Sepúlveda alleges furthermore, it should be known, that the more
> imperfect things should cede—by nature—upon encountering more
> perfect things, such as matter cedes to form, the body to the soul, and
> sentiment to reason, which is certainly something that I do not deny.
> However, this is true when the two things are found to be united
> by nature, "in acto primu," as when matter and form, which gives
> "being" to the thing, occur in one single thing, as for example, when
> the body and the soul converge in the formation of a human being
> or when both feelings and reason exist in the same individual. This
> being said, if the perfect thing and the imperfect thing are found to
> be separate and refer to different subjects, in this case the imperfect
> does not give way before the more perfect, for they are not united "in
> acto primu."[45]

On this basis Las Casas denied the possibility of a "natural," hierarchical ordering of the relationship between the Spaniards and the Indians. That is, he rejected the deterministic domestic social model; for him the simple model of the household could not provide a template for a kingdom and its peers. Citing Augustine and Giles of Rome, and refuting Sepúlveda's "for the sake of the well-being of the Indians" argument, he concluded that "in effect, no free people can be obligated to submit to a more educated people, even if such submission would redound to great advantage of the former."[46] Las Casas therefore renounced the use of force against the Indians, either to impose Spanish civil rule upon them (*Quod omnes tangit*) or to evangelize them.

In the latter case his basis was not only legal and canonical but directly scriptural. It appears in his 1538–39 Latin treatise on evangelization, *De unico vocationis modo omnium gentium ad veram religionem* [Concerning the Only Way to Attract All Peoples to the True Religion].[47] Las Casas takes the pertinent principle from Jesus's instructions to his disciples about preaching the faith, which are set down in three of the four books of the gospel. Here is the version from the book of Matthew (chap. 10, verses 11–14, Jerusalem Bible): "Whatever town or village you go into, ask for someone trustworthy and stay with him until you leave. As you enter his house, salute it, and if the house deserves it, let your peace descend upon it; if it does not, let your peace come back to you. And if anyone does not welcome you or listen to what you have to say, as you walk out of the house or town shake the dust from your feet." "Shake the dust from your feet" implies that in the foreign land the Christian is guest, not lord; the Christian priest abroad is likewise an outsider. In the same manner, in Las Casas's canonical view, the Christian prince abroad cannot impose a new ruler on a people without their free and voluntary consent.

The high point of this discussion in Spain is commonly identified with the 1550–51 debate at court in Valladolid between Las Casas and Sepúlveda. Yet it did not resolve the conflict over conquest. Its inconclusiveness (all the formal opinions handed down by the fourteen judges have not been assembled and analyzed) and the fact that afterward the emperor lifted the ban on conquests that he had earlier imposed leave the episode to be popularly seen as an ineffective if not empty imperial gesture, the relic of a noble but failed "struggle for justice in the conquest of America."[48] I view the event not as a landmark in its own right but as part of a longer deliberative process; it distilled and sharpened (making increasingly irreconcilable) the positions of its protagonists, and its convocation responded to the pressing needs of the time.

Why was this royally convened junta called? It occurred, after all, three decades after México-Tenochtitlán fell in 1521 to Cortés, his men, and their thousands of native allies and two decades after the Inca prince Atahualpa was garroted in Cajamarca in 1532. The answer has to do precisely with the fact that by the end of the 1540s civil and ecclesiastical governance was well established in the Indies and the permanence of this arrangement was no more keenly felt than in the control of Indians' lives and well-being at the hands of private citizens, the encomendero class. Although the generation of conquistador-encomenderos was dying off, its surviving members constituted a powerful lobby aimed at retaining for their heirs in perpetuity the encomienda grants that were their sources of Indian labor and economic livelihood. At the same time, the ongoing decline in the native populations and the claims to the encomienda's rewards from royal officials and new settlers squeezed still further the availability of such resources.[49] The forced domination of native peoples and their lands therefore continued to fan out, expanding its frontiers. Because known resources were limited if not contested and because the private pursuit of such private gain showed no signs of diminishing, matters continued to overheat at court in response to developments taking place "on the ground."

In an effort to take action against violent conquest and the rewards it offered to conquistadors and encomenderos, Las Casas read at court in 1542 his "long account" of a briefer one (*Brevísima relación de la destruición de las Indias* [Brief Account of the Destruction of the Indies]) and presented proposals (*Entre los remedios* [Among the Remedies]) that resulted in the same year in the promulgation of the New Laws that abolished Indian slavery and encomienda.[50] Yet in 1545–46 those New Laws were repealed as unenforceable: the viceroy of New Spain, Antonio de Mendoza, supporting the interests of his encomendero-class power base, refrained even from announcing the new legislation, and the just-appointed viceroy of Peru, Blasco Núñez de Vela, was assassinated by encomendero interests as he took office. Also in 1545 Sepúlveda wrote the *Demócrates segundo* justifying wars of conquest against the Indians. Although the faculties of the universities of Alcalá de Henares and Salamanca deemed the work unfit for publication, Sepúlveda got his word out by having a similar work, his Latin *Apologia*, published in Rome in 1550. Las Casas, who had exercised his powers of persuasion with the university professors, now persuaded the court to prohibit the work's importation into Spain, to seek out and burn all smuggled copies, and to prevent its exportation to the Indies.[51]

From the perspective of the ideological battles fought in print and at court, as well as from that of the continuing colonial expansion in the Indies, which was always justified on the basis of evangelizing the Indians, 1550 was precisely the moment to ask (and this was the question laid out before Las Casas and Sepúlveda to debate in Valladolid), "Is it lawful for the Spanish king to wage war against the Indians before preaching the gospel to them?" [¿Es lícito que el rey español haga la Guerra a los indios antes de predicarles la fe?].[52] Sepúlveda answered a brief but resounding "yes;" Las Casas entered a lengthy juridical response of "no."

Sepúlveda and Las Casas disagreed on three central issues: the relationship between the use of force and evangelization, the question of the capacity and appropriateness of the Indians' self-governance, and the character of Spanish dominion over the Indies. Although there were only two combatants in the royally convened junta, Vitoria, already deceased (he died in 1546), was clearly the shadow hovering in the background. With regard to the character of Spanish dominion over the Indies, Sepúlveda followed the prevailing interpretation of the papal bulls in favor of the powers, interests, and duties of secular rule: the Indians were obligated to submit to papal and royal authority, by force of arms if necessary. It was therefore legitimate to make war on them before preaching the gospel. Las Casas rejected the principle of papal authority over temporal matters and interpreted the papal bulls of donation as granting the right to evangelize only. Evangelization, he argued, had to be carried out peacefully, without the use of force. Advocating the political autonomy of Indian communities, Las Casas argued that even subsequent to their conversion to the faith the Indians could legitimately be placed under Spanish rule only by their free will and consent.[53]

The junta at Valladolid did not end the Indies debates or the contentions between the espoused principles and strong personalities of Sepúlveda and Las Casas. In 1552–53 Las Casas wrote his own *Apología* in response to that of Sepúlveda and in reflection upon new insights gained at the Valladolid debate.[54] If, in his 1550 *Apología*, Sepúlveda had accused Las Casas of provoking "a great scandal and infamy against our kings," Las Casas now accused Sepúlveda of "defaming these [Indian] peoples before the entire world."[55] When Las Casas devoted himself to writing his *Apologética historia sumaria* (1560), his great proto-anthropological treatise defending the dignity of Amerindian societies (no worse, often better, that the ancient Greeks and Romans), the stimulus or catalyst for doing so surely came from Sepúlveda's denigration of the Indians at Valladolid. The Spanish historian Francisco López de Gómara also added fuel to the fire by declaring in his 1552 *Historia de las Indias* that those who queried the justice of the conquests could be satisfied of their merit by consulting Sepúlveda's published work in Latin.[56]

The encomienda question, however, raged on: Las Casas and his Dominican collaborators in Peru continued to defend the rights of the Andean peoples against the interests of the encomenderos before the king. When in 1554–55 the encomenderos of Peru offered to buy the perpetual rights to the use of its lands and the services of its native peoples from the treasury-poor, prospective Philip II, the indigenous lords of Peru made a counter-offer, bidding to buy their liberty at a higher price than that offered by the encomenderos. In the end Philip neither accepted the counteroffer nor sold the emcomiendas to private Spanish citizens.[57] Out of this crisis Las Casas proposed in the 1560s that Philip II restore sovereignty over the Andes to the Inca's successors and that Castile abandon its political rule over the Indies altogether.[58]

Thus the discussion on the governance of the Indies, based on the twin platforms of church and state, played out through the middle decades of the sixteenth century. Those who applied the "natural order" of the Aristotelian model of the private household to the public realm of nation and empire (Sepúlveda and the early Vitoria) were refuted by those who conceived the relation among peoples according to criteria of canonical (and civil) jurisprudence (Las Casas and his peers and successors, such as Domingo de Soto). Neither the early Vitoria nor Sepúlveda from first to last considered post-conquest Amerindian polities, once in contact with European Christian invaders and settlers, as legitimate civic or political entities. Here Las Casas's foundation on the discipline of law instead of philosophy or theology stood out; on the basis of law he formulated the restoration of Amerindian sovereignty over their own lands and lives.

Ironically, Sepúlveda's thought is often popularly considered "modern" and Las Casas's "medieval." It is, in fact, just the reverse.[59] Whereas Sepúlveda harked back to Aristotle's theory of natural slavery, he modified its application but never overcame it. Meanwhile, Las Casas, on the basis of the law and its evolving commentary, moved forward, creating juridical rationales for dealing with and respecting the peoples and nations of this previously unknown "fourth part" of the world.

The templates laid down by Las Casas and Sepúlveda constituted the heart of the Spanish polemics on religion and empire that would prevail throughout the sixteenth century and into the seventeenth, and they continued, with unmitigated though sometimes veiled intensity, in the Spanish, creole, and indigenous writings on the Indies from then on and especially in the early nineteenth-century era of Latin American independence. The Castilian thinkers of the mid-sixteenth century did not resolve the issues of the relationship of religion to empire, but their efforts to formulate solutions constitute an essential chapter of the intellectual history of European colonialism's Atlantic legacies. There is no question that the texture, content, and thrust of their thinking appeared in various guises as Europe continued to spread its expansionist, colonialist interests over the Americas.

CHAPTER 2

Cruelty and Religious Justifications for Conquest in the Mid-Seventeenth-Century English Atlantic

Carla Gardina Pestana

Studies of English expansion have concentrated on the justifications deployed for taking the lands of indigenous peoples. Expansion, however, took place not only in the context of the process of dispossessing native peoples while wielding legal and religious arguments; it also occurred in the context of struggles between rival European claimants. If Europeans used their own perceived cultural superiority to the original inhabitants to justify invasion, other ideas—such as the false religion and brutality of rivals—had to be brought to the fore to defend aggression against fellow Europeans and Christians. English activity in the Atlantic entered a new phase in the 1650s, as the state itself orchestrated its first colonial conquests, aiming these takeover bids at colonies already held by other European powers. To justify this new round of conquests—in particular, Jamaica in 1655 and New Netherland in 1664—innovative defenses seemed necessary. When expropriating the land of fellow Christians, besmirching the character of one's opponents helped make the process palatable. The accusation of cruelty drew attention away from inappropriate English maneuvers. Worry over the potential victimization of the English—whether at the hands of the cruel Spaniard or his apprentice, the sadistic Dutchman—created a rhetorical space in which valiant English adherents to civility and true religion could invade first Jamaica and later New Netherland. Cruelty served similar goals in the two cases, despite the varied contexts that gave rise to them and the sharply contrasting logic behind each.

Before the mid-century turn toward taking already established colonies, the English had developed a rationale for earlier acquisitions, which they saw as different in kind from the later cases. By 1655 England controlled more than two dozen "plantations" from Newfoundland to Surinam. Technically speaking, all had been established on lands the Spanish claimed, because Spain claimed everything west of Portuguese Brazil throughout both Americas. Spain's possession of most of the Americas was based on right of discovery as well as on papal decisions dividing the responsibility to evangelize the non-European world between Spain and Portugal (1493–94). English (along with Dutch, French, and other European) governments denied the validity of such broadly construed claims, asserting that territory that had not been visited, much less planted with forts or settlements, could not be said to belong to any particular power. Based on this legal position, English charters for land grants in the Americas or the Caribbean stated that colonies could only be planted on lands not already occupied by the subjects of another "Christian Prince."[1] Native ownership in this conceptualization was not so much challenged as passed over. Debates surrounding the later English invasions differed from those engaged in by the Spanish in the previous century; the Spanish discussion considered the justice of taking native land as well as the proper place of the Indians within the colonial system (see Rolena Adorno's chapter in this volume).[2] English common law required that land be used in precise ways to denote legal occupancy; Indian modes of use as observed by explorers and settlers did not meet the Eurocentric criteria. In particular, native ways of relating to the land were seen as not fulfilling the necessity to "subdue" the earth. According to their own (clearly self-serving) understanding, the English classed lands used by Indians but not occupied by a Christian prince as "empty lands"—*vacuum domicilium*—and therefore free for the taking. Beginning with Roanoke in 1585 and continuing to the establishment of the colony of Surinam in 1650, English colonization had been carried out on such supposedly empty lands.[3]

Having begun by justifying expansion in terms of legitimate entry into unused lands, the English required a new interpretive framework as they opened a new phase of acquisitions, and charges of cruelty came into play. Not satisfied simply to seize other Europeans' colonies and claim them based on right of conquest, the English looked beyond the idea that might makes right. One option, firmly grounded in long-standing European legal systems, was to assert that the colony invaded was already owned by the invaders and had been unjustly taken from them. The English would use this strategy in the conquest of New Netherland. But in that case, as well as in the case of Jamaica, they also deployed charges of abusiveness; they brought religion and ethics into play to undermine the rights of both Spain and the United Provinces.

While it may be unsurprising that English Protestants—who had long hated and feared Spanish Catholics—would castigate Hispanic character in this way, their subjection of the Dutch—their fellow Protestants and erstwhile allies—to the same treatment was more unexpected. The Spanish, as powerful adherents to a church many English considered both wrong and dangerous, were obvious targets. In the 1650s English leaders felt called by God to fight against Catholicism; they assumed that the Lord would favor any struggle against "papist" Spain.[4] On a related note they resurrected the conventional idea that the Spanish were cruel, especially in their treatment of the natives of the Americas. Although the Dutch were Reformed Protestants, a religious position they had shared with the English since the Reformation, religion came into play in the justification to seize New Netherland as well. According to this view, the Dutch were ungrateful toward their rescuers, the English. Like the Spanish, the Dutch were sadistically cruel. They were similarly guilty of atrocities, in this case against the English directly, rather than against proxy innocents, such as native peoples. In order to battle with the Dutch the English had to demonize them, just as they had long done to the Spanish. Although the Dutch started out joined with the English as major Protestant opponents of the Hapsburg kings, their English rivals subsequently recast them as remarkably like their former enemies and oppressors. Yet Dutch cruelty was figured as personal and particular, whereas Spanish abuse occurred on a grand and impersonal scale.

On the face of it the two conquests have little in common. Although both events shifted ownership of minor colonial outposts, the locations of the two differed drastically: Spanish Jamaica rested in the midst of the Caribbean Sea, while New Netherland nestled along the Hudson River on the North American mainland. The revolutionary regime headed by Oliver Cromwell invaded Jamaica, having recently killed a king and conquered both Ireland and Scotland. Nearly a decade later, after the Restoration had ended the revolution, James—the Duke of York and Albany, that martyred king's son, and an implacable foe to the regime that had murdered his father—masterminded the seizure of the northern colony. In capturing Jamaica, Cromwell's fleet invaded a Catholic settlement, acting on a historic spirit of antipopery.

The Duke took a Reformed Protestant colony owned by the Westindische Compagnie (Dutch West India Company, or WIC) at a time when James was a member in good standing of the Protestant Church of England. The Caribbean conquest, although the work of a massive fleet, was badly botched and took fully five years to complete; the staggering loss of life on the English side was attributable largely to disease and malnutrition. James's more modest campaign to the north was completed without casualties in New Netherland proper, although the small outpost on the Delaware River experienced fatalities when it was subsequently assaulted. Whether considering the actors, the objects, or the outcomes, these two efforts appear remarkably different.

Both campaigns nonetheless faced the problem of justification, the need to defend the act of invasion. Although the providential world view in wide circulation at this time seemed to endorse military success, in that victorious combatants could see their triumphs as part of God's plan, most people believed that war would only earn God's favor and indeed could only be fought to a victorious conclusion if its cause was just. The simple act of successful conquest was insufficient in and of itself. The right to invade had in turn to be explained. Contemporaries turned to just-war theory, a venerable set of ideas about when as well as how to wage war, to analyze specific military projects. According to this tradition, which by the mid-seventeenth century drew upon a variety of sources, defensive wars were always acceptable. Offensive wars—of the sort that the English conducted in both of these cases—had to meet certain criteria to be credible. Among the accepted reasons were "to regain from the enemy something which he is forcibly and unjustly detaining" (and the English would use a version of this explanation in the seizure of New Netherland); to right a wrong; to respond to rebellion; or, more controversially as time went by, to combat heresy.[5] Conquests, even when they succeeded, were not automatically defensible, and both in going into war and afterward early modern Europeans expected a compelling case for the legitimacy of a given conflict. Whether at the level of scholastic argumentation or of popular opinion, these ideas—that God would smile on a military endeavor only if it was fought in a just cause—were widespread, and they induced those who mounted seemingly offensive wars to justify them. Although the English did not hold theological debates of the sort the Spanish hosted at their universities in the sixteenth century, they nonetheless worked to justify their decisions to wage war in both Jamaica and New Netherland.

The conquest of Jamaica proceeded on the twin themes of popery and cruelty. Hostility to popery was by the mid-1650s a powerful force in English politics. Having been officially and continuously Protestant since Elizabeth came to the throne in 1558, England expanded its commitment to Protestantism in part through an anti-Catholic campaign, citing executions of Protestants in the reign of Mary I ("Bloody Mary") and underscoring the threat posed by the mighty Hapsburgs under Phillip II of Spain. Fear of "papists" tended to focus less on the small resident Catholic population and more on such Catholic outsiders as the Irish or the Spanish.[6] Cromwell and others who supported the revolutionary regime of the 1650s were vehement anti-Catholics. In a speech to parliament justifying war with Spain, Cromwell rehearsed the history of the Catholic Hapsburgs' enmity to the Protestant English. He alluded to the Irish Rebellion, implying that the alleged massacre of Protestants in Ireland in 1641 had been the responsibility of the Spanish. He then argued that the English state could not have relations with any Catholic state, save the French who "do not think of themselves [as] under such a tie to the Pope." Spanish Catholicism rendered that kingdom the implacable foe of a Protestant England, according to Cromwell's analysis.[7]

These militant visionaries declared themselves compelled to undermine Spain's possession of the best of the New World, replacing brutal Iberian power with benevolent English Protestant rule. Viewing Catholicism as at best erroneous and at worst evil, the leaders of England in the 1650s believed that replacing Catholic colonizers and missionaries with Protestants would save Native Americans from being misled into error and damnation. In commissioning five men to oversee the design, Cromwell asserted his hope that God would make them instruments to rescue the natives from "Popish and cruell Inquisition" and to plant true religion.[8] As John Morrill has pointed out, Cromwell was convinced that "God wanted the English Revolution exported so that the world could be rid of popery and the menace of the Antichrist."[9] During the military campaign in the West Indies the password used by the army was "Religion," a telling indication of how its leaders perceived their project.[10] That God intended to oversee an English victory over popery was axiomatic to these Protestant would-be conquistadors.

Central to their antipopery and particularly to its Hispanophobic version was the idea of Spanish cruelty. The image of the cruel Spanish had circulated in Protestant Europe for a century by the time the English fleet sailed to Jamaica. Such phrases as "Popish and cruel Inquisition" referenced this concept. Accusations of Spanish cruelty cited atrocities in the wars of religion within Europe as well as the mistreatment of Native Americans. The latter theme gained great currency and became central to the so-called Black Legend associated with the Spanish.[11] Ironically, the major evidence for this cruelty came from the pen of a Spanish author who wrote *Brevísima relación de la destruición de las Indias* (Brief Account of the Destruction of the Indies) to persuade the authorities to modify the policies pursued in the colonies.[12] Dominican Bartolomé de las Casas published a detailed denunciation of atrocities in the West Indies. His graphic account described mass murder and torture undertaken in the initial years of the conquest, when private men licensed by the government were free to set their own bloody policies. Las Casas further alleged that such cruelty continued even after the opening years.

Brevísima relación spared no detail in the effort to depict the inhumane sufferings inflicted upon the Indians. Las Casas attributed massive population loss in the Caribbean Islands entirely to "divers kinds of torments neither seen nor heard of before," which the Spanish deployed as they "so cruelly and inhumanely butchered" the "quiet Lambs" they found in the Indies.[13] Many editions, including that produced in England in the 1650s, contained gruesome illustrations of soldiers, wearing the signature helmets of the conquistadors, hacking, roasting, and otherwise slaughtering unarmed and naked Indians. According to Las Casas, "the children they would take by the feet and dash their innocent heads against the rocks, and when they were fallen into the water, with a strange and cruel derision they would call upon them to swim." One captain told Las Casas, after he had burned alive a large group of natives inside a house he had made them construct before carrying off others to forced labor, "I was commanded by those that sent me, that those I could not take by fair means, I should seize by force." In an interpretive gesture heartily endorsed by English Protestants, Las Casas deemed one particularly vicious conquistador "an enemy of God." During a genocidal incident that took place in Guatemala, "witnesses affirm that they have seen a cloud of Indians falling down from the Mountain, which were all bruis'd to pieces." Tossing victims from cliff tops had become necessary when soldiers were "wearied with murdering" them in other ways.[14] Contrasting simple, innocent Indians with sadistic Spanish, Las Casas made a compelling humanitarian case for a change in policy.

Although Las Casas aimed his account at an audience of Spanish officials, the enemies of Spain republished it in other European languages later in the century. Seeking to highlight Spanish perfidy, the Dutch were the first to reprint it (under the title *Seer cort Verhael vande destructie van d'Indien*) at the time of their independence movement. Responding to events such as the vicious sack of the city of Antwerp in 1576, they launched a propaganda campaign against the Spanish. As Benjamin Schmidt explained, Dutch editions of

Las Casas carried "near canonical status among the sacred texts of the Revolt."[15] The Dutch printing was followed by translations into French—*Tyrannies et cruautez des Espagnols, perpetrees e's Indes Occidentales* (1579)—and English—*The Spanish Colonie* (1583).[16] In England the appearance of Las Casas's text coincided with the moment when Elizabeth I's support for the Dutch cause was moving her inexorably toward open conflict with Spain. This publication pattern in which renewed hostilities with Spain sparked a return to the theme of cruelty recurred repeatedly, and Las Casas was republished across Europe in the coming decades. As anti-Spanish polemic, his vivid and enduring depiction of cruelty perfectly served to rally opposition to Spain. Little wonder that hostile Europeans repeatedly dusted off their copies of Las Casas and sent it back to the press for another printing so often after the original reprinting.

Predictably, the English rehashed these themes in the 1650s, another time of heightened animosity toward Spain. In commissioning the commander of the land forces dispatched to the Caribbean, Cromwell laid out the case against Spain in three parts. They claimed "all that part of the world" on the basis of "the pope's donation"; they "exercise[d] inhuman cruelties upon the natives"; and they prohibited trade and settlement, resorting to "destroying and murdering" as well as capturing settlers and traders to enforce their claims.[17] A cynical reading of Cromwell—and one that did not take his religious agenda seriously—might focus on the first of these three issues, as the extent and profitability of Spain's American empire did cause widespread envy. Cromwell's other two points, cruelty to the Indians and the extension of that abusive treatment to Europeans who ventured to the region, were not simply disingenuous. Nor were they minor issues. In his published *Declaration* outlining the reasons England attacked the Spanish West Indies, Cromwell noted that "it would have been as Dishonourable and Unworthy for Us, who, through the goodness and providence of God, were so well furnisht with Ships of War fit for Foreign Service, to have let them lie rotting at home, rather than to have employed them for the just Revenge of so much English (why may we not also say) Indian blood, so unjustly, so humanly, and so cruelly spilt by the Spaniards in those parts." Cromwell was a dedicated providentialist, who suspected that God would provide military might to the godly when wrongs needed to be righted. Why God waited over a century to put the English into a position to address these atrocities, Cromwell did not say. Having implicitly equated the extensive sufferings of the native peoples with more modest sufferings the English were alleged to have endured, he then went on to make a case for the common humanity of all, Indians and

English, to make sense of English intervention on behalf of abused Indians. After traveling thus far down the path of human rights (and responsibility to revenge wrongs done to others on the grounds of common humanity), Cromwell drew back somewhat, stating that the "blood and spoils of our own Countrymen" were sufficient to warrant English intervention.[18] With this point he had circled back around to the sort of wrongs most theorists of just war were considering when they stated that wars might be fought to correct injustice. The catalog of ship seizures and other infractions that fill the later sections of the *Declaration* contained far less bloodshed and far more property loss than the reader might expect, given the Protector's easy equation of the enormity of native suffering with English tribulations.

Further supporting this agenda and following in the tradition of reprinting Las Casas at moments of heightened antagonism toward Spain, translator John Phillips brought out another English edition under the evocative title, *The Tears of the Indians: Being an Historical and True Account of the Cruel Massacres and Slaughters of above twenty millions of innocent people, committed by the Spaniards in the islands of Hispaniola, Cuba, Jamaica, &c.: as also in the continent of Mexico, Peru, & other places of the West-Indies, to the total destruction of those countries,* in 1656. In prefatory statements putting the publication into a context for English readers, Phillips opened with a reference to the "above Twenty Millions of the Souls of the slaughter'd Indians"; but then confided that the cry for blood among them had, "methinks," been silenced by Cromwell's revenge upon the Spanish. An English assault on the Spanish West Indies, according to Phillips, responded "to the will of the most High." Like Cromwell, Phillips linked the alleged massacre of thousands of Protestants in Ireland to atrocities in America, ascribing all to the same perpetrators.

In an awkwardly revealing passage Phillips noted that the English had on occasion been culpable of cruelty as well, but they were redeemed by their reaction to their own brutality. "When our own Case had a small Resemblance of this, how sensible the People were, and how they mourned at the burning of a poor Village; the usual Accidents, or rather, things to be expected, in a tedious and necessitated War."[19] We can easily imagine how the Pequot Indians—all the men, women, and children slaughtered as they fled the flames of their burning village—would have responded to this profession of English restraint and regret, not to mention the Irish who had been subjected to the brutal reconquest campaign led by Cromwell earlier in the decade. The English potential for cruelty was a cause for worry, and Phillips's vague and reassuring mention did not begin to address the problem. Despite these incidents and a growing association of their New World colonies with cruelty, the English construed their own rule as benign in contrast to the "Proud, Deceitful, Cruel and Treacherous" Spanish.[20] Mentioning Spanish cruelty was a routine, even expected, move, as geographer Samuel Clarke indicated. In putting together his *Geographicall Description of all the Countries in the known World*, Clarke interrupted an account of the lifeways of native peoples in various New World locations in order to paraphrase Las Casas's indictment of Spanish cruelty; after a full four pages of atrocity he offered his opinion that recent volcanic eruptions in Peru were divine punishment for this injustice.[21]

Official support for assessments in this vein helped pave the way for a limited resumption of theatrical performance in interregnum London, despite the storied opposition of revolutionaries toward play acting. Sir William Davenant produced an anti-Spanish opera of sorts in London in the later 1650s, exploiting the Cromwellian desire to promote Hispanophobia in support of the war. Davenant, who had been a playwright at Charles I's court before the Revolution and would live to produce plays in Charles II's London, eventually circumvented opposition to theatre by presenting innovative pieces on historical themes designed to please both audiences and the authorities. By 1658 he had already been emboldened to move his historical productions out of a private residence (Rutland House) and into a proper theater. His next effort, *The Cruelty of the Spaniards in Peru. Exprest by Instrumentall and Vocall Musick, and by Art of Perspective in Scenes, &c.*, was "Represented daily at the Cockpit in Drury-Lane, At Three after noone punctually."[22]

Davenant's show exploited the image of Spanish cruelty along with other stereotypes. As the performance opened, Incas were depicted living a wild but simple and harmonious life, enjoying an egalitarian existence among frolicking apes. (Along with other Europeans who wrote of the New World without leaving Europe, Davenant had a sketchy and inaccurate sense of the mega-fauna that he might find in Peru.) The action proceeded through Spanish subterfuge and conquest, which allowed the victorious conquistadors to torture and abuse the natives. One scene was staged with "a dark Prison at great distance; and farther to the view are discern'd Racks, and other Engines of torment, with which the Spaniards are tormenting the Natives and English Marriners, which may be suppos'd to be lately landed there to discover the Coast." In addition to the rack, they employed water and fire tortures on their victims. The Indians complained that, although the Spanish alleged that they came to fight the Indians' idolatry, they would not permit conversion, "because the Christian Lawe makes Converts free." This speech challenged a major justification for the Spanish presence in the Americas, that they brought Christianity and through it the possibility of eternal salvation to the inhabitants. While a baseless accusation against the Spanish—whose missions far outstripped any English effort—this claim resonated with the opposition of the English toward the conversion of their own (usually African) slaves.[23]

After underscoring the natives' sorry condition, the story culminated in a battle in which a combined English and Peruvian force defeat the Spanish. With the help of an ape—who danced joyously once more—the Spaniard was driven into the woods. The English led this victorious campaign, the Indians coming along behind in support of their newfound champions. Davenant presented the English fantasy that their moral and religious superiority would draw oppressed natives to them for succor against the inhumane Spanish. The opera closed with a gratifying if inelegant Incan chorus:

After all our dysasters
The proud Spaniards our Masters,
When we extol our liberty by feasts,
At Table shall serve,
Or else they shall starve;
Whilst th'English shall sit and rule as our guests.

The accompanying dance included the Spaniard paying homage to the English while still displaying "pride and sullennesse toward the Indians"; meanwhile the English and Indians "salute and shake hands, in signe of their future amity."[24] The haughty and tyrannous Spaniard came to a fittingly servile end, while the Indians, rescued from abusive masters, happily embraced the benign authority of the English. The performance promulgated Spanish cruelty and English benevolence, all choreographed to various rousing or doleful tunes. Davenant, eager to stage pieces that would be acceptable in the Commonwealth era, used an experimental form to present the popular theme of Iberian atrocity. Spanish cruelty easily served to justify war, while it helped steel English resolve to fight; it might even have helped Cromwell and his cronies find the stage acceptable.

The attack on the Spanish was fueled by English anti-Catholicism and envy of Iberian successes, supplemented with reference to Spanish depredations against English traders and settlers but especially with the trope of Spanish cruelty toward the Indians. English accounts often glossed over the fact that the Spanish had not, in taking the New World, directly antagonized English men and women. Cruelty to native peoples both indicated the despicable character of the Spaniards and suggested that they might do the same to the English. Davenant's piece put the English in the Americas at the time of the conquest, subjecting them to Spanish torture alongside the benighted natives. In other cases the seizure of English trade goods and of the colony of Providence Island in 1641 was placed on a continuum with atrocities committed against others, suggesting that banishment with only the goods a settler could carry was related to being stretched on the rack.[25] Cruelty and Roman Catholicism went hand in hand in the Spanish case, forming a dialectic relationship that made self-evident sense in the context of English anti-Catholicism. In Davenant's opera as well as in Cromwell's rhetoric, the English slipped back and forth between saving Indians and functioning as their fellow victims. Spanish cruelty was a threat, but it was also an opportunity for displays of English valor and goodness.

Having fine-tuned their justification for expansion based on the cruelty of their opponents in the Spanish case, the English turned this paradigm against a less likely group, their sometimes allies and fellow Protestants, the Dutch. The English had assisted the United Provinces in their efforts to get out from under the Catholic Hapsburg yoke during Elizabeth's reign, which they believed ought to have earned England the right to undying gratitude. That expectation, that the Dutch would continue as grateful junior partners in the anti-Spanish cause, was dashed when the United Provinces used their newfound freedom to develop into the preeminent global merchants. Dutch primacy as traders put them in competition with English interests, which strained relations, undermining the harmony supposedly based on shared religion. Although the anti-Dutch images were arrived at through a slightly different route, contentions of cruelty similarly justified war. English writing made sense of Dutch atrocities not by references to popery but rather through claims of ingratitude and lack of true religion.

Before they marshaled these charges, however, the English announced that they had every legal right to seize the colony of New Netherland in 1664. According to their interpretation, the English crown held rights to all of the coast of North America from the new colony of Carolina north to New Scotland (Nova Scotia). At the time when the Dutch had stolen the area around the Hudson River in 1624, it rightly belonged to the English and was labeled on maps as part of Virginia. Even in 1609, when navigator Henry Hudson, then in the employ of the Vereenigde Oost-Indische Compagnie (East India

Company, or VOC), sailed up the Hudson River to the future site of Fort Orange, or Albany, the area was already part of the newly founded colony of Virginia. Some versions of the history made much of the fact that Hudson was an Englishman who was duped or coerced by the Dutch.[26] In asserting that the Dutch colony founded some time later by the WIC was illegally seated on English land, expansionists neglected to respond to the obvious question: why wait for four decades after the colony's founding to reclaim that stretch of North America? Charles II granted to his brother the Duke of York a vast tract that included New Netherland and the lands along the Delaware River, while both areas housed Dutch settlers and were encumbered by Dutch claims, and he did so without even alluding to the presence of these rival colonizers.[27] The Dutch thought this issue the crux of the matter, and the States General of the United Provinces labeled English assertions to the contrary "ridiculous." During the negotiations leading to the fall of the colony Governor Peter Stuyvesant was shocked to hear the commander of the English forces state the "he would not lend himself to any argument as to his Majesty's right, and whether the Dutch had any title to this place; but said, he left all such to be vindicated by the King himself, for, had his majesty commissioned him to attack Amsterdam, in Holland, he should make no scruple about undertaking the business, leaving its justification to the King."[28] While the Dutch wanted to debate title with a chance to prove the superiority of their own claim, the English merely gestured to their self-evident right as their ships sailed into the bay and proceeded to threaten the Dutch government with force.

Behind the English assertion that they were in fact owners of the colony that the WIC had planted and run for decades was the oft-repeated allegation that the Dutch routinely took that which was not theirs. The Dutch, as the preeminent traders of the mid-seventeenth century, were the object of envy and suspicion. Whereas the English desperately wished to emulate Dutch economic success, they also entertained the notion that the Dutch succeeded through subterfuge. It was axiomatic by the 1660s that the Dutch used foul means to engross the trade of the world. As one pamphlet put it, "The Neatherlanders from the beginning of their Trade in the [East] Indies, not contented with the ordinary course of a fair and free Commerce, invaded divers Islands, took some Forts, built Others, and labored nothing more, than the Conquest of Countries, and the Accruing of New Dominion." It was not so much their success as the means they used to attain it that their rivals found objectionable, according to scholar Steven Pincus.[29] In one arena after another, their English critics alleged, the Dutch worked to eliminate other traders and to exercise complete control. To accomplish their goals they were willing to seize ships, trading posts, and lands; and they would not stop at murder, although their favored method for violently eliminating competition was inciting local people to attack European competitors who posed a challenge to their own dominance of trade. In sending natives to attack the English, the Dutch forgot their shared cultural and religious heritage. Forsaking European and Protestant solidarity, they sanctioned the murder of their fellow Christians.[30] Selfish and unscrupulous, the Dutch behaved in an inhumane fashion in order to secure economic advantage.

In abusing the English in particular the Dutch demonstrated their gross ingratitude. The English loved to remind the United Provinces that their independence had been won with English help during the late sixteenth century. As the beneficiaries of aid in the long war against the Hapsburgs, the Dutch ought to have been eternally grateful. Yet they were not. Instead of adopting a subservient position as clients to their English patrons, the Dutch had the nerve to use their newfound independence to create a global trading empire. As one author petulantly observed, "England, more like a Father then Neighbor to them in all their necessities, are requited by Holland with unsufferable Cruelties, Treacheries, and Tricks." The Dutch even extracted the fish from the waters off the coast of Scotland, sustaining themselves on the herring of others to fuel their meteoric rise. Dutch ingratitude was a recurrent theme. One anti-Dutch poem rehearsed how the English "buoy'd up your sinking States,/ Rescu'd you from that Force, by which you were/ Thrown down into the bottom of Despaire." It continued by sarcastically referencing repeated indignities as examples of the "Kindness" that the Dutch had shown in return.[31] Numerous publications—from broadsides to books—limned the history of Dutch ingratitude. In *His Majesties Propriety and Dominion on the British Seas Asserted*, the author, who was apparently the author and translator Robert Codrington, labored to demonstrate Dutch ungratefulness, which involved him in a detailed discussion of Elizabethan military interventions. John Crouch's verse pamphlet expostulated:

Who shed their rich blood for your Infant State;
First to procure your Freedom, than your Hate.
Doe not so farr degenerate, to conclude
Your utmost Period with Ingratitude.[32]

It was maddening to the English to think that they had helped raise up the United Provinces only to have those states turn on them and treat them with such contempt. In the England of the 1660s some authors thought that the Dutch failure to acknowledge their indebtedness might be related to their republicanism. Supporters of the Stuart monarchy understood the recently ended revolution as arising from (among other things) ingratitude to the royal family. By extension the republican United Provinces, infamous for their lack of gratitude, might owe this character flaw to the nature of their polity. A small, insignificant country "that scarce deserves the name of land, As but th'off-scouring of the British sand," the Dutch ought to know their place and acknowledge their obligations to the English.[33]

The final accusation made against the Dutch, and repeated with remarkable frequency, was the charge of cruelty. The Spanish were widely believed to have abused the Indians, which formed the core of English accusations against them. In the Dutch case, however, atrocities had been perpetrated directly on English bodies, or so it was commonly thought. In 1623 agents of the Dutch VOC arrested, tortured, and executed ten English employees of the English East India Company along with one Portuguese man and nine Japanese men in Amboyna (modern-day Ambon, Maluku Province, Indonesia). According to the Dutch the men had plotted to seize Amboyna fort and massacre the occupants; the English asserted that false confessions were tortured out of innocent men. The incident had been a cause célèbre from the time the first pamphlet recounting the events was published in 1624. The major account, *A True Relation of the uniust, cruell, and barbarous proceedings against the English at Amboyna in the East-Indies*, was frequently reprinted in various editions; furthermore, as was typical of early modern publication practices, much of the text was imported into the publications of other authors.[34] Amboyna quickly became well-known, the word often appearing in print, reference to it always denoting Dutch tyranny, cruelty, and duplicity. Well before John Dryden wrote a play about it for the occasion of the third Anglo-Dutch War in the 1670s (for which he drew heavily on the 1624 version of events), Amboyna was embedded in the English cultural vocabulary.[35]

In the English telling, the events at Amboyna pitted cruel tyrants against innocent, honorable men. The situation in Indonesia was tense, as the Dutch and English traders differed over the implementation of an agreement that divided the local trade into shares, with the English as junior partners. The Dutch became suspicious of the English on the island when a Japanese soldier asked questions about fortifications. The authorities arrested him. They then proceeded to torture the over-curious soldier as well as an alcoholic English surgeon they happened to have in custody, to extract confessions of a conspiracy to take the Dutch factory. Based on these confessions the Dutch arrested all the English in the town and seized their goods. VOC officials tortured the prisoners in order to corroborate the confessions they had already heard. The original English account, which served as the basis of other publications over the decades, detailed the torture methods used, including the rack, water, and fire. Leading questions structured the interview sessions, and their tormentors encouraged men not only to lie but to agree to events that were obviously impossible—such as meetings that occurred when some of the conspirators were not physically present in Amboyna. One man who said he would confess whatever they wanted was accused of mocking the proceedings, since the authorities wanted the conspirators to hit upon the right admissions without underscoring the spurious nature of the entire effort. The tragic hero of the tale was the English leader, Captain Towerson, who acted honorably throughout but whom the Dutch especially sought to implicate in the conspiracy. As the account movingly described, many who gave false confessions later asked for Towerson's forgiveness.

A *True Relation* made a strong case for English blamelessness and virtue. The condemned men used various means (including notes appended to bills that they paid as they awaited death and interviews with men who had been accused but released) to communicate their innocence. Before the execution they forgave each other and their captors. While the Dutch Reformed clergyman called in to minister to them in their last hours refused them communion because they would not ask forgiveness for their purported crimes, they awaited execution in prayer and psalm singing.[36] Their deaths were described using the imagery associated with martyrdom: they all "with great Chearfulness suffered the fatal stroke."[37] Remarkably, the English tale even suggested that God showed his displeasure with the outcome in a gesture reminiscent of Christ's death on the cross. Whereas various gospel accounts relate that during the crucifixion the sky grew dark while the moment of Christ's passing was marked by earthquakes, in the case of the Amboyna martyrs, "at the instant of the Execution, there arose a great darkness, with a sudden violent gust of Wind and Tempest."[38] Along with the Christian demeanor of the martyrs, this climatological validation was presented as further indictment of the Dutch. The popular view of Amboyna circulating in England and the English Atlantic world affirmed English piety and depicted Dutch inhumanity.

While the English version of events at Amboyna equated the Dutch with the Spanish and thereby made it easier to countenance war with an erstwhile ally,

Dutch cruelty in the standard narrative differed in notable ways from Spanish cruelty presented in Las Casas, the main text in that tradition. Spanish atrocities, as reproduced from Las Casas, had been acted out on such a vast scale as to be almost incomprehensible. Las Casas did enumerate the murder of native elites, often by name and always by rank, in order to make the case that the conquistadors, usually lowly men themselves, overturned the social system with their indiscriminate violence against members of the indigenous nobility. The vast majority of victims, however, were nameless Indians, described as poor and innocent. Las Casas peppered his account with frequent reference to the murder of women and children. The cruelty to the Indians amounted to genocide, and the reader experienced the challenge typically associated with ideologically driven mass murder: it is difficult to comprehend the enormity of such evil. Spanish cruelty thus took on an unreal quality, events so monstrous as to be difficult to grasp. Spanish acts of cruelty, as recounted by English authors, became atrocities in part because of the sheer volume of the bloodshed; Daniel Baraz has argued that early modern quantification of cruelty helped render some acts unacceptable simply on the grounds of scale, regardless of the reasoning behind them. English use of Las Casas, emphasizing as it did the unimaginable scale of the destruction, fit this shift.[39]

Dutch cruelty at Amboyna occupied the opposite extreme on the continuum. The English victims appeared as individuals, named and quoted. They had flaws and failings. Some of them betrayed their fellows and subsequently had to seek forgiveness. Far from a scene of genocide, the crime at Amboyna was the work of a few men who targeted other specific individuals. The reader identified with the English victims, not only for their Englishness but also through the specificity of their stories. Modern readers might find that the hero of the tale, the ethical and resolute Captain Towerson, presaged the eighteenth-century sentimental literature surrounding the tragic hero John André.[40] The author of A True Relation did not render the other, non-English victims in the same loving detail, although the presentation of them and their plight was sympathetic. It was also more specific than most of Las Casas's descriptions of victims of native genocide. A True Relation listed all twenty of those killed by name and birthplace, including not only the one Portuguese man but the nine Japanese as well. Dutch cruelty as exercised at Amboyna constituted specific acts of brutality against individual sufferers, and the details allowed the reader to empathize with the individual victims to an extent not possible for the readers of Las Casas. If English readers stood ready to believe that the Spanish reached new heights in inhuman brutality, they might have needed to be persuaded that the Dutch were capable of similarly unconscionable acts. The writing on Amboyna made the case by documenting Dutch viciousness against named sufferers, many of them English but all of them identified as particular people.

Amboyna loomed in the background as the English seized New Netherland and moved toward wider war with the Dutch. When King Charles sent commissioners in 1664 to visit his colonies in New England, he explained his plan to take the Dutch colony and the thinking behind the move. Making reference to Amboyna, Charles II linked Dutch actions there to a more general tendency to steal what belonged to others. In order to prevent the Dutch from using New Netherland as a base from which to conduct similarly heartless operations in the region, Charles declared his intention to regain the land and thereby eliminate their threatening presence.[41] Armed with the conviction that the Dutch would abscond with the property of others, and would do so violently without qualms, the English felt justified to become the aggressors in their stead. Preemptive war was defensible on the grounds that the Dutch could be expected to encroach on other people's property and to resort to sadistic cruelty to reach their goals.

Another arena in which the English were simultaneously confronting the Dutch was the west coast of Africa. The king dispatched a small fleet there early in 1664, to counter claims that the WIC held the right to all trade on the so-called Gold Coast. Under the command of Sir Robert Holmes, the English fleet took most of the WIC forts and trading posts, leaving only the fortress at Elmina in Dutch hands. When the Dutch retaliated by secretly assigning a larger force to retake its possessions and to expel the English from all of their outposts, the English did not view this as the predictable response to their own act of aggression. Instead they interpreted it within the framework of Dutch atrocity. Rumors flew through London that the triumphant Dutch force—which managed to reduce the English presence to the same level at which Holmes had previously left the Dutch, with only one fort on the coast—had murdered all the English present, including women and children. When dealing with the Dutch, the English expected cruelty at the service of greed.[42] They did not see their own efforts at aggrandizement in the same light, thinking their aggression warranted when they were dealing with the sadistic and selfish Dutch. Anti-Dutch propaganda pressed the point that the United Provinces and the various Dutch trading companies routinely stole and murdered.

Despite this campaign some English continued to feel uncomfortable with the prospect of fighting Dutch Protestants. Hostility to the idea of making war upon coreligionists had helped bring the first Anglo-Dutch war to a close. At that time newly elevated Lord Protector Oliver Cromwell used the treaty negotiations to exact restitution for the Amboyna incident, thereby further undermining the case for anti-Dutch action.[43] Some would argue that with Amboyna finally resolved, the reasons to fight were not sufficiently compelling.[44] Supporters of the war effort addressed the issue of a shared religion in order to forestall such objections. The Dutch were not good Christians, critics averred. Their supposed willingness to use torture offered some evidence in defense of that view. As the Restoration Church of England abandoned its historical commitment to Calvinism for a softer theological position on the availability of salvation, some even ventured to denigrate the Dutch church, reformed in the Calvinist strain, as a flawed Christianity. In the Restoration era Calvinism was increasingly associated with the civil wars and regicide, calling the religion into question more generally. The natural alliance that Cromwell saw between his own faith and that of the Dutch did not so obviously prevail when the Restoration Church of England was substituted on the English side of the equation.[45] Regardless of the worth of their specific brand of Protestantism, the Dutch cared more for trade than for religion and demonstrated their lack of commitment to the latter when, for instance, they offered not to raise the issue of conversion when trading with Japan. Their policy on this issue was much appreciated by the Japanese, who gained trade partners without having to submit to a missionary campaign, and it distinguished the Dutch from other prospective European traders who had not agreed to this criterion. Unlike Davenant's unfair accusation that Spanish colonial policy actively avoided native conversion, the claim leveled at the Dutch had a basis in fact. In this fashion even liberty of conscience within the Netherlands and throughout their global trade networks was taken as evidence that the Dutch were irreligious. Their critics asserted that they permitted all religious expressions out of lack of commitment to their own faith.[46]

The case in favor of seizing the colony of New Netherland relied only lightly on the alleged English ownership of that region and focused instead on flaws in the Dutch character. Their penchant for cruelty, their unscrupulous acts in pursuit of profit, and their religious faults—whether their Calvinism, their wanton permissiveness, or their irreligion—all contributed to the justification for English aggression. The English took Dutch forts along the Gold Coast of West Africa and the colony of New Netherland, telling themselves that the Dutch were not to be trusted. The Dutch would grab that which was not theirs and would gain the advantage through sadistic acts of torture without a second thought. Their reprehensible behavior was a far cry from the obsequious gratitude that would have been an appropriate stance to adopt vis-à-vis the English who had rescued them from Hapsburg tyranny. The Dutch, who in their long battle with the Spanish had taken the lead in promulgating the Black Legend of Spanish variant, were themselves the target of similar accusations. Dutch cruelty—like Spanish cruelty—could be trotted out at any turn to explain why a colony was subject to invasion or why war ought to be declared.

The adaptability of this use of cruelty was remarkable. If the Spanish—the original conquistadors in the Americas and papists to boot—were the obvious targets in the Elizabethan era and afterward, accusations against them made sense in the context of English anti-Catholic rhetoric. That the Dutch—fellow Protestants and occasional allies—could be demonized in similar terms revealed the flexibility of such indictments. To prepare people for war, pamphleteers cited the mistreatment of the Indians—occasionally, as in the case of Davenant's dramatic presentation, adding English victims to the tableau— or the torture and murder of English traders in Southeast Asia. That these events occurred a century earlier (as in the case of the abuses recounted by Las Casas) or decades before (as in the Amboyna incident) made little practical difference. That restitution had finally been received for the East Indian outrages was of no consequence. Although his father and grandfather had done little to gain satisfaction for the indignities at Amboyna (which had only been achieved by his father's nemesis, Oliver Cromwell), Charles confidently used the Amboyna grievance as if the abuses there had direct relevance to his own day or to Dutch comportment in North America. Encompassing Protestant torturers into the established trope of papist cruelty would seem a stretch. The extension to the Dutch became possible because the Dutch tortured Englishmen. Suffering English bodies stretched on the rack, with water forced down throats, hit far closer to home—even if the events occurred in the distant East Indies—than all the tales of butchery of Indians on Hispaniola. Hispanophobes depicted Spanish cruelty occurring on a scale so vast as to be unimaginable, and on some level the English no longer had to be able to imagine it since they simply believed it. Harder to sell was the phenomenon of the Dutch sadist. That vision was presented with such dense detail as to be easily corroborated. English victims named and quoted were able to remake Dutch Protestant allies into vicious, irreligious torturers. As scholar Ayanna Thompson noted, Dryden's *Amboyna*, while contributing one among a number of torture scenes in the historical tragedies of the Restoration era, was unique within that genre in its display of English victims.[47] Inhuman Dutch actions when perpetrated on the English themselves raised the public's ire sufficiently to countenance war against the United Provinces.

The roles the English imagined for themselves were sometimes unspoken but always revealing. Most obviously, they vacillated between savior and victim. In the rhetoric surrounding the Spanish such fluctuation was literally on display. On the one hand the English rescued the Indians, as in Davenant's rendering, or they sailed on to the scene belatedly to vindicate their suffering; on the other the English shared the cruel fate of the natives, being tortured on the rack along with them or being subjected to supposedly equivalent abuses when they attempted to trade. With the Dutch, the English at Amboyna clearly served as victims, and it was only through the subsequent declaration of war that they might avenge those atrocities. Whether fellow victims, saviors, or avengers, the English were always godly in the general sense of virtuous and good Christians. The meaning of godliness—which took on something of a sectarian taint in the minds of Cromwell's opponents—shifted, and the ostensible English commitment to godly behavior even declined somewhat, at least in the Restoration court.

Still the English rhetoric continued from the era of the revolution through the Restoration to cast the English as the better Christians. That they were superior to Spanish papists appeared self-evident (at least before James's conversion to Catholicism). Their better religiosity in relation to the Dutch had to be constructed more consciously, through intimations of Dutch irreligion and cruelty. That the rhetoric, so strongly associated with Catholics, could be applied to fellow Protestants supports the point that Barbara Fuchs has made in Chapter 3 in this volume about the constructed nature of religion difference. The necessity—or perhaps the opportunity—to deploy difference in this fashion outlived the transitional period of the Reformation, coming into use again in the seventeenth century.

In order to take the land of another Christian prince (or of an upstart republic) the English defamed the character of those they attacked. In their construction the English were never intentionally cruel; when they found themselves being unkind, they were unique in that they felt remorse. Implicitly the English construed themselves as better colonizers, a people whose imperialist turn was justified by their superior character. Imperial ambition drove a wedge between coreligionists and former allies, as the justifications developed to deal with the Spanish conditioned the later conversations about facing the challenge posed by the Dutch. Applying the different logic of Spanish and Dutch cruelty—one cosmic in its proportions, the other focused and personal—the English managed to arrive at the same place. That space allowed, even required, English expansion and the seizure of the colonies of others.

CHAPTER 3

Religion and National Distinction in the Early Modern Atlantic

Barbara Fuchs

—In memoriam Richard Helgerson

This essay is an attempt to think through the fragile and purposeful nature of religious difference in the sixteenth-century transatlantic world of Spain and England. For this early period religious difference between Catholic Spain and Protestant England is often taken as a given, when in fact such difference was very much up in the air and often pressed into service to make a point about national distinction. As Jorge Cañizares-Esguerra has recently argued in *Puritan Conquistadors*, the worldviews of English and of Spanish settlers in the New World had much in common, from their belief in the presence and power of Satan in the Americas to their sense of a providential national election.[1] Cañizares-Esguerra shows that "British Protestants and Spanish Catholics deployed similar religious discourses to explain and justify conquest and colonization: a biblically sanctioned interpretation of expansion, part of a long-standing Christian tradition of holy violence aimed at demonic enemies within and without."[2] In his encyclopedic *Empires of the Atlantic World*, J. H. Elliott reminds us that the English conceived of their providential mission in the Americas in the same terms as the Spanish, even borrowing their vocabulary to describe the *reduction* of native peoples to Christianity.[3] We fail to recognize these similarities, however self-evident, partly because of the increasing parochialism of New World history, as Elliott points out,[4] and partly because the radical difference of an ultra-Catholic, inquisitorial Spain is so ingrained in the Anglo-American worldview.

Beyond the actual connections that Cañizares-Esguerra and Elliott note, there are many moments over the course of the sixteenth and seventeenth centuries at which the English either return to or contemplate a return to Catholicism. Moreover, the mimetic pressure for a belated England to imitate Spain in its imperial expansion often elides any religious distinctions. In keeping with the new critical attention to *sameness*, this essay revisits the deliberate use of religious difference as an ideological tool in the effort to distinguish England from Spain as an imperial power. Conversely, I show how often England's own understanding of its place in the transatlantic world was fundamentally indebted to Spain, despite whatever confessional differences the Reformation may have introduced. I do not mean to suggest that the similarities between the national and imperial identities of Spain and England were any less constructed than the differences. Instead, my intent is to problematize religious difference in the transatlantic world as a stable, fully established distinction, through a concerted effort not to read later divergences back into the sixteenth century. By analogy with the body of work that has interrogated teleological readings of early modern English imperialism and of the nation itself, reminding us of how uncertain and contradictory ideology appears in the moment of its emergence, I suggest that religious difference is often far more tactical and situated than we have recognized.[5] In order to recover this sense of the contemporary confusion and blurring of boundaries, my reading focuses not on religious discourses per se, which are the most categorical in their prescriptive account of differences between Catholicism and the reformed Church, but rather on the broad spectrum of texts—accounts of the New World, real and imaginary encounter narratives, national epic—that consider religious difference in the context of transatlantic expansion.

Eden on Eden

In the mid-1550s, during the brief Catholic interregnum of Mary Tudor and Philip of Spain, the humanist Richard Eden translated Peter Martyr d'Anghera's 1516 *De orbe novo decades* into the *Decades of the Newe Worlde or West India* (London, 1555). Although Christianity had undergone successive shock waves in the interim between original and translation, Eden's version manifests a striking avoidance of religious difference, the better to signal the translator's adherence to the new regime in England. In the exhortative preface to his translation Eden imagines English goals as fully aligned with those of Spain, in a *Christian* mission to convert the native peoples of an Edenic New World.

There are several important erasures in Eden's framing of Martyr's text: first, the peoples of the New World are described as a *tabula rasa*, all too ready to be imprinted upon by European Christianity: "These simple gentiles lyvinge only after the lawe of nature, may well be lykened to a smoothe and bare table unpainted, or a white paper unwritten, upon the which you may at the fyrst paynte or wryte what you lyste."[6] Second, the fissures in that Christianity are minimized, despite the abundant resistance to Mary's restoration of Catholicism in England. Praising the Spaniards for their conversion of New World peoples, Eden chides, "Even so I do thinke them no trewe Chrystian men that do not rejoyce with the Angels of heaven for the deliverie of these owre brootherne, owre flesshe, and owre bones, from the handes of owre commune enemie the oulde serpente" (50). In a persuasive reading Andrew Hadfield argues that, in the interest of dampening Protestant criticisms of Spain, Eden strains to avoid in his preface the ambiguity that often characterizes Martyr's own account of Spanish conquests.[7]

Instead, Eden takes the English to task for not doing as much as the Spaniards have done:

> Howe much therfore is it to be lamented, and howe greatly dooth it sounde to the reproche of all Christendome, and especially to such as dwell nerest to these landes (as we doo) beinge muche nearer to the same then are the Spanyardes (as within xxv dayes saylinge and lesse) howe muche I saye shall this sounde unto oure reproche and inexcusable slothfulnesse and negligence bothe before god and the worlde, that so large dominions of such tractable people and pure gentiles, not beinge hytherto corrupted with any false religion (and therefore the easier to bee allured to embrace oures) are nowe knowen unto us, and that we have no respecte neyther for goddes cause nor for oure owne commoditie to attempte summe vyages into these coastes, to doo for our partes as the Spaniardes have doone for theyrs. (55)

It is not clear from Eden's somewhat ambiguous and heightened rhetoric whether English "commodity" takes precedence over "God's cause." What is evident is that he imagines shared goals for England and Spain that both comprise and transcend religion. Author and reader, Spaniards and Englishmen, are united in their position vis-à-vis the unnamed "false religions" that might corrupt the peoples of the New World. But their shared Christianity is only part of what brings them together; they also share a responsibility to act "before the worlde" in pursuit of profit. Yet in urging the English to do "for our partes as the Spaniardes have done for theyrs," Eden shatters the sense of unitary purpose that animates his religious rhetoric.

Eden denies Spanish greed, as critics of the conquest might have it: "They have taken nothynge from [the native peoples of the New World] but such as they them selves were wel wyllynge to departe with, and accoumpted as superfluities, as golde, perles, precious stones and such other." Indeed, he claims the Spanish conquest as "bondage...much rather to be desired then theyr former libertie" (57), given that the Spaniards protect them from cannibals. (As Hadfield has shown, Martyr's text offers episodes that complicate the very distinction between Spaniards and cannibals, underscoring the voraciousness of Spanish greed for gold.)[8] Ultimately, then, Eden must acknowledge Spanish greed, although he insists that it does not undo the importance of Christianization: "Even so although summe wyll obiecte that the desyre of golde was the chiefe cause that moved the Spanyardes and Portugales to searche the newe founde landes, trewly albeit we shulde admitte it to bee the chiefe cause, yet dooth it not folowe that it was the only cause, forasmuch as nothyng letteth but that a man may bee a warrier or a marchaunte, and also a Christian. Therefore what so ever oure chiefe intente bee, eyther to obteyne worldely fame or rychesse, (althoughe the zeale to encrease Christian religion ought chiefly to move us) I wolde to god we wolde fyrst attempte the matter" (57). As Eden moves seamlessly from *their* to *our* "chiefe intente," he also acknowledges that Christianization may be only a by-product of the search for riches in the New World, yet—and this is where the text reveals its true ideological investments in "worldely fame or rychesse"—that recognition does not make imperial expansion any less to be desired or devoutly pursued.

In rebutting accusations against Spain, Eden's preface acknowledges, however unwittingly, that not all readers would accept his enthusiastic version of the *conquista* as an exemplary Christian enterprise. Indeed, the text seems to have retained enough ambiguity that Eden's intended official audience was unconvinced: in the same year that the translation was published he was both accused of heresy and relieved of his official duties at the Treasury. One might hazard that some readers found in Eden's enthusiastic calls for England to stoop to and imitate Spain an unavoidable irony. Such is the reading proposed by Claire Jowitt, who deems Eden's preface "a carefully encoded critique of the uneasy English political situation of the 1550's," designed to goad the English to action.[9] Yet beyond the undecidable question of Eden's intimate religious conviction, it seems clear that his account of England's difference from Spain—in its failure to pursue an empire—and its similarity—in a fully shared and unfragmented Christianity—is strategic. Eden's powerful admonition to England to emulate Spain's empire holds whether that admonition is born of true admiration and belief in Christian unity or of revulsion and Protestant dissimulation.

Loose Change: Gold and Virtue

Despite Eden's mimetic desire for empire and his readiness to enlist England in Spain's Christianizing mission, there is from early on in the history of European expansion across the Atlantic a particularly English hesitation in the face of New World temptations, even before the Reformation makes it desirable to mark that hesitation as Protestant. This vacillation, which Jeffrey Knapp in *An Empire Nowhere* describes as a paradoxical kind of *contemptus mundi*, is perhaps most evident in Thomas More's *Utopia*, where the refusal of gold and of the cupidity associated with it are key signs of virtue.[10] More's island of Utopia is itself a colonized space, yet its conquest by the eponymous Utopus occurred long ago and has largely been lost in the mists of time. Gold lust plays no role in that ur-colonization, which is presented instead as a civilizing mission, bringing "its rude and uncouth inhabitants to such a high level of culture and humanity that they now excel in that regard almost every other people."[11] The author thus avoids the obvious moral failings of a colonial enterprise motivated by cupidity, such as would be anatomized by Bartolomé de las Casas in his devastating accounts of Spanish conquests. Although More's Utopians practice a fanciful religion, their attitudes toward gold are highly topical, anticipating the famous attacks of Las Casas and others on the legitimacy of a Spanish dominion whose ostensible spiritual dimensions were vitiated by the lust for gold. As Peter Herman notes, More would have been well aware that by 1516 the "superficially pious intentions of the Spanish and other 'converters' of the Amerindians," which had led the pope to grant Spain dominion over the New World, had come under general suspicion, with the Dominicans in particular denouncing Spanish depredations in the Caribbean.[12]

In contrast with European cupidity in the New World, More's ideal is measure in all things, a Horatian *aurea mediocritas,* except that a crucial aspect of the Utopians' lust-lessness is their disregard for gold: "Meanwhile, gold and silver are so treated by them that no one values them more highly than their true nature deserves. Who does not see that they are far inferior to iron in usefulness since without iron mortals cannot live any more than without fire and water? To gold and silver, however, nature has given no use that we cannot dispense with, if the folly of men had not made them valuable because they are rare" (84). The specific focus on gold as an arbitrary object of value, despised by the Utopians, remits us to the earliest New World encounters. From Columbus's first voyage gold was one of the primary goals of exploration, even if the admiral conceived of that gold as the means for fighting a new crusade against Islam. In Vespucci's letter on his purported first voyage (on which *Utopia* is partially based) he betrays the European interest in gold while ostensibly describing the natives' *dis*interestedness: "The wealth to which we are accustomed in this Europe of ours and in other parts, such as gold, jewels, pearls, and other riches, are of no interest to them, although they have them in their lands, they neither labor to procure them, nor prize them."[13] Vespucci's wondrous account of the natives' disregard for gold contributes to the construction of the New World as a paradisiac place, where the values of the fallen world lose their importance, while simultaneously the gold ignored by the natives lies there for the taking. In Martyr's later description of the "Comogruans," astutely read by Hadfield, the dynamics of gold lust are more complex: what distinguishes the virtuous Comogruans from the Spaniards is that they "no more esteem rude gold unwrought, then we doo cloddes of earthe": what they value is the social worth of the metal once it has been formed into beautiful and significant objects, whereas the Spaniards, who would melt down all such objects, value it only as a commodity.[14]

In More and in his reception there is a kind of mirroring or metalepsis: the virtuous or primitive (depending on one's point of view) disregard for gold initially associated with the indigenous New World subject is transferred to the ideal Utopian and thence to the moderate, ethical English take on conquest. Although *Utopia* was written before the spectacular Spanish plunder of Aztec and Inca riches, More's stigmatization of gold lust is oddly prescient: in Utopia gold identifies slaves and "those who bear the stigma of disgrace on account of some crime"(86). More thus disparages the quest for gold and obliquely criticizes the more rapacious aspects of the imperial enterprise. Yet, as Antonis Balasopoulos notes, the Utopians' deliberate attempts to debase gold in highly symbolic fashion by manufacturing from it everything from chamber pots to slave's chains to children's toys betray their fetishistic relation to it (more akin, I would add, to the Comogruans' focus on social worth than to the Spanish valuing of the commodity). Despite the humor of More's account, gold becomes "an idol on which the ambivalent, psychic dynamic of a community is projected in a fusion of reverence and animosity, worship and abuse."[15]

Some of this ambivalence is apparent as More's paradoxically virtuous Utopians are recalled in later texts. For whatever their doctrinal differences, the Catholic, humanist, temperate More's attitude to gold is reprised in key Protestant figures associated with Elizabethan expansion, as the classical and traditionally Christian virtue of temperance is put in the service of a militant Protestantism. These writers seem to have absorbed what Balasopoulos terms the "productive and positive character of Utopia's detachment from a historical reality which had certainly seemed to exclude England," emphasizing a desirable English difference where gold was concerned.[16]

Utopian lustlessness returns in Edmund Spenser's most explicit meditation on the New World, Book II of *The Faerie Queene*, the "Legend of Temperaunce." Temperance, as David Read usefully reminds us, "is characterized by abnegation—by not doing certain things, acting in certain ways, or following particular paths....Lacking positive alternatives, Spenser faces the puzzle of portraying English colonial conduct primarily by what that conduct is not."[17] Yet as Read himself notes, the vaunted English temperance exists mainly in theory, in those places where England has failed to achieve a colonial foothold. Matters were very different in Ireland, where a most intemperate violence, even by the standards of the day, was the response to Spanish encroachment on England's restive colony.[18]

In *The Faerie Queene*, however, temperance is offered as central to the English gentleman and colonist. In Book II, the knight Guyon, presented with a vision of riches reminiscent of Mexico or Peru, stalwartly refuses Mammon's gold:

Regard of worldly mucke doth fowly blend
And low abase the high heroicke spright,
That ioyes for crownes and kingdoms to contend;

Faire shields, gay steedes, bright armes be my delight;
Those be the riches fit for an aduent'rous knight. (2.7.10)

Strikingly, even as Guyon rejects Mammon's gold, he underscores his imperial ambitions "for crownes and kingdoms to contend," as though an "aduent'rous knight" could achieve such a project in a state of pure disinterestedness. As Read has argued, Guyon seems the "anti-conquistador," "stripped of the usual attributes of conquest," and knows to value power—riches as a means to an end—rather than gold itself.[19] Yet how convincing is the parsing of power over riches? And how might the abundant contradictions in the great Protestant epic's prescription for a gentleman's behavior inform the imperial ideology of Spenser's dedicatee, Sir Walter Ralegh? The rhetoric of temperance, I suggest, sanitizes a longing for imperial plunder that is both morally compromising in its own right and especially problematic in undoing the supposed difference between England and Spain.

In Ralegh's own conflicted *Discovery of the Large, Rich, and Beautiful Empyre of Guiana* (1596), measure and avoidance (however hypocritical) become closely associated with the English alternative to Catholic Spain. The language of virtue is everywhere in the text, even though Protestantism is rarely invoked. In his "Epistle Dedicatorie" to Howard and Cecil, Ralegh denounces those who either "forejudged that I would rather become a servant to the Spanish king, than return" or "who would have persuaded that I was too easeful and sensual to undertake a journey of so great travel."[20] The *travail* of travel instead serves as a test of the virtuous and religious subject, Ralegh argues, as "the gracious construction of a painefull pilgrimage," from which he himself is returned "a begger, and withered" (121).

In Ralegh's account English difference is predicated on Spanish colonial excess, even though the English can only hope for an occasion that will truly test their forbearance in refusing such riches as the Spanish have found before them. Ralegh's fruitless search for Manoa/El Dorado is thus doubly fraught: it requires relying on previous Spanish accounts (although these are all failures) and also mirroring Spanish desires. Ralegh's difference from the Spaniards, he claims, stems from his virtue, but also from his strategic calculation that present excesses will prevent future gains. Thus the obverse of temperance and humility (assuming the opportunities for plunder were really available— it is by no means clear that Ralegh managed to find Mammon) is a fairly Machiavellian calculation: "But I have chosen rather to beare the burthen of poverty, then reproch, & rather to endure a second travel and the chances thereof, than to have defaced an enterprise of so great assurance, untill I knew whether it pleased God to put a disposition in her princely and royall heart eyther to follow or foreslow the same" (123–24). Thus what makes Ralegh's vaunted temperance possible is his *failure* as a conqueror, in contrast to the blatant hypocrisy of a truly successful figure such as Sir Francis Drake, whose pious iconoclasm leads him to the plunder of religious artifacts in the Spanish colonies. Interestingly, religion and conversion are largely absent from Ralegh's text, so that the difference between Spain and England consists mostly of the "temperance of necessity" that I describe above. The desire for conquest and profit meanwhile is fully shared between the two nations.

As Spenser recognized, gold is one of the pressure points in the fraught construction of national difference in a context of imperial competition. Consider those remarkable mimetic moments, in Drake and Ralegh after him, when the English mark their presence in New World territory with the coin of the realm: in "Nova Albion" (somewhere near San Francisco) Drake plants a sixpence "upon a faire great poste,"[21] while Ralegh, in Guyana, distributes shillings for the Indians to wear, ruefully noting that he handed out much more gold than he actually found. While the coins bear the image of Elizabeth, the kindly sovereign touted to the indigenous peoples as an alternative to Spanish tyranny, the English replacement of the Spanish Cross with loose change speaks volumes. Whatever their rhetoric of religious purpose, Protestants are as motivated by greed as the Catholics ever were, if not more. Their vaunted virtue, much like the gold they distribute, is an investment in future conquests. As Ralegh claims with inadvertent irony after showing off Elizabeth's image to the Indians elsewhere, "it had been easy to have brought them idolatrous thereof" (134).

Converted *Pícaros*

In closing I want to revisit a slightly earlier text, a fascinating narrative of national and religious distinction that, like the accounts of Drake's and Ralegh's voyages, was collected in Richard Hakluyt's *Principal Navigations*. I first wrote about the story of Miles Philips a few years ago, when, by a happy coincidence, Richard Helgerson also turned to the same text.[22] Yet we read this narrative of a young boy abandoned in New Spain by Hawkins on his disastrous 1568 voyage in completely different terms. Helgerson focused on the "irreducible core of Protestant Englishness"[23] that Miles found within himself while living among Catholic Spaniards in New Spain and conceived of him as an epic figure, committed to the return home and to that wholeness of self of which dissimulation had deprived him. Conversely, I read the text as a kind of picaresque *relación*, in which Miles had to justify himself to his English readers once he returned home by emphasizing a difference that he did not necessarily experience or embody as he passed for a Catholic and a Spaniard for many years.

How to reconcile these completely different yet plausible readings? The key lies in our shared recognition of the constructedness of national identity and its relation to religious difference. For in both our understandings of the text, religious difference—or the lack of it—is crucial to the construction of national distinction. In this vein I focus on the equivocation produced when Miles and his fellow Englishmen are hauled before the Inquisition as "Lutherans," given that Catholic dogma could not have been unfamiliar to men born in all likelihood to Catholic homes. Helgerson, too, recognizes the newness of this difference on which national identity must hang: "When Hawkins' fleet first sailed, the Protestant Reformation was just fifty years old, and its most recent identification with the English state dated back less than nine years, to Elizabeth's accession in November 1558."[24] Rereading the text with the benefit of Helgerson's interpretation, I would suggest that the key might be to expand our sense of the performance in the text: the slippery Miles does not just pass as a Spaniard or a Catholic; he also learns how to *cobble together* a Protestant English identity. Instead of the humanist core that Helgerson finds within Miles, I find an able bricolage of recollections and experiences into a Protestant subjectivity—even though our end results look very similar.

Moreover, to focus on Miles's agency—authentic or strategic, irreducible or assembled—is to tell only half the story. Both Helgerson and I overemphasize the narrator's "I," whether as emerging heroic self or evasive *pícaro*. Helgerson argues that the simple existence of Miles's narrative and the fact that he resisted marriage and the Inquisitors' surveillance prove his "unbendable sense of who he is and who he wishes to remain."[25] I would argue instead that the Inquisition is also operating under its own notions of difference, as essential for the construction of a Spanish identity in opposition to "Lutherans" (and Jews and Moors) as Protestantism is to the English. The text notes that many of the Englishmen who were abandoned with Miles were able to adapt to local ways, transcending such ostensibly essential differences, and Helgerson takes Miles's refusal of marriage in New Spain or a similar accommodation as basic evidence for his resistant Protestant self. The key passage for Helgerson, in which Miles's "I" virtually erupts onto the page, reads: "For mine owne part, I could never thoroughly settle my selfe to marry in that countrey, although many faire offers were made unto me of such as were of great abilitie and wealth, but I could have no liking to live in that place, where I must every where see and know such horrible idolatrie committed, and durst not once for my life speake against it, and therefore I had alwayes a longing and desire to this my native countrey."[26] What we cannot recover from this solid retrospective telling, however, is the extent to which Miles's own refusal to assimilate is determined by his violent experience of the Inquisition. It is thus due as much to a *negative* mistrust or suspicion of that institution's powers, which others may have been able more successfully to transcend, as to a *positive* embrace of Protestant difference. Thus, though Miles himself may be more or less deliberately dissimulating his allegiance to England, the constructedness of that allegiance as both a result of and a refuge from Inquisitorial persecution is undeniable. Those others who remain shadowy presences in his text clearly found it both expedient and amenable to embrace Catholicism—a religion that they probably knew well and that may for most of their lives have represented no contradiction with Englishness. The spectrum of identities limned by Miles's narrative thus includes everything from his companions who become martyrs to Protestantism and Englishness, put to death by the Inquisition; to Miles's own cautious (and opportunistic) self-fashioning; to the flexible allegiances of those Englishmen who agreed to marry local women.

The mimetic imperative resisted in the accounts of Protestant temperance I first charted, or repudiated in Miles Philips's claims of essential difference after passing in New Spain, underscores the tremendous energy required to forge Protestant difference out of England's very similar motivations and experiences. Yet we have largely accepted these Elizabethan claims of Protestant difference in the New World, overlooking just how strong are the mimetic pressures on the ground, as it were, as well as the Old World rapprochements that undo any sense of fixed alterity—the constant stream of texts and persons that circulate between Protestant England and Catholic Spain even at the most fraught periods. Ralegh, Spenser, and their circle were steeped in Spanish texts and Spanish ideas. For James, Spain would represent an attractive allegiance, and royal alliances were repeatedly considered between the two nations. But this closeness is belied by the powerful rhetoric of a temperate Protestant alternative to the rapacious, Inquisitorial Spain of the

Black Legend. In Spenser or Ralegh a rhetoric of virtue or temperance that is particularly English becomes as important as Protestantism in the construction of national identity, while in the Miles Philips text the vocal refusal of Catholicism, however suspect and unmatched by any positive content of Protestantism, becomes key. What transforms these complex texts, with their varying degrees of difference, into a heroic version of an English Protestant alternative to Spain in the New World is as much the retrospective construction of that difference as any inherent distinction.

CHAPTER 4

The Commonwealth of the Word

New England, Old England, and the Praying Indians

Linda Gregerson

Six months after the trial and execution of Charles I and two months after the formal declaration of an English commonwealth, amidst deliberative and legislative action on such urgent matters as the settling of army accounts, reforming of the admiralty, assessment and collection of taxes, impressment of sailors, billeting of soldiers, fen drainage, coinage, abolition of the Deans and the House of Lords, pursuit of the war in Ireland, and the sale of forfeited royal and bishopric lands, the Parliament of England turned its attention to a project we may at first imagine to be more remote. On the strength of reports from certain godly ministers in the field and with the intent of furthering their fledgling mission, Parliament established a corporation, the Society for the Propagation of the Gospel in New England, and appointed sixteen members to its governing board.[1] The New England Company, as it came to be called, was endowed with certain legal powers and obligations within the Commonwealth: it could sue or plead, be sued or impleaded in courts of law; it could purchase land and tenements in England and Wales, gather rents, receive and invest the proceeds of charitable donation. Its mandate, the purpose of these accumulations and investments, was the maintenance of ministers for the conversion of the Indians in New England; the provision of clothing, tools, and other materials conducive to the settlement that was thought to go hand in hand with conversion; and the foundation of "Universities, Schools, and Nurseries of Literature" for educating the natives and their children.[2]

Parliament's Act of July 27, 1649, "for the promoting and propagating the Gospel of Jesus Christ in New England," construes a profound continuity and reciprocal obligation between the radically reconstituted commonwealth of England and Wales and the "many hopeful Towns and Colonies" of New England. The authors of the Act refer to the North American settlers not merely as coreligionists but as conationals, part of an extended first-person plural. Since the godly "of this Nation" have largely exhausted their own estates in the course and labor of New England settlement, it becomes the duty of those still living within the ancient boundaries of the nation to support the work of conversion with money and material supplies: the authors "conceive our selves of this Nation bound" to help. Accordingly, the act mandates a national collection "through all the Counties, Cities, Towns and Parishes of England and Wales." Ministers are instructed to read the act in the presence of their congregations "upon the next Lords-day after the same shall be delivered unto them, and to exhort the people to a chearful and liberal contribution." Nor is this exhortation intended to die a quiet death beneath the cover of a general appeal. Following their solicitation from the pulpit, ministers and their delegates are instructed to go from house to house to every inhabitant of their parish and "to take the subscription of every such person in a schedule to be presented by them for that purpose."[3]

Despite some skepticism (monies collected earlier on behalf of the New England missionary enterprise had been poorly accounted for) and some confusion (the most prominent of the New England ministers continued to encourage private donations that bypassed the Society), this charitable fundraising gradually assumed significant proportions. Between the establishment of the New England Company in 1649 and the Stuart Restoration of 1660, charitable donation to the Society exceeded £15,900.[4] This amount was supplemented, as the Society exercised its rights to invest in urban and county real estate, by an additional £4,000 in rents. On the American side of the Atlantic, authority to disburse the money raised in England and Wales was vested in the Commissioners of the United Colonies, a confederate body that had been established in 1643 (some six years before the founding of the New England Company) to protect the common interests of the Plymouth, Connecticut, New Haven, and Massachusetts colonies.[5] In addition to bills of exchange and goods intended for direct distribution among the Indians (chiefly clothing, tools, and books), the Commissioners received from London a wide variety of merchandise intended for resale, having persuaded the Society in England that mercantilist activity of at least this limited scope would be the most effective means of transferring dispersible income across the ocean. The Society refused, however, to transfer its principal for reinvestment in New England, as the Commissioners urged it to do; primary investment was to remain firmly situated in England and Wales.

The business of North American conversion thus involved a reciprocal cultivation and survey of Old and New England: on the one side counties and parishes were systematically canvassed for benevolent donation, according to "schedules" and subscription lists, and properties purchased, administered, and leased; on the other side ground was brought under cultivation, meetinghouses and dwellings were built, and fourteen "Praying Towns" established for the furthering of Christian community among the Algonquian tribes of eastern Massachusetts. These networks of exchange and affiliation may seem to have been modest in scale, tenuously inscribed upon the political and economic landscapes that sustained them. But they were far from modest in philosophy or intent, and they were born of trauma and upheaval on both sides of the Atlantic. Even modest parcels of land, for instance, bore an immoderate weight of history: the Society's holdings in England and Wales included a significant proportion of Royalist estates sequestered in the course of civil war;[6] the "Praying Towns" in Massachusetts were conceived in part as a last and fragile bastion against European encroachment. For the Algonquians, ravaged by English disease and English appropriation, had no effective means of securing (English) title to traditional tribal grounds in the context of traditional land use; the colonists recognized no proprietary right to lands that remained uncultivated. "Take care," John Eliot exhorted the Commissioners, "that due Accommodation of Lands and Waters may be allowed them [the Algonquian tribes], whereon Townships and Churches may be (in after-Ages) able to subsist; and suffer not the English to strip them of all their Lands."[7]

But the deepest reciprocities between the faithful of England and Wales and their counterparts in New England were manifested not in acreage but in written words. John Eliot spent fifteen years learning Algonquian, devising an orthography that could render it on the page, and translating into that language both the Old and New Testaments of the Bible. That Bible, printed in 1663, was the first complete Bible of any kind published in North America. It was also as an instrument for Christian conversion, "without precedent in modern times, for there [had been] no tradition of such Bible translation for missionary purposes" since the patristic era of the Christian church.[8] Tellingly, John Eliot's Algonquian Bible predated the first Irish Bible by twenty-seven years and the first Scots Gaelic Bible by over a century. In addition to the complete Algonquian Bible, Eliot published preliminary translations of the books of Genesis, Matthew, and the "Psalms in meter" (1655–56); Richard Baxter's *Call to the Unconverted* (1663); Lewis Bayly's *Practice of Piety* (1665); an *Indian Grammar* (1666); an *Indian Primer* (1669); *Indian dialogues, for their Instruction in the great Service of Christ, in calling home their Country-men to the Knowledge of God, and of themselves, and of Jesus Christ* (1671); an *Indian ABC* (1671); a *Logic Primer* (based on the *Dialecticae* of Petrus Ramus, 1672); and Thomas Shepard's *Sincere Convert* (1689). All but the *Indian dialogues* were published in Algonquian; a second edition of the Algonquian Bible was completed in 1685.[9] Eliot's petitions for assistance from his English supporters and their New England agents routinely listed paper, type, and journeyman printers among his most urgent requests.

The New England mission also produced a remarkable series of publications printed in London, addressed to the people and Parliament of England, and affording an account of settlement and conversion among the Indians. Four such tracts or promotional pamphlets had been published before the founding of the New England Company, and a fifth appeared before the Society assumed responsibility for their production . Eleven tracts were published in all, each conveying its substance in colorful figures of futurity: *The Day-breaking, if not the Sun-Rising of the Gospell With the Indians in New-England*, and *The Light Appearing More and More Towards the Perfect Day, Or, a Farther Discovery of the Present State of the Indians in New-England, Concerning the Progresse of the Gospel Amongst them*.[10] These pamphlets are a conspicuous patchwork for the most part: letters written by Eliot and other ministers in the field; epistolary endorsements from the president of Harvard College, Commissioners of the United Colonies, and persons of note in Parliamentary England; partial transcriptions of the Indian converts in dialogue with their ministers and fellow congregants; and sermons and exhortations delivered by the Indians in Christian assembly. Among the most distinctive features of these pamphlets are lists of questions propounded by the Indians in the course of their spiritual training. The following questions, for instance, were propounded by the Indians of Natick, near Roxbury, Massachusetts, in 1649, and were duly recorded by John Eliot, their pastor:

> *If but one parent beleeve, what state are our children in?*
>   *How doth much sinne make grace abound? . . .*
>   *If so old a man as I repent, may I be saved? . . .*

*When we come to beleeve, how many of our children doth God take
with us, whether all only young ones, or at what age?*

What meaneth that, Let the trees of the Wood rejoyce?

*What meaneth that, That the Master doth not thank his servant for
waiting on him?*

What meaneth that, We cannot serve two masters?

Can they in Heaven see us here on Earth?

Do they see and know each other? Shall I know you in heaven?

Do they know each other in Hell?

*When English-men choose Magistrates and Ministers, how do they
know who be good men that they dare trust?*

*Seeing the body sinneth, why should the soule be punished, and what
punishment shall the body have?*

If all the world be burnt up, where shall hell be?

What is it to beleeve in Christ?

What meaneth, that Christ meriteth eternal life for us?

What meaneth that, Covet not thy neighbours house, etc.?

*What meaneth that, The woman brought to Christ a box of Oyle, and
washt his feet with tears, etc.?*

*What meaneth that of the two debtors, one oweth much, another but
little?*

*If a wicked man prayeth, and teacheth, doth God accept, or what saies
God?*

At what age may maids marry?

If a man be wise, and his Sachem *weak must he yet obey him?*

We are commanded to honour the Sachem, *but is the* Sachem
commanded to love us?

*When all the world shall be burnt up, what shall be in the roome of it
. . .?*

What meaneth God, when he sayes, yee shall be my Jewels?

(Whitfield *The Light Appearing* 132–33

The treatise in which these questions appear, *The Light Appearing More and
More Towards the Perfect Day,* was published by Henry Whitfield, "late pastor
to the Church of Christ at Gilford in New England," with the explicit intention of countering false reports to the discredit of the New England mission.
The questions that is, are offered as a form of surety, interim report, and
prospectus to an audience of interested investors, the Christian faithful of

Parliamentary England. Whitfield acknowledges discouraging rumors that the New England mission is but "a device or engine used...to cheat good people of their money."[11] Witness to the contrary, says this testimony from the field, the good use to which your money has been put.

"What meaneth that, We cannot serve two Masters?" In the context of the Society for the Propagation of the Gospel in New-England the precept has two primary connotations. First, it asserts the claims of monotheism, that peculiar economy of faith that construes a "jealous" God.[12] It is worth re-minding ourselves that this postulate and its correlative hostility to doctrinal deviation are not the inevitable foundations of religious faith. William Stra-chey reports in *The Historie of Travell into Virginia Britania* (1612) that the king of the Quiyoughcohanock Indians near Jamestown was wont to con-cede that "he beleeved or [*sic*] god as much exceeded theires as our guns did their bow and arrowes, and many tymes...did send to the President at Iames Towne men with Presents entreating him to pray to his god for rayne, for his gods would not send him any."[13] To Strachey's mind the Quiyoughcohanock perversely resist a self-evident logic: we want your god to help us, we concede our gods are false, we give them up. But no; the Quiyoughcohanock gods, it appears, are still very much in the pantheon; they simply will not send rain. "And in this lamentable Ignoraunce," the Englishman writes, "doe these poore sowles live."[14] Thomas Mayhew, preacher of the gospel on Martha's Vineyard, reports the efforts of the "praying Indian" Hiacoomes to convert one of his brethren. How many gods do the English have? asks the neophyte. Just one, says Hiacoomes. "And shall I (saith he) throw away these 37. gods for one?"[15] To the unconverted the bargain is patently a bad one. It is not simply that spiritual wealth is not assessed according to a single universal standard of weights and measures. The very numerability that signifies bounty in one system of faith is fatally discrediting in another.

"What meaneth that, We cannot serve two Masters?" The second assertion conveyed by the biblical precept is the opposition between God and Mam-mon,[16] the pursuit of this-worldly and other-worldly "profit." At the outposts of early modern empire—at the trading ports, in the meetinghouses and vil-lage schools, in the "factories" and on colonial plantations—we encounter the problematic overlay of two systems of circulating wealth: material and spiritual "commodity." The conversion of souls to Christianity confusedly motivates, overlays, competes with, and covers for the conversion of spices, fabrics, and metals into currency and back again. Eliot, minister of the Gos-pel in Roxbury, Massachusetts, reports that the Sachems (or native overlords)

are hostile to the conversion of their dependents and subordinates. "*Cut-shamoquin*... told me that the reason of this trouble was, because the Indians that pray to God...do not pay [the Sachem] tribute as formerly they have done." Eliot protests to his native informant that he has done his best to avoid direct conflict with the local authorities: "Once before when I heard of his complaint that way, I preached on that text, *Give unto Caesar*.... He said its true, I taught them well, but they would not in that point do as I taught them." But when the "praying Indians," or "meeting Indians," as they are called, itemize for Eliot all the labors they still perform, all the goods and money they routinely turn over to their Sachem, the inventory is so impressive that Eliot much "wonders" at what he takes to be wildly divergent accounts. "But the bottome of it lieth here," he concludes upon reflection, "[the Sachem] formerly had all or what he would; now he hath but what they will; and admonitions to rule better."[17] It is not simply that tribute and vassalage may be differently assessed and extracted in different social systems, but that identical measures of tribute and vassalage may be differently assessed and extracted within a *single* social system. Obeisance performed in one spirit may be superabundant; performed in another spirit, it is scant. The preacher's disingenuous stipulation ("Give unto Caesar all that is Caesar's") has venerable precedent, but Caesar and the Sachem have always known that their conflict with Christianity is real and mortal. They too have heard the precept against two masters. When they hear themselves admonished from below, they know they rule on sufferance.

"*If a man be wise,*" asks a convert in Massachusetts, "*and his Sachem weak must he yet obey him?*" The Parliament that sponsored the Society for the Propagation of the Gospel in New-England during the early years of Eliot's ministry had concluded in January 1649 that conscience obliged them to kill a king. Far from resolving the divergent constructions of faith and allegiance, material interest and corporate identity that had pitted Kirk against Prayer Book, Ulster planter against Irish Catholic, Cavalier against Roundhead, Parliament against the king, and the army against Parliament, the dismantling of monarchy and the Laudian church had unleashed yet further convulsions of centrifugal dissent. There were those who saw a providential, even an apocalyptic, link between turmoil in the old world and the new. "For the *Shaking of all Nations*," writes Edward Reynolds, "maketh way for the coming of him, who is the desire of all Nations."[18] And J.D., "Minister of the Gospell" in Old England, writes: "These godly persons who fled into *America* for shelter from *Prelaticall persecution*, doe now appeare to be carried there by a sacred and sweet providence of Christ."[19] Sixteenth-century England had been a noted haven for religious refugees; by the middle of the seventeenth century this trend had been dramatically reversed, with more than twenty thousand English emigrants having left the country to escape religious persecution.[20] Eliot was himself among the nonconforming churchmen who had fled the established Church and shores of England in order to practice his faith more freely; his mission to the Algonquian was a consequence, not the instantiating motive, of emigration.[21] So the Lord "counterplots the enemy in his designes," J.D. asserts, "making the late Bishops persecuting of the Godly tend to the promoting of the Gospel."[22] "The Lord," writes Joseph Caryl, "*who is wonderful in Councel, and excellent in working*, hath so wrought, that the scorching of some of *his people* with the *Sun of persecution*, hath been the enlightning of those who were *not his people* with the *Sun of righteousnesse*."[23]

One of the more convoluted debates among planters and preachers on both sides of the Atlantic had to do with the supposed origins of the American Indians. The debate was not merely speculative, despite its frequent abstruseness, nor was it disinterested: the genealogy of the Indians had direct bearing on the settlers' understanding of their own place in providential design. In 1650 Thomas Thorowgood published the first edition of *Jewes in America, or, Probabilities that the Americans are of that Race: With the Removal of some Contrary Reasonings, and Earnest Endeavors to Make Them Christians*. Like the Rabbi Menasseh ben Israel of Amsterdam and like Edward Winslow, who drafted the act that established the Society for the Propagation of the Gospel in NewEngland and served on the Society's first board of governors, Thorowgood was convinced that the Amerindians had descended from the ten lost tribes of Israel. This theory, argues J.D. in his appendix to *The Glorious Progress of the Gospel, amongst the Indians in New England*, has won "the Generall consent of many judicious, and godly Divines" and "doth induce *considering minds* to beleeve, that the conversion of the Jewes is at hand."[24]

Despite a passage in the Massachusetts Charter declaring that conversion of the native populations was "the principal end of this plantation," New England ministers had been slow to begin their evangelical work. And despite a general conviction, based on prophecies in the books of Daniel and Revelation, that the millennium would be signaled by two mass conversions, that of the Jews and that of the Gentiles, the faithful disagreed on which conversion would precede the other and what this boded for active proselytizing. Eliot appears to have embraced the lost-tribes theory for a period of seven years or so, but his mission to the Algonquian both preceded and outlived that period.[25]

The debate over tribal origins was dizzying in its complexity and confused in its practical import but clear, for all that, in its foundational assumptions: the fate of England's exiled population of believers, of the gospel among the Amerindians, and of the English Reformation on its own native soil were indissolubly entwined. In letters addressed to fellow ministers in England and Wales in October 1649, leading divines of Oxford and Cambridge endorsed the labors of the New England Company as "not at all relating to, or ingaged in the unhappy differences of these sad and discomposed times,"[26] that is, as a means of advancing the interests of the church while healing division within it. And for significant contingents in the army (a large source of the Society's monetary support) and in Parliament, the New England church of the Puritan diaspora afforded a template for work that had yet to be accomplished at home. To their minds the New England church was bound to cast its beacon in two directions: its mission extended outward to the Indians, whatever their origins, and backward to the stalled Reformation in England.

The logic of eschatology was also entwined in New England with the fiduciary logic of mercantilism and plantation. Plantation requires that there shall be some palpable return on investment, some aggregate influx of wealth to the metropolitan center that sponsors exploration and development. In its trade with the Orient early modern Europe had had to reckon with an embarrassing imbalance in consumer demand: while the East afforded great quantities and varieties of merchandise much coveted in Europe, Europe appeared to have very little that the East coveted in return. Hence the pivotal usefulness of New World gold: it was not only desirable in itself; it could also promote the circulation of moveable wealth in other parts of the world. Possessed of the one true faith, of course, Christian Europe could tell itself that it possessed a pearl worth all the wealth of the heathen nations combined and indispensable to the well-being of those nations, if only they could be brought round to the proper understanding. Eliot's letters, writes J.D. in an appendix, "are as a discovery of a far more precious *mine* in *America*, then those *Gold* and *Silver* ones of *India*: For they bring tidings of the *unsearchable riches of Christ* revealed unto poor soules in those parts."[27] And, writes Joseph Caryl, "This gaine of soules is a *Merchandize* worth the glorying in upon all the *Exchanges*."[28]

The problem with this impeccable rebalancing of the books is that it could not be made to work out very neatly in pragmatic terms. The New England mission to which John Eliot and Thomas Mayhew devoted their lives had to offer its underwriters the spiritual satisfaction of performing good works in lieu of material profit. The work of the gospel in Roxbury, in Natick, on Martha's Vineyard, in Pawtucket, is "difficult, not only in respect of the language, but also in respect of their barbarous course of life and poverty; there is not so much as meat, drink, or lodging for them that go unto them to preach among them, but we must carry all things with us, and somewhat to give unto them." Eliot dwells, as well he might, upon the practical difficulties that attend conversion among a population afflicted with much material want. And he appears to feel it as an advantage that he can offer the Algonquian a double advancement, both material and spiritual: "They shall flock unto the Gospel, thereby to receive externall benificence and advancement, as well as spirituall grace and blessings." From a less sanguine perspective, however, the practical difficulties Eliot describes are compounded by the further difficulties they engender, difficulties both heuristic and political. Christ preached among the Gentiles as a poor man, as Eliot himself points out, "a poore underling, and his servants poore,"[29] yet his English servants come to the Indians armed with relative riches and power. Is it not possible that their example will be misleading? That the material incentive will obscure or deform the spiritual? The Commissioners of the United Colonies cautioned Eliot that the Indians might "onely follow Christ for loaves and outward advantage Remaining enimies to the yoak and goverment."[30] Acknowledging the real and present danger of material bribes, one anonymous promoter of the New England mission tried to distinguish its methods from those of the Catholic competition on these very grounds: "If wee would force them to baptisme (as the Spaniards do . . .) or if wee would hire them to it by giving them coates and shirts . . . wee could have gathered many hundreds, yea thousands it may bee by this time . . . ; but wee have not learnt as yet that art of coyning Christians."[31]

According to Edward Reynolds, the Indians may measure the truth of (Reformed) Christianity and the disinterestedness of its promoters by the latter's opposition to worldly riches. Joseph Caryl thumpingly concurs: "How much it doth become Christians to let Heathens see that they seek *them* more then *theirs*; That the gaining of them to Christ is more in their eye, then any worldly gain."[32] But the Indians are not certain how to read this. "*What meaneth God*," they ask in Massachusetts, "*when he sayes, ye shall be my Jewels?*" To covet the souls of the Indians, rather than their furs and precious metals, is for Caryl to be absolved of mercenary motive, to be found pure. But at some ideological distance his words induce something of a chill. Add to the peculiar imperatives of monotheism the peculiar imperatives of a proselytizing church and you have a formidable institution hungry for expansion. The

English faithful construed their mission as a merciful corrective to the murderous depredations they associated with the Spanish conquest—and thus with Roman Catholicism. But the harms engendered in the name of faith have never been exclusive to a single church. Hypocrisy and cynical self-interest on the part of the proselytizers afford tempting interpretive "solutions" to the historical conjunction of material exploitation, violent demographic shifts, and Christian conversion. If sheer bad faith afforded a fully sufficient account, the interpretive conundrum would evaporate. To my mind it does not.[33] "In the old law," writes William Strachey, "the elected Iew accompted every Iew his neighbour only, yet synce the time of Grace, we are taught to acknowledge every man...to be...our neighbour." Under the new law the faithful are instructed to "Goe, and baptise all Nations,...that all Nations might be...Partakers of...Redemption."[34]

The planters in New England needed money for seed, tools, settled shelter, books, paper, schools, and journeymen printers. "I finde it absolutely necessary," writes Eliot, "to carry on civility with Religion."[35] The civility he describes has two main branches: (1) that which Eliot calls "cohabitation," the establishment of settled communities among the Indians so that they may function as congregations, and (2) literacy. Neither project is simple: land must be brought under cultivation, the habits and techniques of husbandry must be introduced, a language must be written down, the Bible translated. But the pragmatic difficulties of settlement and education, daunting as they may be, pale beside the epistemological difficulties of propagating a text-based religion among a people who have no tradition of literacy. The problem was especially keen for Protestant missionaries, who could not rely on the liturgical and sacramental mediations of the Roman Catholic Church. This was what the Reformation had been *about*. Christ is represented in a book, as the Word that at once fulfills and supersedes an earlier testament, the mere letter. But what can this mean to those for whom the letter itself is an innovation? The central textual strategy of the Gospels, the parabolic logic that overturns while relying on an earlier textual tradition, assumes mind-boggling complication in the New England plantation. John Eliot—he who transcribed the questions reprinted above—reports in 1658 on the exegetical progress of his converts. In a time of sickness and bad harvest the Indians of Natick gather together for a day of fasting and prayer. The "exhortations" they offer and that Eliot records are more elaborate than the questions of a decade earlier: the Indians have now been trained to perform their own ritualized *explication de texte*, and this at a time when they have "none of the

Scriptures printed in their own Language, save *Genesis*, and *Matthew*, and a few *Psalmes* in Meter."[36]

The Indian Waban takes his text from Matthew: "*I will have mercy and not sacrifice; for I came not to call the righteous, but sinners to Repentance*" (Matthew 9:13). "What!" says Waban. "Doth not God love them that be righteous? Doth he not call them to him?...Is not God righteous?" Answer: "These words are a Similitude.... The righteous here are not meant those that are truly righteous, but those that are Hypocrites; that seem righteous, and are not; that think themselves righteous, but are not so indeed."[37] The Indian John Speene takes his text from Matthew as well (Matthew was the only gospel the Indians had so far): "*I... baptize you with water... but he that cometh after me...shall baptize you... with fire.*" This too is a similitude. "You all know what fire will do; for when your Tobacco-pipes are filthy, foule, stinking, unfit for your use, you cast them into the fire, and that doth not burn them up, but burneth up all their filth, and maketh them clean and sweet, & fit for your use. So our hearts are filthy, and unfit for Gods use, but cast our hearts into the word, for there the Spirit is, and then the Spirit of God will burn out all our filth and sin, and make us sweet, and fit for the Lords use."[38] The God of the Englishmen speaks in figures, and nowhere so insistently as through the mouth of his Son.

Thomas Mayhew, out on Martha's Vineyard, records a homelier scene, less bookish, that he takes to be evidence of progress in spiritual understanding among his converts. A five-day-old child of "meeting Indians" has died, and Mayhew beholds a remarkable change in the ceremonies of passage: "Here were no black faces for it as the manner of the Indians is, nor goods buried with it, nor hellish howlings over the dead, but a patient resigning of it to him that gave it;...and as we were going away, one of the Indians told me he was much refreshed in being freed from their old customes, as also to hear of the Resurrection of good men and their children to be with God."[39] Conversion installs its own sort of double-entry system, one in which God's creatures are always and hopelessly in debt on account of their sins but capable of being "redeemed," bought back for salvation by Christ. The paradox of the Protestant ethic, whatever it may have done for capitalism, involves the profound discrediting of "works." In order that the macroeconomic vista be one of hope, the microeconomic vista must be one of despair: I can never make good on my debt to God; it is presumption (and a deadly sin) to think I can. According to what logic then, should Reformed Christians invest in the propagation of the gospel?

"Come forth ye Masters of money," writes J.D. in his appendix, "part with your gold to promote the Gospel. . . . If you give any thing *yearly* . . . Christ will be your *Pensioner*. If you give anything into *banke*, Christ will keep *account* thereof, and reward it. . . . [W]hat ever you give will be well and wisely improved."[40] That is, contributions to the New England plantation for which he canvasses will be a *good investment*. But wasn't it the founding purpose of the Reformation to remind the faithful that they cannot buy their way to heaven? Whitfield, though he publishes *The Light Appearing More and More Towards Day* in order to promote plantations, paints a rather darker picture of what the investor may hope to secure: "Brethren, the Lord hath no need of us, but if it please him, can carry his Gospel to the other side of the world . . . and leave us in Indian darknesse."[41] Eliot finds something of a middle ground: "Your faithful and unwearied paines about the Lords work for the good of his dear children here, and for the furtherance of the kingdome of Christ among these poor Indians, shall doubtlesse be had in remembrance before the Lord, not through merit, but mercie."[42] Not through merit: even from within the project of missionary conversion, the point is not that the Indians need the Englishmen (efficacious grace comes from God alone, and God is not dependent upon the English instrument). The point is rather that Englishmen, cast out of England by oppression and civil turbulence, or remaining in England only to see their hopes of a purified church give way to new forms of tyranny and fragmentation, require a missionary project among tribes more dispersed than their own (when he did not hold firmly to the lost-tribes-of-Israel theory, Eliot seems to have held with the alternate theory that the Amerindians derive from Tartarian or Scythian tribes).[43] They required this not in order to obtain grace (grace cannot be earned) but to achieve an interim consolation, that of community. With no guarantee that they would constitute the community of the saved, the agents of the Christian mission could perform the work that marked them as the community of the hopeful.

The modern nation is a back-formation, part of the retroactive logic of empire. Hence our common recourse to the colonial periphery when we try to understand what the nation is and how it is perceived by those who claim to constitute it. The community for which John Eliot and Thomas Mayhew proselytized was universalist and transcendent, a community that rendered national boundaries and nationalist ideology obsolete, and yet it was a community whose fate was indissolubly linked for many seventeenth-century Englishmen with the fate of their own emergent nation. The church was one, but its restoration to unity required a state-based bastion of Reform.

The Word was one, but the unifying instrument of Reform was a multiplying vernacular. The constitutive paradox of early modern Britain was at once an uncertain union of asymmetrically empowered ethnicities, cultures, languages, and administrative units and an uncertain union of secular and religious aspiration. This paradox was profoundly aggravated by the transatlantic colonial encounter. Historians and sociologists have begun to argue for the inseparability of state formation and empire building in the early modern period.[44] While emphatically sharing that view, this essay also suggests that the experience and experiments of colonialism are in many ways more complex than the language of empire would allow.

To a twenty-first-century reader the catechistical exchanges reported by Eliot as part of his effort to bring certain eastern Algonquian tribes into the one true faith contain a devastating cultural and political critique of his enterprise. The temptation is to imagine that only we are alive to the full weight of this critique and the full irony of these exchanges, but we would be better advised to underestimate neither the Algonquian nor the ministers who evangelized among them. Some of the "questions" propounded by the Indian converts are not at all ambiguous in the force of their critique: "*Doe not Englishmen spoile their soules, to say a thing cost them more then it did? and is it not all one as to steale?*" Yet John Eliot duly records this question, along with others that cut to the contorted roots of Christian faith: "*I see why I must feare Hell, and do so every day. But why must I feare God?*" And, "*If God made hell in one of the six dayes, why did God make Hell before Adam had sinned?*"[45] It is far too crude to imagine that only the perspectives of postcolonial postmodernity can offer purchase on the full complexity of these questions, the circumstances in which they were propounded, and the (heavily mediated) circumstances in which they came to the attention of the faithful back in Parliamentarian and early Restoration England. "Let me give you a taste of their knowledge by their Questions," Eliot writes.[46] They are, to his mind, very good questions; they accrue to the credit of both his converts and his mission. Why should we imagine he could only believe this if he believed his Algonquian interlocutors to be missing the point? At the outposts of early modern empire, in the prayer meetings as in the frankly mercantilist and military centers, we see the groundwork laid for the devastating exploitation that is still our heritage. At the same time, the improbable, even preposterous labors the New England congregations represent testify to a baffling component of good faith, and on both sides: a vision of commonwealth that considerably challenges our present analytical vocabularies.

PART II

Colonial Accommodations

CHAPTER 5

Catholic Saints in Spain's Atlantic Empire

Cornelius Conover

The Atlantic fleet in September and the mail ship in May brought Mexico City "news and mercies" from Europe.[1] Residents bombarded travelers and new royal administrators with questions about the latest current events and court gossip in Spain. Even more important for the Catholic Empire of Spain, boats carried mercies in the form of royal decrees and devotional privileges like beatifications and canonizations.[2] From the arrival of the fleet of 1628, Mexico City learned that Pope Urban VIII had beatified the very first holy figure born in the Americas—its own native son, Fr. Philip of Jesus. The Discalced Franciscan was one of twenty-six martyrs killed in Nagasaki, Japan, in 1597.[3] Mexico City rejoiced at the "great mercies that God Our Lord has given the city with a hometown saint" and celebrated with days of festivities.[4] Yet while Philip gave expression to local pride, his cult was far from an expression of municipal sovereignty. Preacher Miguel Sánchez in 1640 reasoned that Mexico City had produced a saint, "knowing that any one of her creoles could be . . . a Philip Martyr for his Philip King."[5] Since Sánchez used the term *creole* to mean people of Spanish descent who were born in Mexico, Philip symbolized the loyalty of grateful colonial subjects. More startling, the passage also suggests a religious understanding of Spanish imperialism. Surely Sánchez and his audience knew that martyrs sacrificed their lives for God and not for the Spanish king across the Atlantic?

An analysis of municipal devotions in Mexico City from 1625 to 1670 shows that Spanish imperialism guided the long-established process of devotional change in Catholicism. Over the course of the seventeenth century Catholic liturgy in Spanish territory showcased Hispanic saints and the royal family to reinforce Spanish dominion over the Americas.[6] The Spanish Empire then solidified imperial rule by skillfully integrating elements from the Catholic Church. Because works on religion in the Spanish Empire have focused on personnel or hagiographies rather than liturgy, this shift to an imperial religion has gone unnoticed. The cult of the *beato*, or blessed, Philip of Jesus in Mexico City provides a case study to analyze imperial Catholicism within a local municipality. In examining such local holy figures Latin American historiography has emphasized how they have given voice to local identity and contributed to the formation of an autonomous political consciousness.[7] I argue, to the contrary, that cults of saints actually reinforced imperial ties between Mexico City and the Spanish crown. Church documents show that municipal officials adopted Spanish saints and royal devotions while rejecting holy figures from foreign lands and even saints from other Spanish American cities.

Spanish Saints in the Catholic Reformation

Striving to introduce uniformity and orthodoxy into Catholic worship, sixteenth-century reforms cleared the church's liturgy of many saints. The simplified order of worship and new centralized bureaucracies ironically facilitated the manipulation of the liturgy by Spanish imperialists. The cult of saints received special attention from reformers working within the Catholic Church. During the Middle Ages, Christians of parishes, monasteries, or convents could integrate a new saintly veneration into their churches without authorization from Rome.[8] The result of centuries of incremental additions, as reform-minded Catholics of the sixteenth century noted, was little unity in liturgy across the Church, and many questionable practices centered on the cult of saints.[9] As part of the Tridentine-era reforms, church officials issued a new Roman Catholic breviary in 1568, vastly paring down the number of saints.[10] By requiring that all parishes use the Roman breviary, officials in Rome effectively eliminated much of the particularistic content of Catholic worship.[11] Roman prelates also introduced new restrictions on bishops to prevent them from just adding back excised holy figures. Beyond being simply unpopular, these steps threatened to arrest any devotional change, an ability that had traditionally kept Catholicism relevant to parishioners.

Rather than forswearing the power to modify worship, the Catholic Church shifted the responsibility to authorize new devotional privileges to Rome. In order to obtain new ceremonial honors for their favorite holy figures, inter-

ested parties like cities, orders, and monarchs now had to send representatives
to lobby the new Congregation of Rites in Rome.[12] While beatification and
canonization are the two most recognizable designations in the cult of saints,
these existed within a complex, hierarchical system of liturgical privileges. As
a feast gained more solemnity, it occupied more liturgical space in lessons and
prayers—sometimes for a period as long as eight days, an octave. At the very
pinnacle of the liturgy were the universal feasts of precept, with an obligation
to hear mass and rest from work.[13] This system of finely graded privileges allowed Catholicism to reflect the strength of a saintly devotion with precision.
The pope could extend particular liturgical concessions to any geographic
unit of the Catholic world: empires, nations, orders, archdioceses, dioceses,
parishes, churches, cities, and even chapels and altars.[14] In sum, the liturgy of
the Catholic Church provided a devotional system as complex and diverse as
its faithful. As evidence from Mexico City suggests, the papacy quickly abandoned its goal of a universal order of worship and began to exercise its newly
centralized authority to make particular liturgical concessions.

In the case of Philip of Jesus and the other Nagasaki martyrs, the Roman
Curia was quite willing to award extra liturgical concessions beyond those
inherent in beatification. The relative ease with which agents procured these
privileges stands in marked contrast to the rigorous process of beatification
and canonization. For instance, because the Nagasaki martyrs were only
beatos, or blessed, only the Franciscan order and the diocese of Manila could
celebrate the feast day. To lift this restriction the Jesuits asked and received
permission to say a common office to their three martyrs at their secular
masses.[15] Likewise, Mexico City and Avila, Castile, which were the dioceses
where Philip and Pedro Bautista were born, received the privilege of celebrat-
ing mass to their native sons in secular churches.[16] These seemingly technical
privileges actually eliminated the Catholic Church's restrictions on these beatified saints. In the archdiocese of Mexico City the cathedral and all parish
churches could include Philip of Jesus in their ritual calendar. Effectively, the
pope made the *beato* Philip a canonized saint in Mexico City.

Even though the Roman Curia authorized liturgical modifications as the
highest authority in the Catholic Church, local officials exercised a surprising
degree of power over devotional arrangements. In order to integrate Philip of
Jesus into the liturgy in Mexico City, the guardian of the Discalced Franciscans, Fr. Francisco de la Cruz, presented the bull of beatification in turn to
the archbishop, the Mexico City cathedral chapter, the viceroy, and the city
council.[17] From the archbishop and cathedral chapter, Fr. Francisco obtained

ecclesiastical endorsement of the bull and the *beato*'s formal integration into the calendar of worship for the archdiocese. From the viceroy and the city council Fr. Francisco received monetary support and commands for obligatory citywide participation in Philip's feast-day festivities. The *beato* enjoyed the broad support of municipal authorities and gained entry into worship without difficulty. Not every privilege approved by Rome sailed through local officialdom as easily.

Liturgical data show that despite the ostensible centralization of the Roman Catholic Church in the sixteenth century, the papacy actually played only a minor role in determining the saints venerated in Mexico City. Throughout the entire seventeenth century Mexico City integrated only one saint promoted by the pope into its standard liturgy, St. Gertrude of Helfta.[18] The role of the papacy in Mexico City's devotional culture was primarily reactive in terms of sponsoring new holy figures and passive in terms of encouraging devotions to existing saints.[19] For instance, Urban VIII expressed his motives for beatifying the Nagasaki martyrs as wanting "to conform, in so much as in God we can, with the pious wishes of... the Discalced Franciscan friars, and by their letters the very dear children in Christ don Philip y doña Isabel Catholic monarchs of Spain, and all the city of Manila, and China, or Macao."[20] Cities, monarchs, or religious orders initiated and pressed for liturgical change while the papal authorities approved or rejected them.[21] Moreover, the pope was largely absent from the personal decisions of Catholics when selecting a saint. This general principle found expression in a much-used sacramental guide, which advised parish priests ministering to the infirm to place an image of Jesus Christ, the Virgin Mary, or "the favorite saint of devotion" before an ailing person.[22] Priests expected that parishioners would have their own special celestial intercessor to resolve a particular problem like illness or to demarcate identity traits like occupation. By allowing some freedom of choice, the Catholic Church injected adaptability into an otherwise hierarchical religion. When the Catholic Church permitted this flexibility in devotions, it made itself vulnerable to the manipulation of outside forces. In the seventeenth-century Spanish Empire no one individual was more influential than the Spanish king.

Spanish Catholicism

By taking advantage of the inherent flexibility in Catholic worship, Spanish imperialism with the king at its center created a liturgy that showcased

Spanish saints and the monarch himself. Spanish kings employed a range of powers, from formal decrees to informal force of example, to promote liturgical change. An analysis of the liturgy of colonial Mexico City demonstrates exactly how Spanish Catholicism developed and what principles guided its creation. The influence of this imperial religion was critical for the cohesion and longevity of the Spanish Empire. Spanish Catholicism in its objects of veneration and its order of worship inculcated a religious unity among diverse peoples and projected imperial values across the Atlantic to the Americas.

The Spanish king had more control over Catholicism in the Spanish Empire than did the pope. This trend started in the times of Ferdinand of Aragon and Isabel of Castile who imposed Catholicism as a means to unite the disparate peoples in their kingdoms, including those in the newly conquered Americas.[23] In order to evangelize the vast conquests, as kings argued successfully to the pope, they needed to control most aspects of the Catholic Church in the Americas. The monarch could authorize the creation of all ecclesiastical institutions and dioceses in the realm as well as present candidates for ecclesiastical appointments. As Latin American historiography has long established, these two key provisions ensured that the king distributed patronage and that loyal subjects were positioned strategically in bishoprics. The king's power over religion in his empire, however, extended far beyond these personnel decisions.

The Spanish king heavily manipulated the very substance of Catholicism, particularly the cult of saints. Using his power and influence in Rome, monarchs promoted Spanish religious figures with remarkable success. Spanish saints accounted for roughly half of all the beatifications and canonizations in the seventeenth century.[24] Likewise, Spanish holy figures earned a disproportionate share of liturgical privileges over the same period.[25] Because of this royal intervention in Rome, formal worship began to reflect more Spanish influence. In practical terms Spanish saints dominated public celebrations in Mexico City. Local officials used their approval power to ignore foreign holy figures and to promote Spanish ones. Among all newly named saints in the seventeenth century the Mexico City religious community celebrated only one non-Spanish saint out of roughly seventy-five.[26] Even this celebration for the Franciscan martyrs of Gorkum had Spanish connections because they were killed across the river from Spanish Flanders in 1572. The trend toward imperial saints was all the more remarkable because the Spanish king did not prohibit the worship of foreign saints nor in every case decree that his subjects acclaim the Spanish saints.

Spanish religious imperialism explains the preponderance of Spanish saints in colonial Mexico City. In several specific instances this force was most visible. For instance, in referring to the celebration for St. Raymond of Peñafort, the councilmen vowed to fete the occasion appropriately, "attentive to the fact that Raymond was a Spanish saint..., that his canonization was due to his majesty King Philip our lord..., and that this city is very obligated to this Holy Religion."[27] In choosing predominantly Spanish saints, secular and religious leaders of Mexico City considered themselves to be following instructions from the king himself. On other occasions Mexico City adopted devotions in simple emulation of the king. On January 1, 1655, the cathedral began a three-day celebration dedicated to the Holy Host because "that is how it is done in Madrid, [in] his majesty's court."[28] While the king was the single most important influence, Mexico City also imitated Spain more generally. Mexico City voted to celebrate the happy event of another new Spanish saint, stating that "his holiness had dignified the saint Xavier, Spaniard, which had caused all Spain great joy and rejoicing."[29] In 1653 the University of Mexico elected to hold a feast of the Conception of the Virgin Mary "in imitation of all the Universities of Castile."[30] In voluntarily choosing to imitate the king and metropolis, leaders of Mexico City exhibited a conscious colonialism. Municipal authorities took for granted that Spain and particularly the king represented the spiritual center of the Spanish Empire and for that reason alone were worthy of emulation. The flexibility of the cult of saints allowed leaders to incorporate their understanding of the Spanish Empire into Catholic liturgy. As a result of religious imperialism and sheer numbers, Mexico City's Catholic devotions turned inward toward the Spanish Empire.

Despite the Roman Curia's tightened control over the liturgy during the Catholic Reformation, the Spanish king could raise a saint's ranking by decree or simply by influence of example. For instance, Philip IV ordered an annual feast dedicated to the Holy Host to commemorate the Spanish armada's victory over the French on November 23, 1653.[31] Three years later Philip IV decreed that his subjects celebrate a feast to Our Lady of Patronage to commemorate Spanish military triumphs and to ask for peace and victory over the enemies of Spain.[32] This festivity became known as the "king's feast" and formed a permanent fixture in the liturgy.[33] The Spanish king could also name patron saints for all or part of his empire, which he did for St. James (Santiago) and St. Joseph.[34] Monarchs, like all Catholics, also chose favorite saints, but the ambiguous boundary between the king as person and the king as monarch often made personal selections into imperial ones.

Spanish Catholicism went beyond featuring more Spanish saints, even to the point of integrating the monarch on the same level as canonized holy figures. Mexico City cathedral prelates referred to the king's birthday celebration as an "intraoctave of the saints."[35] Mexico City celebrated masses for the health of the monarch, for marriages within the royal family, and especially for the birth of a male heir, as in April 1658, when authorities threw a three-day party for the birth of a new heir to the throne.[36] The close integration of Catholicism into Spanish imperial rule proved remarkably effective in giving the king authority and devotion rivaling those of the Catholic Church. As the legal scholar and political theorist Juan de Solórzano wrote in the mid-seventeenth century, "We are the vassals of very Catholic Kings: [and as such] we respect their actions and determinations."[37] While Catholicism was not created in order that kings might exercise dominion over the consciences as well as the external actions of their subjects, in the Spanish Empire it certainly served those ends.

Through decrees and by example Spanish kings inspired a Catholicism that reinforced a religious-like loyalty toward the metropolis. Much to the benefit of the crown, it also established a common vision to unify an otherwise disparate people. However, not even Spanish kings could alter the inherent flexibility of the cult of saints. I have argued that the cult of saints strengthened Catholicism by providing the means for a diverse polity to express differences. For this to occur a local arrangement had to obtain. The cult of Philip of Jesus in Mexico City provides a case study to examine how officials negotiated between diverse factors like Spanish and Catholic tradition, religious directives emanating from the Roman Curia and Madrid, influential personalities, and even natural events to forge its municipal devotional culture.

Philip of Jesus and Catholic Colonialism

To observe Philip's first feast day on February 5, 1629, the Mexico City municipal council organized and financed a lavish celebration. In the morning the city council met with the viceroy and his officials outside city hall to walk together in procession to the cathedral for Philip's office. The streets had been cleaned and hung with lights. At each intersection, as the council ordered, fireworks were lit. Altars also lined the route; trumpets and clarions played. Ecclesiastical officials had carte blanche from the city council to deck the cathedral with fragrant candles. In the afternoon officials held a masquerade. Later that night there was another procession when fifty of the most important government functionaries (and their horses) left the city center dressed in their finest formal outfits.[38] All told, the city earmarked four thousand pesos for the celebration, which thus ranked among its biggest expenditures of the year.[39] It was an extravagant occasion but not an unusual one in the Spanish Empire.

The system of imperial rule in the Spanish Empire prompted celebrations like those for the *beato* Philip. Urban centers like Mexico City emulated the king's patronage of religious events and, in fact, celebrated both God and king simultaneously. According to the councilmen themselves, they sponsored religious festivals because it was their "duty as a viceregal and a Catholic city."[40] The officials that took part in the festivities also represented both religious and secular powers in an arrangement typical of the heterodox nature of the Spanish colonial administration. The group that collaborated for the first celebration of Philip's feast was typical: Franciscans, the archbishop, the viceroy, the cathedral chapter, and the city council. This small cadre of men, numbering fewer than twenty, exercised outsized influence on the devotional culture of the viceregal capital. Surprisingly, the archbishop and cathedral chapter functioned primarily as institutional gatekeepers for the authorization of new privileges. Viceroys exerted only a temporary force on the devotional culture lasting no longer than their term in office.[41] Among all colonial institutions, the Mexico City council exercised the largest influence in initiating or supporting devotions. The councilmen's sponsorship of Philip's feast, as described above, was typical of their involvement in the cult of saints of Mexico City.

In exchange for their support civic officials expected the *beato* Philip to intervene for Mexico City in the celestial court to shield it from any harm. As the Spanish-born Viceroy Cerralvo had remarked upon hearing the news of Philip's beatification, this "son could also be a father for this republic protecting it in everything."[42] City leaders assumed that Philip of Jesus, precisely in his capacity as a saint, would watch over and protect their city by intervening in the heavenly court. This particular attitude formed the very core of the relationship that people and cities established with their saints. By offering the hope of a miracle saints intimately connected to people and their cities during their hour of need.

Unfortunately for the devotion to Philip of Jesus, neither his religious virtues nor miraculous ability seemed up to snuff. The authoritative account of the Nagasaki martyrdoms made it clear that Philip was not a heroic leader but rather a last-minute addition unequal to the others in virtue.[43] At one point in the narrative the *beato* tried to avoid his execution on three separate occasions. Rome was willing to overlook these inconvenient details of the Mexican's biography because he was part of the virtuous Nagasaki martyr group, but since Mexico City venerated only Philip, his merits had to stand on their own. Also damning were two disastrous events that followed immediately upon his beatification. Only months after the announcement of Philip's beatification, Dutchman Piet Heyn captured the Atlantic silver fleet off Cuba. The city council estimated the loss at nine million pesos and promptly canceled all public religious functions.[44] They made an exception for Philip's first feast, but their faith in his protection was misplaced. Misfortune struck again, this time from flooding. The city council expressed alarm in mid-August 1629 after eight days of rain.[45] As the waters rose, the councilmen appealed in vain to their patron saint of water, St. Gregory Thaumaturgus.[46] The flood covered the streets and caused adobe houses to crumble. The waters reached such a level that religious services were held on rooftops of the buildings that remained.[47] Residents did not blame Philip of Jesus for the terrible destruction, but it was an inauspicious beginning for his cult. Apparently, his addition to the heavenly hosts could not guarantee the preservation of his city. The series of disasters threw into question his miraculous power at a critical time when his reputation as a celestial intercessor was still forming.

Despite Philip of Jesus's defects, the city council voted to make him a patron saint of Mexico City. The election in January 1630 seems to defy normal logic since the *beato* had so obviously failed to fulfill the primary saintly function of offering protection.[48] An analysis of the sacred patrons of Mexico City confirms that the city's saints did not serve strictly religious ends. Certainly, the vice-regal capital had some patron saints that protected people and property, such as St. Gregory Thaumaturgus for floods and St. Nicolas Tolentino for earthquakes.[49] However, the city rarely invoked them when disaster threatened.[50] Rather, in times of crisis during the late seventeenth century Mexico City depended on the Virgin of Remedies.[51]

Instead of choosing patron saints for their intercessional ability, Mexico City's leaders selected them for political reasons. The city council adopted St. Hippolytus, for example, to mark the day the last defenders of Tenochtitlán surrendered to the Spanish conquistadors. That celebration developed into an occasion to commemorate the Spanish conquest and the benefits of Spanish civilization. In addition, Mexico City took two favorite saints from the Madrid court as sacred patrons, St. Teresa of Ávila and St. Isidor Labrador, in imitation of pious trends of the metropolis.[52] Political pressure from within Mexico City also led the city council to adopt patron saints. By the 1650s

Mexico City had a patron saint from nearly every major religious order.[53] At each saint's feast the order enjoyed the exclusive attention of the city councilmen, who donated funds for the ceremony and attended in their formal attire. The Jesuits, sensing that their order was excluded from the city's prestigious ceremonial calendar, demanded a patron saint from their ranks. The city council bowed to their request and adopted St. Francis Xavier in 1659.[54] The flexibility of the cult of saints ensured that a powerful constituency of the city council could be appeased.

The celebrations of the cult of saints in Mexico City were public demonstrations of a larger system of political rule in Spanish Catholicism. The bias toward Spanish saints and the Spanish king reinforced colonial loyalty with religious devotion. Ironically, the cult of saints proved such an effective forum for imperialism ironically because municipal leaders retained significant ability to modify the devotional culture. This flexibility made the veneration of saints a useful feature of the colonial world by allowing municipal leaders to incorporate imperial directives, pious trends, and pressure from powerful social groups. In the case of Philip of Jesus leaders rapidly integrated him as one of their chosen patrons, where he served as the local representative amid imperial saints and political appointees. The very malleability of the cult of saints that allowed Philip of Jesus's rapid rise, though, also meant that his favored status was not guaranteed, especially considering his uninspiring performance as municipal protector.

Devotional Change in Mexico City: Philip of Jesus After the Flood

Mexico City remained flooded for five years, during which time the city canceled all public ceremonies. For the fledgling cult of Philip the long interim broke its early momentum. The flexibility of the cult of saints and the ability of local officials to modify devotions meant that the *beato* Philip's cult was subject to neglect, even abandonment. In fact, the great majority of the roughly ten thousand saints in Catholicism had no public or even private following.[55] Philip might have joined this undifferentiated mass if not for the efforts of one energetic creole canon of the Mexico City cathedral, Dr. Luis Herrera. As this essay has established, the king and colonial institutions were particularly influential in creating Spanish Catholicism while the pope was less so. However, even individuals like Herrera could modify the devotional culture of Mexico City. The canon was particularly astute in his promotion of Philip of Jesus. As a senior member of the Catholic Church in Mexico City, he knew exactly where to turn for support, the right rationale to emphasize, and the key components of a successful saintly devotion in colonial Mexico. In imperial terms the cult of saints created a structure dominated by the king, but one that also retained the ability to capture the energies and pious aspirations of individuals.

After the floodwaters receded, Herrera, chancellor of the Mexico City cathedral, began to resuscitate the devotion to Philip. No record remains to explain the canon's decision to champion the cult. Perhaps the strongest connection between the two was that each was born and raised in Mexico City.[56] They may have even attended the same grammar school. His dedication to a particular saint was not unusual, but Herrera's privileged position allowed him to advance Philip from his own personal cult to an institutionalized public devotion. Herrera specifically targeted the two institutions within the colonial system that were most likely to cooperate with his campaign on behalf of Philip: the Mexico City council and the king himself.

Herrera mobilized the rationale of Catholic tradition and of Spanish imperialism to win broader support for Philip of Jesus. After receiving permission from his ecclesiastical superiors, Herrera first approached the Mexico City council. In January 1636 he presented the council with a proposal of three parts. First, he wanted to restore public funding for Philip's feast day procession. Herrera tried to prick their conscience by chiding the council members that they had a sworn obligation to sponsor the holy figure's feast day.[57] Flatteringly, he confided that their attendance at that event ranked equal to that of the viceroy and the archbishop. Second, Herrera wanted the councilmen to donate money for a church building named for Philip. He suggested that the council could purchase the San Juan Letrán School (one of the rumored birthplaces of the *beato*) for that purpose. In making the request Herrera invoked the city's responsibility to maintain celestial goodwill. He felt that the martyr as prominent titular saint would serve as a good example for the youth; perhaps then God would reward the city with divine favor, such as more saints. Finally, the clergyman asked that the city council join the cathedral chapter and Archbishop Manso de Zúñiga to obtain a relic of the *beato* "to be placed in the land where he was born."[58] Herrera knew that each of the proposals would add a crucial element to Philip's cult. The city council's money and prestige would solidify the martyr's feast as a premier religious event. A building would provide a geographic center for the *beato*'s devotion. A relic would booster his miraculous presence. After listening to Herrera the city council thanked him for his zeal and set up a committee to research his suggestions.

Although Herrera had appealed to the council's religious duty, their patriotic sentiments, and their vanity, the councilmen made their decisions based on cost. Writing to the Philippines for a relic was essentially free, and the council approved sending a letter.[59] For the feast of Philip public lighting, fireworks, and comedies cost about two hundred pesos a year and passed "with great contentment."[60] Purchasing a building implied an expense of hundreds of thousands of pesos plus yearly maintenance and was voted down. The council suggested that Herrera find a private donor. Even for a hometown holy figure in Mexico City, religious sentiment was bounded by economic considerations.

In Herrera's promotion of Philip of Jesus he next turned to the Spanish king. After the city council refused to provide funds for the parish named for the *beato*, Herrera petitioned Philip IV for approval to create a chapel for the martyr in the cathedral.[61] He emphasized to the king the great devotion to Philip of Jesus and the people's desire to have a place for his image. In making these claims Herrera may have taken liberties, given there is no evidence that supports a widespread popular cult. However, the canon's understanding that the king was the greatest patron of Catholicism in his empire was well founded. By 1640 the monarch approved the application and even authorized the use of royal funds to adorn the chapel.[62] It was a tremendous coup for Herrera and gave the cult of the *beato* a permanent focal point in a premier location in the cathedral. Thanks to Herrera's efforts and his knowledge of the religious principles of the Spanish Empire, the cult of Philip had heightened prestige, increased visibility, and more money. Philip's popularity had advanced so much by the 1650s that he was the subject of blasphemy among such distinguished company as St. Ignatius Loyola and St. Peter Martyr.[63]

While the Spanish king did occasionally intervene directly in the cult of saints, he left the implementation to municipal dignitaries. This decentralized approach to devotions guaranteed that social demands and city politics would come to bear on Philip of Jesus, which was the case in 1640. The trouble had its origin in the arrangement of the celebration itself. The martyrs' feast took place over eight days, each with a different sponsor.[64] Civic and religious authorities negotiated among themselves for their octave assignment, which also signaled the hierarchy among the institutions. In October 1640 a conflict broke out between authorities when the cathedral chapter discovered that the Franciscans and the viceroy were planning to upstage the cathedral's celebration of Philip's feast day.[65] The canons fumed in their chambers and sent an emissary to the Mexico City council, which then sent a delegation to the Franciscans.[66] The friars quietly agreed to return to the customary use, and the canons were mollified.[67] Questions like these arose because neither the pope nor the king established the ceremonial order nor customarily intervened to defend it.[68] The public religion of saints' cults provided an acceptable social space to work out matters of hierarchy within the colonial ruling order.

Herrera's knowledge of Spanish Catholicism, especially the explicit promise of the secular government's patronage, allowed him to convert his personal saint into a permanent fixture in Mexico City's devotional culture. In a larger sense Herrera's successful promotion of Philip of Jesus demonstrated why the cult of saints was such an effective imperial system; namely, it could accommodate the ambitions of powerful individuals without threatening the authority of the king. In particular, Herrera shrewdly promoted permanent institutional commitments to the *beato* Philip, and as a result neither the cathedral nor the city council could abandon the martyr's cult. With its place in the public eye guaranteed, Philip's cult began to specialize and in so doing carved out a particular niche in Mexico City's devotional culture.

Creole Saints: The Beato Philip, the Virgin of Guadalupe, and St. Rose of Lima

From the 1630s Philip of Jesus's feast increasingly became a public occasion to extol the splendors of Mexico City and the glories of its natives. However, rather than being a reaction against Spanish predominance, the cult of the martyr allowed residents to assert their importance to the empire and to Catholicism. In other words Philip of Jesus and another local saint, the Virgin of Guadalupe, captured the energy of local patriotism and used it to reinforce loyalty to the Catholic Church and to the Spanish State. As a final piece of evidence that the cult of saints in the Spanish Empire allowed the expression of both imperialism and local identity, this section concludes with an analysis of the cult of St. Rose of Lima, a saint born in Peru. Even though both St. Rose and the *beato* Philip were holy figures born in the Americas, Mexico City's leaders balked at integrating a saint from a colonial competitor. To them "creolism" represented conflicting municipal identities rather than a general rise in a commonly shared American sentiment. Saints were not symbols of a larger colonial resistance to imperial power.

Thanks to Herrera's efforts Philip of Jesus earned a place in the mainstream of Mexico City's rich public life. In the liturgical calendar the *beato*'s feast followed Candlemas on February 2 and immediately preceded Lent. Each year on February 4 for the feast vesper the cathedral received the statue of Philip from the friary of San Francisco in a lavish procession of friars, silversmiths, and musicians along a route with triumphal arches and altars.[69] The canons of the cathedral chapter accepted the image and carried it to the high altar. The next day the archbishop performed Philip's office in his chapel. The centerpiece of the office was the sermon, a work by a specially chosen cleric for the gathered orders of Mexico City society. These sermons demonstrate how the cult began to develop within the larger religious life of the Spanish Empire.

To the preachers Philip represented Mexico City, and his feast day allowed them to indulge in adulation of the urban center and of its natives. In 1652 Jacinto de la Serna described the attributes of his Mexico City in a poem of adoration:

> You are beautiful, in your streets, your plazas.
> You are rich for your Gold and Silver.
> You are noble and illustrious for your noble and illustrious sons.
> You are Jerusalem, Saintly City, and birthplace of St. Philip.[70]

Serna put into words a sweeping vision of the grandeur of Mexico City, magnificent enough to resemble even the birthplace of Christ, the origin of the Christian faith. Within this depiction of a glorious Mexico City, Philip embodied the people: as one cleric stated, "the creole nation crowns itself with his glories."[71] Since the seventeenth-century audience would have understood "creole" as an individual born in the Americas to parents of Spanish descent, the phrase implied that Philip symbolized all native-born Americans. In actuality the constituency of the martyr was limited to only those people born and raised in Mexico City. In a 1638 sermon Philip was lauded as "our *insigne* martyr from our Mexican earth, product of her education and culture."[72] By virtue of Philip's martyrdom and beatification all native-born inhabitants of Mexico City received papal validation of their innate worth and of their piety. In their sermons preachers also exceeded simple praise to voice a more divisive nativism. In 1639 cleric Jacinto Caxica challenged Mexico City: "Why do you search for protection and favor from strangers when you have it secured in your own; if you have a religious son and saint, what do you want from other powerful figures?"[73] Here was evidence of a fierce local pride that rejected outsiders. Surprisingly perhaps, given the great control of the king in

Catholicism, the flexibility of the cult of saints allowed, even encouraged, the discordant sentiment of local boosterism.

Rather than an expression of autonomy, Philip of Jesus provided a metaphor to clerics to show how Mexico City fit into Catholicism and the Spanish Empire. Theologian Miguel Sánchez described two Philips, "one Philip, a Catholic Monarch, Caesar of Christianity, Atlantis of the Church, and King of the Spains...and another Philip, Mexican martyr among the gentiles."[74] The *beato* gave Mexico City the opportunity to praise its natives and their role in Catholicism but to acknowledge as well that its martyr contributed to the glory of God, of the king, and of the Spanish Empire. Because Spanish Catholicism unified disparate peoples across the empire, it also provided a common basis for comparing and for ordering colonial cities. As Luis Vaca Salazar argued from the pulpit in 1638, "God has given the city a canonized saint who is a native. Before Philip, Mexico City had to confess itself inferior to others...now it is among the most *insigne* of the world."[75] In the opinion of civic leaders Mexico City now stood in the company of religious cities like Madrid and Seville and ahead of colonial competitors like Puebla and Lima that had no native saints. The cult of saints ensured the loyalty of municipalities because it served a social need of leaders of municipalities like Mexico City to distinguish their city in the esteem of Spain's imperial system.

Philip of Jesus gave the people of Mexico City their own place in the Catholic liturgical calendar among Spanish saints, the Spanish king, and the central mysteries of the faith. Mexico City had other options for expressing creole identity, the most famous of which was the Virgin of Guadalupe. In contemporary times no saint has come to represent the Mexican people like Guadalupe, but in the seventeenth century her cult was still developing. By some measures, particularly in publications, it lagged behind that of Philip of Jesus.[76] Over the longer run Guadalupe's reputation as a miracle worker made her chapel outside the city a regional pilgrimage site. Philip's more political and social following did not have the same popular appeal in the seventeenth century. The case of these two holy figures followed the general rule that saints with a strong supernatural reputation tended to establish stronger and more lasting devotion, which partially explains the enduring popularity of European saints in the Americas.[77] In reality residents of Mexico City needed a saint to express municipal pride only occasionally. One of those times, though, came in the 1660s.

Starting in the 1660s, both Mexico City and Lima, Peru, began intense efforts to press for greater liturgical privileges for their municipal devotions.

Their campaigns showed how city leaders used the cult of saints to accommodate pious devotion and municipal patriotism within the wider Catholic Church and Spanish State. Mexico City chose to promote Philip of Jesus and the Virgin of Guadalupe, while Lima pressed for its favorite saint, St. Rose of Lima. Both Philip and St. Rose were "creole" saints born in the Americas, but evidence suggests that leaders of Mexico City understood that these saints represented their respective municipalities rather than all native-born Americans. In 1664 the Mexico City cathedral voted to ask Madrid and Rome for a list of new concessions for the cult of their *beato*—a church, a jubilee for his chapel, and relics, especially of the martyr.[78] Two years later the cathedral initiated a cause to lobby Rome for formal recognition of the Guadalupe cult.[79] To the great disappointment of civic leaders none of Mexico City's petitions prospered in Rome. Even worse, exactly at a time when Mexico City fruitlessly searched for more validation of its stature through the cult of saints, it had to confront the remarkable success of Lima's promotion of St. Rose.[80] In only four years, from 1668 to 1672, she was beatified, canonized, and made a universal patron of the Americas. Soon thereafter the Spanish king decreed that her feast be included in the *fiesta de tabla*, which implied mandatory attendance for all his royal government.[81] The saint from Lima put Mexico City's leaders in a predicament. They were accustomed to taking devotional cues from the Spanish king, but always before saints had come from the Spanish peninsula.

The reactions of municipal dignitaries in Mexico City to St. Rose of Lima showed the deeply entrenched system of imperial religion based in Spain and emanating across the Atlantic. Although Mexico City celebrated St. Rose with processions and octaves, her rapid rise sparked jealousy, soul searching, and hurried self-promotion.[82] The religious values of St. Rose did not run contrary to those of Mexico City. The capital had embraced the cult of St. Teresa of Ávila, also a miraculous mystic. The problem for Mexico City was that the Peruvian Rose did not come from Spain like St. Teresa but from a colonial competitor. To counter the Rose phenomenon the Franciscans of Mexico City briefly revived an obscure devotion to a holy woman named St. Rose of Viterbo.[83] Perhaps the most sustained response was liturgical. After the publication of a biography on St. Rose in 1670 the cathedral dusted off the project to petition for more privileges for Philip of Jesus, in this case a modest request for a special prayer.[84] By 1674, after St. Rose of Lima's many distinctions and honors, the cathedral's expectations were higher. The dean of the cathedral suggested that the chapter request that Philip be made a patron saint of all

New Spain, "just like the admirable Virgin St. Rose of Santa Maria, native of Lima."[85] The vote passed unanimously, and the canons sent their petition to Rome. The canons' grand designs for Philip of Jesus soon encountered obstacles. In 1678 the cathedral's representative in Rome reported that he had learned that the pope would have to canonize the *beato* before he could receive such a high distinction as patron of New Spain.[86] This requirement effectively ended the cathedral's promotion of Philip as regional saint within the Roman Curia. Canonization implied a rigorous and expensive process in the best of circumstances. As city leaders discovered, the *beato*'s cause faced even longer odds. Much to their surprise the Mexico City cathedral chapter read that Philip's canonization should be undertaken in conjunction with the hometowns of the other Nagasaki martyrs.[87] Philip's story had become so immersed in its local context that leaders in Mexico City had completely forgotten that he was part of a group of martyrs beatified jointly. The canons knew that in Spanish Catholicism, however, the pope was not the only authority with the power to bestow new liturgical distinctions.

Frustrated in Rome, Mexico City's leaders petitioned the king to obtain more liturgical recognition for Philip and renown for themselves. The cathedral asked that the king make the celebration of Philip's feast equal to that of "St. Rose," which suggests that the desire to distinguish the cult of the Mexican martyr came less from devotion than from colonial competition.[88] The king could not designate the *beato* patron saint of New Spain, which was a right reserved for the pope, but neither was he powerless. In 1689 Charles II effectively raised the liturgical rank of Philip's feast by requiring that his royal officials, the archbishop, the cathedral chapter, and the city council attend the celebration.[89] The phrasing of this royal decree underscored the king's role in Spanish Catholicism, as well as the larger understanding of saints among his subjects. Charles hoped that the city's son could supplicate "Our Lord for the conservation and aggrandizement of all the City and Kingdom."[90] First, the king was responsible for the promotion of religion in his realm. Second, he expected that this act would protect the prosperity of the entire Spanish Empire. Third, the two most important entities in the cult of saints were city and empire. Holy figures with regional affinities like St. Rose of Lima were not natural fits within the system of Spanish devotions.

Holy figures like Philip of Jesus and Guadalupe allowed municipalities to express local identity and effectively channeled social desire for recognition in the Spanish Empire. The complex system of liturgy provided an outlet for self-promotion but reinforced authority in the hands of the Spanish king and Roman pope. The king was more responsive to municipal politics, and his active sponsorship of local cults earned goodwill across the far-flung territories of his empire. As the example of Philip and St. Rose showed, Spanish Catholicism worked better to create ties between individual cities and Spain or Rome rather than among colonial cities themselves. Even in Mexico City, however, the respect for the religious directives of the king overcame the initial negative reaction to St. Rose of Lima. Leaders of Mexico City did eventually integrate her into the municipal devotional culture, but she entered the municipal pantheon on the city's own terms. The cathedral chapter decided to build an altar to her in the chapel of Philip of Jesus.[91] It was a small gesture to local patriotism but one that signaled an ongoing negotiation between pious trends, imperial decrees, and municipal politics.

Conclusion

The cult of saints in colonial Mexico City not only sheds light on the process of religious change in the seventeenth-century Catholic Church but also on the working arrangement of Spanish imperial rule. By dominating the traditional process of devotional change the Spanish king inspired a shift in Catholic worship in the Spanish Empire to emphasize more of its own saints and the Spanish king. Key religious functions in the liturgical calendar celebrated not just Catholic piety but also conferred an aura of sacredness on the secular power of the Spanish State. Within this Spanish Catholicism, however, individuals like Herrera and civic leaders such as the city councilmen retained the power to modify municipal devotions. Cults to Philip of Jesus, St. Rose of Lima, and the Virgin of Guadalupe gave voice to local patriotism, a fact much noted by historians. While these creole saints did embody municipal pride, they did not represent a declaration of cultural or political autonomy. Evidence suggests that leaders used these holy figures to assert their city's contribution to the Spanish Empire and Catholic Church.

The practice of Catholicism in the Spanish Empire and the content of the religion implied a complex negotiation, even a strengthening of imperial ties. This finding complicates the tendency in academic literature to overemphasize religion as a locus for early autonomous sentiment. The king, rather than a source of oppression, was a close ally of municipalities to encourage favorite devotions—even more so than the pope in Rome. For Mexico City, competitors were other colonial cities like Lima, which calls into question the notion of colonial resistance organized around the charismatic figure of a saint. The process of religious observance in municipalities like Mexico City exemplified an Atlantic system of religious belief that reinforced Spanish imperialism rather than an uninterrupted development toward autonomy.

CHAPTER 6

A Wandering Jesuit in Europe and America

Father Chaumonot Finds a Home

Allan Greer

Historians find it hard to resist the lure of the Jesuits. From the time of Ignatius to the dissolution of the order in 1773, members of the Society of Jesus played a central role, not only in the religious life of early modern Europe but also in its scholarly, scientific, educational, and political life. More important to colonialists, the Jesuits fanned out across the globe, and in their efforts to convert the heathen nations they developed a deep acquaintance with the languages and cultures of America, Africa, and Asia. Dedicated missionaries with a complex relationship to European *imperium* in the Americas, they sought to bring indigenous peoples under Catholic rule, while they simultaneously fought to protect their native flocks from the rapacious exploitation of colonizers.[1] These pioneering ethnographers and natural historians flooded Europe with information on hitherto unfamiliar lands and peoples far across the seas. Intellectuals among them, such as José de Acosta and Joseph-François Lafitau, even developed elaborate theories of cultural difference.[2] Some of the Jesuits' most spectacular achievements in cross-cultural infiltration occurred in China and India; Matteo Ricci and Roberto di Nobili are the best-known names among hundreds of Jesuits who worked their way into the heart of Confucian and Hindu cultures, respectively.[3] There may be disagreement as to how far the Jesuits succeeded in their evangelizing projects, but no one doubts their importance as Europe's antennae on the wider world.

But who were the Jesuits and what motivated those who left their homes to spend decades—often their entire adult lives—in strange lands? One might say that they were driven by evangelizing zeal, stoked by a sense of Catholic Christendom under siege—from within by the Protestant upheaval, from without by Ottoman invasions—as well as by the opportunities afforded by the period's voyages of discovery to outflank opponents, taking true religion to the far corners of the globe.[4] But while such strategic considerations perhaps explain the order's missionary policies, they hardly provide a full account of the Jesuit mentality. What made these religious travelers tick? Can we get beyond the rhetoric of self-presentation by which Jesuits appear in their own published writings as authoritative observers with an integrated point of view and a self-consistent subject position? Not for purposes of anti-heroic debunking but in order to improve our understanding of the religious encounters documented by missionary writings, we need to interrogate the missionaries' portrayal of themselves and their motives, as well as their accounts of exotic societies. And when we look closely at individual Jesuit lives, we sometimes encounter far more uncertainty, internal contradiction, and a yearning sense of incompletion than the assured tone of the *Cartas annuas* or the *Jesuit Relations* would lead us to expect.[5]

What follows is a modest contribution to the enterprise of getting to know the overseas Jesuits. It traces the life of one seventeenth-century missionary, Pierre Chaumonot, from his childhood in France to his death at an advanced age in Canada. Chaumonot was not an eminent Jesuit; neither was his career in any sense typical. However, it is well documented, thanks largely to a detailed autobiography he penned—not for publication—at the age of seventy-seven.[6] The close-up look that the autobiography affords us, when supplemented by personal correspondence and other sources, reveals a surprisingly uncertain, fragmented personality; a life of dislocations; and a heart constantly in search of something irretrievably lost. At the same time, as will become evident, Chaumonot embodied all the strength and resilience that one would expect of an early modern Jesuit missionary.

To refer to the subject of this chapter as "the French Jesuit, Pierre Chaumonot" is to raise difficult problems at the outset. He may have been French by birth, but his nationality shifted over the years, and for a time he lost all knowledge of the French language. Baptized "Pierre Chaumonot," he used that name only as a child; as an adult, he was known by a series of aliases: Pietro Calmonotti, Petrus Calmonottus, Pierre-Joseph-Marie Chaumonot, Aronhiatiri, and Héchon.[7] Constantly on the move, Chaumonot/Calmonotti/Héchon made his way through seventeenth-century France, Italy, and North

America, observing customs, learning languages, and, like a good Jesuit, absorbing knowledge, human and divine. Through an arduous lifelong itinerary, this wandering Christian made his way across rivers, mountains, plains, and oceans, reinventing himself as he went.

Chaumonot's journey began with a crime. Born in 1611 in the Burgundy village of Ste-Colombe,[8] the second of five children in the family of a poor wine-grape grower, Pierre was sent to be educated at the Jesuit college in the nearby town of Châtillon-sur-Seine. He lodged with his uncle, a local priest, and made rapid strides in mastering Latin, the first of a series of languages he would acquire over the years. During his "rhetoric" year—about the time he would have been twelve or thirteen years old—he became interested in music and took singing lessons from a fellow student. Having exhausted the musical resources of Châtillon, the two classmates conceived the idea of pursuing their training with the Oratorian fathers at Beaune. And so Pierre ran away, pausing first to steal one hundred sols from his uncle's purse to cover travel expenses. Taking back roads to escape detection, the two companions walked 130 kilometers to the southern Burgundian city. They duly enrolled with the Oratorians and studied music until the stolen funds ran out, at which point Chaumonot wrote to his mother, asking her to send more money so that he could continue. The boy's confidence in his mother's capacity to understand, forgive, and nurture is quite striking; he would never see her again, but he would not lose his faith in the power of maternal love (even as he discovered a substitute mother in the Virgin). At the time, however, his expectations were rudely disappointed as his letter fell into his father's hands and instead of help he received a stern paternal summons to return home and make amends for his misbehavior. Only then, according to his recollections some sixty years later, did Chaumonot realize that he had done wrong. His only thought was to flee the wrath of offended justice, and so he turned, not northward toward his parents and his home, but in the opposite direction.

Alone and penniless now, and about twelve or thirteen years of age, Pierre Chaumonot left Beaune on the highway to Lyons. "And so I decided to travel through the world as a vagabond rather than accept the humiliation I deserved as a thief."[9] Though the avoidance of punishment provided the original impulse, his mind soon formulated a redeeming sense of purpose for the voyage: he would undertake a pilgrimage to Rome! After all, the Vatican lay no more than 1,250 kilometers away, beyond the Alps, in a country where he knew no one and could not speak the language. On his first day he fell in with two journeymen from Lorraine who approved of his pious design and began initiating him into the ways of the road. They taught him the art of begging door to door, and soon he was part of the multitude of vagabonds wandering across the face of seventeenth-century France. As far as I can tell, he never saw parents or home again. He would later thank the lord for detaching him from the bonds of domestic affection, but an undercurrent of yearning for family runs through his autobiography.

Chaumonot's own account of his adventures along the highways of Savoie and northern Italy is filled with picaresque detail.[10] He parted company with the Lorraine journeymen at Lyons, where he was barred entry to the city for lack of a passport (later on he persuaded a passing priest to lend him his papers and to help him forge copies in his own name), and then acquired a new travel companion with whom he pressed forward into the mountains. He begged, he stole, he slept in farmers' haystacks and pilgrim hostels, he shivered through cold alpine rains, he narrowly escaped forced induction into the army (being so small that his saber dragged on the ground helped here; this was also the occasion when he perfected the technique of bursting into tears and begging for mercy), he was set upon by dogs and pelted with rocks by suspicious peasants, he walked until his shoes disintegrated and his clothes hung in tatters, and fleas tortured him constantly. Along the way his Jesuit education in Latin came in handy more than once: it helped him in his efforts to cadge food and shelter from clerics and religious communities; it also helped him communicate with hostile Italian villagers: "Nos sumus pauperes peregrini," he called out, and their attitude softened as they gave him the benefit of the doubt as a religious traveler.

By the time he reached Ancona, on the Adriatic coast, the hardships of life on the road had taken a heavy toll on Chaumonot's body and on his spirits. "I was then barefoot, having been forced to discard my worn-out shoes when they cut my feet. My rotten shirt and my torn clothes were full of vermin; even my uncombed scalp was covered in horrible scabies which oozed pus and worms and stank strongly."[11] Feeling dejected and disgusting, the poor pilgrim plodded on to Loreto, site of a great baroque shrine dedicated to the Virgin. The shrine was built around a modest house, supposed to have been the very dwelling in Nazareth where Mary had been born and where Jesus had grown up. During the Middle Ages it had been magically transported to the coast of Dalmatia, before flying over the Adriatic to its resting place near Ancona. Chaumonot prayed fervently at the altar, and then on leaving the church he encountered a mysterious young man clad all in white. The stranger approached him, removed the boy's hat, wiped his infested scalp with a clean towel, and then vanished. Instantly, the noisome scabs and vermin disappeared and Pierre was cured; he concluded that an angel had performed this miracle. Credit went to Our Lady of Loreto and her shrine. Even apart from its role in curing his afflictions, the resonances of home, hearth, and family were enough to give Loreto a central and lasting place in the heart of this lonely wanderer.

Continuing on his journey toward Rome, Chaumonot came to rest in the Umbrian town of Terni. A kindly old doctor there took pity on the foreign beggar who appeared on his doorstep and brought the boy into his household as a servant and protégé. He spent some time there, comfortable and well treated by his master, but eventually restlessness overtook him and he hit the road once more. He had been reading about the ancient hermit fathers of Egypt and had vague plans to become an anchorite, living off wild herbs in some far-off spot. Instead, he found himself in Rome, his original destination when he had left Burgundy long ago. Confused and more alone than ever, he retraced his steps to Terni, where he was welcomed back into the doctor's household. By now he was fluent in Italian and was beginning to be known as Pietro Calmonotto. He retained much of his Jesuit learning and so found work tutoring the children of a neighboring family. When the children went off to the local Jesuit college, Pierre/Pietro accompanied them, and before long he was back in the bosom of the Society of Jesus.

Over a period of years (the autobiography provides no precise chronology) Chaumonot's status appears to have shifted from servant/hanger-on to college student as the Jesuits of Terni, recognizing his talents and previous learning, encouraged him to pursue his education and consider a priestly calling. In his memoirs he frankly discusses his hesitation about joining the society and his flirtation with other religious orders; it was the assurance that Jesuit vows were not irrevocable that convinced him finally to take the plunge. (If he changed his mind in the future, he seemed to be thinking, he could always bolt—but as it turned out, he stuck with his commitment to the Jesuits for more than sixty years.) He returned to Rome to begin his novitiate at the age of twenty-one and then went on to the colleges of Florence and Fermo to continue his training.

As a student, Chaumonot had been wracked by self-doubt and moral anguish. Troubled by erotic impulses, he indulged in orgies of self-flagellation and other penances. After entering the society his sense of himself as a stranger expressed itself through a fixation on his humble social origins.

Other student Jesuits seemed to him "all young men of distinguished birth," whereas he sprang from peasant stock and, worse still, had lived as a beggar and performed the services of a lackey. Feeling guilty, in addition, for dissimulating his humble origins, Pierre consulted his confessor at the Florence college, who helped him devise a ceremony to purge his pride and dishonesty. Before the entire college the young student underwent a public interrogation that brought out every part of his background that made him ashamed. To complete the performance the confessor ordered him to climb up on a chest and sing a peasant song in his native patois. After that humiliation, Chaumonot declares, he never again felt any discomfort about his social origins. Indeed, he had achieved a lasting basic spiritual serenity that he described, characteristically, in maternal terms: "I often felt myself being caressed by Our Lord, like a child caressed by his mother who puts him gently to sleep sucking the milk from her maternal breast."[12]

Having completed his novitiate, Chaumonot continued his Jesuit training through his twenties, studying philosophy and theology, while teaching basic Latin to boys enrolled in the colleges of Florence, Fermo, and Rome. In Rome he made friends with a young French Jesuit, Father Joseph-Antoine Poncet, who lent him a copy of one of the early *Jesuit Relations*,[13] containing Jean de Brébeuf's account of his efforts to proselytize the Hurons. The impressionable Chaumonot was entranced, focusing on the hardships and suffering of missionaries and on the patience and humility required to "instruct and convert these barbarous nations."[14] He decided to volunteer for the New France mission, hoping to accompany Poncet. Securing permission to transfer to the Province of France and to join the mission in Canada was no simple matter, but Chaumonot was relentless in pressing his case with the Jesuit authorities. He submitted his request to the general of the order in the form of an *indipeta*, a petition requesting a transfer or overseas posting; in it he argued that he was suited for work among the savages because he was humble and restless for activity; more studious and cultivated priests, he modestly suggested, were better suited for service in Europe.[15]

Finally, permission was granted, but before setting off for Canada in 1639, Chaumonot and Poncet planned a pilgrimage, going on foot from Rome to Loreto in order to revisit the shrine where, years earlier, a poor waif had been cured by an angel sent by Our Lady. Since the days of Ignatius Loyola, Loreto was very much a Jesuit project; the order provided multilingual confessors at the shrine, and many Jesuits made pilgrimages there.[16] The night before he departed for Loreto, Chaumonot had a strange dream. "In the dream, I saw a person that I took to be my mother, but her blackened, swarthy face aston-ished me." He was convinced that the vision was a signal from the Virgin, "who wished to act as my mother."[17] The dark skin, he assumed, had to do with her dark-colored image at Loreto, though his unconscious mind may also have been alluding to the natives of New France.[18] In his autobiography the Jesuit makes no mention of the fact that his real mother died less than a year after this dream, never having seen her son since he left home almost two decades before.[19] By then his yearning for nurturance had been trans-ferred almost fully into the religious realm. He was devoted to Joseph, as well as to Mary, and had received many "favors" from that father figure at difficult moments during his Jesuit education after having discovered that he was the patron saint of Canada. In 1639 he obtained permission to change his name to Giusseppi-Maria Calmanotti (later modified to Pierre-Joseph-Marie Chaumonot). Thus he integrated into his parentally deprived personal iden-tity a complete substitute family.

Back in Rome, Chaumonot conceived a plan to build a replica in Canada of the holy house of Loreto; he even extracted a donation of twenty-five écus from the niece of a cardinal to pay for the construction! Clearly he was touched, not only by the religious ideal of a loving father and mother but also by the image of the cozy little house where Jesus passed his child-hood.

Hastening with Father Poncet to the port of Dieppe in 1639, Chaumonot had an opportunity to relearn the oral French he had largely forgotten over the years. There is a gap in the autobiography for the period separating his de-parture from Rome and his arrival in Quebec, and so we must consult other sources to get some idea of his experiences traversing the Atlantic. We know that he made the crossing on board one of three French ships that embarked from Dieppe on May 4, 1639, carrying the Counter-Reformation payload of the century: along with Poncet, Chaumonot, and a third Jesuit on this voy-age, there was the religious benefactress, Madame de la Peltrie, with a pio-neering contingent of Ursulines, including Marie de l'Incarnation, as well as the first three hospital nuns bound for the new colony.[20] It was a horrendous, three-month crossing in the overcrowded little vessels, featuring storms, fog, illness, and a very close brush with an iceberg. Landing at Quebec, Chau-monot was allowed two days to acclimatize, and then he had to climb into a birch-bark canoe for another arduous journey, this one up the St. Lawrence and the Ottawa rivers to the inland country of the Hurons, hundreds of miles from the nearest European outposts. It entailed five-and-a-half weeks of constant paddling against the current, portaging around rapids, and camping out among clouds of mosquitoes.

No wonder that Chaumonot's stated view of travel was rather grim. His autobiography and correspondence contain no talk of picturesque vistas, wonders of nature, or curiosity satisfied; instead travel is depicted, as it was in the epic of Gilgamesh and many other ancient myths, as exile and punishment: a cross to be borne.[21] As teenage runaway and as adult missionary, he saw himself as a suffering pilgrim. Or rather that is the spirit in which he constructed his personal narrative. He traveled so widely and so willingly and clearly absorbed so much from the environments through which he passed that his motives and responses must have included more joyful dimensions along with the penitential element.

Life among the Hurons, where he would live for the next eleven years, presented a whole new set of challenges. Chaumonot arrived at a low point in the history of Huron-Jesuit relations. A terrible smallpox epidemic was raging through the native population, and many Hurons noticed that the missionaries remained mysteriously exempt from illness. "As this contagion did not attack the French, we were taken for sorcerers who were causing this affliction and thus they chased us out of most of their cabins."[22] Far from converting to Christianity, they were shunning the Black Robes as hostile and dangerous agents. A newcomer still learning the native language, Chaumonot was sent to accompany a more experienced missionary, Paul Ragueneau, who was touring stricken Huron villages, attempting to baptize the dying and preach to the well. People literally plugged their ears, jeered, and shouted at the unwelcome visitors; sometimes they brandished hatchets and chased them away. On one occasion a man who was enraged by the Jesuits' attempts to capture the soul of his sick daughter knocked Chaumonot unconscious with a large rock. In a scene reminiscent of his childhood encounter with an angel at the Loreto shrine, another Huron healed his damaged skull, making incisions to reduce the swelling and then bathing the wound with a soothing solution of water and herbs.[23]

Meanwhile, the missionary was struggling to master the Huron language, "the most difficult of all the languages of North America," under the most adverse conditions imaginable. His busy colleagues simply told him to plunge into native longhouses and ask the names of objects. More often than not his inquiries met with silence, rebukes, or laughably inaccurate translations. "So repelled was I by these visits that I felt I was heading for the torture rack every time I entered a cabin; that was how much I dreaded the mockery that they subjected me to."[24] In spite of his repugnance Chaumonot persevered and made rapid progress, achieving complete fluency in Huron within a few years. "It pleased God to give such blessing to my work that there was not an expression in Huron or a subtlety of the language that was unknown to me." Huron provided him with an entry to other Iroquoian languages, and he later found he could swiftly master the languages of each of the Five Nations, as well as other related tongues.[25]

In November of his second year in New France, Chaumonot was chosen to accompany Jean de Brébeuf on a winter mission to the Neutral nations of southern Ontario. In the course of a four-and-a-half-month visit, he learned enough of the Neutral language, an Iroquoian tongue similar to Huron, to compose a guide to the grammar and vocabulary.[26] The Neutrals had had little contact with Europeans in 1640 and at first gave the Jesuits a cordial reception, but after Huron messengers arrived warning that the Jesuits were sorcerers who spread deadly contagion, they were violently expelled.

Chaumonot remained at the mission in the Huron homeland continuously for eleven years, passing the prime of his life there from age twenty-eight to thirty-nine. It was an ordeal, though certainly not the first hardship he had encountered in an eventful life. Besides the hostility and danger, he suffered from the cold climate and the unfamiliar native food. In an early letter to Jesuit colleagues in Rome he compares *sagamite*, the corn porridge that formed the staple of the Iroquoian diet, to wallpaper paste and notes that it gave him a chronic stomach ache.[27] Eventually, he grew accustomed to Huron ways, just as he had acclimatized to other foreign customs in his childhood. The natives bestowed on him the name Aronhiatiri, and so he could add that appellation to his already substantial list of personal identifiers.[28] Over the course of the 1640s the Jesuits' fortunes improved, and a faction of the Hurons accepted Christian baptism; Chaumonot appears to have played a leading part in this success.

As a seasoned missionary, toward the end of his first decade in the Huron country, Chaumonot found himself in charge of the large village of Ossossané, otherwise known as the mission of La Conception. With the leading clans of Ossossané largely converted, he had the satisfaction in the winter of 1648–49 of learning that the village council had decided to institute a Catholic regime and prohibit all ceremonies and customs that were contrary to the faith. He was proud to report that this resolution was scrupulously followed. The test came in March 1649 when a shaman from a neighboring village ordered a curing ritual for a sick person that, following established Iroquoian custom, involved group copulation. Put to the trial in this way, Christian morality won out over approved medical procedure, and the shaman was sent packing before he could organize the now-prohibited ceremony. Father Chaumonot's triumph was complete, but it was short-lived. Three days later an Iroquois force attacked Ossossané, killing or making captives of most of the inhabitants.[29]

While the fortunes of the Jesuit mission had been improving, the Hurons were losing ground in their military struggle with the Five Nations.[30] The spring of 1649 saw devastating Iroquois attacks from which the Hurons could not recover. Chaumonot joined thousands of Hurons fleeing for their lives. For a time they took refuge on Ile St. Joseph (Christian Island) in Georgian Bay, where the frightened and demoralized survivors faced slow starvation. The missionary accompanied one contingent of refugees to Quebec and then dwelt with them at a refugee village on the nearby Ile d'Orléans. In a solemn ceremony of resuscitation the Hurons renamed Chaumonot once again. Henceforth, he would be "Héchon," the name and persona previously assigned to the fallen martyr and senior Huron missionary, Jean de Brébeuf. Though Chaumonot/Héchon served in several other parts of New France over the years, he would be drawn back repeatedly to this Huron community, following it through its successive relocations in the vicinity of Quebec. In the life of this deracinated wanderer, long ago cut off from his family, the need to belong seems to have been a powerful force.

For several years, however, his attention turned to the Hurons' traditional enemies, the Iroquois. After years of bloody conflict between the Five Nations and the Huron-Algonquin-French alliance, the Iroquois offered peace in 1655. The Onondagas, the central Iroquois nation, were particularly insistent that a Jesuit mission be established in their midst. Since the truce was fragile and uncertain, and since any French living in Onondaga territory would become defenseless hostages in the event of renewed hostilities, this undertaking was extremely perilous. Leadership of the Onondaga expedition fell to Chaumonot, an experienced missionary by this time and one recognized for his ability to establish a rapport with natives. The *Relation* for 1655–56 expressed it in these terms: "[He] possesses the language, the heart and the mind of the savages."[31] And so, it seems, he did. Not long after arriving at Onondaga, Chaumonot had occasion to address the assembled *royaners* (league chiefs) of four of the Five Nations. (The Mohawks were still at war with the French at this time.) He spoke at length, on important diplomatic issues as well as religious matters, presenting gifts of value and symbolic meaning with each of the main points of his discourse. The Jesuit account of this event leaves the impression that Chaumonot, now a mature missionary with sixteen years of experience among the Indians of North America, had fully mastered not only the language but also the oratorical styles of the Iroquoian peoples.[32] He had, in other words, attuned himself to "the heart and the mind" of another culture.

During his residence in Onondaga, Chaumonot visited the villages of the Cayuga and Seneca and stayed there long enough to add the languages of those nations to his linguistic repertoire. In Chaumonot's account the highlight of this expedition was a debate before a Seneca council in which he condemned "the plurality of wives" and argued the merits of monogamy. He failed to convince the men on this point, but the women of the village, he reports, were so pleased with his performance "that they wished to thank me with a great feast which they held in their town."[33] He was back at Onondaga when war broke out between the Iroquois and the Erie people. Having witnessed the ravages of Iroquois warfare when he was among the Hurons, he now had the chance to observe that same phenomenon from the attackers' point of view: the preparations for military expeditions and the awful treatment of captives brought back to the village for torture, adoption, and execution. Chaumonot's, mostly unsigned, contributions to the *Jesuit Relations* remain a precious source for the study of Iroquois culture early in the contact period. No better description than Chaumonot's can be found of the Iroquois festival of *Onnonhouarori*, a time when reason was temporarily overturned and people enacted dream-inspired scenes suggesting murder, arson, and cannibalism.[34] When war resumed between the Five Nations and the French in 1658, Chaumonot and his colleagues made a perilous and hasty retreat back to Quebec.

Even though his knowledge of native customs and languages was unparalleled, Chaumonot is not usually numbered among the great Jesuit ethnographers of New France, such as Paul LeJeune and Jean de Brébeuf. This was partly a function of his "humility" in declining to contribute texts in his own name, but it also reflects his special approach to the task of writing the Other. LeJeune and Brébeuf both penned elaborate texts on, in one case the Montagnais and in the other the Hurons, following the classic tradition of ethnographic description. Since ancient times genre conventions had become established for analyzing the various aspects of a "savage" society: its government, religion, marital customs, morals, and so on. The tone was objective,

detached, and authoritative, and the scope exhaustive, as though a given society were fully knowable and reducible to data arranged in a prefabricated
matrix.[35] Chaumonot did not write in that vein, although his texts in the
Jesuit Relations and other writings are rich in ethnographic observations. His
descriptions of Huron and Iroquois ways come as part of narratives of personal experience, travel, and exploration; the tone is more subjective, the topics arise in somewhat random order depending on the structure of the story
in which they appear, and there is no implicit claim to be revealing the whole
truth about a particular nation. Chaumonot does not exactly write about Indian societies as an insider—he is fully aware of the gap separating himself as
a European missionary from the natives among whom he lives—but neither
does he write from the lofty perspective of the scientist.

In discussing the Ursuline mystic Marie de l'Incarnation, Natalie Zemon
Davis identifies a divergence in the attitudes of male and female missionaries
toward the Indians of New France. Women like Marie tended to be more
warmly positive, focusing on individuals and stressing their similarity to the
French, their shared potential to be good Christians. Because they were men,
and therefore had a different experience of contact with indigenous nations,
the Jesuits took a comparatively detached view, as evidenced by their systematic ethnographic writings, analyses that convey a certain sense of distance
separating the observer and the observed society.[36] In general terms Davis's
point is well taken, and yet it is possible to detect what might in this context
be called a "feminine" outlook on the part of some men of the Society of
Jesus, and none more so than Father Chaumonot. Like Marie, he can be
quite personal about individual Indians, sometimes allowing himself to be
carried away with enthusiastic admiration for exemplary Christian converts.
The *Jesuit Relations* for 1651–52 contain a letter reporting to a Jesuit colleague,
now returned to France, on the tragic death of six Hurons, drowned when
their canoe capsized in the St. Lawrence. One of those killed was Joseph
Taondechoren, a paragon of Christian virtue. Chaumonot dilates upon Taondechoren's virtues in the clichéd style of the "pious savage" trope,[37] but his
account nevertheless conveys a sense of warm human connection. "Ah, what
a loss....Although you were eye witnesses to his virtues when we lived with
him, sharing the same cabin, the same fire and the same table—or rather
the same pot, since tables are not used in that country." A sense of personal
knowledge, respect, and even intimacy pervades the missionary's portrait of
the life and death of his Huron friend, counteracting, even if it does not erase,
the stance of racial and clerical superiority.[38]

One of the most remarkable Chaumonot texts is an unsigned memo on the Iroquois dated 1666 and attributed to him on the basis of the handwriting. This is a unique ethnographic study, one whose very structure defies all the conventions of the genre as practiced by Jesuits and secular writers, French, English or Spanish. "The Iroquois Nation is composed of nine families," it begins, "and these form two bands, one of them made up of four families and the other of five." Not only has this author abandoned the standard ethnographic descriptive grid (government, ceremonies, men's work, women's work, etc.), he has approached the constituent elements of the Iroquois nation in a manner quite unlike that of other European observers of the time, not to mention scholars of the present day. Instead of identifying five tribes or nations (Mohawk, Oneida, Onondaga, Cayuga, and Seneca), each with its own distinct territory and language, he speaks consistently of "families" ("clans" in the vocabulary of modern anthropology). He lists them, noting their Iroquoian names, giving French translations, and carefully arranging them in their respective "bandes" (moieties, as anthropologists would now say). "The first band, Gueyniotiteshesgué, which means the four families,"[39] includes the Turtle (Atiniathin), the wolf (Enanthayonni or Cahenhisenhonon), the bear (Atinionguin), and the beaver. This is not how the shape of the Iroquois League appeared to most outside observers; rather it is how Iroquois society looked from the *inside*—a network of interconnected kin relations.

There is another respect in which Chaumonot's memo appears to be shaped as much by Iroquoian as by European sensibilities. Text actually plays a secondary role here: at the heart of the document is a series of iconic images, schematic drawings showing animals representing clan totems, some gathered round a fire in council, others carrying weapons of war; there are also pictures of warriors escorting captives and other symbols indicating success or failure in battle. Chaumonot's French text takes the form primarily of an explanatory legend, while the drawings carry the main weight of communication. So deeply immersed was this missionary in the Iroquoian culture of the Hurons and Iroquois that he drew heavily on native semiotic systems, even when conveying messages to fellow Frenchmen.

At the same time, it has to be said that the 1666 document, found in the colonial archives rather than any religious collection, seems to be essentially a piece of military intelligence designed to help the French conduct war against the Five Nations. The document concentrates primarily on customs relating to warfare (e.g., "When they go off to war and they wish to inform other parties which might pass by the same route, they draw the animal of their family with a hatchet held in the right paw")[40] and the treatment of captives. It focuses on "families" partly because war parties were formed through the mobilization of men within and between the clans; moreover, captives were distributed to specific clans for adoption or execution. The document itself gives no explicit clue as to its purpose, but we must surmise that it was part of a process of consultation in which French officers planning their 1666 campaigns against the Iroquois gathered useful information from a leading Jesuit expert. That Chaumonot should be drawing on his knowledge for hostile purposes is hardly surprising: he knew which side he was on in the cruel and bloody struggle pitting pagan Iroquois against Christian Huron and French. His insight was all the more valuable because it was to a considerable extent an insider's view, the combined product of a flexible mind, an adaptable identity, and a long immersion in Iroquoian cultures.

But Chaumonot was by no means cut off from the French settler society that was taking root on the banks of the St. Lawrence. For a time he served as chaplain to the troops stationed at a fort at the mouth of the Richelieu River, and for several years in the late 1650s he lived in the infant town of Montreal, ministering mainly to the French population there. It was at this time that he joined forces with Madame D'Ailleboust, the widow of a governor-general of New France, to found the confraternity of the Holy Family, a colonial devotional sodality devoted to imitating the familial virtues of Mary, Joseph, and Jesus. In retrospect Chaumonot saw this as one of the most important achievements of his long missionary career: "For my part, it had been fourteen years and more that I had harbored an ardent and almost constant desire that the divine Mary should have a large number of spiritual and adoptive children to console her for the pain she suffered for the loss of her Jesus."[41] The poignancy of these displaced sentiments expressed by a man who had left his mother at a tender age, never to see her again, requires no elaboration, nor does the consistent preoccupation with the holy family of Jesus.

In later years Chaumonot was again placed in charge of the refugee band of Huron converts near Quebec. After a series of relocations the Indians ended up several miles northwest of the city, and, as they labored to build their cabins and clear fields to grow their corn, their missionary priest was busy realizing another long-standing dream. He had never forgotten the shrine of Loreto and the image of the Virgin there. Before he left Rome for New France a pious lady there had given him a sum of money to buy the first bricks that would build a New World replica of the *santa casa*. Now he was determined to realize that ambition, and with Jesuit funds supplemented by private donations from France and Canada he managed to construct a modest chapel precisely modeled on the childhood home of Jesus, the one that had flown from the Holy Land to Dalmatia and then across the Adriatic to Italy. This was in 1674. Father Poncet, now back in Europe, arranged for a copy of the image of the Virgin of Loreto to be made and dispatched to Canada. With Father Chaumonot presiding for most of what remained of his long career, the Indian mission of Lorette established itself as a center of pilgrimage for French Canadians and natives seeking miraculous cures for their ills. The wandering Jesuit passed his last years in a religious atmosphere redolent of mother, home, and family.

His had been a long journey. Between his Burgundian childhood and his old age at Lorette, Chaumonot had traveled thousands of miles, across broad stretches of two continents. It was no tourist's itinerary of superficial observation. Each time this wanderer encountered a foreign culture, he immersed himself deeply and fully, adapting himself to the novel situation and learning to see it, at least to some degree, from the inside. Language is the ground on which Chaumonot apprehended the diverse human environments through which he passed. Raised using French, or more precisely a regional patois, he used Latin as a linguistic passport during his youthful travels; later he learned Italian to the point where it almost crowded out his native language. Once in Canada he set about learning the complex inflections of Huron. Later he achieved fluency in Onondaga, as well as a very good working knowledge of Neutral, Cayuga, Seneca, and Oneida. Throughout New France, Chaumonot became the acknowledged master of indigenous languages, and within the Society of Jesus he acted as the repository of linguistic knowledge and the instructor of neophyte missionaries.

> As he possessed a perfect knowledge of the Indian tongues, notably Huron and Onondaga, he was the principal missionary at almost every mission where he found himself and was responsible for most of the good that was done there. He trained many of our missionaries. All members of our society who will ever learn Huron will learn it thanks to his precepts, his [guides to noun and verb] roots, his speeches and several other fine [manuscript] works that he has left us in that language. The Indians themselves admit that he spoke it better then they, this according to people who generally pride themselves on

speaking well and who do indeed speak with great purity of language, eloquence and fluency.[42]

These linguistic skills need to be seen as something more than a neutral instrument for boring into a foreign culture. Yes, he possessed an obvious talent for languages, a "gift from God" as Chaumonot would have put it, and, yes, he must have applied himself to linguistic study with great dedication. But when we bear in mind the circumstances in which young Chaumonot acquired his fluency in Italian and Huron, we have to recognize these languages as evidence of his own (at least partially) transformed identity; learning Italian and Huron was an integral part of the process of *becoming* Italian and then Huron.

One of the striking markers of Chaumonot's shifting identities is the long list of names by which he was known at different stages of his life and in different circumstances. Pierre Chaumonot became Pietro Calmonotti in Italy, though within the confines of the Jesuit colleges he was Petrus Calmonottus. So intense was his devotion to the holy family that he changed his name to Giuseppe-Maria Calmonotti, alias Joseph-Marie Chaumonot. During a decade passed in Huronia, he was Aronhiatiri to the natives. After 1650 he became Héchon, an appellation applied not only by the Hurons but also on occasion by the missionary himself when he signed letters to colleagues in France. These name changes may seem a superficial matter, but I would suggest that we consider them from an Iroquoian point of view: among the Hurons and Onondagas an individual might acquire a succession of names as he or she went through different life stages and as his or her status changed. Names were more than a convenient personal identifier: they were the sign of a particular persona and situated the individual within a web of kin and community. Similarly, Chaumonot's changing names suggest something deeper than simple translation; they betoken shifting allegiances and affiliations.

Chaumonot's metamorphoses mark him as a remarkably adaptable figure, though by no means unique in the context of his time.[43] We might admire his talent for adaptation, but we must also recognize that change was often imposed upon him as a brutal necessity. The hungry, penniless boy attacked by stone-throwing peasants had to learn the customs and language of Italy simply to survive. And this formative cross-cultural experience in the Old World must have played a part in equipping him for the more forbidding challenges of cultural difference that the New World had in store for him.

The connecting thread that seems to have preserved some sense of continuity for him over the long run was the Catholic faith and the Society of Jesus. An anchor of stability in some respects, religion was also the register through which Chaumonot expressed the anguish of severed connections and personal discontinuity. His Marian devotion, his dedication to the Holy Family, his lifelong fixation on the little cottage where the boy Jesus enjoyed the love of parents, all suggest both consolation and inconsolable loss.

CHAPTER 7

From London to Nonantum

Mission Literature in the Transatlantic English World

Kristina Bross

Sometime before 1647 in the Massachusetts Bay Colony, an Algonquian woman and her husband decided to join a community of recent converts to Christianity. Some of them had begun living together in the town of Nonantum, and this couple found reason to move there also: perhaps they had lost kinfolk in the several plagues that swept through native communities since the English had come; perhaps the members of their families who had survived the plagues had become "praying Indians," and this couple wished to remain with them. Perhaps they had lost land to English settlers, or felt that they soon would, and hoped to make land claims based on new Christian identities. Perhaps they wished to enter the colonial economy and knew that praying Indians were being given new tools and being taught new skills. This latter possibility is probably at least a part of the reason they joined the praying movement; after the move the woman supported herself with traditional skills—she made and sold baskets—and with new ones—she was given a spinning wheel and learned to use it. Then again, perhaps they had heard the missionary John Eliot or one of the new converts preaching, and had simply felt their spirits incline to join the movement.

In any case, sometime before 1647 an Algonquian woman and her husband moved their belongings to the praying town of Nonantum: "They fetched all the corne they spent, sixteene miles on their backs from the place of their planting."[1] And then, sometime in 1648 this woman, middle-aged, with several grown children, died from an infection contracted during the birth of another child. According to English mission literature, she made a proper deathbed speech—proper in that it adhered to the genre as it was being worked out by Puritans in Old and New England—and then, away from the minister's gaze, she also called her adult children to her and admonished them to stay with the praying community rather than return to live with non-Christian relatives after her death.[2]

We know these details of her life because at mid-century New England writers published a series of tracts in London to promote their efforts to convert coastal Algonquians to Christianity, and in the fourth of those tracts, *The Glorious Progress of the Gospel Amongst the Indians in New England* (1649), the missionary John Eliot described the pious life and "good death" of this unnamed woman.[3] Something about her story was compelling to the English missionaries and their supporters, who were busy exchanging their views across the Atlantic about Indian missions, English national identity, and God's cosmic plan for English and native peoples alike. Eliot devoted considerable space to it in his letter to a well-wisher in England—so much so that he worried he was "too tedious in this Story" (B4r). John Dury, minister, millennialist, and agitator for religious toleration, found her story inspiring enough to single it out in his commentary on New England's mission work, included as an appendix to *Glorious Progress*. Readers could also have encountered this woman's story in a curious tract edited by the well-connected Baptist minister Henry Jessey, *Of the Conversion of Five Thousand Nine-Hundred East Indians on the Isle of Formosa*, to which he appended a postscript concerning the New England mission effort. The colonial print archive thus contains several views of this Algonquian woman's life and death. Her story survives because whatever her personal sorrows, hopes, and achievements, Englishmen understood it to be useful confirmation of various, even competing theological beliefs, millennial hopes, and political designs.

The print archive that encodes various English interpretations of her life bears the traces of at least one other key telling of the woman's story. The print record, although produced and preserved by the Englishmen whom it served, mediates the story she herself crafted. At most we can but speculate about that version, but if we broaden our definition of the colonial archive to include material as well as print culture, there are clues to suggest that even as she was afforded a significant place in the English transatlantic religious world as it was described in the mission tracts, the woman saw her praying life and deathbed speech as a sign of the persistence of her local community and of the emergence of praying towns as decidedly "Indian places" in that transatlantic world.[4] Taken as a whole, the record of her "pious life and good death" affords us an unusual opportunity to trace the influence of one individual on transatlantic literature, to compare the use to which Native American figures were put by members of the transatlantic Protestant community—including Christian Indians—with different political and theological interests, and in particular to chart the differences between colonial and metropolitan beliefs.

A New England Theme

John Eliot and Edward Winslow were the colonists who brought the woman's story to England in 1649, and the account recorded in *The Glorious Progress of the Gospel* establishes a colonial theme for metropolitan variations. Eliot was minister to an English congregation at Roxbury, Massachusetts. He spent much of his life ministering as well to the praying Indians, whom he helped settle in towns set aside for them throughout the Massachusetts Bay Colony.[5] Winslow, a Plymouth colony divine, was appointed New England's agent and went to London in 1646 to solicit support for the colonies. As part of this campaign, he published *Glorious Progress*. Their combined gloss on the Algonquian woman's life and death demonstrates the pragmatic value the mission had for the colonies. Christian Indians are offered as evidence of the importance of colonization. They are meant to persuade Englishmen and women to open their hearts and purses to support the colonies, and both men contextualize their account of the woman's life and death with discussions of what observers in England should do to support the cause.

In a letter dated November 12, 1648, Eliot writes that he decided to report on the Algonquian woman's death because she "was the first of ripe yeares that hath dyed since I taught them the way of salvation," and "of the dead I may freely speak." Eliot reports on her deathbed scene in brief: "She told me she still loved God, though he made her sick, and was resolved to pray unto him so long as she lived, and to refuse powwowing. She said also, that she believed God would pardon all her sins, because she believed that Iesus Christ dyed for her; and that God was well pleased in him, and that she was willing to dye, and beleeved to goe to Heaven, and live happy with God and Christ there" (B3v) . The reader, by evaluating her deathbed speech for orthodox beliefs, has confirmation that Eliot's catechism was taking hold among those he taught. In addition to her professions of belief about the saving power of Christ and about God's mercy, a key component of her statement—an element particular to the deathbed confessions of Indian converts—is the repudiation of "powwowing," that is, of traditional healing practices. Reports of the "good deaths" of Indian converts regularly included this assertion that Christian Indians would rather die than resort to "heathen" medicine, however effective.[6] That the woman eschews powwowing confirms Eliot's assertion, published in a previous tract, that "they have utterly forsaken all their *Powwaws*, and given over that diabolicall exercise, being convinced that it is quite contrary to praying to God."[7]

Here Eliot paraphrases the woman's deathbed confession, but in the next paragraph he allows her to speak in her own words. She offers a "deathbed charge" to her children, another element that I have identified as conventional for Indian dying speeches: "When I am dead your Grand-father and Grand-mother and Unkles, etc. will send for you to come and live amongst them and promise you great matters and tell you what pleasant living it is amongst them; But doe not beleeve them, and I charge you never to hearken unto them, nor live amongst them; for they pray not to God, keep not the Sabbath, commit all manner of sinnes and are not punished for it: but I charge you live here, for here they pray unto God, the Word of God is taught, sins are suppressed, and punished by Lawes; and therefore I charge you live here all your dayes" (B4r). His account does not describe her motivation in giving these instructions. Eliot claims that he learned of them only when her prophecy came to pass, when the extended family, as expected, reached out to the young women, and their stepfather brought the case to Eliot for counsel. Whatever her reasons, Eliot is careful to assure his readers that her instruction to her children was her own idea. The shift in point of view is significant. By paraphrasing her deathbed confession he implies that he is present in her final moments, actively ministering to her, and we can attribute her sound theology to him. By switching to the first person for the charge to her family and making clear that he is not present at that scene, he implies that her desire for the family to continue in Nonantum is independent of her English minister. Thus, she supports Eliot's efforts to resettle Christian Indians in lands set aside for their use and to isolate them from "wild" Indians, a project Eliot describes in detail in the succeeding pages. The change in narrative style assures readers in England that praying Indians are both good Christians under the influence of sound ministers and also voluntarily choosing a "civilized life."

Eliot goes on to capitalize on the woman's "good death" by making it clear that if well-wishers in England approve of the mission and its results, as illustrated by what he calls the "exemplary" life of this woman, they must reach deep into their pockets to support efforts to evangelize and civilize.[8] In another letter included in *Glorious Progress*, Eliot writes to a "*Gentleman* of New-England" explaining that if the mission is to succeed, "it [is] absolutely necessary to carry on civility with Religion: and that maketh me have many thoughts that the way to doe it to the purpose, is to live among them in a place distant from the *English*, for many reasons; and bring them to co-habitation, Government, Arts, and trades: but this is yet too costly an enterprise for *New-England*, that hath expended itself so far in laying the foundation of a Common-weale in this Wildernesse" (16). It is a canny argument. Because this plan is addressed to a fellow colonist, readers are eavesdropping, as it were, on a discussion among colonial insiders.[9] The notion of New England exhausting itself in "laying the foundation of a Common-weale" makes the colonists' endeavor parallel to that of Parliamentarians charting the course of the rising Commonwealth, but because Eliot does not make a request for metropolitan funds, his words seems a simple self-description rather than whining. Eliot's role is that of eyewitness. It is up to Winslow, New England's agent in London, to make the direct appeal.

Indeed, Winslow, acting as the missionary's editor and the colonies' agent, is quick to follow Eliot's lead. His preface wastes little time in getting to the point. On the first page he rehearses the legislative action that was sparked by the publication of the mission tract *Cleare Sun-shine of the Gospel* a year earlier: Parliament had taken note of the good work among the Indians in New England and had referred the matter to the Committee on Foreign Plantations. Parliament now had an act before it, "for the Promoting and Propagating the Gospel of Jesus Christ in New England." The act would establish a corporation charged with raising and dispersing funds in support of New England's evangelism efforts.[10] Winslow uses *Glorious Progress* to urge its ratification. Like Eliot in the letter to his friend in New England, Winslow also suggests that there are parallels between the great work of Parliament and the more humble work of the colonies: "As God hath set a signall marke of his presence upon your Assembly, in strengthning your hands to redeem and preserve the civill Rights of the Common-weale: so doubtlesse may it be a comfortable support to your Honours in any future difficulties, to contemplate, that as the Lord offered you (in his designe) an happy opportunity to enlarge and advance the Territories of his Sonnes Kingdom: So he hath not denied you...an heart to improve the same" (A4v). This is a remarkable passage, the references to current events subtle yet clear. Political and theological concerns are masterfully imbricated. It even includes a veiled, threatening prophecy. The year of publication is 1649; Charles I was executed in January of that year. Winslow was in London, well aware of recent events and the anxious mood of even the most committed regicide. He begins with encouragement (God has strengthened parliamentarians to "preserve the civ-ill rights of the Common-weal"); the House of Commons had followed the king's execution with acts to ensure that there would be no royal succes-sor and that a representative government would be the ultimate authority in England.[11] In an echo of Eliot's letter to his fellow colonist, Winslow parallels these political actions with mission work in New England: as Parliamentar-ians are establishing Christ's kingdom (as opposed to the corrupt kingdom of Charles I) in England, so too are New Englanders expanding Christ's territo-ries into the colonies. The most surprising moment in this passage, however, has to do with potential failure rather than celebration. If Parliament's more worldly ends are frustrated, if England encounters "future difficulties," Win-slow suggests, they will always be able to draw comfort from their support for the propagation of the gospel in New England, an apolitical, enduring, divinely inspired effort. While the phrase "future difficulties" is appealingly vague and low key, its import could not have been lost on readers. Winslow is addressing avowed regicides: their "future difficulties," should the political wheel turn again, would include imprisonment, arrest, and execution as trai-tors.[12] It is perhaps a stretch to see Winslow here as offering actual refuge in New England should the Commonwealth fail, but several of the men who passed judgment on Charles I would indeed fly to the colonies for safety after the Restoration.[13] Whether or not Winslow foresaw such events, this passage demonstrates that as a colonial agent he wished to be cautious, and he wished to anchor the colonial mission effort in cosmic rather than temporal events, even as he appealed for concrete, worldly support.

Metropolitan Variations

Winslow's caution extends to the most exciting theological speculations about the significance of American evangelism, that it was a harbinger of end-times, and it is caution on this theme that most differentiates colonial from metro-politan authors, at least at this moment in New England's mission history.[14] Nevertheless, although I see the main text of *Glorious Progress* as a pragmatic argument for funding, Winslow does make reference to the more enthusiastic discussions of Native Americans then circulating among metropolitan observers: "There are two great questions...which have troubled ancient and modern writers....What became of the ten Tribes of Israel...[and] what Family, Tribe, Kindred or people was it that first planted, and afterward filled that vast and unknown Countrey of America?" (A3r). Winslow's two questions frame a theological debate about the identity of Native Americans and the role they were to play in cosmic events. The debate turned on whether Indians were Gentiles or Jews. If Gentiles, their conversion was laudable, just as the saving of any English soul was to be desired. If they were Jews, however, their conversion was potentially earth shattering. Millenarians read scripture as prophesying a general, worldwide conversion, but more specifically they believed that the conversion of Jews would accompany the particular historic moment of Christ's second coming. Thomas Brightman, "the most famous contemporary commentator on the Book of Revelation," whose most important innovation was to map the prophecies of Revelation onto human history, projected that the fall of the antichrist (Rome) would occur in the year 1650, after which the conversion of the Jews would occur.[15] Monumental events, such as the execution of Charles I and the establishment of the Commonwealth, seemed to confirm that the end-times were imminent. If it could be proven that "Jews in America" (as one tract was titled) were becoming Christians, it would be an important sign that Brightman was right.[16] Winslow, of course, was familiar with these predictions and speculations, and although he himself offers further evidence that such theories may be correct, noting especially the "juncture of time" between Indian conversions and calculations about the date for the end-time conversion of the Jews (A4r), he hedges: "I confesse questions are sooner asked than resolved."[17]

Compare his measured enthusiasm with that of John Dury's breathless tone in his appendix to *Glorious Progress*. Dury begins by stating his agreement with those divines who were convinced that Brightman's prophecy of imminent end-time events was being fulfilled: "The palpable and present acts of providence, doe more than hint the approach of Jesus Christ: and the Generall consent of many judicious, and Godly Divines, doth induce *considering minds* to beleeve, that the conversion of the Jewes is at hand." Second, he writes that he is convinced that Indians are Jews: "The serious consideration of the preceding Letters, induceth me to think, that there may be at least a remnant of the *Generation of Jacob* in *America* (peradventure some of the 10. Tribes dispersions)" (D3v). Their conversion in New England thus supports millenarian speculation. The logic of the proof is straightforward: the Bible tells us that Christ's return will be accompanied by the conversion of Jews. All the signs indicate that Indians are Jews, and lo, here is proof of their conversion. Ergo, the Second Coming is upon us!

Although Dury himself is convinced that the end-times are nigh, he recognizes such beliefs are controversial. Nonetheless, he asserts, the reports from New England should be received with gladness by even the most skeptical Christian reader, who can at least agree that "the work of God among the Indians in America, is *glorious*" (D4v). At this point in the appendix he turns away from high-flying theological speculation to a more immediate understanding of the praying Indians' significance. And here we get a hint of the reasons for his own interest in the Algonquian woman and her dying speech. He too is lobbying Parliament for ratification of the act to support New England evangelism, and he notes that "as Ministers, so Statists do finde personall examples, the most powerfull motives to practick doctrines" (E2r). He seems to be offering both a description of his own practice here and advice for ministers and "statists" who will subsequently join him in advocating for the New England mission: find a real convert who can drive your point home.

Dury may have understood his own rhetorical practice as using Christian Indians as "personal examples" to achieve practical ends, but a closer look at his appendix suggests that the Algonquian woman has a more important place in his remarks. For several pages he lists in good, plain, rhetorical style the many pieces of evidence regarding praying Indians' divine role that he has derived from the colonial letters included in the main body of the tract. He turns at last to the woman's dying speech and spends nearly as much time on it as on all the preceding anecdotes, making a five-point explication of her testimony. He then goes on to apply the example of godly Indians, most especially the unnamed woman, to English readers, castigating them for hypocrisy and lukewarm faith. In essence, she becomes the text of a sermon that he delivers. He notes her speech; "opens" it with his five points, just as a sermon opens scripture; then suggests its uses for his readers (a marginal note usefully identifies this section as the "application," as in countless printed sermons). And among the applications for Dury's readers is his direction of the "heads of our Tribes in Old England" to pass the "Act for the Promoting and Propagating the Gospel of Jesus Christ in New England." Thus the woman's story has been altered from a simple anecdote of Indian godliness, attested to by colonial eyewitnesses, to a sermon text, made to provide lessons not for native colonial subjects in New England but for Parliamentarians and for (other) "apostate" but still important English readers in London and throughout the Commonwealth (E2).

I have been reading Dury's version of the Algonquian woman's story as "metropolitan" rather than "colonial," but perhaps, like Winslow's, his interpretation is better classified as in-between. After all, he was recruited by colonial agents to write his appendix, and it is clear that he read the reports from New England carefully and followed them closely as he prepared his gloss on colonial experiences. For a more purely metropolitan viewpoint we must turn to the version produced by Henry Jessey and published in the 1650 tract *Of the Conversion of Five Thousand and Nine Hundred East-Indians*.[18] As editor of the tract he extends and intensifies the metropolitan trend toward radical theological interpretation that we see in Dury's treatment.

Of the Conversion is one of the innumerable Interregnum-era texts produced by busy London printers, and at first glance it seems unlikely to shed much light on the relations between New England and the metropole. The main text is a simple sketch of Dutch mission work in Taiwan containing little concrete detail. A postscript promises information about New England's missions, but rather than offering new facts and stories it summarizes previous publications about the topic—the first three of the so-called Eliot tracts, including *Glorious Progress*. For the scholar interested in New England the original publications about New England's evangelism would seem to be a much better source.

Indeed, *Of the Conversion of Five Thousand and Nine Hundred East-Indians* has attracted very little critical attention. A closer look, however, reveals the tract as a valuable part of the seventeenth-century transatlantic archive. It was written by a Baptist minister seeking to affirm his place in the chaotic religious and political landscape of England in the 1650s. It is representative of the Americana produced in the wake of the English Civil Wars, it is a concrete response to Cromwell's Western Design, and it provides an intriguing example of the ways New England was understood by metropolitans. *Of the Conversion*, though a slim pamphlet, has much to reveal about the uses to which ordinary conventions of mission writing were put by readers far distant from New England's colonial settlements. Moreover, despite its titular subject, it indicates with remarkable clarity New England's pivotal role as part of an incipient English empire.

There is little on the title page of Jessey's tract to suggest that the reader will find new or useful information about New England. The pamphlet's cover announces that the tract is primarily concerned with Formosa (present-day Taiwan) and with Dutch missionary efforts there. Jessey was an ecumenical minister, interested in global Christendom, and so had good reason to take note of his Protestant brethren's work in the eastern missionary fields.[19] Moreover, English interest in the Netherlands was high in the early 1650s. English observers closely followed the struggle of the Low Countries to cast off Spain's rule, charted rising Dutch Republicanism, and agitated for a Dutch declaration of support—on either side—in the English civil war. Further, just two years after the tract's publication rivalry between England and the Netherlands would erupt into the first Anglo-Dutch war. Nevertheless, despite the tilt of the title toward the Dutch and the East Indies, Jessey's real interest here clearly is in the New England missions and the "West Indies." While the discussion of America is ostensibly confined to a "Post-script," the bulk of the publication concerns New England. The report on New England is a robust twenty-six pages compared with the paltry eighteen of the "main" text, and the context in which Jessey places his discussion pertains specifically to England's national and religious concerns.

The title page of the tract (figure 7.1) can be taken as a key to the tract's purposes. As befits the titular subject, most of the page is devoted to describing the tract's treatment of the Formosan mission. Nonetheless, the font size of "East-Indians" matches that of "West-Indians," giving the tract a visual balance to the page. The "proof text" of the title, that is, the scripture offered as the divine prophecy or description of the human evangelism being reported, is Isaiah 49.12: "Behold, these shall come from farre; and loe, these from the NORTH, and these from the WEST; and these from the Land of SINIM." The east-west balance on the title page along with the use of this particular verse signals the author-editor's belief in an imminent millennial crisis: both elements suggest the worldwide conversion that biblical scholars linked to the Second Coming.[20] The title page suggests that Jessey will extend Winslow's cautious questioning and Dury's abbreviated—if enthusiastic—speculation in *Glorious Progress*. After all, Jessey is publishing in the auspicious year of 1650, the year Brightman had prophesied would be the beginning of the end, and Jessey has proof that the prophecies are being realized worldwide—from the east to the west. If we dip into the text itself, we immediately find additional millennialist proof texts. Jessey dedicates the pamphlet to "his Christian Friends...that pray of the Coming in of the fullnesse of the Gentiles, that so all Israel may be saved" (A2r), a clear reference to the millennial belief that first Gentiles, then Jews would convert as worldwide Christianity

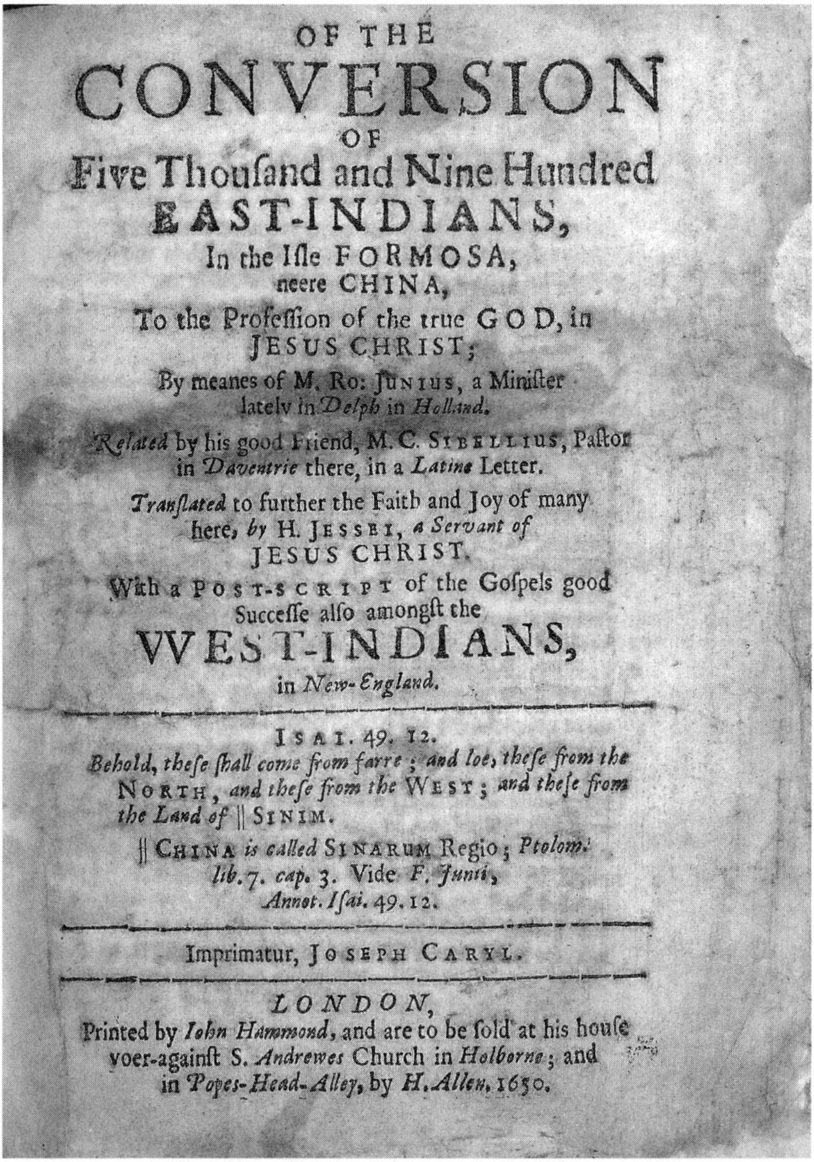

OF THE

CONVERSION

OF

Five Thoufand and Nine Hundred

EAST-INDIANS,

In the Ifle FORMOSA,
neere CHINA,

To the Profeffion of the true GOD, in
JESUS CHRIST;

By meanes of M. Ro: Junius, a Minifter
latelv in *Delph* in *Holland.*

Related by his good Friend, M. C. Sibellius, Paftor
in *Daventrie* there, in a *Latine* Letter.

Tranflated to further the Faith and Joy of many
here, *by* H. Jessei, *a Servant of*
JESUS CHRIST.

With a POST-SCRIPT of the Gofpels good
Succeffe alfo amongft the

WEST-INDIANS,

in *New-England.*

ISAI. 49. 12.
Behold, thefe fhall come from farre ; and loe, thefe from the
NORTH, *and thefe from the* WEST; *and thefe from
the Land of* ‖ SINIM.

‖ CHINA *is called* SINARUM Regio; *Ptolom.*
*lib.*7. *cap.* 3. Vide *F. Junii,*
Annot. Ifai. 49. 12.

Imprimatur, JOSEPH CARYL.

LONDON,

Printed by *Iohn Hammond*, and are to be fold at his houfe
voer-againft S. *Andrewes* Church in *Holborne*; and
in *Popes-Head-Alley*, by *H. Allen*, 1650.

Figure 7.1: Caspar Sibelius, *Of the Conversion of Five Thousand and Nine Hundred* (1650).
Reproduced by permission of The Huntington Library, San Marino, California.

manifested itself. The three verses then cited in the opening of this dedicatory letter are all passages understood to foretell global Christianity. Most significant, he quotes Malachi 1:11, "From the rising of the sun even unto the going down of the same my name shall be great among the Gentiles," a verse I have traced as foundational to New England evangelism in this period.[21] This title page iconographically illustrates these prophecies, presenting the calling of Gentiles and Jews from Formosa, the east—the rising of the sun—to New England, the west—its "going down."

All of this coding might seem so much esoteric speculation, but the east-west mapping in this tract is more than theological wish fulfillment. The balance of east and west on the page—seemingly a straightforward representation of Christian prophecy—also points to particular political views. The title's claim to discuss "West-Indians, in *New-England*" strikes a discordant note. At this time the West Indies could refer to all of the Americas, but it was most often used to refer to the islands in the Caribbean or sometimes to Spanish holdings more generally.[22] One need only consider Abraham Cowley's description of his mistress's body to realize that impoverished New England did not fit: "Mine too her rich *West-Indies* were below, / Where *Mines* of gold and endless treasures grow."[23] If Jessey had described New England as the West Indies in his title alone, the phrase would not be worth remarking, but he insists on the description, rewriting the New England mission tracts he excerpts in his postscript to make *them* reflect the term. He inserts it twice into the title of the New England tract *Glorious Progress of the Gospel*, once on the introductory page to his postscript and once on the title page reproduced in the body of his publication. He edits the tract's discussion of the local progress of Christianity so that it appears that New England colonists themselves use the phrase. In the original, Eliot contrasts our "Southern Indians" on Martha's Vineyard with "our Western Indians" on the mainland who are more pious (B4v). Jessey cuts the reference to "southern" Indians so that Eliot appears to refer to West Indians. And throughout passages written in his own voice, he consistently labels Indians in New England "western" (14, 33, 34).

This forced symmetry matching New England's "West Indians" to Formosa's "East Indians" might seem just a rhetorical tic were it not for the larger foreign policy context of its moment. I see the repeated westering of New England Indians as a tactic to associate settler-colonial evangelism (which Jessey supported spiritually, politically, and financially) with Cromwell's increasing interest in expanding England's power into New Spain, a project that became known as his "Western Design." Throughout the 1650s Cromwell yoked together prophecy and politics, determining a course of action that would commit English military power to the West Indies.[24] These policy debates culminated in 1654 with the launch of the English fleet to attack the Spanish in Hispaniola. The attack failed miserably, though the English were able to take the much less fortified Jamaica.

New England could not avoid responding to these developments at its doorstep, as it were. Although John Winthrop had preached in his 1630 sermon "A Modell of Christian Charitie" that the eyes of the world were upon the colonists, in the 1640s, during the civil wars, England's attention had been on events at home. Now that the king was dead and the Commonwealth established, that attention could once again be paid to "foreign" as well as "domestic" concerns. As these events played out, the Bay Colony was increasingly positioned as peripheral to more important concerns.[25] In 1656 Cromwell even commissioned an agent, Daniel Gookin, to encourage New Englanders to consider moving to Jamaica to shore up English control there. The commission empowered Gookin to offer ships, land, farm animals, and military protection to any who would remove forthwith to Jamaica, "it being his Highness Pleasure that the work of Transporting should be begun before September next."[26] His actions must have confirmed the colonists' sense of being situated on the periphery, both geographically and politically.

Given this context, Jessey's tract ingeniously and disingenuously promotes New England's mission as already having established a foothold in the West Indies: there will be no need to divert populace or money from New England; colonists there are already competing with Catholic Spain for colonial control of West Indian bodies and souls, and they are winning. Dury, too, hints at this argument in his appendix to *Glorious Progress*. Like Jessey, he makes praying Indians "western" Indians: "The Gospel in its advancement amongst these *Western Indians,* appears to be *not in word only* (as it was by the *Spaniards* among their Indians) *but also in power, and in the Holy Ghost, and in much Assurance*" (D5r).[27] Later mission tracts produced by colonists similarly take this tack and position New England as already accomplishing Cromwell's goals, successfully countering Spain's influence on the natives of the West Indies. Jessey's is an extended use of such a rhetoric.[28]

This reasoning can help us understand the element of Jessey's title that seems most risible today, the inflated-sounding number of Dutch conversions in Formosa. Indeed, the tract later claims that some 17,000 are "affected." The numbers are similar to English reports of Spanish claims to mass conversions; national evangelical competition was ratcheted up in

1648 with the publication of *The English-American* by Thomas Gage, an apostate Dominican who had returned to England arguing that the corrupt Spanish rule in the colonies was precarious and that England should take control of Spanish holdings. England, he assured his readers, would easily be able to conquer Hispaniola, would even be greeted as liberators by the oppressed natives. Gage became one of Cromwell's advisers, and he was instrumental in convincing the Lord Protector that England would be acting as God's agent in expanding its colonial holdings into Spanish-held territories. Like other English travel writers before him, Gage reported the influence of Catholic missionaries on thousands of Native American souls, but he dismisses Catholic claims of mission success as proof of Catholic hypocrisy. He argues that empty ritual had supplanted true understanding, and fear of mistreatment had driven many Indians to profess a belief they did not possess. The claim to mass Protestant conversions in Jessey's tract thus has contradictory overtones: the huge numbers claimed by Catholics were widely discredited by English writers, but they were impressive and worrying nonetheless. Jessey tries to have it both ways in his tract. New England's converts appear to be impressively well-informed and pious, though colonial writers could only report modest success. Worldwide, however, the mission efforts of the "reformed" churches are doing well, as evidenced by large numbers of converts in the east. Thus, the main text does not celebrate so much a Dutch as a Protestant response to the overwhelming Jesuit presence in the East Indies, even as the postscript serves as a pointed attempt to insert New England into England's anti-Catholic, anti-Spanish policies in the West Indies.

Jessey's religious and political hopes for the mission are perhaps more pronounced than that of many settler-colonists. But on the matters of Indian identity and New England's role in the Commonwealth as a rising empire, the differences are a matter of degree only. Even the colonial divine Thomas Shepard, who was openly skeptical about the Christian Indians' Jewish origins and of prophetic signs and portents, was willing to allow mission reports to feed the religious fantasies of metropolitan supporters.[29] Important supporters such as Jessey promised to greatly further New England's cause. Jessey was a close friend of Massachusetts governor John Winthrop. He seriously considered emigrating himself and made monetary donations to the Massachusetts mission. In *Of the Conversion* he clearly sought to forward his friends' efforts, offering them "free publicity."[30] He was also a Cromwellian and, according to historian Murray Tolmi, helped establish "respectable non-conformity" during the Interregnum.[31]

Despite these credentials, fairly orthodox for the Interregnum, Jessey was also a Baptist, a millenarian, and a philo-Semite.[32] His publication is marked by his diverse interests, and as a consequence, it also rereads and re-presents New England mission writings in ways that probably would not have made their original authors entirely comfortable. The tract's most significant break with previous mission publications lies in its treatment of the Algonquian woman first introduced to English readers by John Eliot in 1649, a treatment in line with Jessey's early publications.

Jessey's earlier publishing history and religious affiliation suggest one reason that he may have been especially interested in the testimony of the Algonquian woman. His reputation as a writer was built on the publication in 1647 of *The Exceeding Riches of Grace Advanced by the Spirit of Grace, in an Empty Nothing Creature, (viz) Mrs. Sarah Wight*, an account of the sufferings and conversion of a young woman, which included extensive transcriptions of Sarah Wight's religious debates and prophecies.[33] *Exceeding Riches* is an early and prominent example of Jessey's ecumenical willingness to understand voices coming from unlikely sources as prophetic, as harbingers of cosmic events. Indeed, near the end of the tract he advises those who have not yet felt as moved by the spirit as Sarah Wight to "pray for more powerings out of his Spirit upon his sons and daughters, as he hath promised to doe in the last dayes."[34]

Of the Conversion thus follows *Exceeding Riches* in taking seriously and giving space to women's religious experiences and voices. In *Of the Conversion* Jessey transforms the spiritual example of the unnamed Indian woman into a first-person account that offers readers a pattern for their own faith and a confirmation of the millennial expectations suggested by his title page, with its significant choice of scriptural proof text. Jessey's alterations to Eliot's original suggest that he sees her testimony as of a piece with the experiences of Sarah Wight and other radical believers whom he pastors in London.

As we have seen, when Eliot presented the unnamed woman's experiences in *Glorious Progress*, he did so initially by paraphrase: "She told me she still loved God, though he made her sick, and was resolved to pray unto him so long as she lived, and to refuse powwowing." Compare his version to the same moment in Jessey's rendition: "she said, *I still love God, though he made me sick. I resolve to pray to him, whilst I live: and no* Pawaw. ---- *I believe God will pardon all my sins, because* Iesus Christ *died for me: and God is well pleased in him. I am willing to die, I shall goe to Heaven, and live happily with God and Christ there"* (27). Whereas Eliot's version emphasized his mediating role, Jessey renders this moment as an example of the woman's religious agency. She speaks for herself, the repeated, insistent "I" making her voice especially strong. Jessey's changes in his account of the woman seem intentional and unusual. Unlike this moment of clear editorial interference, Jessey leaves most of the speeches that Eliot reports elsewhere as they originally appeared, changing third to first person in just a couple of instances. All sense of this moment as confirmation of Eliot's influence as a missionary is dropped. Instead, the woman is presented speaking in her own voice, testifying to her own faith, just as any good Protestant experiencing an "easy death" should do.

As I noted earlier, Eliot describes her death-bed charge to her children as focused on keeping her family within the bounds of English authority. He reports that acting on her own, she warns her daughters against the blandishments of their relatives and charges them to remain in Nonantum. By contrast, in Jessey's version the emphasis is on her beliefs and experiences: "Before her Death, she called her up-growne Daughers, with her other Children, and said to them; I shall now die; Then your Grand-father, and Grand-mother, and Unckles,—will send for you, to come back to live there, and promise you much.—But I charge you, never goe; for they pray not to God, nor keep Sabbath: sinne, and not punished, etc." (27). Here, rather than the weight that Eliot's version puts on the proto-reservations of the praying towns (in Eliot's version she says "*here* they pray unto God"), all emphasis is on the sinfulness of her extended family. The effect is a focus on the dying woman— she prays, keeps Sabbath, subjects herself to church discipline—rather than on Eliot's work, with an immediacy not fully realized in the original publication, an immediacy that may have appealed especially to readers who had made Jessey's earlier account of a prophetic woman so popular.

It is important to recognize this context because it points to the ways that the New England tracts, excerpted, revised, and summarized by a writer whose beliefs were more extreme than most New England authors, result in a flexible figure of the praying Indian and of native women put to diverse uses by Englishmen.[35] In Eliot's original version he takes pains to demonstrate that the Algonquian woman's behavior was strictly according to English social norms. As Eliot would have it, she was eager from the first to inhabit a proper gender role, willingly silencing herself in public. In addition to her deathbed scene he offers one other anecdote from her Christian life. At a meeting she joins a number of converts posing "spiritual questions" to Eliot.

Although she stands out—she was "the first woman that posed a question"—
her behavior is unexceptional: she finds a way to stay silent in public; the
question was "by another man propounded for her." Both the method of
questioning and the content of the question reveal her willingness to subject
herself to male authority: "When my Husband prayeth in his house my heart
thinketh what he prayeth, whether is this praying to God aright or no?" Eliot
approves: "I thought it a fit question for a woman" (B3v). Jessey cuts this
detail, and unlike the picture of a quiet, safely orthodox woman that Eliot
paints, Jessey's treatment of her makes her something else—someone whom
Eliot and perhaps not even the woman herself would have recognized. By giving the Algonquian woman a strong, even unique voice in the New England
mission, Jessey offers his readers more evidence of the "powerings out of his
Spirit upon his sons and daughters" that they had encountered in *Exceeding
Riches*. If this American daughter is not exactly prophesying, she is certainly
speaking publicly and forcefully of Christ and salvation.

A Nonantum Life

Consideration of English uses of the Algonquian woman's story shows how important native figures could be to debates over the most significant events of the
time, from regicide, to imperialism, to millennialism, even to individual minis-
tries. However valuable these accounts for our understanding of the transatlantic English community, they offer no direct encounters with their subject. The
problem, of course, is to recover any sense of native experiences through such
heavily mediated accounts. Indeed, on the face of it, there seems little more to
glean from the printed accounts of the woman's testimony than the facts of the
woman's move to Nonantum and her death in 1648. But in addition to Eliot's
description of her Christian beliefs, he does give us another important detail of
her life: she makes and sells baskets. This detail is key to my speculation about
the woman's own sense of her conversion and removal to Nonantum.

Christian Indian women used their traditional skills as basket makers
as part of their bid to become members of the colonial economic system.
Indeed, non-Christians also adapted such traditional technologies to new
markets.[36] In 1671 Daniel Gookin notes the basket-making practices among
praying Indians: "Some of their baskets are made of rushes; some of bents,
others of maize husks; others of a kind of silk grass; others, of a kind of wild
hemp; and some of barks of trees; many of them, very neat and artificial, with

the portraiture of birds, beasts, fishes, and flowers, upon them in colours."[37] His description is tantalizing; what might the "artificial"—read "artful"—decoration of such baskets have communicated to their makers, to others in the community, to their purchasers? The meaning of such basketry design is, in the words of Stephanie Fitzgerald, a Native American studies scholar, "imbued with cultural and spiritual power."[38]

We may never be able to recover a separate "native" versus a "Christian" meaning to the basket's artistry: indeed, the effort would be misdirected, since the baskets created by the Algonquian woman in Nonantum were produced or possessed by people who were in a native Christian community. Nevertheless, the fact that this woman made and sold baskets has the potential to tell us something new about her, to alter our understanding of her deathbed confession and of the woman's participation in the transatlantic discourse I have been tracing. Even without any surviving record of her production, we know that she produced texts with meanings that could not be fully contained by Eliot or the colonial print archive. Not that colonial writers didn't try: Eliot mentions the woman's basket-making ability—along with her willingness to spin—because it makes clear her membership in the colonial labor economy. In the tracts he regularly touts his converts' ability for hard, English-style work, contrasting them with "lazy" traditionalists. But basket making, like beading and wampum making, has an important cultural as well as practical meaning. It has been and continutes to be an important signing practice for native women.[39] Even if we cannot make positive statements about the meaning encoded in her basket designs, the fact that she made them, coupled with the provocative arguments offered by recent scholars of native material culture in the colonial period, allows us to reconsider the print archive.

We know that historically wood-splint baskets encoded references to colonialism, traditional spirituality, tribal histories, and politics. For instance, Ann MacMullen and Stephanie Fitzgerald analyze space-place in Mohegan basket designs of the early nineteenth century. Although their conclusions differ, they agree that these baskets often represent the Peoples' migration—originary, cyclical, or forced. Could this woman, though creating her baskets years earlier, likewise have represented her own or her community's recent history, particularly the move to Nonantum? Christian converts were most readily drawn from badly splintered tribes and displaced families. Praying towns were attractive because they could consolidate remnant families and help survivors form new connections.[40] Moreover, a few years after the woman's death men from Natick record their attachment to the praying town as a place in their confessions before the Christian church: indeed, quite often they explain that their decision to convert to Christianity was initially driven by their love of the place where they lived and their hope that conversion would allow them to remain, and Eliot tells us that when this woman and her family moved to Nonantum, they traveled sixteen miles with their goods and provisions on their backs.

Given the effort she spent to get to Nonantum, given her interest in and willingness to commit herself to the praying life, it should come as no surprise that she enjoins her children to respect her decision and remain with the praying Indian community. But it is perhaps too easy to read this as colonial ventriloquism on the part of the missionaries. Rather than focusing only on her concern with God's law, a sense of traditional native basket design that may have included representation of native lands, spaces, and movement should direct our attention to the repetition of her directions to her children: "I charge you live here... I charge you live here all your dayes." While Eliot interprets her emphasis on Nonantum as an example of her thoroughgoing conversion to English mores and Christian rule, it may be that her deathbed charge to her daughters—her grown daughters by a first husband, a charge delivered out of the hearing of the English missionary—has to do with her interest in Nonantum as a new Indian place.[41] As much as Eliot wants to see her life and death as adhering to conventional English norms, her desire for her children to remain in Nonantum (and her husband's desire to see her dying wish fulfilled) may not be the expressions of piety that Eliot imagined them to be. We would do well to remember that among coastal Algonquian peoples women could traditionally hold positions of both political and religious authority.[42] Perhaps the woman's desire that her children remain in Nonantum reflects her establishment of a new matrilineal social structure, one that was not as well understood by her English missionary interpreters as it was by her neighbors in Nonantum's pan-Indian community, drawing as they would on various traditions of women sachems and female agricultural practices that knit women to the land in particular ways.[43]

My reading here is highly speculative, of course, but I think the effort worthwhile, because at the very least it reminds us that an individual Algonquian woman had an encounter with an English missionary that sparked a wide-ranging exchange among colonial and metropolitan writers. Such speculation should also remind us that the seventeenth-century transatlantic religious world included places with such names as Nonantum and Natick no less than Boston and London. It should remind us that disruption, fears, and hopes were characteristic of all reaches of that transatlantic world. National and personal upheaval compelled Jessey to search out millennial meaning in colonial reports, prompted Eliot to immigrate to New England, moved Winslow to return to London to represent the colonies, and also led an Algonquian woman to walk some sixteen miles with all her possessions on her back to join with a new and untested religious community. We may not share Eliot's, Winslow's, or Jessey's sense of what her decision signified. We may not be able to do more than speculate about her own understanding of that choice. But we must surely recognize her choice for its historical and especially for its human value.

CHAPTER 8

Dreams Clash

The War over Authorized Interpretation
in Seventeenth-Century French Missions

Dominique Deslandres

"The dream is the oracle that all these poor Peoples consult and listen to, the Prophet which predicts to them future events, the Cassandra which warns them of misfortunes that threaten them, the usual Physician in their sicknesses, the Esculapius and Galen of the whole Country,—the most absolute master they have."[1] By these words, written at the beginning of the seventeenth century, the superior of the Huron mission, Jean de Brébeuf, drew the contours of a culture of dreams that he failed to find legitimate; neither did he believe it compared favorably to that of the ancient Greeks and Romans—as his Jesuit colleague, Joseph François Lafitau, did almost a century later in *Moeurs des sauvages amériquains comparées aux moeurs des premiers temps.*[2]

There is, though, a centuries-old continuity in the Western approach to dreams that masks the disagreement of Brébeuf and Lafitau over Huron dream culture.[3] Dreams have always had a special place in monotheistic traditions, where they were supposed to put the dreamer in contact with the supernatural world and introduce him to a knowledge that is inaccessible to ordinary consciousness. Since antiquity, European philosophers and theologians have agreed on the necessity of understanding dreams, as their interpretation was the key to foretelling the future or to learning the ways of God.

Of course, the Catholic Church paid careful attention to the phenomenon and tried to discern good dreams from bad ones, condemning oneiromancy—the art of divination through dream—which was associated with witchcraft and other superstitions.[4]

Moreover, one must recall that the practice of "incubation" (sleeping in the temple of a deity in order to be informed or healed by this deity), which was widespread among the Greeks and Romans,[5] was well-known to seventeenth-century scholars and churchmen—the very men who described at length similar practices performed by the Amerindians. So what does it mean that Brébeuf and his Jesuit companions made this comparison with antiquity but failed to use it in a favorable assessment of Amerindian aptitude for conversion to Catholicism? On the one hand, does this reflect a kind of momentum in the semantic shock between French and Amerindian cultures?[6] In other words, can we understand this refusal on the part of the missionaries, who were actually at the beginning of their missions, as the incapacity to grant the same origins—or assign humanity—to the Amerindians? On the other hand, can we understand this failure as a defense of a "new religious deal" promoted by the Council of Trent that would eventually lead to the condemnation—and eradication—of all types of paganism, including that of the ancient pagan philosophers?

These questions are all the more important because during the "Century of Saints" (corresponding in France to the years 1600–1660), most Catholic mystics and reformers were themselves subject to night dreams, daydreaming, and other "private revelations" that were often the basis of their vocation.[7] Most of the French missionaries recalled having a vision or a dream that dictated their involvement in the mission. But how did they receive the accounts of dreams expressed by those coming from the profane world? Were they open to their authenticity or, on the contrary, closed to their dangers? How were these dispositions carried over the Atlantic in the meeting of very different peoples?

This is what this paper seeks to explore. Its setting is in effect France and New France—its colony in formation—both of which were the theater of an intense and simultaneous campaign of evangelization. The aim here is to underline the French missionaries' rationale about the convert's belief in dreams, visions, and premonitions and to show how they dealt with and tried to convert the other's imaginary world in what can be called an essential war of the seventeenth century.

The Double Setting: France and New France
in the Seventeenth Century

At the end of the religious wars of the Reformation, when the kingdom of France was at last at peace, the reconstruction of the country lay in the hands of the religious elite. Education, health, social care, and missions were the tools of this reconstruction, and the clergy, regular and then secular, were the main agents of change. And very soon Capuchin and Jesuit missionaries literally patrolled the whole country, which they called the "Black Indies of the interior" since they found there peasants as ignorant of the Christian faith as were the pagans of Canada, Constantinople, or Madagascar. In fact, as I have shown in earlier work, mere chronology shows how interwoven were the internal and external missionary initiatives: often the same agents, using the same methods of conversion and expecting the same results, were active on both sides of the Atlantic.[8] Ultimately, these missions aimed to pacify the very diverse peoples inhabiting the French early modern space; as will be shown, this was an uneasy process.

Discovered by the Frenchman Jacques Cartier in 1534, New France was initially confined in essence to the St. Lawrence Valley, with colonial economic exploitation and settlement really only starting after the Peace of Vervins in 1598. Although Quebec City, founded ten years later, was at the heart of the colony, it remained a simple fur-trading post for many years. Eventually, the French settled along the banks of the St. Lawrence River, despite the raids against them and their Amerindian allies by the Iroquois Five Nations. The settlers were quickly drawn into Amerindian conflicts, taking sides against the Iroquois. In 1615 and 1625 first Recollect and then Jesuit priests started missions for the nomadic people around Quebec City—referred to as Algonquians by modern anthropologists—who traded fur with the settlers. The missionaries soon discovered the existence further west and south of Quebec City of semi-sedentary peoples who they felt were the most promising prospects for conversion to Christianity: the Hurons of the Iroquoian family, who constituted the central axis of the fur trade in the west. From 1632 to the erection of the Quebec bishopric in 1658 the Jesuits' religious monopoly in New France was almost total. However, terrible epidemics quickly devastated the Amerindian peoples, who lacked immunity to European diseases. These epidemics decimated Amerindian populations and jeopardized the lives of missionaries, who were often denounced by the natives as "sorcerers" intent on killing them all. We can say that until the conclusion of the Great Peace of Montreal in 1701, the situation was difficult for the French and their allies alike, with epidemics, warfare, risks of the fur trade, low immigration, and the instability of the missions.[9]

Dreams: The Heart of the Problem of Conversion

One of the main obstacles to conversion that the missionaries faced was the belief in dreams. In France, knowing the dangers of a drift in the understanding of religion, they were very careful to check the orthodoxy of the dreams and visions reported by the faithful in confession. For example, the Jesuit Julien Maunoir in his missions in the province of Brittany sorted out his flock's dreams and visions. He distinguished carefully the good ones from the bad ones and was thus able to measure the influence of his preaching. When a dream featured the souls in purgatory, the good angel, the patron saint, or the Virgin Mary while the dreamer led a good life—that is, a life according to the rules of the Council of Trent—the Jesuit was satisfied that it was proof of a genuine change of heart; he "thank[ed] God that He used the imagination of these good people to lead them to a real penance."[10] But when a peasant named Yves Le Goff came to confess that he was visited by frequent apparitions of the Virgin, the missionary asked him to perform a kind of exorcism: the next time the said lady appeared, Le Goff was instructed to present her with his crucifix.[11]

Apparitions, visions, "*songes*," "internal word": all these phenomena, which the post-Tridentine Church considered legitimate, were "private revelations,"[12] which had in common the ability to carry at least an intelligible meaning if not a divine message. But is there any evidence that dreams were a vehicle for expressing opposition to the established orthodoxy in seventeenth-century France? Embedded, as we said, in a long tradition concerning prophetism, the practice of discernment[13] brought prudence to seventeenth-century clerics' concerns: the examples of deviance found in antiquity and the Middle Ages (Gnosticism, Montanism, Joachimism, and others)[14] were still vivid in their minds as they were fighting the new "venom of heresy" spread on their soils through Protestant reforms and legitimately settled in France since the Edict of Nantes in 1598. A basic attitude among the missionaries was to dismiss without appeal the pretense of Protestants claiming to have been "illuminated" by a dream or a vision.

But simultaneously, among Catholics, the intense search for sanctity that characterized the beginning of the seventeenth century[15] forbade the missionaries to condemn altogether the visions and dreams that those they labored among had confessed. The Roman Church considered the phenomenon also as a sign of election and a *sine qua non* of canonization.[16] In fact, everything depended on the religious quality of the dreamer or visionary. Thus, helped by their examination of the depth of their flocks' faith, the missionaries carefully evaluated which visions or dreams were authentic and which ones were not. Since this was a relatively easy task to do in France, one could have supposed that they would have brought this broad approach to the New World.

But strangely enough, in New France the missionaries found themselves at war with the dreams of the Amerindians. For as the Jesuit Jérôme Lalemant pointed out in 1642, "In France a dream is only a dream; but here it is a point of Theology, or an article of Faith,—it requires great grace to set it at naught."[17] The superior of the Huron mission, Jean de Brébeuf, explains his remark, quoted above in the introduction to this essay:

> If a Captain speaks one way and a dream another, the Captain
> might shout his head off in vain,—the dream is first obeyed. It is
> their Mercury in their journeys, their domestic Economy in their
> families. The dream often presides in their councils; traffics, fishing
> and hunting are undertaken usually under its sanction, and almost
> as if only to satisfy it. They hold nothing so precious that they would
> not readily deprive themselves of it for the sake of a dream. If they
> have been successful in hunting, if they bring back their Canoes laden
> with fish, all this is at the discretion of a dream. A dream will take
> away from them sometimes their whole year's provisions. It prescribes
> their feasts, their dances, their songs, their games,—in a word, the
> dream does everything and is in truth the principal God of the
> Hurons. Moreover, let no[one] think I make herein an amplification
> or exaggeration at pleasure; the experience of five years, during which
> I have been studying the manners and usages of our Savages, compels
> me to speak in this way.[18]

Thus, when confronted by Amerindian dreams, the missionaries felt not only powerless but also insecure. They may condemn visions as stupid fables, even as diabolical perversions, for they know perfectly well that they are dangerous; as Paul Le Jeune put it, "One may die for God in dying because of a dream."[19]

In effect, the widespread belief among the Amerindians encountered by the missionaries was that dreaming of killing someone put the dreamer under an obligation to carry out the killing. Already in 1627 Charles Lalemant warned that "there is no security for our lives among theses Savages.... if during the night they dream they must kill a Frenchman, woe to the first one whom they meet alone. They attach a great faith to their dreams."[20] The missionaries felt powerless in the face of this Amerindian belief in the power of dreams. They had already risked their lives in confronting the physical dangers of following the "Savages" to their country; now they had to be aware of a more powerful but more ethereal danger.

Besides, the Amerindians' dreams were a source of exasperation because those who had these dreams pretended that they were premonitory. "Some of them will tell you two days before the coming of a ship the hour of its arrival, and will give no other explanation except that they have seen it while asleep."[21] Such premonitions were ridiculed by the French: as the explorer Samuel de Champlain saw it, these premonitions were the results of mere coincidence or worse, of devilry.[22] But the French were never wholly reassured. All their reports exhibit their ambivalence: on the one hand, they claimed that these dreams were only fables, but on the other hand, they hastened to report them in great detail and tried very hard to convince their readers—and themselves—of their ineffectiveness.[23] This attitude can be explained by the European traditional approach to dreams and visions: no risk can be taken.

Dreaming and Resisting

In fact, the dreams of the Amerindians constituted the main field of symbolic shock between the nations of the Old and the New Worlds. With the dreams that they recounted to the Europeans—and to which the Europeans attached great importance—the Amerindians narrated their resistance to the spiritual invasion they were undergoing, their demands as well as their fear and help-lessness. For example, from 1636 on, Brébeuf reported dreams and visions that contradict his teachings on paradise and hell:

> It is the devil that deceives them in their dreams; thus he speaks by
> the mouth of some, who having been left as dead, recover health
> and talk at random of the other life, according to the ideas that this
> wretched master gives them. According to them the Village of souls

is in no respect unlike the Village of the living,—they go hunting, fishing, and to the woods; axes, robes, and collars are as much esteemed as among the living. In a word everything is the same: there is only this difference that day and night they do nothing but groan and complain. They have Captains, who from time to time put an end to it and try to moderate their sighs and groans. God of truth, what ignorance and stupidity! *Illuminare his qui in tenebris, et in umbra mortis sedent.*[24]

Le Jeune reports that an Algonquian pretended to have been resuscitated: "This good man, sitting up, related that he had come from the country of souls, which is situated where the Sun sets, and that he had not seen any Frenchman there,—this place being destined only for Savages. 'It is in my power, said he to live again upon earth; but I prefer to go away to the country of souls, rather than to remain among men.' So saying, he lay down and died again."[25] This is a good way of expressing one's disagreement with the new Christian belief.

Five years later the dreams and visions were more precise, more cutting in their denunciation of the Christian discourse. And the missionaries of Huronia reported a whole series of rumors, founded on tales of apparitions or daydreaming. As Paul Ragueneau wrote in 1645, "In order, then to sap the foundations of our faith, they have tried to shake them by falsehoods which they invent, and with which they fill the whole country."[26] The anthropologist Bruce G. Trigger has accounted for a real traditionalist movement that spread at that time among the Hurons that aimed to refute the new Christian beliefs.[27] Thus the Algonquians circulated the rumor that they had found distant cities inhabited only by souls who told them "that these things which are said of Paradise and of Hell are fables." Other news circulated "that there has appeared in the woods a phantom of prodigious size, who bears in one hand ears of Indian corn, and, in the other, a great abundance of fish; who says that it is he alone who has created men . . . he also said that to believe that any one of them was destined to a place of torments and to the fires, which are not beneath the earth, were false notions—with which nevertheless we treacherously strive to terrify them."[28] And a Huron Christian woman, buried in the French cemetery, was said to have risen again and to have proclaimed

that the French were impostors; that her soul, having left the body, had actually been taken to Heaven; that the French had welcomed it

there, but in the manner in which an Iroquois captive is received at
the entrance to their villages,—with firebrands and burning torches,
with cruelties and torments inconceivable. She had related that all
Heaven is nothing but fire, and that there the satisfaction of the
French is to burn now some, now others; and that, in order to possess
many of these captive souls, which are the object of their pleasures,
they cross the seas, and come into these regions as into a land of
conquest, just as a Huron exposes himself with joy to the fatigues and
all the dangers of war, in the hope of bringing back some captive. It
was further said that those who are thus burned in Heaven, as captives
of war, are the Huron, Algonquian, and Montagnais Christians,
and that those who have not been willing in this world to render
themselves slaves of the French, or to receive their laws, go after this
life into a place of delights, where everything good abounds, and
whence all evil is banished; she had chosen to return into her body,
as long as was necessary to warn those who were there present of such
terrible news, and of that great misfortune which awaited them at
death, if they continued to believe in the impostures of the French.[29]

Through these examples we can see how difficult it was for the Jesuits to
counter the collective resistance expressed by rumors; the same difficulty
arose when they tried to counter the individual resistance manifest in visions and dreams. Thus a sick woman refused to be baptized because her
dream forbad it on pain of death; another had a dream that forbad him to
pray; still another was threatened in his dream by a devil because he had
converted.[30] The missionaries tried their best to discredit these "ordinary
dreams" among their converts. And always they met with the same problem:
the stubbornness of the Amerindians, who "are extremely attached to their
dreams," which "are the whole Theology of these poor Barbarians."[31] In response, the missionaries strove very hard to demonstrate the falseness of the
dreams, especially in cases when the sick dreamed about what could heal
them and when the whole tribe hastened to satisfy their desires to speed their
recovery.[32] In these situations the Jesuits tried all sorts of strategies: they
ridiculed the dreams,[33] and they pretended to have competing dreams—as
did father Le Jeune, who relates, "I had an idea that this dreamer might
play some bad trick on me and abandon me, to prove himself a prophet. For
this reason I made use of his weapons, opposing *altare contra altare*, dream
against dream. 'As for me,' I replied 'I have dreamed just the opposite; for

in my sleep I saw two Moose, [. . .].' 'In fact,' the Jesuit adds 'I had had this dream some days before.'"[34]

The missionaries also refused to answer the demands expressed by the dreams and sometimes even blackmailed the dreamers (if they fail to heal, they will convert); but these tactics only earned them the hostility and the suspicion of the Amerindians. And in their eagerness to prove their point the Jesuits proposed to pray, meditate, and make vows to God to ask for the recovery of the sick. For the Jesuits these spiritual actions constituted "experiences, to shake and overthrow their belief in dreams";[35] for the Amerindians they appeared as powerful communications with spirits, the very one performed by sorcerers.[36]

But the idea was to succeed in convincing the Amerindians to abandon their belief in the power of dreams. Disowning visions became proof of an authentic conversion, and all the Jesuits eagerly reported these signs.[37]

> This good Christian, having returned some months ago from a
> journey that he had made to the Khionontateronons, whither he
> had gone to assist our Fathers in the preaching of the Gospel, seeing
> himself wearied with travel, took a sweat (this is a certain kind of bath
> which these savages use, by which they refresh themselves). Having
> entered this bath, it was a pleasure to hear him, not singing of dreams,
> and war songs, as all his fellow countrymen do on this occasion, but
> animating himself to a new combat, resolving to die for the defense of
> the Faith, promising God to scour the whole country, and announcing
> everywhere his holy name.[38]

The Ursuline Marie de l'Incarnation describes the same effect on a neophyte: "The man who had the vision could not help but preach to his fellow countrymen about what he saw. That is our Lord who appeared to him, showed him his sacred wounds, made him see the glory of the blest and the sentence of the damned, with the just reason He had to chastise men, who do not make good use of the blessing of the Redemption."[39]

Better yet, some converts began to ridicule their own dreams and those of their tribesmen.[40] The missionaries happily applauded this new attitude without realizing how native belief in dreams mirrored their own, for dreams, visions, and apparitions were part of what can be called the frame of mind, that is, the *episteme* of the Jesuit missionaries.[41] They firmly believed in them, and they showed a deep attachment to those of their countrymen, especially the premonitory dreams, such as those of Isaac Jogues, Charles Garnier, and Jean de Brébeuf—whose vision announcing his own impending martyrdom was so powerful that his companions "by a movement of God" had him bled by a surgeon in order to be sure to have a relic.[42] The Ursuline Marie de l'Incarnation, who dreamed of settling her convent in Quebec City; her fellow nun Marie de Saint-Joseph; and the Hospitalière Catherine de Saint-Augustin all reported visions and dreams that foretold their future.

The missionaries did not fail to notice the fervor that the Amerindians displayed when they obeyed their dreams. But for them this fervor was badly directed; as Brébeuf writes: "They have a faith in dreams which surpasses all belief; and if Christians were to put into execution all their divine inspirations with as much care as our Savages carry out their dreams, no doubt they would very soon become great saints."[43] The missionary view of the world was essentially dualist. They never ceased to refer to God's and the Devil's actions. So the dreams of the pagan Amerindians could only be inspired by the Devil. However, when a convert reported a vision, when a neophyte had a dream that led to conversion or to prophecy, the missionaries took him very seriously, though not without first checking the veracity of the report. Thus, when the Montagnais Nenaskoumat, an exemplary convert, reported that he had seen paradise and hell in a "great communication he had with God," Le Jeune hastened to reassure the correspondent to whom he described the event:

Now I can assure Your Reverence that we did all we could to discover [if] this were an imposture or a dream. We had sounded him several times and on different occasions until believing that he had his soul upon his lips, we reminded him of this vision, threatening him with severe punishment if he lied in a matter of so much importance. This poor frightened man, trying to raise himself to a sitting posture, said to us with a steadfast eye, "I assure you in all truth that the thing is as I have described it to you. I have not lied to you in life; I will not lie to you at my death." Regarding this, what can one say except that the God of Paradise bestows his blessings upon the Barbarians as well as upon the Greeks.[44]

Other dreamers were converted by their visions, as was the Huron woman who asked Brébeuf to baptize her after having dreamed of "a young man clothed in a robe as white as snow, and as beautiful as a Frenchman, who was going about baptizing all our village; I took great delight in looking at him; and now I pray thee to baptize me." The Father instructed her as to the nature of dreams and explained to her the Catechism, "with much consolation on the part of both. The knowledge she had of the pains of Hell, and of the joys of Paradise, made her desire and ask for holy Baptism with more insistence."[45]

Some years later Jérôme Lalemant was ready to believe in the prophetic dream of a Huron who announced the conversion of the western peoples of America:

> I have wondered whether I should relate here a vision, or if you will, a dream that this man had. Whatever be the name by which it is called, here is the account he himself has given of it. "I saw" he said, "a cross in the Sky, all red with blood; and our Lord stretched thereon, with his head to the East and his feet to the West. I saw a crowd of people advancing from the West, whom our Lord attracted by his loving looks, and who did not dare to approach his sacred head, but remained respectfully at his feet. Remaining silent and quite astounded in the midst of that company, I heard a voice commanding me to pray. I did so, in holy awe, and felt in my soul emotions of fear and of love that surpass all my thoughts." He had the same vision on three different occasions; but I would have paid no more heed to it than to a dream, were it not that the impressions that it has left in his heart are supernatural. These peoples of the West must come to adore the cross of Jesus Christ.[46]

We see in these cases that the missionaries have the same attitude in France and in New France toward the religion of their flock, the same care in noticing the intervention of supernatural powers and their effects on the souls of the peoples they encounter, and the same refusal to consider legitimate the religions of the others: the peasant's or the heretic's or the Amerindian's beliefs are only shallow dreams, stupid beliefs, or bad customs, merely superstitions that must "be changed into true religion." But the task was equally difficult on both sides of the Atlantic, so much "indeed the obstinacy of heretics is a true illustration of the callousness of our Savages."[47]

CHAPTER 9

"For Each and Every House to Wish for Peace"

Christoph Saur's *High German American Almanac* and the French and Indian War in Pennsylvania

Bethany Wiggin

Although Britain did not officially declare it for another three years, in 1753 war already filled colonial Pennsylvania's air. Periodicals teemed with speculation about its outbreak; talk of war and peace saturated even apparently apolitical publications, such as the *High German American Almanac*:

> Newcomer: The Germans will soon be half English and say "Hau di thu?"
>
> Resident: What does that mean?
>
> Newcomer: I'm not quite sure myself, but I'd certainly like to know.
>
> Resident: When the first settlers came to Pennsylvania and found no houses, no horses, no cows, no fruit, no mills, no salt, and no bread, they had it hard. When blessed friends met out of love to see whether they might serve and help one another, then their first greeting was "Hau di thu?" (how do you do). And when someone didn't want to complain, he answered: "Indifferent!" That is to say: tolerable or so-so. By the next year they had planted Indian corn; some must have had a whole day's journey to carry their corn to be milled and then to get home again. Their neighbor women would likely have come, each glad to have a little flour for her small child (because older

children could eat their corn cooked), and so the man's little bag of flour was soon used up. But out of love for his neighbors' children, he would again take that burden upon his own shoulders and walk to the mill. If he ran into a good friend who asked "Hau dost thi" or "Hau di thu," then he answered: "Pretty well," that is to say: acceptably well. But because in the following years these and other people lived, and live, in great plenty, they ride past one another on fancy horses. One says "Hau di thu?" and the other also says "Hau di thu." And so no one knows how the other fares, and it's now become a habit.

Newcomer: What did the ancient fathers likely have for a greeting when they came together or when they met each other?

Resident: Even today the Jews say "Schoulum Legum" (I wish you peace). And Christ greeted his apostle with these words: "Peace be unto you" (Luke 24: 36) and said to his apostles: "When you enter a house, so first speak: Peace be to this house" (Luke 10:5).

Newcomer: I think it's strange that this greeting has grown so out of use, it seems to me that it's still necessary today for each and every house to wish for peace.[1]

The *Almanac*'s author and publisher, Christoph Saur (1695–1758), recognized the present as a time of war; nonetheless, he used the reach of his German-town press to campaign for a time of peace. Of the reams of broadsheets, pamphlets, newspapers, primers, devotional materials, and more issued by the Germantown press, Saur's almanac likely enjoyed the largest readership among the colony's German speakers, somewhere between a third and a half of Pennsylvania's total population.[2] The popular almanac's potpourri of information, entertainment, opinion, and practical advice truly contained something for every reader—for sectarians and Church Germans, for those who lived in town and "im Busch" (in the backcountry), for women and men, for young and old. Even for those who could not read, the *Almanac* provided something: letter patterns for anyone wanting to learn German and English letters, both in script and in type.

Beginning in the issue for 1751, the *Almanac* also began to include lengthy dialogues between an *Einwohner* (resident) and a *Neukommer* (newcomer) such as that given at the outset of this essay. In part, these dialogues were designed to answer practical questions for those thousands of newly arrived migrants who stumbled out of crowded ships' holds onto Philadelphia's busy docks. Furthermore, the dialogues were calculated to urge all Germans to keep the peace on the eve of what would become the French and Indian War. As Saur's Newcomer plaintively echoed his more experienced German American interlocutor in the almanac for 1753, "It's still necessary today for each and every house to wish for peace."

This article focuses on Saur's "wish for peace," exploring how his popular almanac crafted a pacifist rhetoric to reach explicitly political ends. The printer's millennial and martyrological tendencies, subtly explored by Jan Stievermann,[3] hardly precluded a pragmatic political engagement. Even a parable extolling the plain virtues of early colonists contained a political lesson. No meek martyr, Saur wrote to persuade the colony's flood of new arrivals to support Quaker-led politics in and out of the colonial assembly.

All colonial players sought to harness the power of language for their own ends, whether in contexts of direct diplomacy or in printed ephemera. For some two decades Saur managed to dominate the sizable market for German-language printed materials in the colonies, and he provided critical support to his Quaker allies in Pennsylvania. The Quaker majority in the provincial assembly had long been backed by a firm alliance between German colonists— many of whose more influential members were "sectarians," members of the German Peace churches—and the colony's founding sectarians, English Quakers. But unlike previous German migrants to Pennsylvania, new German arrivals were overwhelmingly "Church Germans," members of either the Lutheran or Reformed (Calvinist) Church.[4] The *Almanac* preached to them, teaching that any "wish for peace" could only be realized if they cleaved to the party of "sectarians." Churchmen (*Pfaffen*), Saur taught, let slip the dogs of war.

With Quakers, and then to a lesser extent with Delaware (Lenape) Indians, the Saur press made common cause. Pennsylvanian society was stretched, rewoven, and often torn by the mass influx of primarily German and Scots-Irish colonists, who occupied land whose ownership was already hotly contested by various European and Indian parties. Colonists and Indians alike began to think reductively in categories of "red" and "white." Writing against this racialization of colonial society, Saur and his allies cleaved to a vision of a shared past whose plain virtues they constantly extolled. Against the terrifying specters of what Peter Silver has aptly called the "anti-Indian sublime,"[5] Saur venerated the early colonists and particularly the colony's founder, William Penn.

While the peace Saur wished for might have failed, the oppositional political community forged by his writings nonetheless endured, as I hope to demonstrate below. This essay's first section situates Saur's rhetoric in the fraught atmosphere of Pennsylvania's mid-century politics. In the 1740s and 1750s Saur himself provided the target for ad hominem attacks; he hardly shied from firing printed salvoes in return. A detailed exploration of Saur's rhetoric in the *Almanac* occupies the essay's second section, and it shows the printer deeply engaged in political life. This reading of the *Almanac* helps document a concerted albeit belated strategy planned by Pennsylvanians, both Indian and European, who worked for peace across languages and ethnicities.

Wolves, the Winds of War

Saur carefully formulated his rhetoric in the 1750s to address the crisis that was rapidly engulfing Pennsylvania politics. Although long in the making, the crisis was immediately precipitated by a Delaware attack on Moravians— Germans, Christian Delawares, and Mahicans—at Gnadenhütten on Penn's Creek and by Governor Morris's ensuing request on November 24, 1755, that the Pennsylvania Assembly provide for defense against further expected raids.[6] The assembly's majority Quakers had long contested plans proposed by the colony's Penn family Proprietors, now Anglican, and their governors who steadfastly refused to allow taxation of the family's considerable land holdings. Morris's requests that the Assembly fund military operations had already often foundered on this disagreement over property taxes.[7] But after still more attacks in 1755 and the arrival of a delegation of the "Dutch mob" from the backcountry, the Quaker Party's already tenuous commitment to pacifist principles cracked.[8] Reports of battles to the west and the taking of captives dominated the rapidly approaching fall elections, which were certain to determine the colony's degree of support in battles against French and Indians. All knew that winning the "German vote" would decide the outcome.

Unlike earlier groups of European migrants to the Quaker colony, the thousands of Germans arriving at mid-century had not been moved primarily by considerations of conscience. Neither freethinkers nor sectarians, the great majority of these new arrivals belonged either to the Lutheran or to the Reformed Church, both of which had begun to expand their institutional presence in the mid-Atlantic only in the 1740s, in response to what Aaron Fogleman aptly calls "the Moravian challenge."[9] In search of fabled American plenty many recently arrived Germans pushed their way into Indian territory, squatting on land west of Pennsylvania's border, even after the colony's border had been aggressively expanded by the 1737 Walking Purchase.[10]

But perhaps no one was more eager to break Quaker Party control of the Assembly than the author of *A Brief State of the Province of Pennsylvania*, a clergyman in the Church of England named William Smith (1727–1803).[11] Published anonymously in 1755 in London, Smith's pamphlet made a splash across the Atlantic world.[12] How was it, the pamphlet quizzed, that Pennsylvania, "esteemed one of the richest Colonies in *North America*," could also be "the most backward in contributing to the Defence of the *British* Dominions in these Parts, against the present unwarrantable Invasions of the *French*?"(5). Smith neatly placed the blame for the colony's apparent lack of love for Britain at the door of the Quaker-led Assembly. Outlining a theory of populations, wealth, and government, Smith labored to delegitimize the Assembly's authority: "But in Proportion as a Country grows rich and populous, more Checks are wanted to the Power of the People" (8–9). Clearly no friend of republican forms of government, the Anglican Smith opposed "the Power of the People," especially if those people were pacifist Quakers: "Possessed of such unrestrained Powers and Privileges, they [Assembly men] seem quite intoxicated; are factious, contentious, and disregard the Proprietors and their Governors. Nay, they seem even to claim a kind of Independency of their Mother-Country, despising the Orders of the Crown, and refusing to contribute their Quota, either to the general defence of *America*, or that of their own particular Province" (12). Should the Quakers' "disregard" for right authority and their insufficient filial piety not yet prove convincing to his readers, Smith laid his trump card: the Quaker Assembly was in league with "a *German* Printer, who was once of the *French* Prophets in *Germany*, and is shrewdly suspected to be a *Popish* Emissary" (28). This villain, Smith asserted, was "Saüer," whom the Quakers "took into their Pay" (29). Christoph Saur was, as any reader of his papers would have easily seen, no more a crypto-Catholic than were Quakers.[13] But for a jittery audience Smith's charges played well enough—in London and in the American colonies, to English and apparently to German readers.

Saur found it necessary to take on Smith's pamphlet directly, and he rushed a two-page broadside into print. Smith, according to Saur, might call himself a "protector of our freedoms" [Beschützer unserer Freyheiten] as part of a cheap appeal to those Germans already subject to or fearful of further Delaware attacks along the Susquehanna River and in the region known as the Tulpehocken.[14] But, Saur reminded his German readers, Smith had questioned not just Saur's loyalty but that of all the German colonists. The Germans, Smith had asserted, "give out that they are a Majority, and strong enough to make the Country their own; and indeed, as they are poured in upon us in such Numbers (upwards of 5000 being imported this last year) I know nothing that will hinder them, either from soon being able to give us Law and Language, or else, by joining with the *French*, to eject all the *English* inhabitants" (31). Saur's 1755 broadside aimed squarely at Smith and all those who misleadingly called themselves "watchmen, guardians, protectors of our freedoms" [Wächter, Guardiane, Beschützer unserer Freyheiten].[15] Such would-be guardians, the broadside rhymed in verse obviously hastily penned, "want to introduce unchecked power into this land / with freedom on their tongue, they forge slavery's bonds" [Will unumschränckte Macht, einführen in diß Land/ Führt Freyheit in dem Mund, und schmiedet Sclaven=Band]. Smith questioned German loyalty to English law and had recommended stripping all non–English speaking Pennsylvanians of their voting rights and had urged that printed German be outlawed.[16] Saur's broadsheet advertised that in fact all the freedoms originally guaranteed by founder William Penn stood threatened.[17]

While the Quaker Party, backed by Saur, retained its majority in the 1755–56 elections, the results nonetheless irremediably transformed the party itself—and with it all of colonial politics.[18] More strictly pacifist Quaker Party members, including Israel Pemberton, soon resigned their seats, paving the way for the election of delegates who, while not strictly committed to pacifism, had nonetheless been handpicked by resigning Quakers.[19] Furthermore, upon resigning their seats, Pemberton and others continued their work outside the Assembly, immediately organizing the Friendly Association for Regaining and Preserving Peace with the Indians by Pacific Measures. The Friendly Association began that same spring to meet with Delaware and Six Nations spokesmen, and its vigorous activities belie persistent notions of Quaker quietism. As Jane Merritt too has remarked, "Although they made a principled and public withdrawal from politics, they were able to transfer their power to the supervision of Indian trade and diplomacy."[20] Now outside the assembly, under the aegis of the Friendly Association, Quakers and their German allies pursued pacifist politics by other means.

The Friendly Association, "among the most enlightened, open-minded groups founded in provincial America," Silver has written, also "lent itself perfectly to the vilification of Quakers and Indians."[21] Indeed, the association remains better known through its depictions by detractors rather than supporters. Led by Quakers John Woolman, Anthony Benezet, and the wealthy

merchant Israel Pemberton, Jr., the Friendly Association was denounced in
the bloody wake of the so-called Paxton Boys murder of six Christian Con-
estoga Indians eleven days before Christmas in 1763.[22] Cartoons depicted
Quaker "mischief" and drew "King Wampum" (Pemberton) literally sleeping
with the enemy. Yet before the actions of the Paxton Boys the association had
received substantial positive notices, particularly by Saur's press.[23]

Central to the Friendly Association's mission was the recollection of a
shared European and Indian past, a time of amity between early settlers and
the Delaware, a lost idyll symbolized by the person of William Penn. Saur
was an avid supporter of the association and its beatification of the Quaker
colony's founder. Saur's letter dated "germantown 4 mo. 25th 1756" and
addressed to "Friend Pemberton" documents the printer's offer to write to
"friends among the germans," expressing his belief that "many friends who
are against bearing arms will contribute towards a Peacible way and I think
that among them by a voluntary way of subscription more will be geathered
than what many will think." The letter closed with a request that Pemberton
communicate news of further talks immediately so "that the publick may
know." And indeed, a subsequent article in the August 16, 1756, issue of Saur's
newspaper advertised enthusiastically for the association.[24]

Saur's *Almanac*, is documented below in detail, both anticipated the purpose of the association and then after its establishment in 1756 advanced its
work explicitly. As did the association, Saur paired his veneration of Penn
with a thorough critique of the present to express a heartfelt "wish for peace."
Read in the context of the French and Indian War and of the formation
of the Friendly Association, Saur's widely read *Almanac* helps correct retroactive accounts emphasizing the marginal status of pacifist voices.[25] Pacifist
politics were not a concern exclusive to the colony's radical edge or lunatic
fringe. Nonetheless, such leaders of the Friendly Association as Pemberton
and Woolman have often been portrayed as such, often unwittingly. Silver,
for example, writes that Woolman was known for the "'affected singularity'"
with which he "took to going around in a big white hat."[26] Left without further explanation, the description suggests the reformer merely had some odd
fondness for white clothing. And yet we know that this sartorial choice was
made to present a visual objection to the use of slave labor. Wearing undyed
cloth formed an integral part of Woolman's severe critique of the Atlantic
economy and its foundation upon the suffering of enslaved Africans.[27] Pacifism was not a doctrine held only by lunatics, nor was it the exclusive purview
of marginal mystics who truly longed for martyrdom, as Jan Stievermann

has suggested.[28] Peace, Saur's *Almanac* reveals, was preached even by popular works for a popular audience, presented to those German readers who made up nearly half the colony's population.

Sheep, the Talk of Peace

Talk of peace had grown increasingly scarce in Pennsylvania in the 1750s. This was the charge Saur repeatedly leveled throughout the *Almanac* dialogues.[29] Instead, peace had been crowded out by the plenty over which colonists had grown increasingly jealous. When the colony's first settlers had asked one another, "Hau di thu?" the question had expressed "love for their neighbors' children." And returning to the passage from the 1754 *Almanac* with which this article began, early colonists' answers had attested to a shared commitment "to shoulder one another's burden." Indeed, their very language—a part-English, part-German, and profoundly hybrid greeting—had forged a shared community. But today, the Resident lamented, Pennsylvanians trotted past one another on "fancy horses," unwilling to wait for an answer to the old question. Emptied of its original intent, the question now marked merely its own hollowness—"it's now become a habit"—and it signified only the shaky vestiges of what had been a vibrant common undertaking. Imperial greed, fanned by establishment churches, had been its undoing. Only peace, Saur implied over the dialogues' many pages, might reanimate the intention of the original greeting "Hau di thu."

Throughout the dialogues, included in the *Almanac* issues from 1751 to 1758, Saur employed a rhetoric consisting of two parts. Both were designed to win his German readers' hearts and minds to the cause of peace. First, Saur launched a radical critique of the present and of colonial society's increasing prosperity. Chief among the present's many villains are *Pfaffen*, men of the Church—whether Lutheran or Calvinist, Anglican or Presbyterian. With their misbegotten concern for worldly things these men, Saur alleged, have summoned war clouds. Second, to provide an antidote to the woes brought on by material and imperial greed, only fueled by the churchmen who arrived in ever greater numbers, Saur transformed the colony's Quaker foundations into a story of mythical origins, grafting William Penn's arrival in Pennsylvania onto images of the early apostolic church and onto edenic visions of antediluvian, prelapsarian origins. Critiquing the present and urging a return to the teachings of the hallowed Penn and to the orginal intent of the friendly question "Hau di thu," Saur wished for peace to dispel the dark clouds enshrouding the city on a hill.

In the second *Almanac* issue in which Saur's widely read dialogues occur, men of the church lurk behind every disturbance of the peace. Saur's Newcomer first worries about other recent migrants—about their numbers, but still more particularly about their quality. He has heard tell how "it used to be so quiet and peaceful in this land, and neighbors were so united and friendly with one another" [es vormahls hier im Lande so ruhig, friedlich, und die Nachbarn so einig und nachbarlich mit einander gewesen]. Such tales, he suggests, appear ethereal in the harsh light of today when "many neighbors can barely stand the sight of one another" [sich viel Nachbaren einander schier nicht ansehen mögen]. The colony's old atmosphere of neighborliness has become foreign, estranged by the arrival of "so many people who have made their way here because of disgrace there, many condemned as whores and witches" [so viel Leute herein kommen, die wegen der Schande drausen wegziehen, daß viele Huren und Hexen gescholten sind]. Leading this motley band of recent migrants are men of the church, "yes, and on top of that such preachers come to this land who could not stay there because of these and other vices" [ja noch darzu solche Prediger ins Land kommen, die wegen solcher und anderer Laster draussen nicht bleiben können 1752].[30]

Two years later the Newcomer paints churchmen in still more sinister shades. Among the various undesirable elements of colonial society, the *Almanac* styles them as public enemy in chief. The Newcomer pointedly asks the more experienced Resident whether colonists must accept men of the church at all, questioning both the fundamental desirability of new ministers in the colony as well as their right to preach and their claims to authority over other colonists. The Newcomer begins, "A question occurs to me: Because the preachers who come to this land are so bad that they could get no place elsewhere, or had been, or will be, removed from their positions, are we then required by God to accept them all? And is it written by God that we must obey all of those who are authorized to preach and believe everything that they say?" [Mir fält eine frage ein: Weil so gar schlechte Prediger herein ins Land kommen, die draussen keinen Dinst bekommen können, oder abgesetzt worden, oder werden; Sind wir dan von Gottes-wegen schuldig sie alle anzunehmen; ist es dan ein Befehl Gottes daß man allen die da predigen können/ gehorsam seyn muß, und alles glauben was sie sagen?] And he alleges again that men of the church have declared war on the peace colonists previously enjoyed. The Newcomer, he explains, "would so sincerely like to live in peace with all people" [wolte doch mit alen Menschen gern im Frieden leben], but how, he wonders, might he find "a way to remain in peace with them" [ein Weg wie man im Frieden stehen und veträglich mit ihnen bleiben kan] when his neighbors "have been both privately and publicly provoked to hostility by their preachers or neighbors" [von ihren Predigern oder Nachbaren heimlich und offentlich angereitzet werden zur Feindseeligkeit] (1754).

Churchmen have turned colonial society topsy-turvy. It is not the *mundus inversus* of carnival that they have ushered in but a world of nightmarish, apocalyptic reversal: peace replaced by war, pacifism by militarism, friendship by enmity, freedom by slavery, honesty by deceit, simplicity by greed. The Newcomer presses the Resident for further answers, wondering again, "I've heard that such [dishonest] people did not used to be here, and that people spoke and treated one another honestly; but now it's growing out of control here too. What might the reason be?" [Ich hab gehört, daß vor diesem dergleichen hier im land nicht gewesen ist, und die leute haben aufrichtig mit einander geredet und gehandelt; nun aber will es hier im land auch überhand nehmen: Was mag wohl die Ursach seyn?] In answer the Resident explains that the old world has caught up with the new: "Every year many people come from Germany where lying, deceit, cursing, swearing, gorging, boozing, and other depravities rule the day, and all the while most people believe or think that they are truly good Christians" [Es kommen alle Jahre viele Leute aus Teutschland, wo das Lügen, Betrügen, Fluchen, Schwören, Fressen, sauffen und alle Leichtfertigkeit in vollem Schwang gehet, und die meisten doch dabey glauben oder dencken, daß sie gar gute Christen sind] (1754).

Newly founded colonial churches incarnate the many reversals to which the Quaker colony has been subjected. The long-term Resident opines: "In church, the rich sit in the best seats; and at holy communion, the worst oppressors and deceivers are the first in line while the poorest go behind, and at the very last the most innocent drivers of cows and pigs and the executioners of people and animals (who are least able to deceive) must form the tail end; and if one godfearing soul were among this whole group, then he would be despised, ridiculed, have his life turned sour and chased away" [Wan man zur Kirche gehet, so sitzen die reichen auf den besten Plätzen, und wan man zum Abendmahl gehet, so gehen die grösten Schinder und Betrüger forne her, und die aller-ärmsten hinten nach, und zuletzt muß wohl der unschuldigste Kühhirt, Schwein-hirt, Scharff-richter und Vieh-Schinder [die am wenigsten betrügen können] den beschluß machen; und wan ja noch eine Gottfürchtende

Seele darunter wäre, so wird sie verachtet, verspottet und das Leben sauer gemacht und weggetrieben].

True Christianity, replaced long ago in Europe by sorcerers and witches, has now been sent packing in America too. The *Almanac* teaches, "Thus because so many come here, away from that fine Christianity—even those known as witches and sorcerors, many moving away from their hostile surroundings because they think that unknown in a foreign land they can pass for honest and Christian; well, you can easily conclude for yourself what the result must finally be" [Weil dan aus dieser schönen Christenheit viele herein kommen, ja so gar daß die man Hexen und Zauber-geschmäiß nennet, eben darum aus ihrer feindseligen Nachbarschafft wegziehen, weil sie glauben, daß sie in einem fremden Lande als unbekant vor ehrlich und christlich passiren können, so kanst du dir leichtlich den Schluß machen, was endlich draus werden wird]. Less than a year before the first Delaware attack, the old-time Resident pointedly observes that men of the church bear all blame for contemporary troubles: "Truth to tell, the interpretors of scriptures bear the blame for all the fighting and mischief" [Ich kan dir in Wahrheit sagen, daß die Ausleger der schrifft an allem Streit und unheil Ursach und schuldig sind] (1756).

As an antidote to the "fighting and mischief" sparked by the countless churchmen "known as witches and sorcerors," Saur's Resident urges a return to the past. Calls to renew ancient covenants resounded up and down the Atlantic seaboard from the 1730s on, issuing most famously from the lips of those synonymous with the Great Awakening, such preachers as Jonathan Edwards and George Whitefield. But the Great Awakening is a name perhaps insufficient to designate the broad renewal of religious life in Europe and America triggered by the pell-mell multiplication of religious diversity. Sectarians—Quakers, Moravians, Mennonites, Schwenkfelders, Dunkers, and others—orbited in a universe governed by laws of revival and renewal as surely as did Methodists and Presbyterians.[31] Indians also experienced the pull of renewal and their own Great Awakening.[32] Enslaved and free Africans too hardly failed to invoke revivalism's reforming laws, as Jon F. Sensbach's study of Rebecca Proten compellingly illustrates.[33]

Saur, like Quaker reformers, urged a return to Pennsylvania's halcyon days, to a time when William Penn walked the land together with his Indian friends. This vision of the colonial past, as I shall discuss below, was also propounded by Delaware and Iroquois leaders in the mid-1750s. Saur's renewal, like that of Quaker abolitionist John Woolman, was deeply steeped in Christian teaching, employing many familiar images from the Christian Bible. But it also contained a message of tolerance no doubt deeply alarming to the "churchmen" he vilified. Taking on these supporters of the Proprietary Party, Saur's message of tolerance was also highly political. Peace, the *Almanac* proclaimed, would proceed only from the renewal of Penn's founding frame of government, the charter of privileges guaranteeing freedom of conscience. The danger presented by those political foes who stridently sought the abridgment of these freedoms, such as William Smith, had to be recognized and combated.

The articles of freedom are a topic to which the *Almanac* tirelessly returns, devoting particular space to it in the dialogue for 1755. The Newcomer registers widespread concerns among recent migrants that "opinions are so diverse in this country" [so vielerely Meynungen hier im Land sind] and that "freedom of conscience is a harmful thing" [die Gewissens Freyheit schädlich sey]. He continues with vehemence, "Yes, some say that when it lies in their power they will allow no freedom, save for their own religion, and I too am of this opinion" [Ja einige sagen, wan sie zu befehlen hätten, sie gäben keine Freyheit, als nur vor Ihre Religion, und ich bin selbst der Meinung]. But Saur's Resident counters his inexperienced interlocutor's enthusiasm for censorship in all its forms with a discussion of toleration and bigotry. The Resident presents a startlingly robust vision of sweeping religious toleration, and it merits longer quotation. The Resident pokes fun at the Newcomer but only half in jest, "I hardly need ask you for your opinion, for each party is convinced it has the best religion" [Ich mag dich nicht einmal fragen, was du vor eine Meinung hast; dan eine iede Partie glaubt, sie habe die beste Religion]. He continues in a more serious tone:

But what would happen if you were in a land which wanted to force you into thinking and believing what others thought and believed or refused to tolerate your opinion in the land; would you like it? And don't you think it's like this for everyone? What Catholic wants to be forced to think and to believe what the Protestants think and believe and to have to participate in their ceremonies; and what Protestant wants to be forced to think or to believe what Catholics think or believe; and who would hold it against a Jew or a Turk if he was unhappy when someone tried to coerce him into a new opinion. And who could possibly like it if it was in the power of the Jews or the Turks to coerce someone to accept the *Talmud* or the *Alcoran* for pure truth. In truth, it's the same for all. And so one of the most beautiful rules given by Christ says: *And as ye would that men should do to you, do ye also to them likewise.* And I regard it a true *Christian freedom* that *William Penn* gave this land. [Was dünckt dich aber, wan du in einem Lande wärest, da man dich zwingen wolte, du soltest dencken und glauben, was andere Leute dencken und glauben, oder man wolte dich bey deiner Meynung nicht im Lande dulden; solte dir das wohl gefallen? Und dencksty nicht/ daß es einem jeden sey wie dir? Welcher Catolicke ist gern gezwungen, zu dencken und zu glauben was die Protestanten dencken und glauben, und ihre Ceremonien mit zu machen; und welcher Protestant ist gern gezwungen zu dencken oder zu glauben, was die Catolicken dencken oder glauben; und welchen Juden oder Türcken wolte mans verdencken, daß er unzufrieden wäre, wan man ihn zu einer andern Meynung zwingen wolte. Und wem solte es gefallen, wan es in der Juden oder Türcken macht stünde ihn zu zwingen, daß er den *Talmud* oder *Alcoran* vor lauter Warheit annehmen. Gewißlich geht es einem wie dem andern. Darum ist es eine der schönsten Regeln, die Christus gab; Nemlich: *Alles, was Ihr wolt das euch die Leute thun sollen, das thut Ihr ihnen.* Und ich halte es vor eine recht *Christliche Freyheit* die der *William Penn* diesem Lande gegeben.]

The Resident's logic apparently swiftly convinces the Newcomer, for he experiences a radical change of heart after the *Almanac* cites the first and eighth articles of freedom, translating them for those unable to read the English originals. Now the Newcomer too sings Penn's praise: "One must conclude that the *first ruler* of this land must have been a very conscientious man since he *established freedom of conscience so solidly*" [Man solte wohl hieraus schliessen, der *erste Herr* des Landes müsse ein sehr gewissenhaffter Mann gewesen seyn, weil er die *Gewissens-Freyheit so fest gegründet*].

These German hymns extolling the colony's founder rang as notes in a larger concert designed to "un-bury" William Penn and recover his legacy of peace. In the quote from the 1753 *Almanac* that appeared at the beginning of this essay, early colonists addressed one another with words that echoed the newly risen Christ, relocating Emmaus in Philadelphia. If these early settlers were faithfully fulfilling Jesus's command to his first followers to speak of peace with their greeting "Hau di thu," then in a sense William Penn had been their Christ. They were Penn's disciples, and they had worked to cultivate a promised land, a New World garden inhabited by a new people who had shaken off the old Adam. Saur's veneration of the Quaker leader intended to recall Pennsylvanians to that peaceable kingdom planted by the saintly founder and the first generation of English, Dutch, and German settlers with the friendly assistance of their Delaware neighbors. Yet for all its Christian imagery Saur's veneration of Penn was, as we have seen, as much a lesson in religious tolerance and toleration as it was in Christianity. Penn's name in fact had become a valuable symbol upon which many parties could agree.[34]

As early as the 1720s, mediators along colonial frontiers had used the colonial founder's name as an important diplomatic tool. The value of the name's currency rested on a 1701 treaty between Penn and the Conestogas, Shawnees, and Conoys in which all participants pledged to "forever hereafter be as one Head & One Heart, & live in true Friendship & Amity as one People." In the following decades this professed amity had been sorely tested; by the 1750s, "with so many voices clamoring to be heard, conversation [along colonial frontiers] lapsed into cacophony, and finally into war cries and terrified shrieks."[35] And yet across many languages Penn's name ("Onas" for *feather* in Iroquois and "Miquon" in Delaware) provided one of the few signifiers that remained mutually intelligible to diverse colonists and diverse Indians. Scarouyady, for example, an Oneida mediator for the Ohio Indians, praised Quakers of the Friendly Association in April 1756 for their willingness "to stand up as Wm Penn's Children."[36] So strong was Seneca mediator Newcastle's sense of kinship with the children of Penn that he requested to be interred in a Quaker burying ground in Philadelphia in the late fall of 1756 and was granted his wish.[37] And throughout Delaware leader Teedyuscung's negotiations at Easton that year, Merrell writes, "There can be no doubt that the Delaware leader was summoning William Penn to his side once more."[38] If the Friendly Association was "an attempt to revive a lost tradition,"[39] it was also a last-ditch attempt to wish for peace sung by a chorus of many voices in a variety of languages, both European and Indian.

Particularly the Saur *Almanac* for 1757 reveals the common cause the German printer made with the Friendly Association.[40] Composed while negotiations were especially active, the *Almanac* deploys the apocalyptic visions so widely spread after war's outbreak. But the Resident's assessment that "the present time looks still worse" than did the time of Noah prompts no retreat from the cares of the world. Instead, the Resident proves himself obviously well informed about the goings-on of the treaty councils then meeting in Easton, and he launches into a lengthy litany of the many land frauds perpetrated upon all Indians, and particularly the Delaware, since the 1730s.

In the 1757 *Almanac*, Saur did not fail to translate Delaware rage kindled by "Ye Running Walk" of the 1737 Purchase. The Resident explained for all Newcomers, "Just a few years ago, they [the Indians] complained that they had received very little, they had been so disadvantaged by the running of the leapers, that they continuously receive less than previously, and that all of this has been the grounds for suspicion and laid bitter roots" [Sie haben noch vor wenig Jahren geklagt, sie hätten sehr wenig bekommen, sie waren aber dermassen übervortheilet worden durchs Lauffen der Springer, daß sie abermahl wenig und noch weniger bekommen als zuvor, und das hat einen Verdacht und bittere Wurtzel zuwege gebracht]. It was a charge that Teedyuscung had fired at the Proprietors' representatives in Easton in November 1756, and in Merrell's words it "would rock the provincial and imperial world for several years."[41] In addition to the official scribes who recorded the council's meeting many other notetakers recorded their own impressions.[42] Whether he was informed by the various Quakers, Moravians, or possibly by Conrad Weiser, all in attendance at the council, Saur clearly had little sympathy for the Proprietary Party and their imperial land policy.

The 1757 *Almanac* pointedly reminded readers that God had given the land to the Indians, whatever the King of England's claims might be. Nonetheless, such imperial officers as the governor of Virginia did not bear sole culpability for the Indians' just resentment. All landowners were implicated: "We've known for a long time what their land is worth; but we've acquired it any way we could" [Wir wusten schon lang was ihr Land werth ist; aber wir habens zu uns gezogen wie wir gekont haben]. He continued, scolding speculators in particular, "To the Indians, who for seventy long years lived with us in peace and simplicity like lambs or calves, to them we give about a shilling for a hundred acres of land and then sell it again for fifteen, for fifty to 100 pounds" [Wir geben den armen Indianern, die schon wol 70 Jahre wie Schafe oder Kalber um uns herum gegangen in Fried und Einfalt, etwa einen Schilling vor 100 Acker Land, und verkauffens wieder vor 15, 50 biß 100 Pfund]. Returning again to the Golden Rule, he repeated, "Is that Christian? Is that according to the teaching of Christ: *And as ye would that men should do to you, do ye also to them likewise*" [ist das Christlich? ist das nach der Lehre Christi: *Alles was ihr wollet daß euch die Leute thun sollen, das thut ihr den Leuten*]. Answering his own question, he cautioned, "However we might choose to view the Indians, they are still *people*, they are *children of Adam*" [Wir mögen die Indianer ansehen wie wir wollen, so sind sie *Leute*, sie sind *Adams-Kinder*]. And he hammered the point home: "God gave them the land" [Gott hat ihnen das Land gegeben].

Saur's loyalties to the Friendly Association, clearly anticipated in the *Almanac* for 1755 and documented in 1757, also manifested in his letter to Pemberton quoted above and in several newspaper articles in his *Berichte*. All clearly document his belief that since the days of William Penn, Pennsylvanians had subsequently failed sufficiently "to wish for peace." His widely read *Almanac* intended to correct the imbalance. Using the not inconsiderable power of his press, he explained the roots of the Indian grievances that had led to the 1755 attacks. The 1757 *Almanac* addressed particularly those German readers all too familiar with news of grisly attacks on Moravian and German settlements in the Tulpehocken in November 1755. The Newcomer protested the innocence of German frontiersmen and farmers. But there were, the Resident answered, no innocent victims or unwitting bystanders.

German settlers too had profited from lands acquired upon vastly unequal exchanges. The Resident admonished the Newcomer, "Don't blame anyone else, rather we must examine ourselves with a plain eye" [Lege die Schuld auf niemand anders, sondern laß uns nur mit einem einfältigen Auge *auf uns selbsten sehen*]. They too were part of an imperialist system designed to enrich itself, defrauding Indians. Invoking Germans' own folk wisdom, he commented provocatively that "Germans have an old saying: *No knife cuts sharper than a farmer who's become a nobleman*. And furthermore: *If you want to corrupt farmers, take a farmer to do it*" [Die Teutschen haben ein altes Sprichwort: *Es ist kein Messer, das schärffer schiert, als wan ein Bauer zum Edelmann wird*. Ferner heist es: *Wan man Bauren verderben woll, so muß man Bauren dazu nehmen*]. Indians, the Resident averred, "have dealt with people brutally" [haben grausam mit Menschen umgegangen]; but, he added, the Germans have done worse. Thus he reports having "heard a German say: If I should capture an Indian, then I intend to cut some flesh out of his living body which he will eat before my eyes" [habe einen Teutschen hören sagen: *Wan ich einen Indianer gefangen kriege, so will ich ihm fleisch aus seinem lebendigen Leibe schneiden, da soll er mir vor meinen Augen fressen*]. Of this wish to inflict self-cannibalization the Resident poignantly noted, "That is more than *Indian*" [Das ist mehr als *Indianisch*].

Conclusion

Despite these diverse efforts the results from the talks at Easton were ultimately effaced by the events of Pontiac's War (1763–65). Teedyuscung's claims of land fraud had been hotly disputed by Proprietors, and the Delaware leader gradually lost his backing by the Six Nations. He dropped the claims by the early 1760s.[43] In 1765 the Quaker Party finally lost control of the provincial Assembly.

Yet this is not quite the end of the story of those who backed the Friendly Association. The defeat of the pacifist community has often been attributed to quietism and martyrological teachings. Yet in this regard too there is more to the story. On the eve of the pivotal 1765 election Saur's son and heir to the press, Christoph Saur (the Younger, 1721–1784) authored a broadsheet naming those Quaker Party candidates he supported. His pamphlet was not, he emphasized, intended for those quietists who "in faith and trust in God want to absteem [from voting], knowing that the omnipotent divine hand and providence rules all" [im Glauben und Vertrauen auf Gott sich stillhalten wollen, wohl wissende, daß die allesverwaltende Hand und Vorsehung Gottes doch alles regieret]. The younger Saur continued, "to them I don't need to give advice, but rather I wish them steadfast faith" [denen brauche ich auch nicht zu rathen]. But, he protested significantly, "this faith is not for everyone, for most people certainly believe that they need to lend a hand to that which they hold to be right" [weil aber dieser Glaube nicht jedermanns Ding ist, und die meiste Menschen doch davor halten, daß sie auch Hand anlegen müsten zu dem was die dencken recht zu seyn]. Unfortunately, the pamphlet explained, these many people "nevertheless cannot distinguish how to unravel the confused situation to figure out what's right and what's backwards" [und doch die Sache nicht auseinander zu wicklen wissen, was recht oder verkehrt ist]. The situation was indeed "confused," muddled by Benjamin Franklin's attempt to steer a middle course between the colony's Quaker and Proprietary parties by forming a party that advocated direct royal control of the colony.[44] The Saur press thus supplied a list of candidates' names for those who couldn't "unravel" the many puzzling choices on the ballot. Suspicious of Franklin's motives and fearful that the Crown would not uphold William Penn's article of freedom, Saur strongly advocated Quaker Party candidates.[45] But Franklin's initiative split the vote in too many ways, and the Quaker Party lost to the Proprietary Party, supported by an electorate composed increasingly of Church Germans led by those *Pfaffen* whose numbers and influence Saur Sr. had so successfully countered the previous decade.[46]

The sectarian wish for peace with the Indians, informed by an expansive vision of a shared past and future, faded into obscurity. Categories of "red" and "white" men hardened. And yet, from the alliance of men who had worked for peace in the mid-1750s, a durable coalition had been constructed. Together they continued to invoke the Golden Rule, urging its necessary application after 1755 to enslaved black Africans: "And as ye would that men should do to you, do ye also to them likewise."

In 1755, on the eve of the formation of the Friendly Association, the Philadelphia Quaker meeting had made a radical about-face on its teachings on slavery, urged by men who soon went on to found the association: John Woolman and Anthony Benezet. Previously, official Quaker teachings on slavery had inhabited an ameliorist position, one not unlike that widely preached by such reformers as George Whitefield. In 1755 English Quakers were not the only voices raised to protest the African trade. That same year the older Saur had picked up on Whitefield's condemnation of the cruelty of slave owners, featuring it prominently and at some length in his vision of the promised land's end times in the 1756 *Almanac*: "Whitefield has made known the terrible sins in Maryland and Virginia and how masters treat their black slaves" [Der Weitfield hat in Märiland und Virginien die grausame Sünden wie die Herrn ihre schwartze Sclaven tractiren, angezeigt]. And at the same time that the Philadelphia Quaker meeting reversed its position on slavery, Saur Sr. too expanded Whitefield's condemnation of slave drivers in Maryland and Virginia to condemn all Pennsylvanians' entanglement in the trade: "Pennsylvania used to have a reputation across all Europe for its government which carried *Iustice* and *Mercy* in its banner and practiced them too; but how many thousands now shed millions of tears" [Pensylvanien hat einen Ruff gehabt durch gantz Europa daß eine Regierung drinnen sey, welche *Iustice* und *Mercy*, das ist Gerechtigkeit und Barmherzigkeit im Wapen führet und practiciret; aber wie viele tausende vergiessen Millionen Thränen].[47] Still more significantly, four years later, in 1759, the pioneering Quaker abolitionist Anthony Benezet published the first in what grew to be a massive antislavery oeuvre, the seminal *Observations of the Enslaving, Importing and Purchasing of Negroes*. It was hardly coincidental that the title was from the Saur press in Germantown.

In 1755 the friendly greeting "Hau di thu" had been drowned out by the terrifying din of war. Nonetheless, this shared "wish for peace" also survived to found the modern abolitionist movement.

PART III

Violent Encounters

CHAPTER 10

Reconfiguring Martyrdom
in the Colonial Context

Marie de l'Incarnation

Katherine Ibbett

In 1622 the Spanish mystic Teresa of Ávila was canonized and her spiritual autobiography, or *Vida*, one of the most widely read texts of the Counter-Reformation, became even more popular.[1] In France, where it had been available in translation since 1601, it was recommended reading for women seeking to deepen their understanding of the Christian life. The young French Ursuline Marie Guyart (1599–1672), later to take the name Marie de l'Incarnation, wrote in her own account of her spiritual development that her confessor had asked her to read Teresa's text in 1627. At that stage Marie was not yet in the convent and was still full of unfulfilled ideals and mystic leanings. What might she have read in Teresa's text? Early on in the Spanish saint's account of her spiritual development, Teresa describes her own youthful religious aspirations in terms that recall chivalric romance. Discussing her relationship with a favorite brother, Teresa writes:

> We used to read the lives of the saints together, and when I read of
> the martyrdoms that the saints endured for the love of God, it seemed
> that they had purchased the presence of God very cheaply, and I had
> a real desire to die as they had done, not out of any love of God of
> which I was conscious, but in order to reach as quickly as possible

these great blessings that I had read were in heaven. My brother and I would talk together about how we could do this, and we plotted to travel as beggars to the country of the Moors, so that they might behead us there, and it seemed that we might have found a way to do it, if God could give us sufficient courage. To us, the greatest hindrance to this plan was only the fact that we had a father and a mother.[2]

For the young Teresa a relationship with God is best attained through a speedy and glorious death specifically contrasted with the obstacles of a duller domestic existence: only the presence of family impedes the young Teresa's lust for decapitation in foreign lands. But, she goes on to say, this most prosaic impediment eventually brings about an awareness of other forms of Christian sacrifice. Teresa continues: "When we saw that it was impossible to go to any place where they would put us to death for God's sake, we decided to become hermits, and in the garden at home we built hermitages, as well as we could, out of heaps of stones that we would gather together."[3] Though her early desire for a glorious death is thwarted, Teresa settles on ways of Christian living that are a little closer to home and lets other actions and aspirations absorb the heady rhetoric of martyrdom, something that her reader Marie was also to find necessary in her own spiritual trajectory.

Teresa's youthful yearnings for foreign death are affectionately evoked at the opening of *Middlemarch* (1871–72), in which George Eliot "smiled with some gentleness" on the saint and her brother's desire for martyrdom: "out they toddled from rugged Avila...until domestic reality met them in the shape of uncles, and turned them back." Eliot's affection for this image is not merely a celebration of the saint's childish particularity but rather stems from a reflection on the gendering of opportunity. For Eliot the loss of what she calls "epic life" is particular to the position of women, and she launches *Middlemarch* with the image of "a Saint Theresa, foundress of nothing, whose loving heart-beats and sobs after an unattained goodness tremble off and are dispersed among hindrances, instead of centering in some long-recognizable deed."[4] This essay follows Eliot in asking how large ambitions adapt to smaller circumstances and in thinking through the ways in which particular genres make room for women's quotidian heroics as they are "dispersed among hindrances." My Teresa is that young Frenchwoman who was urged to read Teresa's *Vida* and who was later to be hailed by her Jesuit colleague Jérôme Lalemant as the Teresa of Canada. For Marie differed from her Spanish role model in one important way: she did eventually travel to the New World, going as a missionary to New France in 1639 after many years of scheming and dreaming. And unlike Eliot's figure for feminine yearning, Marie was not in any way a "foundress of nothing" but rather is celebrated as an early female missionary in Canada and an important educator and lexicographer. Nonetheless, Marie too was to grapple with the ways in which epic desires could be dispersed by the actual opportunities available. Like Teresa, Marie was to find her initial longing for martyrdom tested by the particularities of circumstance. Even in the New World, where the young Teresa had imagined a glorious death to be hers for the taking, Marie was to find her desire for death displaced by more mundane considerations. Her subsequent reappraisal of the relation between heroism and the quotidian forms a radical reimagining of the question of self-sacrifice, shaped by her experiences in New France.

For Marie, unlike Teresa, the presence of family was no impediment to the dangers of foreign travel. Married at seventeen to a silk merchant, she was widowed shortly after the birth of a son, and even as she managed the family business she began to experience mystic revelations. She entered the Ursuline convent in Tours in 1631, leaving behind an eleven-year-old son, Claude Martin, who was eventually to become a Benedictine and the editor of his mother's voluminous writings: two spiritual relations and countless letters, published to wide acclaim after her death in 1672.[5] The original texts of the two relations (one dating from the convent in Tours and one from her time in Canada) were revised for publication as *La Vie de la vénérable mère Marie de l'Incarnation* in 1677, with "additions" by the editorializing son. That life story was followed in 1681 by an edition of her letters to her family and religious community in France. Far from being an impediment to Marie's dreams of a religious life, Claude Martin was the facilitator of a particular version of it. As editor, he became the manager and mediator of her reputation, and established Marie as a crucial figure in both the Gallican church and the colonial enterprise in Canada. Describing himself in the preface to the *Vie* as merely "un echo qui répond à ce qu'elle dit par ses propres paroles"[6] [an echo who replies to what she says in her own words], Martin was instead a skillful shaper and indeed guarantor of Marie's work: Elizabeth Goldsmith, for example, has argued that Marie alone escaped the influential French preacher Bossuet's condemnation of mystical writing at the end of the seventeenth century because of the particular familial framing of her publications.[7] Claude's careful crafting of his mother's story serves as a reminder that the writing sent from the New World to Europe was packaged for home consumption. It was not merely sent in response to metropolitan interests, however; as Julia Boss has argued, writers in New France also established new generic conventions. Boss describes how the "highly standardized genre" of hagiography was adapted to fit in with the missionaries' understanding of the place of holiness in the New World.[8] Marie's accounts of martyrdom, I argue, evince a similar colonial adaptation of a standard European genre.

The younger Marie's aspirations to foreign death were fostered by two very distinct European Catholic discourses of martyrdom. In 1578 the Roman catacombs had been rediscovered, leading to what Brad Gregory terms the "paleo-Christian revival" of the legends of ancient martyrs.[9] This wave of interest in the figures of the early church gave impetus to the sense that martyrdom was significant for the establishment and development of Christian communities. The Roman Martyrology, a collection of lives of the early martyrs used in the Catholic liturgy, had been revised in 1584, and reached its nineteenth Latin edition by 1613; illustrated editions of the Martyrology, such as that of 1636 by Israël Sylvestre, *Images de tous les saints et saintes de l'année selon le martyrologe romain*, made the martyrological iconography of the early church familiar to a new generation of readers. This memorialization of the martyrs of the early church, culminating in the first publications of the Bollandists' *Acta Sanctorum* in 1643, tended to celebrate brutal bodily assaults, understanding sanctity to emerge seamlessly from the violated body.[10] In these accounts of Christian martyrdom the significance of the martyr's death is predicated upon its visibility: the death must be observed and described in order for it to function within the necessary economy of exemplarity.[11]

A similar story was told in the news sent home from missionaries, and especially Jesuit missionaries, abroad; martyrdom had become, as Marie-Florine Bruneau puts it, a Jesuit trademark that encouraged those at home to fund the missions.[12] This model of martyrdom, in the vein of medieval golden legend, continued to stress the visual exemplar of the wounded body that bears witness to the truth of faith and whose message of salvation is so readily available that it can convert all who look upon it. In 1627 the twenty-six Catholic missionaries who had been killed in Japan in 1597 were beatified, and in Europe their images circulated in cheap prints that served as publicity material for the missions.[13] The news of deaths in New France was reported in the Jesuit *Relations*, which ran from 1632 to 1673, and each death in any given year was described in considerable detail. Such a procedure was deemed necessary for the success of the missions, and not only in terms of garnering funding in France: Paul Perron suggests that during the period from 1642 to 1649, "the mission attained the state when conversion was considered possible if, and only if, the missionaries were persecuted and executed for their faith."[14]

But alongside this model of bloody sacrifice a new rhetoric of martyrdom was making itself heard in Europe, one that redrafted the paradigm of showy suffering to give precedence instead to a martyrdom of the interior. Such language drew upon a redeployment of the terms of martyrdom that was central to Protestant writing during the French Wars of Religion, where if relatively few were massacred, the persecutions of the community nonetheless made martyrs of them all. In this Protestant tradition of martyrology there is less emphasis on the display of the martyr's body and more focus on the suffering of the interior, accompanied by a Pauline insistence that the sufferings of life itself (rather than death alone) constitute martyrdom.[15] In minor ways and in minor genres Catholic writers also began to move toward these more accommodating understandings of sacrifice: in the numerous accounts of holy women that were crucial to the establishment of Counter-Reformation religious communities, even the surgeries or illnesses of nuns who had lived quiet and cloistered lives were sometimes described as a kind of martyrdom.[16] In these reports of convent suffering, martyrdom is located in interior pain and not in external show. The inner life of the holy woman is displayed to the wider community by the accounts of confessors and surgeons, just as Marie's own travails in the convent and in Canada were made known through the efforts of her son as publisher.

When Marie first entered the convent, the language of martyrdom she employed to describe her spiritual life was a sort of sentimental dilution of this latter tradition. Her convent afflictions related predominantly and solipsistically to her inability to find a perfect and peaceful union with Christ. For the young nun struggling to deal with community life after the great and individual revelation of her profession of faith, martyrdom was other people. In her relation of 1633, written in the convent at Tours, she tells of hating religious services and describes how "je ne faisais autre chose, ni jour et nuit, que de me plaindre, et il m'était impossible d'arrêter cette impetuosité, n'ayant point de tout de pouvoir sur moi. Cela se peut vraiment appeler un martyre, mais très aimable, parce qu'il vient du Bien-Aimé" [I did nothing else, day or night, but complain, and it was impossible for me to stop this impetuosity, having no power over myself. That can truly be called a martyrdom, but a lovely one since it comes from the Beloved].[17] In the son's editorial notes to the edition of her writings he published in 1677, these complaints are cast in a more generous and spiritually appropriate light: "Une sainte impatience de n'être pas unie, de la plus parfaite manière, à celui qu'elle aimait uniquement, causait à son âme un désir continuel de sortir de son corps, mais ce désir, ne s'accomplissant point, lui causait ce martyre d'amour, et pour me servir de ses termes, elle mourait de ne pas mourir" [A holy impatience with not being united in the most perfect way with Him whom she loved alone made her soul long continually to leave her body, but this unrealized desire caused her a martyrdom of love, and to use her terms, she was dying to die].[18] Marie's martyrdom then is caused by love, and in casting it in those terms, in 1677 Claude Martin makes it possible for his mother's writing to be received not just by those readers well versed in the mystical tradition but also by those more worldly sorts who some eight years before had thrilled to the allegedly real letters produced by a nun burning for a more earthly passion in the text known as the *Lettres Portugaises*.[19]

In the convent Marie is martyred everywhere: first by the horror of being around others when she longs for a more intimate spiritual bond, and then by the exquisite torture of her relationship with Christ: "Lors que l'occasion m'obligeoit d'aller à la maison des champs, mon esprit étoit extrémement satisfait de se voir libre de l'importunité du grand tracas; mais étant dans le silence, le divin Epoux me faisoit experimenter un nouveau martyre dans ses touches & dans ses embrassemens amoureux" [When I had to go to the house in the country, my spirit was extremely satisfied to be free of importunity and bother; but in the silence that followed, the divine Spouse put me through a new martyrdom in his touches and his amorous embraces]. Her son describes how her love for Christ is "comme un tyran qui fait passer ses Martyrs par diverses sortes de supplices" [like a tyrant who puts his martyrs through different kinds of punishment].[20]

In the convent it is the daily grind of bodily necessity and community living that make for a metaphorical martyrdom, but far from bringing Marie into closer union with Christ, that martyrdom is understood as a cruel separation from the divine. In an extraordinary passage Martin describes Marie's desire to be separated from the bodily world:

> Elle desiroit d'estre separée de son corps ; quoy qu'elle fût dans
> les amours de ce divin & suradorable objet : mais ces divins
> embrassemens étoient interrompus par de petits intervalles du dormir
> & des affaires, qui faisoient comme des petits nuages qui poussez par

un grand vent, passent sous le Soleil, & font de petits ombrages. Enfin
les necessitez du corps faisoient à la dérobée de petits entre-deux,
lesquels pour courts qui peussent estre, étoient une espece de martyre
à l'ame, qui ne pouvoit estre un moment séparée des embrassemens,
ny de la veuë de son bien-aimé.

   [She wanted to be separated from her body, for she was so in
love with this divine and adorable object. But these divine embraces
were interrupted by short periods for sleep and other such things,
just as little clouds pushed by a great wind pass in front of the sun
and make little shadows. Eventually these bodily necessities became
surreptitious intervals, and even though they were as brief as could be
they were a kind of martyrdom to her soul, which could not bear to
be separated for one moment either from the embraces or the sight of
her beloved].[21]

In the convent Marie understands the divine to be radically separate from
daily life, and to be experienced only in solitude. This relation between the
quotidian and the holy, however, shifts when Marie arrives at what she pre-
sumes to be the potential scene of a more traditional kind of martyrdom.
The Canadian experience, which initially seems to promise a reinscription of
the bloody values of traditional European martyrology, in fact provides the
ground for a new imagining of the martyr's suffering and signification.

   Leaving for the New World from Dieppe in 1639, Marie brimmed with
exuberance about even the worst that might lie ahead, writing to her brother
"la vie et la mort me sont une même chose, et je fais ce sacrifice de moy-même
du meilleur cœur qu'aucune chose que j'aye fait en ma vie" [life and death are
the same to me, and I make this sacrifice of myself in the best spirits of my
life].[22] She began her Canadian adventure with great expectations. Stepping
into the boat, she was to write years later, "il me sembla entrer en paradis,
puisque je faisais le premier pas qui me mettait en risque de ma vie pour
l'amour de lui, qui me l'avait donnée" [it seemed I was entering paradise, since
I was taking the first step that risked my life for he who had given me life].[23]
Soon after her arrival in Canada she wrote to her son that "l'on croit qu'il y
pourra avoir quelques martirs dans les grandes cources qu'il faut faire" [we
believe that there might be some martyrs in the great expeditions that must
be made].[24] Nonetheless, the women missionaries found that what Jacques Le
Brun has termed the "occasion du martyre," or opportunity for martyrdom,
was relatively limited. Bound by the Ursuline rule of enclosure, Marie was to

remain in the convent in relative safety.[25] The duties of the newly arrived nuns were the matter of some debate, and their arrival prompted new reflection on what sort of actions would best ensure the firm foundation of Christianity in the New World; the Jesuit Paul Le Jeune speculated in 1636 that "the charity [of nuns] would do more for the conversion of the Savages than all our expeditions and words."[26] The work of the nuns, that is, was understood to supplement in quieter and more charitable form the bolder actions and discourse of the male missionaries. Marie's letters and their reflections on martyrdom form a particularly trenchant reflection upon the relation between these two kinds of Christian action.

By the mid-seventeenth century the genre of Catholic martyrology had largely become frozen into a saintly rictus. The accounts of the deaths of saints that were most widely known followed a very repetitive format and did not on the whole broaden the audience's understanding of sacrifice in the way that Protestant martyrologies of the religious wars had sought to do. Marie's accounts of the clashes between the missionaries and the Iroquois, however, suggest that the realities of colonial encounters were beginning to reshape the martyrological genre. This is particularly evident in her discussions of the Jesuit Isaac Jogues (1607–46), a missionary who was eventually to die for the faith but whose life along the way illustrated for Marie something of the accommodating flexibilities of colonial sacrifice. In these accounts the older, bloodier model of martyrdom so familiar from the Jesuit relations is supplemented by an understanding of the sufferings of life rather than death.

The biographical particularities of Jogues made him an especially resonant figure for this supplementary notion of sacrifice. Jogues was initially captured by the Iroquois in 1642 and was tortured and kept as a captive. He then escaped, returning to France where his story was widely told and admired, and then shortly after he returned to Quebec again. Jogues was captured again and killed by the Iroquois in 1646.[27] His story thus encompasses two great seventeenth-century genres, the one—martyrology—a chiefly European genre in thrall to earlier narrative models, and the other—the captivity narrative—a North American development that pulled disparate influences together to make a new kind of text about the New World experience of trial and redemption. Scholars have insisted on the American particularity of the captivity narrative and on its importance to the development of an understanding of an American literature.[28] But Marie's account of Jogues makes room for the captivity narrative's distinctively American traits in the midst of a purportedly more traditional martyrology sent home to readers in Europe.

In a letter written in 1644 she describes how Jogues "y a souffert plusieurs martires bout à bout, dont Dieu l'a délivré pour nous le rendre vivant" [suffered there several martyrdoms one after another, from which God delivered him to us, alive]. His captivity makes him "un vray martir vivant qui porte en son corps les livrées de Jésus-Chris" [a true living martyr who carries on his body the livery of Jesus Christ]. This living martyrdom, however, is not a lesser model; instead Marie suggests that it is a new and exceptional exemplar set apart from the standard martyr. We might remember Teresa of Ávila, who thought as a child that the martyrs were buying the love of God at a bargain rate. A similar reckoning is made by Marie, who estimates that "il y a des milliers de martyrs qui sont morts à moindre frais" [there are thousands of martyrs who died at less cost] than Jogues's suffering in life. In these accounts the old models of bloody and showy death still retain narrative significance, but they are supplemented by a more fluid understanding of sacrifice that weighs the value and function of a life. Marie's account of Jogues's suffering in captivity suggests that in staying alive the priest is able to bring about the work that was previously imagined only as the fruit of martyrdom: "Il a trouvé nombre d'occasions impréveues qui luy ont fait envoyer au ciel nombre d'âmes.... Et mesme durant qu'il estoit captif, sa grande modestie tenoit les barbares en admiration et le croyoient plus homme" [He found many unexpected occasions which let him send a number of souls to heaven. And even during his captivity, his great modesty was admired by the barbarians, who believed him all the more of a man]. In these descriptions admiration signals the potential for conversion. But here that admiration is no longer reserved for the moment of death; instead it extends to the ways Christians live their lives. Marie's discussion of the implications of Jogues's eventual death creates a rhetorical triptych that shows how the definition of martyrdom is expanded in these situations: "Nous pouvons meme dire qu'il est trois fois Martyr, c'est-à-dire, autant de fois qu'il est allé dans les Nations Hiroquoises. La première fois il n'y est pas mort, mais il y a assez souffert pour mourir. La 2. Fois il n'y a souffert, et n'y est mort qu'en désir, son cœur brûlant continuellement du désir du martyre. Mais la troisième fois Dieu lui a accordé ce que son cœur avoit si long-temps désiré" [We can even say that he is three times a martyr, that is to say as many times as he went into the Iroquois Nations. The first time he did not die, though he suffered enough to do so. The second time he suffered and died only in desire, his heart burning continually with the longing for martyrdom. But the third time God granted him what his heart had so long desired].[29] The tripartite structure of Jogues's suffering has an evident rhetorical significance.[30] But it is also a Trinitarian reflection on suffering, describing three ways to be close to God: to suffer, to desire, to die.

In describing the death of the Jesuit Jean de Brébeuf (1593–1649) Marie seems similarly to give weight to both understandings of sacrifice. She begins by insisting on the fact that his life was already a form of sacrifice: "Mais remarquez que depuis qu'il étoit en ces contrées, où il a prêché l'Evangile depuis l'an 1628, excepté un espace de temps qu'il fut en France, les Anglois s'étant rendu les maîtres du païs, sa vie avoit été un martyre continuel" [But note that since he was in these lands, where he has preached the Gospel since the year 1628, except for the time he was in France when the English had taken charge of this country, his life had been a continual martyrdom]. However, Marie then continues, "Or voici comment le martyre de ces saints Pères arriva" [Yet here is how the martyrdom of these holy Fathers came about], and launches into a story of bloody detail taken chiefly from the Jesuit Relations ("Les uns leur coupent les pieds et les mains, les autres enlèvent les chairs des bras" [Some cut off their hands and feet, others ripped the flesh from their arms]) that would not be out of place in late medieval martyrology.[31] The "Or" forms a hinge between the two forms of narrative validation: in the first it is the life that makes a martyr, and in the second it is the form of death that signifies most. In this new form of martyrology, itself a form of supplement to the more voluminous and official Jesuit *Relations*, both accounts are needed, each one supplementing the other. But Marie makes clear that death is no longer necessary for sanctity and that a new kind of suffering in life particular to the situation in which the missionaries find themselves is pushing aside the Jesuit insistence on martyrdom: "Les Révérends Pères qui étaient demeurés vifs avaient plus souffert que ceux qui étaient morts. A la vue de ces âmes consommées en vertu, dans lesquelles Jésus-Christ vivait plus qu'elles ne vivaient elles-mêmes, et dont la sainteté était si visible à tout le monde, chacun était ravi" [The Reverend Fathers who had stayed alive had suffered more than those who had died. To see these souls consumed by virtue, in which Jesus Christ was more alive than they were themselves, and whose sanctity was so visible to everyone, all were ravished by it].[32] In Marie's description the old model of the body whose sanctity is visible in death is taken over by the saintly but still living and working bodies of the survivors and endurers who are left to construct the religious community in Canada.

The emplotment of New World deaths puts particular pressure on the highly systematized genre of European martyrology. This can be seen in a letter of 1647 in which Marie writes of the eventual death of Jogues. After being stripped naked and beaten, the missionaries are told that the next day they will be decapitated. The Iroquois who threaten this at first and inadvertently almost cater to that same desire for glory and union with God that drove the infant Teresa to long for that fate: "Vous mourrez demain, mais consolez vous, on ne vous brûlera pas; vous serez frappez de la hache, et vos têtes seront mises sur les palisades qui ferment notre village, afin que vos Frères vous voient encore quand nous les aurons pris" [You will die tomorrow, but console yourselves, we will not burn you; you will be executed with an axe, and your heads will be put on the fence around our village, so that your brothers will see you when we have captured them].[33] Though the Iroquois promise death, they also in this promise follow the Christian paradigm of martyrdom as exemplarity to the letter. This is how, according to generic tradition, Christian martyrdom should be: visible and open to interpretation by those who seek to follow. In this instance the Iroquois, who imagine that the decapitated head is a deterrent, do not understand that it is in fact precisely such iconography that spurs the Christians to further action. This sort of incomprehension is central to the "insider" pleasure of reading martyrology, in which the reader can delight in the empty threats of the tyrant. It features repetitively in seventeenth-century French martyr tales, especially those dealing with Christians in the Roman Empire. In Pierre Corneille's martyr tragedy *Polyeucte*, for example, written five years before Marie's letter, the Roman governor Félix who threatens the Christians with death does so without realizing that for the Christian death is the point of the salvation story; he must be instructed by his patient daughter Pauline, a better reader of the changing social climate, that this strange new sect longs to hear just such threats. Félix, like the Iroquois as recounted in this passage, is unable to recognize the new Christian genre in which he finds himself.

But the following day, Marie suggests, events in New France ensue somewhat differently: the Iroquois reassert control of the story. This brutality, it turns out, belongs to a different genre yet again: "Mais sur le soir un Sauvage de la Nation de l'Ours menant le Père Jogues dans sa cabane pour le faire souper, il y en avoit un autre derrière la porte, qui l'attendoit, et qui lui déchargea un coup de hache, dont il tomba mort sur la place" [But in the evening a savage from the Bear Nation took Father Jogues in his cabin to give him supper, and there was another one behind the door, who was waiting for him. He let fly with a blow of his axe, from which he fell dead on the spot].[34] No onlookers are there to be converted; no body is left to be collected and venerated, although the head is later put on a palisade as initially promised. The old stories of Roman colonizers crushing indigenous martyrs, so celebrated elsewhere in Counter-Reformation culture, have been overturned by these summary executions. Now that the colonizers are naming themselves martyrs, the paradigm is changed. There is no room for the confessional claiming of Christianity in a trial scene that shows off the stalwartness of faith. Instead the Iroquois are feared not because they threaten death but because the guerrilla warfare–style death that they threaten is so out of keeping with martyrological tradition.[35] Marie writes, "L'on est tout effraié, parce qu'ils se cachent dans les broussailles, et se jettent sur le monde, lors qu'on ne pense pas à eux" [we are all frightened, because they hide in the bush and throw themselves on people when they are not expected]. Another letter of 1650 describes with sadness how one priest was seized on a journey: "pris et massacré, sans qu'on ait pu sçavoir par quels ennemis, ni ce qu'ils ont fait de son corps" [taken and massacred, without us knowing which enemies did this nor what they have done with his body].[36] The unmarked death disrupts the memorializing economy of Christian sacrifice.[37]

Yet if the unmarked death renders the visibility of martyrdom problematic, Marie's work points to different forms of action that will eventually displace the martyr's act of bodily witnessing. Marie's letters suggest that the locus of transmission of Christianity moves from the staged and public exemplarity of the glorious death to quieter scenes of pedagogy and publication. In Marie's work the Christian sufferer is not on the frontier but in the schoolyard: the essential task of these new martyrs, principally female, is education. Traditionally, the martyr faces his or her death with constancy, a word that frequently recurs in the more conventional Counter-Reformation corpus. But as Marie ages, the constancy given to her by God is marshaled to a different end: reading and writing. Conventional martyrdom had always had something of the pedagogical about it, since it aims to inspire those who look on to follow. But for Marie the realities of the colonial convent make the reader and writer, not the torture victim, into the privileged agent of religious transmission. In an account of her daily work she tells her son how constancy and strength is needed to tackle not the scenes of death she had initially imagined but rather the difficult tasks of learning languages: "ces langues barbares sont difficiles, et pour s'y assujettir il faut des esprits constans" [these barbarian languages are difficult, and to subject oneself to them one needs constant attention]. Learning words from the dictionary is, for the young Sisters, an imitation of Christ: "ce leur est une peine, ce leur sont des épines" [for them this is a punishment, these are thorns].[38] Describing the laborious work she has undertaken in lexicography and translation, she writes that the divine gives her strength in her weakness.[39] There is a generosity to her more accommodating understanding of sacrifice that is not always present in the writing of her Jesuit colleagues: in one more fastidious account of French suffering in New France, a Jesuit insists that it is martyrdom enough to be around the natives, describing their importuning cries and the miserably insipid food they offer as forms of torture.[40] Marie's writing is less dismissive of indigenous habits, and instead she insists that a new model of Christian endurance has come to supplement the older version in a way that is particular to the question of life and death in the New World, suggesting that in New France the great solitary action is no longer enough to compel the establishment and spread of Christianity.[41] Marie's description of a hardworking life as martyrdom serves to remind its readers at home in France that the expansion of Christendom would necessitate a more flexible understanding of exemplarity that relied on the long-term labor of religious women.

In its mixing of letters and relations Marie's colonial martyrdom also revolves around a very particular incarnation of the Word, underlining the complex ways in which, as Patrick Erben's essay in this volume suggests (see Chapter 11), martyrdom is bound up with the status of the book. Julia Boss's description of the ways in which New France's deployment of hagiography differed from that of the metropole underscores the importance of the book in the early religious life of Quebec.[42] Boss describes how the religious institutions of New France stored hagiographic texts as treasures in their own right alongside bodily relics, suggesting that the isolated colonists were particularly "susceptible to a strain of belief in which a book could become the physical site of saintly holiness." For the colonists, she argues, "the project of canonization was inescapably a project of publication."[43] The son's editions of Marie's writings bear this out. Though Marie is not physically tortured in martyrdom, her son as editor nonetheless makes the case that her book itself underwent a trial. In 1650 the Ursuline convent was destroyed in a fire, and Marie abandoned her manuscript of the second *Relation* to the flames, fearing that if she threw it out of the window, the wrong reader might find it. Marie presents the loss of her book as a form of abandonment of the self that displays deep humility. In Marie's own formulation, quoted by her son in the *Vie*, the incident becomes a sort of trial by fire that marks the sublimity of her relationship with God: "Il me sembloit que j'avois dans moy-méme une voix interieure qui me disoit ce que je devois jetter par la fenestre & ce que je devois laisser perir par le feu, je vis en un moment le neant de toutes les choses de la terre, & il me fut donné une grace de dénuëment si grande que je ne puis exprimer son effet ny de paroles, ny par écrit" [It seemed to me that I had an inner voice that told me what I should throw from the window and what I should leave to perish in the flames. I saw in a moment the emptiness of all earthly things, and I was given so great a grace in destitution that I cannot express its effects in speech or writing].[44] The burnt book becomes evidence of Marie's own martyr-like sufferings, signaling her readiness to renounce the affairs of the world.

The son's attention to this burnt offering as a turning point in Marie's spiritual life is particularly striking because Marie's account of the event is so closely paralleled by her description of the renunciation of her son, the future editor, an act that allows her to enter the convent. In her memory of this incident she describes a similar loss of self and submission to divine will: "Il me fallut dépouiller de tout désir et demeurer nue au pied de la croix, me résignant de tout mon cœur à ce que sa bonté en ordonnerait" [I had to strip myself of all desire and remain naked at the foot of the cross, resigning myself with all my heart to what his goodness would command me to do].[45] In her son's framing of the entry into the convent Marie is martyred by the loss of her son, as at the moment of the fire her willingness to submit a denuded self to divine command is the mark of her saintliness. Martin casts this loss of earthly desires as the ultimate maternal selflessness, and in the *Vie* he stages a dialog between mother and son where the child grants his mother freedom to leave and recognizes his own religious vocation. The adult son as editor comments, "Voilà le testament que cette bonne mere fit à son fils, qui depuis ce temps-là fut le fils de la Providence" [Here is the testament that this good mother made to her son, who since this moment became the son of Providence].[46] In imagining Marie's words as a testament Martin presents her entry into religious life as a form of death to the world, evoking a kind of witnessing that recalls that of the martyr's witness to faith. The publication of the letters further emphasizes this figure of the suffering mother. At the head of a letter originally sent to her son in July 1669, Martin attaches the title "Description touchante de sa vocation à l'état Religieux, et de la conduite de Dieu sur elle et sur son Fils" [A touching description of her religious vocation and of the conduct of God toward her and her son]. The sentimental title absolves Marie of agency in her familial relations: God acted upon her and her son as he acts upon the martyr who accepts her fate. Marie writes, "Sçachez donc encore une fois qu'en me séparant actuellement de vous, je me suis fait mourir toute vive" [Let me tell you again that in separating myself from you, I made myself die a living death]. This death involves the recognition of a radical separation of body and soul: "Il me sembloit qu'on me séparât l'âme du corps avec des douleurs extrêmes" [It seemed that my soul was separated from my body with extreme pain].[47] But it is crucial to remember that these letters are published as part of a retrospective reflection on the part of the son which moves beyond the pain of maternal loss in order to reveal a greater truth. In the *Ecrits* the son writes of himself as the perfect sacrifice: "Ce fils était un Isaac et un unique, que Dieu lui avait donné pour éprouver sa foi et son amour; mais aussi, il ne lui donna pas moins de force et de courage pour l'immoler qu'il en avait donné à Abraham pour lui sacrifier le sien" [This son was an Isaac and an only child that God had given her in order to test her faith and her love; but He also gave her as much strength and courage to immolate him as he had given to Abraham so he could sacrifice his own]. Thus the material presence of the son is instrumentalized in order to bring about the illumination of what the son describes as "lumières surnaturelles" [supernatural light],[48] that is to say, a higher order even than natural law.

Of course, Martin's presentation of these touching scenes recalls the suffering mother of Christ who gives her son up for the good of the world, making the son as editor appear in a presumptuously privileged position. But the sentimentality of the separation, which suggests that maternal sacrifice can be understood as a form of martyrdom, perhaps also opens up ways in which even readers comfortably at home in France—even those not going so far as to abandon their children at the door of convents—might imagine their lives of domestic selflessness as Christian sacrifice. Rather than understanding the quotidian as an impediment to martyrdom, as did Teresa of Ávila and the young Marie, these martyrological framings of Marie the teacher and mother make life in a minor key a central part of Counter-Reformation exemplarity. In Annette Kolodny's famous assessment of women's relation to the frontier in the seventeenth-century Anglophone American colonies, women are said to imagine the landscape in terms of an "idealized domesticity," which displaces the image of the hero conquering virgin land and looks instead to what Kolodny terms "an imagined bourgeois west."[49] Marie's rewriting of martyrdom and her son's positioning of her sacrifice show how even the most extreme situations could be cast in terms suitable for a bourgeois domestic ideal; Marie's story is not at all the story of a bourgeois west but rather of a frontier made palatable and even imitable for the bourgeois west of France. Marie's colonial martyrdom, I argue, grants space for those whose lives are "dispersed among hindrances," as Eliot puts it, to consider their sufferings as martyrdom.

Marie begins her Canadian adventure with the desire to die for the faith, and she writes home in hopes that she may be slotted into the preassigned genre of martyrology. But as she establishes herself in the daily life of the mission, she learns to write of what comes after the desire for death. Emily Wilson has recently identified a concern with what she terms "overliving," or living too long, in the tragic tradition, arguing that in such texts as Milton's *Samson Agonistes* tragedy is the failure to die and the subsequent reckoning with the continuation of life.[50] Marie's own tragic overliving becomes the basis for a new and newly quotidian theology, in which patient toil is finally recognized alongside more traditionally heroic exploits. Christian stories of the self traditionally begin with one narrative, the inimitable and yet always to be followed life of Christ, in which the dead body that seems to mark the end of the story is shockingly resurrected in time for a sequel. In its turn European martyrology, the story of the imitation of Christ, stutters the first part of that story over and over again, only to leave the second part untold; death marks the consummation and final frontier of its narrative. But when the scene shifts to the colonial frontier, to the very place the old genre might be expected to thrive, the end of the story is dissolved and in its place comes a new narrative that makes the frontier, geographical and otherwise, into a site of life not death, an ongoing story rather than one whose end is brought about by the usual apotheosis. Marie's metaphorical language of martyrdom travels to a place in which it could become actualized. Yet when it does not, another way of understanding a suffering life makes good the loss. In this colonial martyrology the sufferer gets to tell the tale herself, and she who writes the letter wears the crown.

CHAPTER 11

Book of Suffering, Suffering Book

The Mennonite *Martyrs' Mirror* and the Translation of Martyrdom in Colonial America

Patrick M. Erben

When the brutalities of the French and Indian War came upon Pennsylvania in 1755, Governor Denny indignantly reported the slaughter of frontier inhabitants, buttressing his calls for a colonial defense: "Four dead Bodies, one of which was a Woman with Child, were brought to Lancaster from the neighbouring Frontiers, scalped and butchered in a most horrid Manner, and laid before the Door of the Court House for a Spectacle of Reproach to every one there, as it must give the Indians a sovereign Contempt for the Province.... The poor Inhabitants where these daring Murders were committed, being without Militia or Association, and living among Menonists, a numerous Sett of German Quakers, came supplicating me for Protection."[1] Ironically, the Mennonites—pacifists who called themselves "defenseless" or "non-resistant" Christians—were suddenly implicated in the death of fellow Pennsylvanians. In Denny's rhetoric the "poor Inhabitants" were literally and syntactically surrounded by Indians and Mennonites, presumably needing "Protection" from both. Yet the blame heaped upon the Mennonites recalled the public ostracism they had experienced since the beginning of the Anabaptist movement in Europe around the year 1525. The stance that made Pennsylvania Mennonites so suspicious to government and neighbors alike reflected more than two centuries of passive resistance against civil and religious authority. The history of Mennonite persecution and martyrdom had been collected in various martyrologies, most notably the magisterial *Bloody Theater* or *Martyrs' Mirror* compiled by Jan Thieleman van Braght in 1660 and republished in 1685 with 104 illustrations depicting the violent torture and deaths of hundreds of Anabaptists in early modern Europe.[2] About ten years before Denny's incriminating plea, the German-speaking Mennonites of Pennsylvania had commissioned the "Brethren" of the Ephrata Seventh-Day Baptist community to translate and reprint the Dutch *Martyrs' Mirror* (1748–49).[3] When war arrived in 1754, Mennonites seemed resolved to follow the example of the "blood witnesses" and face the attacks of imperial invaders and the anger of their neighbors with equal fortitude.

The translation and printing of the *Martyrs' Mirror* in mid-eighteenth-century Pennsylvania poses a number of intriguing questions for the study of empire and religion in the early modern Atlantic world: how did Mennonites successfully resist government persecution and social pressures? How could Pennsylvania Mennonites prepare themselves for the possibility of renewed persecution and bridge the distance—in both time and space—from the coreligionists who had experienced martyrdom? How did nonconformist or nonorthodox religious communities like the Mennonites retain or restore a sense of separation from the world? The threats of warfare, the possibility of mandatory armament, and thus the erosion of Pennsylvania's freedom of conscience all required church leaders to create more than a theoretical awareness of theology, beliefs, and church discipline; the peculiar identity of the Mennonites as a suffering church once again had to become a lived faith.

In positing the Pennsylvania *Martyrs' Mirror* as a key to understanding the transplantation, translation, and reception of Mennonite beliefs and practices in the New World, especially their resistance to imperial war and violence, my essay examines the interaction among text, material book, religious beliefs, and communal formation. Martyr books—collections of prison letters, prosecution documents, and above all, stories and images of the torture and death of stalwart believers—had always served to fortify nonconformists in their pursuit of "Truth," build a communal identity, and preserve the memory of the so-called blood witnesses for later generations. While relying on recent scholarship examining discourses of martyrdom as memory devices and community-building technologies, I investigate how a martyr book could appeal to the spiritual and emotional sensibilities of rising Anabaptists and help them accept personal suffering. How could American Mennonites make a transition from witnessing—as readers—the suffering of others to witnessing "truth" as actors in the "Bloody Theater" of Anabaptist martyrdom?[4]

Pennsylvania Mennonite leaders contemplated these questions when rumors of war and calls for colonial militias challenged the principle of "defenselessness," recognizing the key role translation played in continuing their faith and public conduct.[5] In carefully selecting an able translator—Peter Miller of Ephrata—and even more meticulously checking his work, the Mennonites emphasized their sensitivity regarding the precarious nature of transferring spiritual content originally embodied in the suffering of the martyrs through arbitrary linguistic signifiers. The act of translation highlighted the question of how a book could recapture the spirit of suffering originally inscribed in the bodies and accounts of those experiencing or witnessing martyrdom. The task of translators, printers, and readers would be to create and receive the Pennsylvania *Martyrs' Mirror* not merely as a faithful translation of Van Braght's 1660 compilation but also as a physical and spiritual manifestation of martyrdom.

The translation, production, and reception of the 1748–49 Ephrata *Mirror* underscored the central metaphorical and physical link between suffering bodies and texts. Of course, Van Braght's vivid descriptions as well as the elaborate illustrations of Dutch engraver Jan Luyken had already represented the "holy martyrs" as sacred texts to be read, interpreted, and emulated. Van Braght's collection and Luyken's images recreated a palpable sense of martyrdom for a generation of Dutch Anabaptists for whom suffering had become a thing of the past. The producers of the Ephrata *Martyrs' Mirror*, however, made it clear that the suffering observed in those stories had to be translated *back* to the bodies of those producing the new German-language edition. This "suffering" *for* the *Martyrs' Mirror* authenticated the text not only as a correct translation of the Dutch original but also as an expression of Anabaptist faith and community. The 1748–49 translation produced at the Ephrata Cloister refracted the original Anabaptist martyr stories in the context of imperial warfare, and it turned the book itself into a fulcrum of suffering: its translators and printers emphasized their suffering for and during its production, later readers attempted to join their own images with the representation of the martyrs, and the book visually oozed blood—in red ink and hand-drawn images. Beyond the *topos* of "body as text" fundamental to all martyr books, Pennsylvania Mennonites received the Ephrata *Martyrs' Mirror* as a sacred body. It became the ultimate emblem of nonresistance when unbound copies were confiscated during the American Revolution to serve as cartridge wadding. Many copies disappeared, while some returned in a mutilated state, thus continuing the tradition of physical martyrdom in lieu of their Mennonite owners. By examining the production history, personal copies, and local narratives surrounding the Pennsylvania *Martyrs' Mirror*, this essay demonstrates how translation in text and image created a new crystallization of martyrdom for New World Anabaptists—the suffering book.

The centrality of the *Martyrs' Mirror* in the transplantation of Mennonite culture and community to North America thus emphasizes translation, translingualism, transnationalism, and interdenominational approaches to migration and settlement over linguistic, national, and religious exclusiveness. In America the images and stories of Anabaptists suffering for their stance of nonresistance dislodged the use of religion as a justification for imperial violence. The *Martyrs' Mirror* instead became a powerful symbol of religion as an active agent for peace and coexistence, championing defenselessness over aggression, peacefulness over violence, and a community based on empathy for the suffering of others over an imperialist fervor for self-glorification and mutual annihilation. The absence of the Mennonites' story and the story of the transmission of the *Martyrs' Mirror* from mainstream histories of imperialism in the Atlantic world, however, casts the coupling of settlement, expansion, and violence as a foregone conclusion that would inevitably be repeated in later generations and in different theaters of war. The story of the Pennsylvania *Martyrs' Mirror* demonstrates the only lesson that could break this vicious cycle: defenselessness, pacifism, and the peace testimony. My interpretation of the Pennsylvania *Martyrs' Mirror* as the textual and spiritual embodiment of the Mennonites' stance of suffering for peace thus contributes to an alternative history of religion and empire in colonial America and the Atlantic world; I thus hope to dislodge a hegemonic narrative that continues to cast religion primarily as a justification for imperialist expansion and violence.

Most of the German sectarians who settled in Pennsylvania in the late seventeenth and early eighteenth centuries had experienced some kind of persecution. Anabaptist sects such as the Mennonites received the most severe treatment by Catholic and even orthodox Protestant rulers and church authorities throughout the sixteenth century and into the early seventeenth century. Historians estimate that the number of Anabaptist martyrs executed in the Netherlands falls between 1,500 and 2,500, with similar numbers for other states where such persecution occurred, including the Palatinate and Switzerland. Civil and religious authorities persecuted Anabaptists primarily for their practice of adult baptism and other challenges to church doctrine, as well as such civil disobedience as the refusal to bear arms.[6] Through their interpretation of the New Testament and their experiences of suffering, Mennonites and other nonconformist German sects arrived at a "theology of martyrdom." Not technically a religious creed, this interpretation of martyrdom sought to explain the purpose of suffering for Christians, insert it in an eschatological scheme, and define the principles—such as defenselessness—that warranted a stance of martyrdom.[7] Revered as the ultimate martyr, Christ demanded radical discipleship from his followers, who would literally and spiritually take up the cross in order to defend the "Truth." Even though persecution and martyrdom should not be actively sought and would never merit salvation, they were regarded as prominent signs of election and the surest way of "imitating" Christ. Martyrdom became a political statement when discipleship led to confrontation with state or ecclesiastical authorities.

For Anabaptists, suffering and martyrdom sanctioned the existence and formation of religious community. Paraphrasing a quotation from the ancient Christian writer Tertullian, the *Martyrs' Mirror* stated, "The blood of the martyrs is the seed of the church."[8] In turn, the stories of sacrificed believers or "blood witnesses" became sacred texts. Just as the martyrs followed Christ's sacrifice, martyr texts continued the tradition of the Scriptures in chronicling a history of persecution. According to Brad Gregory, the Bible was both an implicit and explicit subtext, as collectors of the martyr stories "added uniform marginal biblical citations." The goal of the earliest martyrologies, Gregory argues, was "to show how snugly present persecution fit its scriptural template."[9] Van Braght made the coherence between biblical martyrdom and Anabaptist persecution and suffering even more explicit by adding an entire volume of accounts chronicling martyrdom from Christ through the time of the apostles, the persecution of early Christians, and up to the Anabaptist movement. The blood shed by those who followed Christ would metaphorically and spiritually be poured onto the pages of the martyr books, infusing them with the spirit of martyrdom.

"Translating" the spirit of martyrdom onto the printed page became more difficult as certain Mennonite communities were no longer persecuted. In the fifteenth century martyrologies represented the immediate experience of regional Anabaptist communities. In the early seventeenth century Dutch Mennonites in particular began to enjoy toleration and prosperity, thus lacking a constant infusion of martyr spirit. Doctrinal disputes and regional differences, moreover, seemed to call for the articulation of a unifying tradition of martyr histories. In response martyrologies expanded their geographical reach to encompass a variety of Anabaptist traditions. In 1615 the Dutch

Mennonite Hans de Ries published the largest martyr book yet, *History of the Martyrs or Genuine Witnesses of Jesus Christ*, and his 1631 expanded edition for the first time carried the title *Martyrs' Mirror*. De Ries also introduced the use of elaborate title pages featuring execution scenes.[10] For his 1660 *Martyrs' Mirror*, Van Braght collected and authenticated previously published or unpublished martyr stories from different regions and traditions, added a lengthy volume recounting martyr stories from Christ onward, and prefaced everything with an introduction that posited the martyr stories as evidence of the continuous unfolding of an eschatological battle that required a rigorous stance of discipleship. For the 1685 edition of Van Braght's collection Dutch-Mennonite artist Jan Luyken contributed 104 engravings depicting in graphic detail the violence perpetrated against ancient and modern martyrs. Luyken's illustrations tried to harness the emotive and subliminal power of religious iconography to recreate the spirit of martyrdom for Mennonites who had never witnessed any martyrs' deaths.

While removal in time and place from actual martyrdom explains the constant addition of new devices, I argue that martyrologists and Anabaptist readers were struggling with a larger phenomenon inherent in the "translation" of writings purportedly imbued with the spirit of God. For early modern Anabaptists, actual martyr scenes created a surplus of spiritual and emotional power that could be captured in martyr stories and martyr books. Once actual martyrdom ceased, this surplus disappeared, and the collectors, editors, and readers of martyr books had to ask whether and how words and images could transmit the spirit of suffering. Mennonite authors and illustrators thus created a new iconography for a generation of Anabaptists who had potentially lost the ability to "read" unmediated martyr stories. Even before the Dutch *Martyrs' Mirror* was first translated into German at Ephrata, martyrology had become a feat of translation.

Once the Anabaptist faith spread beyond its original homelands, Mennonites also began to use translations of their "confessions" (statements of theology, social ethics, and church policy) to increase understanding of their beliefs among outsiders. For instance, the 1632 Dordrecht "Confession of Faith" was consecutively translated into German, French, and English.[11] The first English translation, published in Amsterdam in 1712, was specifically designed for the use of coreligionists who had immigrated to Pennsylvania. In the preface the publisher casts translation as a tool of interdenominational communication and exchange, allowing Mennonite immigrants to position themselves in a new culture and language:

Therefore it hath been thought fit and needful to translate, at the
desire of some of our Fellow-believers in Pensylvania, our Confession
of Faith into English, so as for many years it hath been printed in the
Dutch, German, and French languages: which Confession hath been
well approved of both in the Low-Countries and in France, by severall
eminent persons of the Reformed Religion; And therefore it hath been
thought worth the while to turn it also into English, so that those
of that Nation may become acquainted with it, and so mighe have a
better opinion thereof and of its professors; and not onely so, but also
that every well-meaning soul might enquire and try all things, and
keep that which is best.[12]

Mennonite immigrants could now share the fundamental articles of their
faith with their English-speaking neighbors. Yet the English translation not
only fulfilled the purpose of outward justification; it also reminded Mennonites of their faith's theological and spiritual principles. In paraphrasing
Paul's dictum from the first letter to the Thessalonians, "Prove all things;
hold fast that which is good" (I Thess. 5. 21), the preface establishes a principle
guiding the contact with other denominations and cultures in moments of
religious and ethnic diversity *and* the process of translation itself. Repeated
in the translation of the "Appendix" to the Dordrecht Confession published
in Philadelphia in 1727, this motto asked Mennonites in the New World
to "hold fast" to the most treasured ideals of their faith—such as nonresistance—while reaching out to other groups in order to establish points of
spiritual contact and understanding (which others could "try" and "keep that
which is best").[13]

Pennsylvania Mennonites began to question the resilience of the province's
founding principle of "freedom of conscience" when rumors of war reminded
them of the conditions they had left behind in Europe.[14] Although the War
of Jenkins' Ear (beginning in 1739) and King George's War (1740–48) did not
directly affect Pennsylvania, these larger imperial conflicts raised widespread
calls for a militia and caused great alarm among Mennonites.[15] Consequently,
they assiduously supported Quakers in the Assembly, lobbied for quick natu-
ralization, and wrote petitions against military service.[16] Pennsylvania Mennonites also asked their wealthy coreligionists in Holland for support. A 1745
letter by the leaders of the Skippack congregation expresses the Mennonites'
fear that their dearest religious principles might be curtailed: "We acknowledge our misstep in coming to so distant a land without sufficient assur-

ance concerning freedom of conscience. . . . It cannot be known, now that the flames of war seem to be mounting higher and higher, whether cross and tribulation may not all the sooner fall to the lot of the nonresistant Christian. It therefore becomes us to arm ourselves for such cases with patience and endurance, and to make every preparation for the steadfast constancy in our faith."[17] The "cross and tribulation" Pennsylvania Mennonites feared was not so much the threat of war itself but rather the possibility that "we would . . . be compelled against our consciences to take up arms and meet the foe with weapons with a heavily burdened conscience." Mennonites anticipated that the governor would require military service in violation of their pacifist stance, thus undermining the freedom of conscience that had originally drawn them to "so distant a land." Thus, they sought the spiritual weapons Anabaptists had traditionally wielded in their battle against the "wolves" of the world: martyr books. Their letter asked for assistance from the Dutch congregations in translating and publishing in German Van Braght's *Martyrs' Mirror* "so that our posterity may have before their eyes the traces of those loyal witnesses of the truth, who walked in the way of truth and have given their lives for it."[18] Evidence of stalwartness in the face of persecution in the past would strengthen Pennsylvania Mennonites for the future. Yet the stakes for Pennsylvania Mennonites requesting aid from Dutch Anabaptists were even higher than they had been for Van Braght in 1660 and Luyken in 1685. The *Martyrs' Mirror* translation requested by the Skippack Mennonites needed to become far more than a symbolic device providing the youth with an understanding of their "heritage": it had to continue the physical link between past, present, and future suffering. Pennsylvania Mennonites had to create a threefold translation. They desired a linguistically accurate translation from Dutch to German. Theological content needed to be transferred without distorting articles of faith. Most important, the translation and translators needed to carry the spiritual meanings *and* physical experience of suffering and martyrdom into a new edition, printed for readers in the New World.

The problem of translation was thus foremost on the Mennonites' minds. Although the Skippack congregation had "greatly desired to have this work published for a number of years," they rejected offers from the German printer Christoph Saur, who had published the first American edition of the Mennonite hymnal *Ausbund* (1742).[19] The letter to the Amsterdam congregation hinted at several reasons for not employing Saur: "The establishment of a new German printing office has renewed the hopes, but the bad paper used here for printing has caused us to reconsider. Besides, up to this time, there has not appeared, either among ourselves or others, anyone who understands the languages well enough to make a faithful translation. We have for certain reasons not been able to entrust it to those who have volunteered and promised to do it, for however much we are concerned to have it translated, we are equally concerned that the truth remain unblemished by the translation."[20] Saur's paper may not have been particularly poor by colonial standards, but the Mennonites wanted to have the "sacred" text of their "blood witnesses" produced in the highest possible quality.[21] Second, Saur clearly did not have the linguistic acumen to translate such a lengthy text from Dutch into German. Most important, the Mennonites feared that the spiritual "truth" embedded within the original martyr stories might be corrupted through the translation. Saur was a radical Pietist with Dunker ties. German Baptists or Dunkers favored baptism by immersion, while Mennonites did not. Saur had also been criticized—especially by Lutheran and Reformed ministers— for inserting "apocryphal" texts from the so-called Berleburg Bible favored by radical Pietists into the Lutheran translation accepted by orthodox Protestants. The Mennonites' worries about translation, therefore, went deeper than a potential distrust of Saur's skill, his paper, and his fidelity as a printer. Translation for the Pennsylvania Mennonites carried the charge to transmit the spiritual essence of radical discipleship, and they wondered how such a translation could inspire a similar stance among their youth. Skippack Mennonites eventually contacted the German Seventh-Day Baptist community at Ephrata—founded by the radical Pietist Conrad Beissel around 1732—to aid with the translation and printing of the sacred martyrology.[22] Here the Mennonites found an able translator in the former Reformed minister Peter Miller, who was one of the few university trained members of the Ephrata "cloister," purportedly spoke seven languages, and became later in life a member of the American Philosophical Society.[23]

Beyond Miller's credentials the Ephrata community also qualified because its members had designed an entire lifestyle imitating martyrdom. Beissel and the celibate brothers and sisters at Ephrata generally subscribed to a mystical theology advanced by seventeenth-century German mystic Jacob Boehme. Accordingly, the supposedly male and female qualities of God had once been united in an androgynous Adam; the fall of man was actually the sexual differentiation into male and female, with the divine "femalety" of God—the "virgin Sophia"—leaving both man and God.[24] All human beings, but men in particular, had to overcome their supposedly male self-will and attempt to reunite with the "virgin Sophia," or divine wisdom. The path to this mystical reunion at Ephrata was designed to lead through a variety of activities and principles aiming at self-denial: a monastic lifestyle and dress, various strategies of "self-mortification" (including deprivation of food, drink, and sleep, as well as celibacy), continuous hard work, rigorous singing schools designed to purify the human voice, *Fraktur* writing (a type of manuscript calligraphy), and a printing press that incorporated the production of paper, ink, and type as well as bookbinding. While hard work was championed among Mennonites as evidence of an obedient and virtuous life, Ephrata Brethren and Sisters substituted self-mortification, asceticism, and hard work for the lack of outward persecution to create a similar stance of suffering.

In spite of certain differences between the two communities that were highlighted in differing views about baptism (Ephrata practiced immersion, Mennonites did not), both Mennonites and Ephrata Brethren and Sisters similarly inscribed suffering and martyrdom in the physical objects and conduct of their lives. Similar to the plain dress and lifestyle of the Mennonites, the Ephrata "cloister" attempted to manifest a metaphysical ideal of suffering in a *physical* reality. Even before the *Martyrs' Mirror*, Mennonites and Ephrata Brethren had collaborated on printing Mennonite devotional books that included several martyr stories, thus initiating a transfer of theological content and spiritual symbolism.[25] Indeed, the Ephrata-Mennonite collaboration ensured the "translation" of early modern martyr-book culture to the New World through the confluence of similar traditions.

Beissel championed translating and printing the *Martyrs' Mirror* as another means of purifying and perfecting the earthly selves of the Brethren. According to the chronicle of the community, *Chronicon Ephratense*, Beissel "was the instigator of this work, [and] never allowed a suspension of work or carnal rest in the Settlement, and therefore seized every opportunity to keep all those who were under his control in perpetual motion, so that no one might ever feel at home again in this life, and so forget the consolation from above, which purpose this Book of Martyrs excellently served."[26] The *Chronicon* thus describes this effort as a distillation process that infused the resulting volumes with a renewed spirit of suffering: "When this [work] is taken into consideration, as also the low price, and how far those who worked at it were removed from self-interest, the biographies of the holy martyrs, which the book contains, cannot fail to be a source of edification to all who read them."[27] Granted, the continued insistence on the translation and publication of the *Martyrer-Spiegel* as a work of physical and mental exhaustion could be interpreted as vanity or self-pity. Yet Miller and his associates genuinely imitated the martyrs represented in the book to achieve a spiritual union with Christ, the ultimate martyr.

The production costs and work hours must have been overwhelming by any standard. According to the *Chronicon*, fifteen Brethren worked on the project, "nine of whom had their work assigned in the printing department, namely, one corrector, who was at the same time the translator, four compositors and four pressmen; the rest had their work in the paper-mill. Three years were spent on this book, though not continuously, for there was often want of paper."[28] According to Miller's testimony to the Swedish minister Israel Acrelius, seven hundred copies of an original printing of twelve or thirteen hundred had been sold in 1754.[29] The binding of the *Martyrs' Mirror* was apparently completed in stages or on demand. This assumption is also supported by the many variants of the Ephrata *Martyrs' Mirror* still in existence, especially in the inclusion or exclusion of frontispieces and illustrations. Although the *Chronicon* does not mention Luyken's illustrations, it is apparent from the extant copies of the *Martyrs' Mirror* that the publishers either did not attempt or were unable to secure Luyken's copperplate etchings. In any case the sheer size of the translation and printing enterprise involved in the production of the *Martyrs' Mirror* placed the Ephrata Brethren in a mood of suffering and discipleship.

In his new preface to the Ephrata *Martyrs' Mirror*, Miller casts the translation and printing of the book as a form of *imitatio*; accordingly, he emphasizes that the Brethren did not regret the "pains, the work, the industry, and the diligence in this important and lengthy endeavor, especially as the memorial of the sacrificed confessors…always encouraged us to continue, so that we finally completed the work to the greatest enjoyment of others and ourselves." Linking them spiritually and physically to the subjects of the book, the translators and printers' own sacrifice made the translation of the *Martyrer-Spiegel* a worthy representation of the original sacrifice of the martyrs. Here translation allows readers to partake in the spiritual drama revealed or "mirrored" in the *Martyrer-Spiegel*. The preface explicitly exhorts the readers to gain—through the pain and suffering invested in the volume—a palpable sense of the original sufferings represented. Miller concludes: "Attentive reader! Thus receive this work—for which we have spared neither trouble nor industry—and perceive in reading this book the same taste and awakening by the blessed blood witnesses which others have enjoyed in the translating and printing thereof; then will your life and death serve discipleship, which had been the aim of this [work]. [Signed:] The publisher of this book."[30] The preface imagines a reception of the text through both sensory ("taste") and spiritual ("awakening") experience, expanding communication to a supra-linguistic dimension. The translation of martyrdom thus reaches deep into a common language that ultimately transcends language itself: the imitation of the suffering of Christ and in turn the suffering of the saints who followed his example. The Ephrata *Martyrer-Spiegel* created a community of martyrdom that extended both spiritually and physically from the "blood witnesses" in the book, to the translators and printers at Ephrata, to the Mennonite readers.

Mirroring Miller's preface, the Mennonites' endorsement of the translation and printing at the end of the volume resumes the theme of *imitatio*.[31] The two Mennonite leaders in charge of inspecting the work, Dielman Kolb and Heinrich Funck, express their belief that "the Lord will kindle through his H. Spirit in the hearts of all men a desire and hunger for this book, so that they may not mind the little money, but purchase the same, take their time with it, and read it with devotion, so they may see and learn, how the faith in Christ must be built, and how one's life and conduct may serve to follow the defenseless lamb, and thus to inherit the eternal kingdom with Christ and his followers."[32] The book in front of the reader is not merely a material artifact but a living testimony of those individuals who as "martyrs" or "saints" had followed Christ, asking readers to do the same. Kolb and Funck's afterword projected what the Mennonites valued the most in the translation: preserving the spiritual meanings of the martyr stories. Yet the book is also a physical object that answers the "desire and hunger" Pennsylvania Mennonites had for the martyr stories and their palpable presence in their lives. It is both a spiritual essence and nourishment.

The Mennonites' endorsement also echoes the Pauline principle of "Prove all things; hold fast that which is good" evoked in the earlier Mennonite confessions. Most revealing is the way in which the Mennonites judge the value of the translation: "They [Funck and Kolb] have not found one point in the whole work that does not contain the same sense and foundation of faith, as it was conceived in Dutch. They have certainly found different words where they halted and which, they thought, might have been rendered more pleasantly in both the Dutch and the high-German. One should not be surprised that in such a large book a word here and there is not captured in the most precise manner, but no one should be accused in this regard, for we are all human beings who frequently err."[33] Just as the English edition of the Dordrecht Confession advised readers to shy away from a literalist judgment of both the translation and the faith itself, the inspectors of the *Martyrs' Mirror* emphasize that they expect a spiritually sound translation in which the spirit of the martyrs remains intact, even while the precise wording might have been changed or even improved. They distinguish language as a realm subject to human fallacies from the realm of divine inspiration and meaning, which can be carried into another language (and even another continent) through the spirit of suffering and martyrdom.

Finally, Kolb and Funck ensured that the chain of suffering continued by the Ephrata Brethren during the production of the *Martyrs' Mirror* would remain unbroken. Although styling themselves less self-consciously as martyrs than the Ephrata Brethren did, they nevertheless emphasized their hard work—a key ingredient in the Mennonite ideology of discipleship—in checking the entire text: "Since Henrich Funck and Dielman Kolb have a special love for this book, they have both—with the agreement of the congregation—dedicated the time and attention to comparing one sheet after another with the Dutch book. During this work, they did not skip one verse."[34] The linguistic and theological authentication is thus buttressed by the two readers' emotional attachment to the book as well as their own physical and mental exertions in proofreading such a large volume.

The theme of discipleship also stands at the center of the first of two frontispiece engravings, which appear in parts 1 and 2 of the Ephrata *Martyrs' Mirror*. The first frontispiece transmits the spirit of martyrdom by tracing the progression of the martyr's life (Figure 11.1). The numbers and letters scattered throughout the image seem to correspond to a key that is not extant in any of the known copies and was possibly never bound with the volume. Evoking the Book of Revelation, the future martyrs are greeted by the "Beast" or Anti-Christ on the right, and Christ, personified as the "Lamb of God," on the left. These spiritual opposites frame the "narrow path," which Mennonites believed they had to walk in order to reach salvation. At this stage discipleship means forsaking the temptations of the "World," depicted through the drinking, dancing, and carousing on the right. The fact that martyrdom begins with obedience to the law of the Scriptures is also pointed out by the figure of Moses on the left, donning the Decalogue. Yet obedience and faithful adherence to the law does not grant salvation; it leads the future martyrs toward Christ and to the ordinance of baptism. The exhortation "Den solt ihr hören" [Him you shall hear/obey] is spoken by Moses and by the voice from heaven, thus combining the Old Testament typological anticipation of Christ and the New Testament revelation of Jesus as the son of God and new lawgiver.

Figure II.I. First frontispiece of the Ephrata *Martyrs' Mirror* (1748–49). Mennonite Heritage Center, Harleysville, Pennsylvania.

The moment of baptism completes the conversion of the new disciples and places them in violent conflict with the "World." Having been converted from those *seeking* Christ into disciples *following* Christ, they literally and figuratively take up the cross and proceed toward their martyr's death. The execution scene hints at the kind of torture and violent deaths suffered by the "blood witnesses" and illustrated in their gory details by Jan Luyken; nevertheless, this frontispiece places more emphasis on the larger process of discipleship rather than on the martyrs' death. That martyrs die for their faith, however, becomes clear, as they are—delineated as souls rather than bodies—lifted into heaven, where they are received by the "Lamb" and a group of angels and led to the heavenly paradise. The presence of the divine light of God is depicted as a double circle of the sun, with the Tetragrammaton in the center.

Much of the scholarship on the *Martyrs' Mirror* usually repeats the notion, first published by Pennsylvania historian Samuel Pennypacker, that this frontispiece is absent from many extant copies because Mennonites doctrinally objected to the depiction of baptism by immersion and asked to have the frontispiece removed or not bound.[35] I have consulted several Mennonite historians and archivists, who all either argued that the immersion theory does not hold water (pun intended) or at least that there is no evidence to corroborate it. Instead, the fly-leaf inscriptions on many extant copies of the Ephrata *Martyrs' Mirror* demonstrate that many copies, including the frontispiece, were owned by several prominent Mennonite ministers and families (e.g., the Burkholder family *Martyrs' Mirror* at Muddy Creek Farm Library).[36] Thus, it seems more likely that the followers of *both* traditions of radical Protestantism—the Anabaptists and the Pietists—could find elements of their specific denominational attitudes toward discipleship, suffering, and baptism in this image. Thus, the frontispiece may be a truly Pennsylvanian mélange of denominational practices and local adjustments to other faiths. Rather than Ephrata subverting Mennonite church order with ideas of baptism by immersion and more esoteric notions of suffering, the Mennonites' more socially confrontational concepts of martyrdom may have impressed and influenced the Ephrata "cloister."

Facing the title page to volume 2 is a second frontispiece that seems to be only extant in two copies, owned by the Historical Society of Pennsylvania and the Muddy Creek Farm Library (Figure 11.2). Whatever the reasons for its exclusion, the second frontispiece further elaborates on the theme of blood sacrifice. The banner surrounding the central image cites Matthew

Figure 11.2. Second frontispiece of Ephrata *Martyrs' Mirror* (1748–49). Historical Society of Pennsylvania.

11:30, "Mein Joch ist sanft und meine Last ist leicht" [My yoke is easy, and my burden is light]. For those attempting to follow Christ, suffering—even martyrdom—is an "easy" or "light" burden, because it allows them to become "meek and "lowly" like Christ, thus accomplishing perfect imitation. The imagery going along with this motto, however, was probably too heavily imbued with the mysticism of the Ephrata cloister to pass the Mennonite test. Christ, on the left, is joined by Mary, on the right, who is represented in a pseudo-Catholic manner with the crescent (above her head), designating her role as both birth mother and mother of God. Both frame the central scene of the cross, adorned with a winged heart hovering over a chalice. Most likely, this grouping is an iconographic representation of Beissel's belief, propounded in his *Dissertation on Man's Fall*, that the female qualities of love and sacrifice embodied in both Christ and Mary joined to restore the original "divine femalety" or "virgin Sophia."[37] The lilies sprouting from the cross further represented the "divine femalety" embodied in Christ's sacrifice and emulated by the so-called spiritual virgins at Ephrata.

Even if Mennonites had little sympathy for such mystical speculation and transgendering of orthodox Christian spirituality, they nevertheless participated in an emotionally, even sensually charged veneration of martyrdom and the martyr books encapsulating this spirit. Most surprising, one copy formerly owned by a Mennonite family is complemented by a series of engravings of Jesus and the martyred apostles.[38] The drawings were created and potentially colored by the eighteenth-century German artist Paul Decker (1685–1742) and engraved and published by engraver and art dealer Martin Engelbrecht (1684–1756; Figure 11.3).[39] Friedrich Schott's catalog of Engelbrecht engravings mentions a sixteen-sheet series of Jesus, Mary, John the Baptist, and the apostles (page 107, #2248–63). The numbering of the plates exactly matches the numbers in this copy of the *Martyrs' Mirror*, although the sequence there was changed to match the order in which the specific martyred apostles appear in the text. Moreover, the engravings of Mary and the apostle Thomas were omitted, as neither was martyred. The rearrangement and omission of two images demonstrates that the engravings were not made for the purpose of including them in the Ephrata *Martyrs' Mirror*. The inscriptions provided a German and Latin motto for each martyr and an epigrammatic poem in both languages.[40] How these plates ended up in a specific copy of the *Martyrs' Mirror* is unclear, but most likely the Ephrata Brethren were responsible for the insertion, as the engravings are bound with the rest of the book and not pasted in later. Yet the bright coloring of these plates seems completely out of

Figure 11.3. Unique illustration in copy of Ephrata *Martyrs' Mirror* (1748–49). Lancaster Mennonite Historical Society, Lancaster, Pennsylvania.

place for Mennonites, and even the more eccentric Ephrata artists are known for more subdued colorings in their manuscript hymnals.[41] The Latin inscriptions, moreover, reflect more the learned and elite culture of late-humanistic Europe than the anti-academic sentiments of radical Protestant and Anabaptist immigrants in Pennsylvania. The insertion of these plates may be an anomaly, representing the zeal of a single Ephrata brother who used existing connections to Germany to receive these devotional drawings. Potentially, they may have been the accidental by-product of an undocumented effort by the Ephrata Brethren to gain Luyken's original plates for the Ephrata edition of the *Martyrs' Mirror*.

Yet these engravings also fit into the larger trend of personalizing individual copies of the *Martyrs' Mirror* among both the members of the Ephrata community and among Mennonite families, treating the book as their most prized treasure. Viewed within the larger range of personalized inscriptions in individual copies of the *Martyrs' Mirror*, the presence of these colored engravings demonstrates the range of approaches different readers took toward the transmission of martyrology to the New World. These particular engravings may have served a specific individual for the sensory heightening of the interaction with and appreciation of the *Martyrs' Mirror* and the suffering represented in it. Similarly, elaborately wrought Fraktur writings placed the reader—represented by the owners' names written in colorful lettering—spiritually and physically in the midst of the spiritual drama unfolding inside the book (Figure 11.4).[42]

Evidence for the idea that the translation of suffering created a spiritual fulcrum around which various linguistic groups and religious denominations revolve also exists in the drawings an Ephrata brother named "Amos" inscribed in his personal copy of the *Mirror*. Amos's manuscript insert continues this supra-linguistic language of suffering with Christ and for Christ embodied in the frontispieces and the martyr-book tradition in general. The hand-drawn image, of course, not only reflects the artist's contemplation of the mystery of Christ's suffering and atonement but also his active involvement in it. Brother Amos placed himself in the very center of this spiritual drama. The depiction of the apostles and Mary mourning under the cross—especially their dress and demeanor—closely resembles similar images of Ephrata Brethren and Sisters elsewhere in the Cloister's manuscript illuminations. The Ephrata Brethren attempted not just to disseminate the *Martyrs' Mirror* but to continue writing it. Translation, printing, and manuscript illustration, in other words, created a spiritual community extending from Christ, to the apostles,

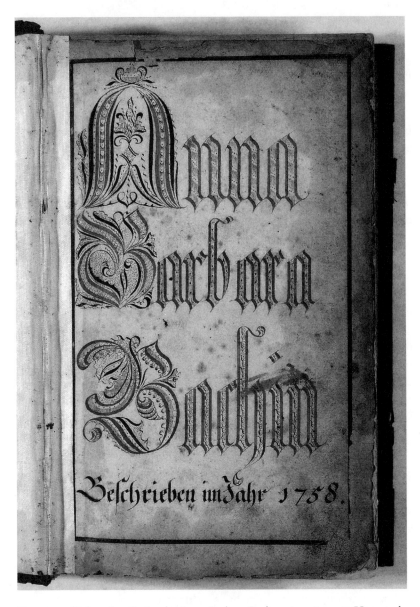

Figure 11.4. Fraktur inscription by Anna Barbara Bach, written in 1758. Historical Society of Pennsylvania.

Figure 11.5. Manuscript illustrations in Bruder Amos's (Ephrata) copy of the *Martyrs' Mirror* (1748–49). Schwenkfelder Library, Pennsburg, Pennsylvania.

to the martyrs of the Protestant Reformation, especially the Anabaptists, and, finally, to the Ephrata Brothers and Sisters. Amos even seemed to interlace the blood shed by the "holy Martyrs" with the writing and illumination of his name (Figure 11.5).

In spite of such appreciation by Pennsylvania Mennonites, a sizable portion of the 1748–49 Ephrata edition remained unbound and unsold at Ephrata, when the Continental Congress authorized their confiscation to produce cartridge wadding for the revolutionary army in 1776. At this juncture the Ephrata *Martyrs' Mirror* turned from a book representing suffering and martyrdom into a martyred or suffering book. Coinciding with a vehement backlash against loyalists and pacifists suspected of being Loyalists, the confiscation of the *Martyrs' Mirror* demonstrated to Mennonites and other German peace sects symbolically and physically the need to withdraw from a society that had promised complete liberty of conscience but now abridged this civil right for the sake of attaining political freedom. The *Chronicon Ephratense* gives the best-known account of this event:

> This book eventually met with strange experiences during the
> Revolutionary war in America. When there was a great lack of all
> war-material and also of paper, the fact was betrayed that there was
> a large quantity of printed paper in Ephrata, which then was pretty
> soon confiscated. Many protests were raised against this in the
> Settlement, and it was alleged, among the rest, that this might lead to
> evil consequences on account of the English army. They resolved not
> to give up anything voluntarily, but that it would have to be taken by
> force. Consequently there arrived two wagons and six soldiers, who
> took possession of all the copies of the Book of Martyrs, after making
> prompt payment for them. This gave great offence in the country, and
> many thought that the war would not end favorably for the country,
> because the memorials of the holy martyrs had been thus maltreated.
> At last, however, they were honored again, for some sensible persons
> bought in all that were left of them.[43]

The key phrase is that "the memorials of the holy martyrs had been...mal-treated." In other words the books containing the stories of the martyrs had become martyrs themselves. The fact that popular opinion feared this action as a token foreboding a negative outcome of the war hints at the spiritual power and significance invested in the translations of the *Martyrs' Mirror*.

Mennonite scholar David Luthy discovered a fly-leaf inscription in a *Martyrs' Mirror* copy owned by a Mennonite named Joseph von Gundy.[44] Gundy condemns the confiscation vehemently and provides a useful account of the purchase of the remaining copies by Mennonites after the Revolution:

> This book was printed in [Ephrata] in Lancaster County.... It was
> *seized* by Congress in 1776 and *taken unbound* to Philadelphia.
> Approximately 150 or a few more were made into cartridges and shot
> against their [former] [English] brothers, making a murder book out
> of it until their own conscience told them it had not been printed
> for such a purpose. Then the government made a pronouncement to
> the lovers of this volume that if they would repay them their money
> and the cartage, they would have back the remaining books. This we
> did, sending them payment in 1786 when Congress money was worth

so little that this book unbound did not cost me over four shillings and six pence or half a dollar and ten pence. Thus, 175 books were returned, many of which were no longer complete and also damaged which I myself saw. But I was lucky that this copy is not lacking a single page. As it is here, it cost me $1.60.[45]

Crucially, Gundy describes the fate of the books as either martyrdom or captivity. Just as the Anabaptist martyrs of old resisted and died for their convictions, the unbound copies of the Ephrata *Martyrs' Mirror* were literally killed by being shot from muskets; in a sardonic irony the testimony of pacifists aided the taking of life, thus making it a "murder book." Just as the Franconia-conference Mennonites had feared conscription into military service above any threats to their physical lives, Gundy regards the spiritual perversion of the book as a worse offense than its physical destruction.

The remaining copies of the Ephrata *Martyrs' Mirror* literally and spiritually became the equivalents of the suffering bodies of the ancient and Anabaptist martyrs, and Gundy's fly-leaf inscription becomes virtually the very last account of an "Anabaptist martyr"—the book itself. Gundy's prose, therefore, describes the confiscated copies like the bodies of martyrs. First, they are "seized and taken." In German the combination of the past participles "genommen...geführt" makes the metaphor of "book as martyred body" even stronger; *geführt* (past participle of the word *führen*, to lead) is not normally used with an impersonal object, such as books, but rather with a person or animal. In other words, for the German writer here the taking of the copies of the *Martyrs' Mirror* is a type of captivity that resembles the arrest and imprisonment usually experienced by the martyrs represented within the book. Gundy makes this analogy even stronger and more explicit. The adverb *ungebunden* [unbound] seems to contradict the notion of captivity (the books are not bound). Of course, *unbound* refers to the pages of the volumes: they are not yet bound into individual books; they are loose assemblies of Mennonite martyr stories. To understand what this implies to the Mennonite sensibility can only be appreciated by visualizing what a bound copy of the Ephrata *Martyrs' Mirror* looks like. Luthy describes the book as "bound between oak boards covered with leather, the book weighed thirteen pounds. It was the largest book printed in colonial America."[46] Among all of the specimens I have seen, the *Martyrs' Mirror* is always dressed in a type of iron-clad lockbox worthy of the Mennonites' most treasured spiritual possession. Thus, for the copies of the *Martyrs' Mirror* to be taken *unbound* to Philadelphia means that they are as unprotected and "defenseless" as the actual martyrs were when they were "seized and taken" by the respective authorities. Like captives being redeemed, the confiscated *Martyrs' Mirrors* only return because the Mennonite admirers of the book pay a "ransom" to secure their "release." This analogy also provides an uncanny echo of the captivity and release (or death) of many European frontier inhabitants among the Indians, giving the suffering of the books both a European and an American context.

Thus, the metaphorical and physical connection between the *text as body* and the *text as martyr* climaxes at the moment of return, not the moment of confiscation. Like the martyrs within the book (who were tortured, dismembered, and executed), the books themselves return mutilated and dismembered. Of the copies purchased back by Mennonites, Gundy explains, "many...were no longer complete and also damaged *which I myself saw.*"[47] Gundy here becomes a witness to the martyrdom of these volumes in the same way that the disciples became witnesses of the sacrifice of Christ through the observation of his wounds. At the same time, Gundy describes the book in which he inscribed this account as miraculously intact: "I was lucky that this copy is not lacking a single page." His good fortune is that, besides having a complete copy with all the stories, he "owns" an even more precious relic: the book that survived in spite of its captivity. The completeness of Gundy's copy, of course, also makes it free from the spiritual stain of having been actively used for musket wadding. His copy is one of the few that has survived with an "unburdened conscience."

What has emerged throughout this analysis is the mutually reinforcing or reciprocal relationship between textuality, translation, and the ideology of martyrdom in the transmission of the Mennonite *Martyrs' Mirror* to Pennsylvania. Ultimately, all martyr books must bridge the gap between a physically palpable and spiritually immediate sense of faith and discipleship—the willingness to follow Christ in death—and the potentially arbitrary nature of language. Removed in time and space from the immediacy of blood sacrifice, American Mennonites also had to negotiate the exigencies of translation. For the translators, readers, and owners of the Ephrata *Martyrs' Mirror*, suffering not only became the subject to be represented and translated, but in turn it was also the key or language that made such a crossing possible. In the process of translating and transmitting the Mennonite *Martyrs' Mirror*, suffering and martyrdom were both signifier and signified, simultaneously the subject to be represented and the language representing it. The *Martyrs' Mirror* was a book of suffering, as well as a suffering book.

The Ephrata *Martyrs' Mirror* became a fitting representation and manifestation of the martyrs' suffering and sacrifice because at all stages of the production and reception process it established both physical and spiritual connections: the translator and printers suffered for its completion in emulation of the martyrs; the readers who checked the translation completed an equal labor of love and sacrifice; owners and readers adorned individual copies with elaborate *Fraktur* writings or drawings that positioned the "self" in the midst of the spiritual drama unfolding inside and outside the book; and finally the book itself participated in the continuation of "defenseless" resistance to persecution and violence by literally being torn apart by war. During the eighteenth-century wars for empire (including the Revolutionary War), America became a "Bloody Theater" not unlike the scenario described in the texts and illustrations of the *Martyrs' Mirror*. Although a quantifiable assessment of the effect the Ephrata *Martyrs' Mirror* had on "arming" Mennonites in their actual resistance to militarization and imperial warfare exceeds the scope of this essay, the book's dissemination and reception most certainly created a textual body that translated martyrdom and pacifism into the New World.

CHAPTER 12

Iconoclasm Without Icons?

The Destruction of Sacred Objects in Colonial North America

Susan Juster

The conventional story of New England religion begins with a litany of what was *not* there: to quote David Hall, "no cathedrals, no liturgy, no church courts, no altars or candles, no saints days or Christmas, no weddings, no pilgrimages nor sacred places, nor relics; no godparents, or maypoles, no fairy tales, no carnival."[1] To which the observer of Europe's bloody and protracted wars of religion—the violent underbelly of the Protestant and Catholic Reformations that tore the continent apart for nearly two centuries—would add: no pogroms; no religious riots on the scale of the infamous St. Bartholomew's Day Massacre in Paris in 1572; no "stripping of the altars," desecration of saints' images, or other orchestrated acts of iconoclasm both popular and official; no (with four notable exceptions) executions for heresy, blasphemy, or any other religious crime; no burning of witches or infidels or *auto da fes*; no forced conversions or mass expulsions of dissenters; no Inquisition. There is, of course, a direct connection between the two lists: it is hard to be an iconoclast without icons to smash, to hunt heretics effectively without an Inquisition. Religious violence on a mass scale needs large groups of people willing to kill and to die for their faith, helpfully concentrated in towns for easy access to one another—not scattered settlers and isolated plantations.

And yet, consider the following example: on a cold winter night in February 1714 some "wicked and Sacrilegious" persons broke into Trinity Church in New York, the temporal and spiritual home of the Church of England in the colonies, and left the sanctuary in shambles. Having "broke into ye North Window of the Steeple" the vandals "broke down the window of the Vestry room did cut or tare off the Sleve of one of the Surplices that was in the said Room, and did Rent and Tare another to pieces and not being contented with that did carry the same Surplice with several common prayer books and Psalm books into ye Church Yard and having spread the Surplice on the Ground and put the common prayer books and Psalm books round it left their Ordure on the Sacred Vestments as the greatest outrage and most Villanous indignity they could offer to the Church of England Her Holy Priesthood and in defiance of God and all Religion."[2] The desecration of Trinity Church was widely (if implausibly) attributed to the Anglicans' "Implacable Enemies" in the colony, those pesky Quakers who had been tormenting local ministers for years. This incident is but one of many in the Anglo-American colonies in which religious *things*—churches and their ecclesiastical paraphernalia, sacred texts, gravestones, local "shrines"—were the object of violence by individual settlers or communities animated by a sense of sacred rage. This chapter examines a series of attacks on churches and other sacred objects during the period from 1620 to 1760 in order both to gauge the extent of iconoclastic behavior (previously presumed to be nonexistent in Anglo-American historiography) in the British mainland colonies and, more ambitiously, to examine the nature of iconoclasm itself in a colonial environment, where the traditional targets of organized iconoclastic raids were largely absent.

Moving back and forth from a consideration of iconoclasm in Reformation-era Europe and the American colonies, the larger aim of the chapter is to ask how traditions of sacred violence that were developed in one historical context thrived in altered, sometimes unrecognizable, form in New World colonies. Understanding the roots and forms of religious violence is a heuristic as much as an empirical challenge, since what differentiates one form of violence from another is often a matter of interpretation: when is a war a just war or a holy war? When is a death at the stake a martyrdom rather than an ordinary execution? How do we tell the difference between the destruction visited by nature and neglect on religious buildings and deliberate vandalism? When is an image an idol? Of all categories of religious violence, iconoclasm may be the most heuristically sensitive, since the relationship between signs and things is at the very core of the act. The iconoclast acts out of a belief that legitimate rites and ceremonies have become corrupted into false idols and vents his rage at the external object (the statue, shrine, painted window) in whose material form the corruption is encased. In the spirit of the inter-disciplinary approach adopted by this volume as a whole, I read episodes of colonial iconoclasm with reference to semiotic theory, cultural anthropology, and literary criticism while remaining firmly rooted in the historical specific-ity of settler communities in British North America.

It is entirely fitting that Trinity Church was the object singled out for attack in New York City in 1714. The church—its physical structure, furnishings, and ornamentation, as well as the sacred (or sacrilegious, depending on one's point of view) doings within—was a primary target of Protestant iconoclasts in the Reformation era. Nothing more symbolized the corruptions of the me-dieval church than the majestic cathedrals that towered over Europe's towns and ancient cities, the site of so many of the degraded ceremonies (commu-nion, baptism, the sign of the cross, the churching of women) that for ardent Reformers marked the Church of Rome as a malignant presence in their communities. The revisionist historian Eamon Duffy calls iconoclasm the "central sacrament of the Reformation," a claim suggesting deep chains of meaning linking the outward expression of rage against the material face of medieval Christianity in orchestrated acts of violence to the theological, litur-gical, and psychological currents that underwrote such repugnance of *things*.[3] The Reformation didn't invent iconoclasm, of course, and a long Augustinian tradition of philosophizing about the role of images and their concrete mani-festations in religious worship provided a sturdy theoretical foundation for the confessional battles over religious objects in the sixteenth and seventeenth centuries. The commonplace notion that images were the "books of the illit-erate" sanctioned a range of representational practices in which the laity was instructed in the timeless truths of Christianity through the contemplation of mimetic scenes. Seeing was truly believing in the visual culture of the me-dieval church, and as the range of devotional objects proliferated in the cen-turies leading up to 1517, so too did critiques of images as creating dangerous idols of the mind, which threatened to become a substitute for the real thing. "It is evident that millions of souls have been cast into eternal damnation by the occasion of images used in place of religion," warned the Puritan martyr Nicholas Ridley before being led to the flames in the infamous Marian per-secutions of the 1550s.[4]

As historians of the Reformation have argued persuasively, the attack on images was part and parcel of a larger campaign to replace the incarnational structure of medieval Christianity, with its emphasis on the physical presence of God in the world via the sacrament of communion and the miracles wrought by saints, with a representational culture anchored in the Word.[5] Text-based practices, such as reading Scripture and hearing sermons, replaced the "superstitious" ceremonies and rituals of the mass and the cult of saints, with far-reaching aesthetic consequences: the theology of *sola scriptura* was translated into an aesthetic of the plain—whitewashed meetinghouses instead of baroque churches, hard wooden benches instead of richly furnished pews with embroidered seat cushions and tapestries, simple block-print books instead of rosary beads and stained-glass windows, vernacular sermons on practical subjects instead of Latinate treatises on arcane doctrinal controversies. This was an epistemological as well as ecclesiological transformation of epic proportions. As the literary scholar James Simpson puts it, "a whole world of once numinous objects" had become "inert, oppressive things."[6] A dense semiotic universe rich with visual, aural, and tactile clues all pointing to the manifold presence of the divine in the world was reduced to a stark landscape of naked souls trembling before a remote and inaccessible deity. God was to be heard, not seen or felt or engaged in the physical world after 1517. This is, to be sure, a one-sided description of the changes wrought by the Reformation in the fabric of medieval piety. To focus, as I have, on the visual and material impoverishment of post-Reformation Europe is to ignore or slight the tremendous intellectual and psychological richness of a word-centered regime that produced such literary wonders as John Milton's epic *Paradise Lost* and Shakespeare's *Merchant of Venice*. Nor does it take into account the extraordinary invigoration of the inner life, the legendary soul struggles of ordinary men and women like Bunyan's Pilgrim and the London artisan Nehemiah Wallington whose spiritual agonies and triumphs, recorded faithfully in journals and diaries, helped birth a new literary genre, the modern novel.[7] Moreover, the severe visual anorexia of Reformation culture did not last long beyond its formative generation: by the seventeenth and certainly the eighteenth centuries the material life of Protestant communities had recovered much of the depth and texture it had lost in the zeal of early Reform (witness the elaborate illustrations of such foundational texts as John Foxe's *Acts and Monuments* and the Mennonite *Martyrs' Mirror*, described in Chapter 11 in this volume). Nonetheless, the notion of the Reformation as a powerful negative force, in which a visually rich material world was destroyed in the name of a severe and uncompromising commitment to the unadorned Word, is not fundamentally wrong.

Everywhere the Reformers seized power in early modern Europe, especially in the Calvinist countries of France, England, and the Netherlands, the destruction of images followed upon theological innovations as sure as thunder follows lightning. Great outbreaks of iconoclastic fervor occurred in the Swiss canton of Basel in 1529, in France in 1560–61, and in the Netherlands during the "Wonder Year" of 1566–67. England alone experienced three waves of iconoclasm before the great "deluge" of the 1640s, during the reigns of Henry VIII, Edward VI, and Elizabeth I.[8] John Weever's doleful survey of the iconoclasm committed in the early years of Elizabeth's reign, *Ancient Funerall Monuments* (1631), narrated the destruction. "Under colour of this Commission, and in their too forward zeale, they rooted up and battered downe, Crosses in Churches, and Church-yards, as also in other publike places they defaced and brake down the images of Kings, Princes, and noble estates.... They despoiled Churches of their Copes, vestments, Amices, rich hangings, and all other ornaments,...leaving Religion naked, bare, and unclad."[9] The brutal matter-of-factness of the journal of William Dowsing, who was commissioned by Parliament to enforce its ordinances of 1641 and 1643 "for the utter demolishing, removing, and taking away of all Monuments of Superstition and Idolatry," is an eloquent testament to the efficiency of the iconoclastic campaign that had so denuded England's ecclesiastical landscape by the 1640s. An entry on December 26, 1643, read, "We beat down about 110 Superstitious pictures, besides cherubims and ingravings." On January 5, 1643–44, he wrote, "We beate downe 3 crucifixes, and 80 superstitious pictures, and brake the rayles, and gave order to deface 2 grave-stones with Pray for our souls." And then one month later "we brake down 841 superstitious pictures." All entries were recorded without comment.[10]

The long shadow cast by the Roman church and its sacramental culture over the dreams and nightmares of Reformers, Puritans in particular, was felt as far away as the colonial seaports in the seventeenth and eighteenth centuries, despite the absence of anything remotely resembling Europe's chapels and cathedrals in these provincial outposts. Colonial iconoclasts were aided in their righteous desire to contribute to the cause of Reform by the Protestant tendency to conflate the despised physical objects of "popish" worship (altars, saints' images or statues, roods, crucifixes, stained-glass windows, surplices) with the rituals and gestures that had grown up around these objects in medieval ecclesiology (kneeling, making the sign of the cross, bowing before the altar): not only were the altars to be stripped and the roods pulled down, but the entire ceremonial structure of the medieval church was to be dismantled as well before the work of Reform could be complete. A group of lay Presbyterians in New York told the resident Anglican minister that among the other "Idolatrous" ceremonies of the Church of England, "the Sign of the Cross is the Mark of the Beast and the Sign of the Devil."[11] As a group, Puritans excelled at this kind of vicarious violence. Ann Kibbey suggests that what distinguished Puritans most clearly from other English iconoclasts was "their extension of iconoclastic motives to nonviolent symbolic acts," such as refusing to kneel at the Lord's Supper. Symbolic gestures became even more important as targets of iconoclasm as the material legacy of the medieval church was steadily effaced; by the seventeenth century, when there were precious few altars left to smash, symbolic acts of iconoclastic disobedience became the Puritans' "most characteristic trait."[12] The New England divine Samuel Mather, in a sermon he delivered in 1672 in Cambridge, Massachusetts, laid out the logic of Puritan iconoclasm for his colonial auditors. Mather argued for an expansive definition of the sin of idolatry: "Although none but the grosses kind of Idolatry, viz. *graven Images*, are expressly mentioned, yet, *under this one Instance is comprehended all the other sins of the same kinde, all other Inventions of men are included and comprehended under this* [emphasis in original]." The long list of Anglican "idols" he recommended for demolition included (in descending order of venality) the sign of the cross in baptism, kneeling at the Lord's Supper, bowing to the altar, and bowing to the name of Jesus, along with the more conventional targets of surplices, organs, and the Book of Common Prayer. When once a true Christian ventured down the path of idolatry, the road to hell was swift and certain. Like "bodily uncleanness," the lure of idolatry is "insatiable," Mather warned. "If you do but wear a Surplice for peace sake, why not as well admit the sign of the Cross in Baptism, or bow to an Altar, and in a little time you will find that the same Reason is as strong for bowing to an Image, to a Crucifix, and why not as well say Mass too, for the peace of the Church, and then at last swallow down everything, Submit to the Pope, worship the Beast, and so be damned and go to Hell."[13]

Under such a wide-ranging mandate, even so modest a remnant of Romish culture as the red cross of St. George embroidered in the royal ensign— this "badge of the Whore of Babylon," in Captain John Endicott's fighting words—demanded action. In 1634 the zealous residents of Salem, Massachusetts, ripped out the cross in perhaps the first recorded act of iconoclasm in the British colonies. The magistrates, including Governor John Winthrop, were not amused and acted swiftly to censure the unrepentant Endicott. They feared that the action "would be taken as an act of rebellion, or of like high nature, in defacing the king's colors; though the truth were," Winthrop was compelled to acknowledge, "it was done upon this opinion, that the red cross was given to the king of England by the pope, as an ensign of victory, and so a superstitious thing, and a relique of antichrist." In full sympathy with the thought behind the act ("we were fully persuaded that the cross in the ensign was idolatrous"), the General Court nonetheless acted to safeguard the Puritan commonwealth's political autonomy by ordering the ensign repaired—though they did try to finesse the issue by suggesting that the cross might be replaced by a "red and white rose."[14] When archaic relics of popish superstitions cropped up far from the prying eyes of the colony's parliamentary masters, the magistrates exercised no such restraint: the infamous maypole erected by Thomas Morton on his Plymouth plantation in 1623 was "cut down" (by none other than the iconoclast John Endicott) and Morton's house burned by order of the General Court.[15]

Crosses and maypoles, especially those that could be easily removed, were one thing; brick-and-mortar churches were quite another. For much of the first half-century of their existence the British colonies were spared the need to confront in any tangible way the presence of competing versions of Christianity in the form of chapels, meetinghouses, or churches. (The southern colonies present something of an exception to this generalization, which I'll explore below.) But the Restoration of the Stuart monarchy in 1660 and especially the political and religious compromises of the parliamentary settlement known as the Glorious Revolution in 1688 permanently altered the ecclesiastical landscape of British North America. When the king's agent Edward Randolph arrived in Boston in 1686 with his Anglican clergyman in tow, Massachusetts's Puritans were alarmed. "For the first time in New England's history," writes Kenneth Silverman, "a minister had worn a surplice and had publicly read the liturgy from the Book of Common Prayer." More outrages were to follow. On Good Friday the Puritans were forced to allow the Anglicans to use their meetinghouse for their own services, an uneasy arrangement that continued until King's Church opened three years later.[16] The era of Puritan hegemony was over.

In the eyes of "hot" Protestants, such as the Mathers, the elegant brick buildings that churchmen in Boston began to erect in the aftermath of the Restoration were nothing less than an abomination in the eyes of God and a direct challenge to their holy commonwealth. And they seized the first opportunity to make their hatred known. The ouster of the Catholic James

II and the bringing in of the Protestant monarchs William and Mary of Orange in 1688 ignited a mini-wave of iconoclastic fervor in the New England colonies. The call to arms came in a sermon by the inimitable Cotton Mather against the use of the Book of Common Prayer, which Edward Randolph believed "persuaded the people that we were idolatrous and therefore not fit to be entrusted longer with the Government."[17] When the residents of Boston rose up against their royal governor, they attacked the Anglican Church as well. "The Church itself had great difficulty to withstand their fury, receiving the marks of their indignation and scorn, by having their Windows broke to pieces, and the Doors and Walls daubed and defiled with dung, and other filth, in the rudest and basest manner imaginable."[18] The Quaker Thomas Maule corroborated this account, accusing his fellow Bostonians of "breaking the Church Windows, tearing the service Book, making Crosses of Mans Dung on the Doors, and filling the Key-holes with the same."[19] The Anglican minister, Samuel Myles, begged the king to intervene. "We are in a deplorable condition.... Young Mr. Mather informs the people that the reason for our calamities is permitting the little chapel for the Church of England among us. It is insufferable for it to stand, according to him, though it is battered and shattered most lamentably already."[20] Puritan New England was not the only region to experience iconoclastic outbreaks during the Glorious Revolution; the royalist faction in New York fought fire with fire in their battle against the Protestant party headed by Jacob Leisler, who reported the "miraculous deliverance from a fire which had been kindled in three different places in the turret of the church and in the fort. Six thousand pounds of powder were under the same roof with the fire, and the offender is suspected to be a papist who has been there before. Thus the city and people were saved from this hellish design."[21] As in New England and Maryland the campaign to oust the royal governor in New York was waged in explicitly religious terms, as a continuation of the long holy war against Catholic superstition and tyranny that militant Protestants had been engaged in for a century and a half.

And in fact war with Catholic France swiftly followed the installation of William and Mary on the British throne, and fears of Anglican inroads in the Puritan commonwealth became quickly swallowed up by more widespread fears of a revitalized papacy operating just beyond the borders of New England. The military conflict between New England and New France in the 1690s had its iconoclastic moments as well. When the combined forces of British, colonial, and Indian troops attacked the Canadian settlement at Port Royal in 1690, the Catholic chapel was burned along with the houses of royal officials and the town's warehouse. The official report of the expedition made it clear that the destruction of the church was not simply collateral damage but a premeditated act of violence modeled on the iconoclasm campaigns of 1641–43. "We cut down the Cross, rifled the Church, Pull'd down the high Altar, breaking their Images."[22] Governor Bradstreet boasted to his fellow rebel governor, Jacob Leisler of New York, that the fort was demolished and "their Crosses & Images broken down."[23] The booty that the commander of the expedition, Sir William Phipps, brought with him upon his return to Boston included, according to Owen Stanwood, a "variety of Catholic baubles, including surplices, communion wafers, and priestly vestments."[24]

It is not difficult to imagine the reactions of ordinary Bostonians to these "baubles" of popery circulating in their midst. Fears of a vast Catholic conspiracy to subvert Protestantism in Europe and the New World had been part and parcel of imperial expansion from the very beginning, and had received fresh support from the supposed "Popish Plot" of 1678 in England and the revocation of the Edict of Nantes by the French king in 1685. The final decades of the seventeenth century represent something of a high-water mark for militant Protestantism in the American colonies, as settlers from Maryland to New Hampshire rose up against royal governors and a resurgent Anglican establishment while following closely the alarming news from the Continent, which included a brutal Catholic offensive against the Huguenot minority in France as well as more immediate threats at home from the crypto-Catholic Stuarts. Puritans fully anticipated that their New World utopia would not be spared the ravages of renewed Catholic persecution. "The cup is going round the world," Cotton Mather warned in a 1686 sermon. "'Tis come into America."[25] Anti-Catholic polemics poured from the presses of New England with such titles as *A Sermon Wherein is shewed that the Church of God is sometimes a Subject of Great Persecution* (Increase Mather, 1681) and *The Church of Rome Evidently Proved Heretic* (Peter Berault, 1685). Crosses once again despoiled the landscape of New England, though in visionary rather than material form: Thomas Cobbett interpreted the "perfect crosse through the moone" that appeared in the skies over Ipswich, Massachusetts, on Christmas Day in 1682, as a portent of "a vigorous prosecution and spreading of popery, east, west, north & south."[26]

More ominous than these apparitions of popish power was the presence on the borders of British North America of a new kind of Catholic enemy, the Indian tribes allied with New France and New Spain who assaulted frontier communities with special vigor in the half-century of nearly continuous

imperial warfare that stretched from 1690 to 1763 with a brief hiatus in the
1720s and 1730s. The specter of a French-Indian alliance was terrifying on a
number of levels. To begin with, the Catholic French and Native Americans
were both regarded as children of the devil. The trope of Indian diabolism
that can be found in colonial writings from Peru to Maine was not merely a
metaphor for savagery but a literal description of native people's subservience
to a powerful and predatory devil in the eyes of New World Christians. The
devil had been resurrected by the Reformation into a potent malignant force
stalking Europe's villages, enticing thousands of weak-willed Christians into
heresy and witchcraft, and the dense forests of the New World were his natural home. Indians served Hobbomack (the English name for the evil spirit
that they believed to be the twin of Manitou, the Indian god of creation) just
as Catholics served Antichrist (the Pope). Their shared allegiance to the devil
transformed the military threat posed by the French-Algonquian alliance
into a spiritual threat that endangered the souls as well as lives of the English
settlers—a threat that was literalized in the form of New England prisoners
of war who abjured their Protestant heritage to embrace the Catholicism of
their Indian and French captors. The captives' plight, so vividly dramatized
in such spellbinding narratives as Mary Rowlandson's best-selling *The Sovereignty and Goodness of God* (1682), was the plight of the Reformation writ
large in the closing years of the seventeenth century as vulnerable Protestants everywhere seemed at the mercy of a shape-shifting Catholic enemy
who wielded simultaneously a "French ax and an Indian hatchet," in Cotton
Mather's combative phrase.[27]

As the anti-Catholic hysteria mounted, veterans of earlier battles against
the Church of England like Mather became more and more strident in their
rhetoric. He urged his fellow saints to show no mercy toward these "Raven-
ous howling Wolves": "*Turn not back* till they are *consumed*: *Wound* them that
they shall not be *able to Arise*; Tho' they *Cry*; Let there be none to *Save them*;
But *Beat* them small as the *Dust before the Wind*, and *Cast them out*, as the
Dirt in the Streets."[28] Mather's graphic language in this and other wartime
sermons he published in the 1690s resembles nothing so much as the accounts
of Protestant martyrs made famous in Foxe's *Book of Martyrs*, perhaps *the*
exemplary text of the English Reformation. Just as Foxe dwelt in loving detail
on the gruesome tortures suffered by the early Protestant martyrs, so too did
Mather recount *ad nauseum* every split skull, burnt limb, and skewered fetus
among the English victims of Indian butchery.[29] "Those *Devils Incarnate* have
Tyed their *Captives* unto Trees, and first cutting off their *Ears*, have made

them to Eat their own Ears, and then have broyled their whole *Bodies*, with slow Fires, dancing the mean while about them, and cutting out Collops of their Flesh," he wrote with typical enthusiasm.[30] His fellow New Englander Samuel Penhallow, in an unmistakable reference to the disemboweling of pregnant women by Catholic inquisitors depicted in the *Book of Martyrs*, charged that "Teeming Women, in cold Blood, have been ript open" by merciless savages.[31] Under such extremities colonists too could become martyrs in the wilderness of America. "You are Fighting, that the *Churches* of God may not be Extinguisht, and the *Wigwams* of Heathen swarming in their room: You are Fighting that the *Children* of God may not be made *Meals*, or *Slaves* to the veriest *Tygers* upon Earth. To Dy Fighting in such a Service, may pass for a sort of *Martyrdome*."[32]

While there are clear echoes of the Reformation discourse of martyrdom in the literature on Indian war, we have to search harder to find traces of iconoclastic violence. The one clear exception is the burning of Indian Bibles during King Philip's War, which Edward Gray suggests was motivated by the same spirit that led Spanish conquistadors to destroy Aztec pictographic texts during the conquest of Mexico, as tokens of idolatry. By the conclusion of the war in 1676 almost no copies of John Eliot's famed Indian Library survived, as Eliot himself admitted to a Dutch missionary. "In the late Indian war all the Bibles and Testaments were carried away and, burnt or destroyed," he lamented. [33] Bibles, both Indian and English, were disposed of by the Narragansetts themselves, in one notable incident by ripping open the corpse of an Englishman who had tried to shield himself with his Bible "and put[ting] his Bible in his belly" in a macabre echo of Reformation-era violence.[34] The majority were in all likelihood, however, destroyed by furious Puritan militiamen, for whom book burning had been something of a specialty during the English Civil War.

Indian Bibles aside, the material damage inflicted in the Indian wars was largely limited to English houses, gardens, and livestock. But if we are willing to look beyond the concrete to the symbolical, we can detect intriguing evidence of a more penetrating iconoclastic impulse at work in the representation of maimed bodies (Indian and English) that so powerfully punctuates the Puritan narratives of war and captivity. In an important sense Indians constituted "living images" whose destruction was sanctioned by the same reasoning that demanded the stripping of altars and smashing of idols in Reformation Europe.[35] Puritan iconoclasts of the Civil War era, such as the anonymous author of the pamphlet *The Case for all Crucifixes, Printed in the*

Climactericall Yeer of Crosses and Cross-men (1643), laid the groundwork for such a reading by explicitly comparing the destruction of idols to the martyrdom of dissenters in the Laudian regime. "Six years agoe or thereabouts, three Images were defiled all at once, which could breathe, and smell, and heare.... Those three were Pilloried, defaced, stigmatized, in plaine English, markt for Rogues, because they were faithfull and kept close to the Law of their God." Quoting from Judges 8.18, the pamphlet demanded, "*What manner of Images were they, which yee saw (or heard were) so abused?*" The answer: "*living Images*...spoyled and left wounded."[36] The notion of "living images" powerfully captures the fluidity of Puritan understandings of idolatry and its remedy, iconoclasm, as encompassing in different places and different times physical things, symbolic gestures, and flesh-and-blood human beings.

The interchangeability of people and icons, human beings and material objects, can be demonstrated from a number of practices in both the Old and New Worlds. Protestants in the Netherlands "'hung images of saints from the gibbets erected to execute iconoclasts." Statutes of saints were not merely destroyed, "they were tortured," according to Phyllis Mack Crew; "the eyes and faces of the portraits were mutilated or the heads cut off, as at an execution."[37] In England funeral monuments were "hackt and hewne apeece; Images or representations of the defunct broken, razed, cut, or dismembered." The more exalted the status of the deceased, the more vicious the attack; William Hackett, a self-declared prophet, was convicted of treason in the 1590s for having "razed and defaced Queen Elizabeth's coat of Armes, as also her picture, thrusting an iron instrument into that part, which did represent the breast and heart." (Hackett was hanged and in symbolic justice "bowelled and quartered" after his body was cut down.)[38] Iconoclasts in London anthropomorphized the massive Cheapside Cross by dismembering the figure of Christ limb by limb before consigning the remains to the flames, in deliberate imitation of the tortures inflicted on their coreligionists by persecuting prelates. A spate of serio-comic pamphlets lamenting the fate of "Jasper Crosse" who protested "my violent undoing" at the hands of an angry mob in the first year of the English Civil War hit the London streets in the 1640s. "I Jasper Crosse, scituated in Cheap-side, London,...in the yeare one thousand six hundred forty one, when almost everie man is to seeke a new Religion;...was assaulted and battered in the Kings highway, by many violent and insolent minded people, or rather ill-affected Brethren; and whether they were in their height of zeale, or else overcome with passion, or new wine lately come from New-England, I cannot be yet resolved." A second, more serious assault followed in 1643, in which the Cross lost first his nose, then his legs and arms to the mob before finally succumbing to the flames. "I draw no sword, nor do I wear long hair," he cried in self-defense. "They will divide my coat, my flesh, my bones.... You will have flesh for flesh."[39]

When we turn our attention to Puritans in the New World, and in particular to the context of Indian warfare and captivity, we see the same logic at work—"flesh for flesh"—but with a perverse twist. The dismembered Cheapside Cross, torn limb from limb, has its referential counterpart in the dismembered corpses that Indian and English raiding parties alike left in their wake as gruesome reminders of their power to desecrate as well as defeat their enemies. Torture, beheadings, and "hacking and hewing" of living bodies were forms of violence that colonial Americans were all too familiar with from their harrowing encounters with hostile Native Americans, in which the posthumous desecration of corpses and the scalping of the near-dead figured prominently as the most distinctive hallmarks of Indian warfare. During King Philip's War in 1675 two English prisoners were "taken by the Indians, who ripped them up from the bottom of the belly to the throat, and cleft them down the back throughout, and afterwards hung them up by the neck on a tree by the River side, that the English might see them as they passed by." Over time English soldiers proved to be as adept, if not more so, than Indians at using corpse dismemberment as a tactic of terror. When the English troops finally cornered Metacom, the leader of the bloodiest Indian war in American history, they dragged his body—"a doleful, great, naked, dirty beast"—out of the swamp and had him beheaded and quartered. The body parts were distributed among the soldiers as war trophies. Benjamin Church insisted that this was done in deliberate retaliation to the Indians' own customs of bodily desecration: "for as much as he had caused many an English man's body to lie unburied and rot above ground, not one of his bones should be buried." The widespread practice of providing bounties for Indian scalps produced a steady stream of Indian body parts (hair, sometimes with the head still attached) into New England's towns and villages for public display.[40]

The notion that Native Americans functioned on some level as icons to be smashed as well as military and political foes to be vanquished is, I would argue, one particularly good example of what Robert St. George has called the "poetics of implication." "In seventeenth-century New England," St. George writes, "if not among today's practicing historians, word and thing were inextricably linked, referentially interdependent, constantly implicated in each other's ways of making meaning."[41] The rhetorical parallels between descriptions of broken images in European iconoclastic literature and broken bodies in New World depictions of Indian war resembles the referential strategy St. George identifies as "symbolic diffusion," or the entanglement of the material world with the charisma that resides in sacred icons. The dismembered Cheapside Cross, torn limb from limb, has its referential counterpart in the dismembered corpses that Indian and English raiding parties alike left strewn over the colonial landscape.

The superficial parallels between descriptions of broken images in European iconoclastic literature and broken bodies in New World depictions of Indian war, however, mask a fundamental reorientation of symbolic logic: whereas European iconoclasts attacked objects *as if* they were people, New England Puritans attacked people *as if* they were objects. Moreover, European iconoclasts understood the difference between metaphor and metamorphosis: hanging an icon on a gibbet to mimic the persecution of actual people or dismantling the statue of the body of Christ were not acts meant to grant equivalence, but rather constituted a rejoinder, a counterargument to Catholic idolatry. *You treat images as if they were Gods; we will destroy images to show you that they are* not *Gods.* It is more difficult to decipher the logic behind New World bodily desecrations that seem in both form and purpose to imitate some of the characteristic traits of Old World iconoclasm. The theory (and I've been arguing that it's not my theory alone, but a theory with supporting evidence in Puritan rhetoric) that Native Americans were stand-ins for Old World icons is an example of Old World semiotics gone terribly awry. What had been an act of parody in one context had become an act of near-genocide in another context, with devastating consequences for Indians and English alike.

The English knew they had violated important cultural boundaries in their treatment of Native American bodies, including the boundary between legitimate cultural politics and outright savagery. As good Puritans they looked to the scenes of Indian war for providential meaning. What message did God intend by allowing his American children to be slaughtered like sheep? "Now since the INDIANS have been made by our God, The *Rod of His Anger*, 'tis proper for us to *Enquire*, whether we have not in some Instances, too far Imitated the *evil manners* of the *Indians?*"[42] The suggestion that English Puritans have become "Indianized" in the New World brings the iconoclastic metaphor full circle. For as good Calvinists the Puritans knew that the lure of idolatry was a snare that could entrap the most faithful Christians. The jeremiads that poured from New England presses in the late seventeenth century, accusing the settlers of everything from Sabbath-breaking to wearing periwigs, drove home the central message that the very success of the Puritan "errand into the wilderness" had bred new idols: wealth, security, fashionable dress, pride, complacency, sanctimony. In their comfortable homes and prosperous villages New Englanders worshipped false gods of their own, no better than the savages who so tormented them. Their most bitter enemy, the Quakers whom they persecuted viciously until ordered to desist by Charles II in 1661, told them so. "Such a Generation of *Blood-thirsty* men, Ravening after the Prey, after *Blood*, the *Blood* of the *Innocent*, who have been Ancient in your Cruelty, and have long been filling up your measure, who as soon as you had escaped the hands of those you feared in England, & gotten large Farmes about you, you sat down at Rest, and then soon began to exercise Dominion, & became Lords over the Faith of others," accused George Bishop. "Ye bloody *Butchers*! Ye Monsters of *Men*!"[43] Much as they wished to close their ears, New Englanders knew in their hearts that they had become idolaters too.

So far I have been telling a largely Puritan story about the mutability of images and the referential imperative that drove New Englanders to declare iconoclastic war against enemies both visible and invisible, including idols of their own making. What happens to the story if we widen our investigation beyond the well-tilled soil of New England and turn to the middle and southern colonies, where Anglicans ruled with a lighter touch and religious conflict was largely confined to verbal skirmishes? Here, too, we find churches attacked, anti-Catholic rhetoric deployed to justify sectarian violence, and Indians who functioned as stand-ins for more traditional enemies of church and state. Here, too, the crucible of imperial warfare served as the catalytic force converting Old World animosities into New World atrocities. The long and bloody border war between South Carolina and New Spain's northernmost territory, in particular, provided numerous occasions for the expression of colonial iconoclasm in ways that parallel the history of religious violence in New England.

The colonial South had one thing New England did not: actual Catholics who were neither foreign nor Indian. To be sure, there were English Catholics who ventured into Massachusetts during the seventeenth century, but they didn't stay long, for obvious reasons. And they certainly did not leave behind any tangible reminders of their religion, such as chapels or crucifixes, for Puritans to attack. Anglicans, not Catholics, were—as we have seen—the primary targets of Puritan iconoclasm in New England. Further south, however, there was a sizable English Catholic population in Maryland, founded by Lord Baltimore in part as a refuge for his persecuted coreligionists, and a smaller but stable community of Catholics in South Carolina. Catholic worship was discrete and rarely visible, however, in deference to the dominant English prejudice against the "Whore of Rome," which held sway even in Maryland. Baltimore cautioned his first governor in 1633 to "cause all Acts of Romane Catholique Religion to be done as privately as may be, and . . . [to] instruct all the Romane Catholiques to be silent upon all occasions of discourse concerning matters of Religion." The spotty historical record of religious encounters in the seventeenth century suggests these instructions were largely followed, though the rosy picture of religious harmony painted by early promoters—here, extolled George Alsop in 1666, there are no "Inquisitions, Martyrdom, [or] Banishments"—is an exaggeration.[44] Maryland's Catholics and Protestants came to blows in 1645 during Ingle's Rebellion; in 1656, when a Jesuit reported that four men "out of extreme hatred of our religion were pierced with leaden balls" during a pitched battle in the streets of Annapolis, and again in 1689 when the former Anabaptist preacher John Coode roused the Protestant citizens of the colony against their Catholic proprietors.

More typical, however, were symbolic acts of violence, such as that attributed in a Jesuit Relation to an apostate who, to express his newfound Protestant zeal, "was accustomed to smoke [his old prayer-beads] in his pipe with tobacco, after grinding them to powder, often boasting that he was eating up his 'Ave Marias'" (a more playful form of iconoclasm perhaps).[45] Some of our best evidence for this kind of episodic, extralegal sparring over sacred spoils comes from the field reports of the Society for the Propagation of the Gospel in Foreign Parts, the missionary arm of the Church of England, which sent licensed preachers into every colony to combat dissenters and convert the infidels. As was the case in New England, Anglicans were convenient targets for much confessional anger that might otherwise have been directed at Catholics in the British colonies. Anglicans and Presbyterians engaged in an unseemly tug-of-war over the pew cushions in a meetinghouse in Jamaica, Long Island, in 1707. "We had a shameful disturbance, Hauling and Tugging of Seats; shoving one the other off, carrying them out and returning again for more," wrote a disgusted John Bartow to the society.[46] His neighbor Thomas Haliday complained that in his parish the dissenters "most contemptuously carryed away all the Goods of the Church and at the same time told me to be gone that I was a knave and a villain."[47] When Jacob Rice arrived at his Newfoundland outpost in the fall of 1711, he was appalled to discover the sorry state of the church. "You may remember Srs that I told you how ye Church in this Country had been defaced by the Enemy," he wrote. Things now were "in a much worse condition than I then represented it, for the Seats, Pulpits, and Communion Table were all destroyed, the wainscot tore down, the floors ript up, the windows broke to pieces, and ye Church made a common field for Cows and Sheep."[48] Inclement weather and human poverty certainly took their toll on the chapels that were springing up everywhere south of Connecticut in the first half of the eighteenth century, even as the "sacramental renaissance" that historians of Anglicanism have identified was in full swing in the colonies.[49] The pace of reform was slow and uneven: while one rector could boast of the "handsome Pulpit, Reading Desk, Clerks Pew, Communion Table & a Chan. Rail'd in, all made of cedar" that his church sported in 1714, another South Carolinian complained the following year that "we are sadly incommoded in our Church, having no Common Prayer Books or Bible, but such as are miserably Spoiled and warn out."[50] As late as the 1760s, Southern churches were still in a state of disarray, with some "well ornamented" with "rich Pulpit Cloths and Coverings for the Altar" (St. Philips) and a "Steeple 196 feet high" (St. Michaels), while others had fallen "to decay" (St. James) or were "consum'ed by fire" (St. Andrews).[51]

Turning the sanctuary into a sty was one way to demonstrate disgust for a rival religion, and the missionaries had no doubts that this was deliberate vandalism, not mere neglect. John Urmston, a bilious sort in the best of times, blasted the rude Scots-Irish Presbyterians who made his tenure a living hell in the swamps of North Carolina. "This is a Nest of ye most Notorious Profligates upon the Earth," he swore. "All the Hoggs and Cattle flee thither [the Church] for Shade in Summer and Warmth in Winter, the first dig Holes and Bury themselves these with the rest make it a loathsome place with their Dung and Nastiness which is the Peoples regard to Churches."[52] The most pointed attack by dissenters ("a pack of vile, leveling common wealth Presbyterians in whom the Republican Spirit of 41 yet dwells") on an Anglican chapel was recorded by Charles Woodmason. "At the Congaree Chapel, they enter'd and partly tore down the Pulpit." The following Sunday "after the Communion was ended, they got into the Church and left their Excrements on the Communion Table."[53] The theme of filth is a recurring one in these reports of chapel desecrations: recall the crosses formed of dung left on the walls of King's Church in Boston in 1689 and the fouling of the priests' vestments in the 1714 attack on Trinity Church in New York with which I began this essay. Excrement is, of course, a universal motif in the anthropological literature on pollution, but it may have had even greater symbolic weight in a colonial environment where the line between civilization and nature was blurred to begin with and where animals and humans lived in alarmingly close proximity to one another.[54]

Filthy churches, damaged pews and altars, with the stink of swine and other, human, pests befouling the sanctuary: such was a common sight in the American backcountry, if these Anglican gentlemen-preachers are to be believed. Yet for all the damage inflicted, either deliberately or by the ravages of nature, on southern chapels, no sight was more evocative of iconoclastic rage than the charred remains of mission churches that successive waves of imperial and Indian warfare had left behind as monuments of intolerance in the early eighteenth century. In the early years of Queen Anne's War a combined force of 50 colonials and nearly 1,500 Apalachicola Indians under the command of the choleric James Moore attacked mission towns "with fire and sword" over a two-hundred-mile-wide swath of territory in the no-man's land between English Carolina and Spanish Florida.[55] Moore's report of the expedition highlighted the destruction of churches, homes, and the enslavement of thousands of Indian men, women, and children. In the town of Ayaville his troops assaulted the fort by "breaking the church door, which made a part of the fort, with axes." After two hours of fierce fighting "we thought fit to attempt the burning of the church, which we did."[56] It was a scenario that would be repeated in town after town. At Ayubale, after the resident priest promised martyrdom to all who would "fight against the pagans that came to disturb the law of God and destroy the Christian provinces," Moore's forces set fire to the mud-walled church, killing the warriors within and taking prisoner those who fled the flames.[57] In August 1704 Jon Sensbach reports, "more than one thousand Apalachee and Timucuan Catholics had been killed or enslaved," a figure vastly exceeding any casualty figures for religious conflicts elsewhere in the colonies. Sensbach makes a strong case that the Apalachee raids should be considered a species of holy war, in which the destruction of churches and religious objects such as Bibles and crucifixes figured prominently. If we haven't seen this as a religious war before, he suggests, it may have more to do with the ethnicity of the victims than with the nature of the violence itself.[58]

When the formidable Yamassee nation struck the Carolina settlement in 1715, in one of the bloodiest wars on record in the colonial era, they applied the lessons they had learned from the English attacks on Spanish missions, burning churches in remote parishes from Santee to Stono. Fittingly, this "barbarous & cruel war broke out in Passion Week."[59] The spectacle of churches in flames reminded one chronicler of a "Spanish *auto de fe*."[60] The comparison is apt. Like so many of the southeastern tribes, the Yamassees were at one time mission Indians, converted en masse by the Spanish with whom they forged a close political alliance. That alliance had been sorely tested in the decades leading up to 1715, as Spanish depradations drove many converts away from the church. "For every Yamassee or Apalachee who remembered his catechism and wanted his children baptized," Stephen Oatis claims, "there was another who had left Florida with some extremely hard feelings about the missions."[61] Yet even in their newly settled villages, far from the Spanish missionaries who had proved such untrustworthy friends, the Yamassees included within their ranks a large proportion of Catholic converts who regarded their English neighbors as heretics. David Ramsay recorded the speech of an Indian warrior who told him that "the English were all wicked heretics, and would go to hell, and that the Yamassees would also follow them if they suffered them to live in their country." And indeed the Spanish welcomed the defeated Yamassees back into their fort at St. Augustine "with bells ringing" after the English drove them out of Carolina.[62] "So great an eye sore are we to the Spaniards there that when some time since it was reported at ye Havanna that we were all taken or kill'd, they expressed their satisfaction thereat by ringing of bells, bonfires, and other demonstrations of joy from which we conclude the Spaniards will still encourage and insist our enemies all they can to kill and destroy us," warned a committee of the Carolina Assembly in 1716.[63] Clearly, the epic wars of religion between Catholic and Protestant that had reduced so many towns in Europe to ashes were not yet over. The New World had its own "passion play" to stage, this time with an Indian cast.[64]

How far did English colonials in the South reflect on their own culpability in these holy wars? Did they, like their Puritan counterparts to the North, engage in the kind of intense soul-searching that such horrific violence elicited in the jeremiads of Cotton Mather and company? We might expect the "swamp warriors" of the southern backcountry, long depicted in colonial historiography as utterly devoid of religious or even humanitarian sensibility, inured to brutishness by their intimate experience with African slavery and Indian warfare, to pass lightly over the religious symbolism of burnt chapels and tortured Indian bodies. And to some extent our skepticism would be warranted. While the occasional missionary from the Society for the Propagation of the Gospel, like the sensitive Francis Le Jau, agonized over the providential meaning of the Yamassee War, "this Terrible Judgment,"[65] most were more concerned with rebuilding their parsonages and dunning the society for back pay. Here, as in Boston, were Quakers to call them to account: the former governor of the colony, John Archdale, prophesied in 1707 that the English in Carolina would "suffer a sort of Transmigration of the Wolfish and Brutish Nature to enter our Spirits, to make our selves a Prey to our Enemies" for their many sins against the Indians and the Spanish, including the "Plunder of their Churches or Places of Worship."[66] Indians called Christians who displayed such brutishness "mad Wolves, and no more men."[67] The relative indifference of most white Protestants to the carnage inflicted by them or in their name on New World Catholics, Spanish and native, makes it difficult to assign clear iconoclastic motives to their actions. Yet when we consider the Old World background of these settlers, many of whom knew firsthand the brutality of religious persecution (Huguenot refugees, Scots-Irish Presbyterians, Anabaptist and Quaker exiles), and the inflamed religious rhetoric surrounding the early eighteenth-century wars between Protestant England and its Catholic rivals, a good circumstantial case can be made that the Carolina settlers knew, and approved, the iconoclastic message their actions conveyed.

Jump ahead sixty years in time. The American colonies stand on the brink of war with their imperial masters, and John Adams is taking a break from his labors as a delegate to the First Continental Congress to explore the religious back alleys of Philadelphia. Wandering into St. Mary's Catholic Church during Sunday Mass, he writes to his wife Abigail in October 1774, of the "awfull" scene he is witness to:

> This Afternoon's Entertainment was to me most awfull and affecting.
> The poor Wretches, fingering their Beads, chanting Latin, not a
> Word of which they understood.... Their holy Water—their Crossing
> themselves perpetually—their Bowing to the Name of Jesus, wherever
> they hear it—their Bowings and Kneelings, and Genuflections before
> the Altar. The Dress of their Priest was rich with Lace—his Pulpit
> was Velvet and Gold. The Altar Piece was very rich—little Images and
> Crucifixes about—Wax Candles lighted up.... Here is every Thing
> which can lay hold of the Eye, Ear, and Imagination. Every Thing
> which can charm and bewitch the simple and Ignorant. I wonder how
> Luther ever broke the spell.[68]

Performing a kind of verbal iconoclasm for his wife, Adams offers a striking summary of the ceremonies and objects that so enraged Protestants in Europe and the New World during the Reformation era. His description tells us just how far the ecclesiastical landscape of the British colonies had come from its visually and materially impoverished beginnings and just how far the colonists themselves had come in their ability to observe such "baubles of popery" without resorting to violence to eradicate them. Nicknamed the "Last Puritan" by his contemporaries, Adams is a good barometer of changing attitudes toward religious things in late colonial North America. Historians speak confidently of the inexorable march toward legal and de facto toleration of religious difference in the Anglo-American world over the course of the eighteenth century, and the primitive urge to smash altars is usually considered one of the casualties of a modern legal regime—along with the desire to hang sharp-tongued old women as witches. The story of John Adams's tour of St. Mary's is certainly compatible with this progressive narrative, but it also tells us more. It tells us that the material face of Catholicism still had the power to shock, to overwhelm sober Protestant sensibilities with its vibrant color, texture, and richness; that the old argument between images and words as reliable conduits of divine truths was alive and well in late colonial Philadelphia; that enlightened Protestants were still fearful of the bewitching effects of Latin on the "ignorant and simple"; that the cause of Reformation—to "break the spell" of the medieval church—was not yet completely won. Adams took up his pen rather than "fire and sword" to do battle with these cunning idols, and this, too, tells us that an important shift in tactics had occurred between the 1714 vandalism of Trinity Church and the 1774 rhetorical demolition of a Catholic mass. The old ways did not die easily, however, and in fact the Revolutionary War saw an upsurge in iconoclastic violence that rivaled the destruction of Anglican symbols during the Glorious Revolution a century before. A mob in Hebron, Connecticut, tarred and feathered several Anglicans in September 1774 and, in the words of the horrified local minister, proceeded to destroy St. Peters's "Windows and rent my Cloaths, even my Gown, etc. Crying out down with the Church, the Rags of Popery etc." As the empire came to an end, Americans "engaged in an orgy of iconoclastic violence in the streets," writes Brendan McConville: "attacking churches, ripping down tavern signs, beheading royal statues, searching for any imperial symbol to destroy."[69] John Adams was not the "last puritan" after all, it seems.

What in the end are we to make of this long journey from the burning of Pequot Indians in 1637 to the burning of Anglican chapels in the Revolutionary War? However we slice the evidence, it is still incontrovertible that iconoclastic violence in the British American colonies never reached the levels of destruction seen in England, France, Germany, and the Netherlands during the religious wars of the sixteenth and seventeenth centuries. There were simply too few religious objects to attack, even if the will to destroy was there. Merely counting the number of churches vandalized and Bibles burnt and crucifixes ground to powder would yield a rather paltry sum. Their very rarity, however, made these isolated acts of violence exceptionally stark. Considered against the total number of Anglican and Catholic churches in existence in the British colonies, the dozen or so attacks we can document amount to a substantial ratio. This is especially true in the American South, where perhaps one quarter of Anglican parishes reported some form of vandalism or acts of desecration in the fifty years between the first arrival of Anglican missionaries in the 1680s and the outbreak of the Great Awakening in the 1740s. That's a pretty impressive figure.

The one area in which we have seen violence on a mass scale, the killing of Indians and the burning of mission towns, had unmistakable iconoclastic echoes, I have argued, especially in Puritan New England. Here religious and racial enmities were so interwoven as to be analytically inseparable. The most we can say—and it is saying a lot—is that the rage expressed in the desecration of Indian bodies and mission chapels derived in part from a deep well of spiritual anxieties and animosities whose source lay in the bloody European past as much as in the unsettled American present. If we add these thousands of native deaths to our list of the victims of settler iconoclasm, the historical record would suggest that British America experienced its own "deluge" of iconoclasm during the formative years of empire building, despite the material barrenness of its ecclesiastical landscape and the institutional weakness of its orthodox establishments. This is truly "iconoclasm without icons."

Final Reflections

Spenser and the End of the British Empire

Paul Stevens

It might well be argued that Protestant England's British Empire reached its apogee in June 1897 with Queen Victoria's Diamond Jubilee, the sixtieth anniversary of her accession to the throne.[1] What had begun as a series of limited Atlantic enterprises in the sixteenth century had recovered from the humiliating collapse of its first, American-centered empire in 1784 to reproduce itself as an even mightier global polity, an empire whose new center was India and on whose extensive dominions, colonies, and territories the sun never set. Few would have predicted in 1897 that within another sixty years this colossus would have almost completely disappeared: certainly not Second Lieutenant W. L. Spencer-Churchill of Her Majesty's Fourth Hussars. On his way home from India early in that same Jubilee summer, Lieutenant Churchill took a two-week holiday in Italy. The focus of his brief tour was Rome. As he put it years later, as he approached the Capitol Hill, "I read again the sentences in which Gibbon has described the emotions with which in his later years for the first time he approached the Eternal City, and though I had none of his credentials of learning it was not without reverence that I followed in his footsteps."[2] The reverence Churchill felt was for both Gibbon, whose style he painstakingly imitated, and for the Enlightenment historian's elegiac story of decline and fall.[3] Gibbon always meant a great deal to Churchill, but in 1930, when he wrote these words, he perhaps understood Gibbon's sense of loss considerably more than he had in 1897. His middle-aged memoir, *My Early Life,* is suffused with a longing for the past, for an imperial world and the brilliant culture it realized that was now felt to be fast vanishing: "Scarcely anything material or established which I was brought up to believe was permanent and vital," he reflects, "has lasted. Everything I was sure or was taught to be sure was impossible, has happened" (67). From the early 1930s on, almost all Churchill's apparently contradictory passions, including his unrelenting opposition to both Nazi tyranny and Indian democracy, were driven not so much by wild ambition and the desire for personal glory as by the longing to recover the "permanent and vital" world of 1897. His rearguard-looking stance is caught in his Guildhall speech of 10 November 1942, when immediately after the Allies' first comprehensive victory over the Nazis and their Italian partners at Alamein, he declared: "I did not become the King's first minister to preside over the liquidation of the British Empire."[4]

Another sixty years on, over the last decade or so, the term *empire* has acquired a dramatic new currency. Like its cognate term *imperialism*, the term Joseph Schumpeter's work did so much to illuminate,[5] *empire* is a catch-all phrase, usually taken to mean some kind of aggressively expansive entity or polity whose claims to authority are absolute. My principal aim in this essay is to enlist the aid of Churchill's "ancestor," Edmund Spenser, in coming to a fuller understanding of what Churchill might have felt and what we might mean by *empire*. My argument falls into two parts: first, I want to focus on the role Protestantism played in stimulating and shaping English or British imperial expansion; and second, I want to consider what it might tell us about the larger significance of the term *empire*. David Armitage's impressive analysis of empire in his important book *The Ideological Origins of the British Empire* seems an appropriate place to begin because it so quickly gets us to the heart of the matter.[6]

The Origins of the British Empire

It is a measure of Armitage's ambition that he opens his book with a parody of Gibbon's *Decline and Fall of the Roman Empire* that is only slightly self-mocking. According to the logic of Armitage's somewhat arch allusions, the first British Empire in the middle of the eighteenth century had reached a point of stability and definition comparable to that of the Roman Empire in the Age of the Antonines: "The frontiers of that extensive monarchy were guarded by a common religion and by the Royal Navy," he says; "the gentle, but powerful influence of laws and manners had gradually cemented the union of the provinces. Their free, white inhabitants enjoyed and produced the advantages of wealth and luxury" (1). Armitage's purpose is not, however, to explain the decline and fall of this great, albeit imperfect, empire but to reveal its origins.

More important, his purpose is to transume or out-do Gibbon by showing how origins as Gibbon might have understood them, origins as deep-rooted, underlying, or necessary causes, are a fiction. What is remarkable about Armitage's book is its unusually thoughtful emphasis on contingency. He does not doubt that the British Empire in the 1740s identified itself as "Protestant, commercial, maritime, and free" (8), but he sets out to demonstrate that this self-identification was a post-hoc rationalization of characteristics that had actually emerged in a random, bewilderingly complex, and often contradictory manner. There is nothing inevitable, necessary, or natural about Armitage's empire. Deeply influenced by Quentin Skinner's version of Nietzsche, he knows only too well that etiology, the study of origins, can become "teleology in reverse" (5) and is determined to construct a genealogy of empire which avoids that danger. In one sense his book is about how the first British Empire came to be what it was before its collapse during the American Revolution. In another sense it is a sustained polemic against the explanatory force of ideology as identity, that is, an argument against those master narratives that aim to show how a specific system of beliefs might interpellate or, as Gibbon would put it, gently insinuate itself into the minds of men, derive vigor from opposition, and finally erect an empire. Most immediately, it is this polemic that I wish to contest: I wish to do so because in its empiricism it limits ideology to political argument or "sectional interest" and effectively constitutes a nominalist assault on any general theory of empire.

Armitage's method is to proceed both synchronically and diachronically, taking each of the British Empire's defining characteristics and analyzing it as it comes most powerfully into focus. In each case he is determined to show how the characteristic in question, whether it be "empire" itself, Protestantism, or any of the other characteristics he feels relevant, emerged dialogically, almost accidentally as "a contribution to political argument, not a normative, self-conception" (172). For Armitage these arguments are always textual, dominated by a surprisingly limited number of key discourses, and almost always unresolved. They usually "fail to square the circle," as he likes to put it, because they fail to meet Skinner's legitimation principle. Almost all the contenders for the role of "taproot," *arche*, or origin of empire turn out to be vulnerable when subjected to the acid test of Skinner's belief that "what it is possible to do in politics is generally limited by what it is possible to legitimize."[7] Thus, the legacy of Rome, the explanatory force of the term *empire* itself, is extremely limited, for while the language and symbolism of empire could provide early modern polities, especially composite monarchies like Spain or multiple kingdoms like England-Scotland-Ireland, "with the resources for the legitimation of their independence" (34), they could not produce arguments capable of legitimizing the suppression of internal differences, especially those between the three kingdoms of the British archipelago. Similarly, the ability of Protestantism to explain the ideological origins of the empire is limited. Protestantism fails because although the imperatives of Scripture "encouraged and legitimated migration and even evangelicisation," they could not provide a lawful justification for either possession or sovereignty (96). In Armitage's view the breakthrough comes not with a theory or even a political debate but with an event. It is the spectacular growth of overseas trade in the decades after the Restoration that provides the insight that allows British people to rationalize their burgeoning empire. As the growth of trade is seen to encourage and be encouraged by both individual liberty and overseas expansion, so it becomes possible to theorize commerce and legitimize the idea "that liberty and empire might be reconciled within [one] political economy" (147). And so, he concludes, the "association of religious and political liberty with freedom of trade became an enduring ideological foundation of the British Empire" (167).

The chief value of Armitage's learned and forcefully argued book is as a corrective to overly thematic or what he calls "straight line" (24) stories of empire. Armitage's favorite self-representation is that of an iconoclast or Talus-like breaker of myths. The book's most immediate weakness is the iconoclast's overdependence on the flail of the legitimation principle. The principle itself assumes a rationalism in politics that is hard to reconcile with either experience or early modern textual evidence. In this case it consistently underestimates the extraordinary ingenuity of politicians, merchants, and settlers in justifying their behavior. And in doing so it shifts attention away from the crucial category of motivation. Once we return our focus to the desires that drive legitimation, then ideology as identity looms as large as ever. In the book's longest and most fiercely argued chapter, after conceding that Protestantism should have provided "the solvent of difference" in state and empire (61), Armitage concludes that there were in fact "no identifiably or exclusively Protestant origins of British imperial ideology" (99). This is quite a stretch. Only a narrowly held concentration on the letter of Protestant doctrine and the *apparent* limitedness of its specifically legal role in justifying colonial practice could allow such a conclusion. The spirit tells a different story. It reveals the degree to which the Protestant emphasis on the argument of grace pervades English culture, insinuates itself into the minds of men and women in all three of Britain's kingdoms and moves so many of them to imagine a new kind of empire, an empire in which the working of grace manifests itself in what Paul Kennedy calls the "initiative, endurance, and will" of its mercantile class.[8] As the examples of Catholic empires like those of Portugal, Spain, and France make abundantly clear, early modern European expansion cannot be explained in terms of Protestantism alone. That would be absurd. But while no form of Christian belief was immune from the expansive imperatives of the Gospels, in Protestantism, to the degree that God's grace was perceived as a direct and unmediated gift to the individual believer, those imperatives seem to have taken on a peculiar force in shaping England's imperial ideology.

In order to emphasize the relative poverty of that ideology, Armitage quotes D. A. Brading: "What is there in English literature to compare to the letters of Hernan Cortes or the 'true history' of Bernal Diaz" (qtd. 63)? The answer is easy. Consider Spenser or Shakespeare. Consider something as familiar as Shakespeare's universalizing account of the opposition between the law and gospel in *The Merchant of Venice.* There the argument of grace, the quality of mercy itself, is secularized in Antonio's risk-taking merchant adventuring and so made to idealize the very overseas trade that so ironically provides Armitage with the way out of the impasse his overzealous genealogical argument creates.[9] As Antonio explains to Shylock, capital "venture" is a divine thing, a thing not in the adventurer's "power to bring to pass / But swayed and fashioned by the hand of heaven" (I.iii.88–90). And so, for so many of the Elizabethan nationalists who associated themselves with Leicester House, was empire itself. If the circulation of grace as it appears in Shakespeare served to idealize the radical expansion of overseas trade, so the descent of grace as it appears in Spenser served to idealize many things, but, most immediately, overseas military expansion in Ireland and America. My point is that the desires aroused by Scripture, especially as they were politicized, secularized, and increasingly aestheticized, proved a potent inducement to their subsequent legitimation.

The Argument of Grace

The role of grace in stimulating the military origins of British imperial ideology might at first sight seem more than a little counterintuitive. But the Christian emphasis on grace is from the beginning rooted in an act of textual violence against its own cultural origins in the Hebrew Scriptures. Central to the polemical purpose of the gospel is the desire to distinguish its "good news" from the Mosaic law. John's gospel puts it this way: "For the law was [indeed] given by Moses, but *grace and truth came by Jesus Christ*" (John 1:17-18; my emphasis).[10] The assertion that grace in its largest sense— of surplus, forgiveness, going beyond the law, of a giving that produces more and more giving—is peculiar to the Christian scriptures is, of course, a misrepresentation, an act of appropriation, or to use Harold Bloom's term *transumption*. Yahweh's willingness to redeem Sodom and Gomorrah in the Hebrew Scriptures, for instance, and his decision to speak directly to Job, to answer his complaints about the inequity of the law and still justify him, are clearly acts of grace. But since Christian doctrine considers grace the unique result of Christ's redemptive sacrifice, it can only tolerate other accounts of grace as types or imperfect models of its own truth. Its *locus classicus* is the Sermon on the Mount in Matthew 5-7. There, Christ offers a detailed explanation of the relationship between the law and the gospel, that the new dispensation does not mean the abrogation of the law but its fulfillment. It means that not only are we to observe the law but to exceed it: we are to be perfect as our heavenly father is perfect, that is, we are to imitate the grace of his Son in giving, in turning the other cheek, going the extra mile, and most important in loving our enemies and praying for them, especially those who persecute us (Matt. 5:44). This articulation and the general significance of grace is constantly being reinterpreted and developed throughout the epistles, but in the Epistle to the Ephesians it takes a radical turn.

Paul, or whoever it actually was who composed the letter to the Ephesians,[11] wrote it from prison and clearly had great difficulty praying for those who were persecuting him. On the one hand, his account of grace is, as one would expect, expansive, boundless, and utterly inclusive. Grace in the epistle even goes beyond Christ's sermon and completely abolishes the Mosaic law, "*even* the law of commandments *contained* in ordinances" (Eph. 2:15). It does so in order to transcend the critical distinction between Jew and Gentile, and so create, the author says, "one new man" or one humanity in place of two (Eph. 2:15). On the other hand, the letter immediately proceeds to reinscribe difference, articulating an intensely combative determination to identify the other and contest the gathering power of its enemies. Even as it insists that "we wrestle" against spiritual not physical enemies, the distinction collapses as the letter focuses all too ambiguously on "rulers"

and the "spiritual wickedness in high places" (Eph. 6:12). Similarly, even as
the letter welcomes Gentiles into the new dispensation of grace, it reminds
them of what they once were and proceeds to express anything but love for
those who have refused grace: they are degenerate, says the letter—having
their "understanding darkened, being alienated from God through the ignorance that is in them, because of the blindness of their heart," being "past
feeling" and having "given themselves over unto lasciviousness, to work
all uncleanness with greediness," they are clearly beyond the pale (Eph.
4:18-19). Over and again, the focus of the epistle is on the *reception* rather
than the *donation* of grace. Such reception is only possible through faith,
the letter insists, but faith in Ephesians is not so much a matter of belief
as one of strength, muscularity, or will to power: "be strong in the Lord,"
the Ephesians are admonished, "be strong in the Lord and in the power of
his might" (Eph. 6:10). Only by putting on the "whole armour of God,"
the "shield of faith," and the "sword of the Spirit" can the Ephesians hope
to receive the grace that will finally enable them to stand against the Devil
(Eph. 6:11–17). Grace, it is implied, is a surplus of explicitly military power
coming to the rescue. Like Ezekiel's vision or Milton's chariot of paternal
deity, grace has become a matter of shock and awe.

In much the same way that the spiritual tenor of the parable of the
talents is coopted by its economic vehicle, so here the same spiritual tenor
is coopted by its military vehicle, and it is entirely fitting that the Epistle
to the Ephesians should be the principal biblical text with which Spenser
opens his chivalric romance, *The Faerie Queene*. In his prefatory letter to
Sir Walter Ralegh he says, "In the end the Lady told him [the knight soon
to be revealed as St. George] that unlesse that armour which she brought,
would serve him (that is the armour of a Christian man specified by Saint
Paul v. Ephes.) that he would not succeed in that enterprise, which being
forthwith put upon him with dewe furnitures thereunto, he seemed the
goodliest man in al that company, and was well liked of the Lady."[12] My
point here is that Spenser's often monstrous militarism is not simply a
function of his colonial situation, but that there is also a degree to which
his colonial situation is itself an effect of Scripture's totalizing imaginations, especially as they are read and reread in various early modern Protestant communities searching for political guidance. In order to develop
this point we need to look more closely at Spenser and the Protestant "New
English" settlers in Ireland.

Gracious Spenser I: Possession and Sovereignty

The argument of grace is as important as it is because of the enormous confidence it afforded Protestants in their expansive enterprises. As it appears in
a text like Ephesians, grace seems specifically designed to confront and over-
awe the degenerate, whether they be Roman authorities or Irish kerns. The
most persuasive prevailing representation of Spenser is that of a profoundly
conflicted, Mulcaster-educated humanist, whose poetics, to use Richard Mc-
Cabe's telling phrase, "interrogate his politics."[13] From Ciaran Brady to Mc-
Cabe's magisterial book, *Spenser's Monstrous Regiment*, Spenser is taken to
exemplify the tragedy of Renaissance humanism rendered monstrous by its
being "imposed on a colony rather than inculcated in a people" (McCabe 6).
There is much to this view, but its limitation, so it seems to me, is that it tends
to turn Spenser into Conrad's Kurtz; and, as Thomas Herron has suggested, it
underestimates the extraordinary resilience of Protestantism in shaping identity
and behavior.[14] Most important, I would add, it underestimates the power of
grace in reassuring Protestants of their election and so stimulating expansive
action. Whatever despair Spenser might feel on contemplating the heart of his
own darkness, there stands universal truth ready to reassure him about the efficacy of grace, just as she would Redcross Knight: "What meanest thou by this
reprochfull strife?"she asks. "Is this the battell, which thou vauntst to fight." Do
not "let vaine words bewitch thy manly hart, / Ne diuelish thoughts dismay
thy constant spright. / In heavenly mercies hast thou no part? / Why should
thou then despeire, *that chosen art?*" Remember "Where iustice growes, there
growes eke greater grace" (*FQ* I.ix.52–53, my emphasis).[15] Therefore, rise up,
she says, leave this place and take possession of Una's promised land. As John
Bradley has pointed out, the motto over the entrance to the New English castle
at Lismore read "God's providence is our inheritance."[16] Even now at the end
of empire the echoes of the argument of grace can still be heard among Ulster's
Protestants. Forced to confront the might of Gloriana Redux in the form of
Margaret Thatcher, the Reverend Ian Paisley invokes the parable of the mustard
seed. In that parable grace says if you have faith the size of a mustard seed, you
can move mountains: "nothing will be impossible to you" (Matt. 17:20). So in
his December 1985 sermon, "A Prime Text for a Prime Minister," Paisley says
this: "God has a purpose for this province and this plant of Protestantism sown
here in this north-eastern part of this island. The enemy has tried to root it out,
but it still grows today, and I believe like a grain of mustard seed, its future is

going to be mightier yet."[17] Armed with the Word, Paisley has none of Kurtz's self-doubt or sense of horror.

Nowhere is the confidence-sustaining power of grace more crucially deployed than in Spenser's *View of the Present State of Ireland*. The situation of the New English in April 1598 when the *View* was first registered was fast becoming as desperate as that of the Ephesians in Paul's epistle, and the emphasis in Spenser's text, just as it is in Paul's, is on receiving rather than giving grace. At the climax of the dialogue Eudoxus and Irenius have arrived at an impasse. Rational discourse has done all that it can do, and the desire for moral balance that animates the law's governing concept of equity has been cruelly frustrated. It is vain, says Irenius, "to prescribe lawes where no man careth for keeping of them, nor feareth the daunger for breaking of them."[18] At this moment, Irenius could be speaking to Armitage: it is vain to talk of Skinner's legitimation principle when these people will not do what we require of them. Both Irenius and Eudoxus feel that the reformation of Ireland now needs "the strength of a mightier power" (92). That power reveals itself in Irenius's draconian plan to go beyond the law by resorting to the sword. As they begin to discuss it, it is clear that the argument of grace is in Spenser's mind because Eudoxus and Irenius act out the roles of Abraham and Yahweh from Genesis 18[19]—the same passage that Milton uses in *Paradise Lost* to articulate the Son's amplification of the Father's intention that "Man should find grace" (III.145).[20] To do otherwise, says the Son, quoting Genesis 18, "that be from thee far, / That far be from thee" (III.153-54). In Genesis 18 itself Yahweh decides that the degenerate cities of Sodom and Gomorrah are to be cut off. Abraham objects but with a speech act indicating his faith in Yahweh's justice: "Wilt thou also destroy the righteous with wicked?" he inquires. "*That be far from thee* to do after this manner, to slay the righteous with the wicked," he affirms. "And that the righteous should be as the wicked, *that be far from thee*: Shall not the judge of all the earth do right?" (Gen. 18:23-25; my emphasis). Yahweh relents and offers to spare both cities if one righteous man be found in either of them. His grace is evident in his willingness to go beyond the needs of equity and spare the wicked on behalf of the righteous. In any event no righteous are found, and his grace is transformed into the mighty power that saves the angels from sodomy and destroys the cities. In Spenser's text it is Eudoxus who objects and Irenius's response with its telltale emphasis on the phrase "far be it from me" assimilates Yahweh's gracious concession into the words of Abraham's challenge: "By the sword which I named," says Irenius, "I did not meane the cutting off all that nation with the sword, which *farre bee it from mee*, that I should ever thinke so desperately, or wish so uncharitably" (93, my emphasis). In the event, all those who oppose the Yahweh-like power arrogated by Irenius to "the royall power of the Prince" (93) will be cut off and mercy in the *View*, unlike grace in *Paradise Lost*, collapses into justice. That is, in Spenser's text the grace of the Sermon on the Mount collapses into the "imperiall" justice of Artegal and the merciless, providential power of his squire, Talus.[21] But grace does this, it needs to be emphasized, not simply through the distorting pressures of Spenser's colonial situation but through the independent, mediating agency of Christian Scripture itself. As Linda Gregerson puts it, "the subject is formed in subjection *by* the power of words,"[22] and the power of the Word is always there with Protestant nationalists like Spenser constantly shaping and directing understanding and action. This is not to say that the argument of grace functions like some vast monological machine, some mindless "dominant ideology," but that under certain circumstances and in particular discursive communities it provides a repository of rhetorical triggers and strategies of great authority for the legitimation of expansion.

As Scripture moves Spenser, so it does innumerable other English empire builders throughout the seventeenth century. In his widely publicized letter of 1614 to the governor of Virginia, for instance, John Rolfe legitimizes his union with Pocahontas specifically by attributing his love for her to the promptings of grace overturning the Mosaic law's prohibition against marrying outside the nation.[23] In his 1625 tract "Virginias Verger," Samuel Purchas appeals to the gracious donation of dominion in Genesis 1:28 to claim possession and sovereignty in Virginia.[24] In his 1655 *Declaration Against Spain*, Oliver Cromwell appeals to the universalizing argument of Acts 17:26 to claim possession and sovereignty in the Caribbean.[25] In fact, despite Armitage's argument to the contrary, there is hardly a point when English colonial possession and sovereignty in the late sixteenth and early seventeenth centuries is not legitimized by an appeal to some version of the Gospel's argument of grace. Most strikingly, it is the argument of grace that animates James Harrington's theory of empire in his *Oceana* of 1656, a theory that was to play such an important role in the intellectual genesis of the U.S. Constitution.[26] J. G. A. Pocock makes the point this way: "Oceana is to be a commonwealth for expansion, but...there is no hint of ultimate doom," of impermanence or that at some point the empire will exhaust itself and decline; "Harrington seems to have discerned messianic or apocalyptic possibilities for his republic, which permitted him to turn from *virtu* to grace in the completion of his vision."[27] Harrington's imperial republic is imagined as a function of grace at work in the world and its specific political purpose is "patronage," that is, the propagation of balanced popular sovereignty, civil liberty, and liberty of conscience across the globe (332).[28] Such patronage or imperial expansion is understood as an imperative: "if the empire of a commonwealth be patronage, to ask whether it be lawful for a commonwealth to aspire unto the empire of the world is to ask whether it be lawful for her to do her duty, or to put the world in a better condition than it was before" (328). At the climax of this passage Lord Archon, an idealized representation of Cromwell, insists on England's imperial exceptionalism: that the empire of Oceana is our first world, the garden of God, "the rose of Sharon, and the lily of the valley" (333).[29]

Critical as this point is, Spenser's representation of grace has another more important insight to offer. Not only does it stimulate the English to expansion, but even in its very virtue it insulates them against difference and cultural mutability, most significantly by enabling belief to overwhelm irony.

Gracious Spenser II: Immutability

One of the most sacred moments in *The Faerie Queene,* so John Milton and Henry Vaughan clearly felt, was the epiphany of grace on Mount Acidale in Book VI. For Milton, Mount Acidale provides one of the principal sources for his representation of paradise. In Spenser's poem, as in *Paradise Lost,* it is the original *locus amoenus,* "a place, whose pleasaunce did appere / To passe all others," says Spenser. "For all that euer was by natures skill / Deuized to work delight, was gathered there" (*FQ* VI.x.5–6). As Milton's recreation of Acidale in Eden makes clear, discovering this hilltop meadow "bordered with a wood / Of matchless hight" (*PL* 6) is like entering our first world. It is profoundly moving. More than anything else it is the home of innocence and boundless grace. For there, "airs, vernal airs," says Milton,

> Breathing the smell of field and grove, attune
> The trembling leaves, while Universal *Pan*
> Knit with the *Graces* and the *Hours* in dance
> Led on th'Eternal Spring. (*PL* IV: 264–68)

For Vaughan in *Silex Scintillans,* Mount Acidale becomes the home of Christ's grace in the fullness of its regenerative agency.[30] The wind that is heard but not seen in the hilltop's "fair, fresh field" ("Regeneration" 27) recalls Christ's words to Nicodemus in John's Gospel. Grace in the form of the spirit of the Word, that is, Christ himself, cannot be summoned at will: it blows "where it listeth and thou hearest the sound thereof, but canst not tell whence it cometh, and whither it goeth: so is every one who is born of the Spirit" (John 3:8). So it is here on Spenser's Acidale. For as Colin, that is, the poet and creator of the graces himself, explains to Calidore, the graces cannot be summoned; once they have disappeared, "none can bring them in place, / But whom they of them selues list so to grace" (FQ VI.x.20). The Senecan graces invoked on Mount Acidale are being assimilated into Christian revelation and made to exemplify the surplus or circulation of grace as it is imagined in the Sermon on the Mount—giving, not demanding or summoning, produces plenitude. Spenser's graces dance in such a way as to exemplify boundless liberality—that "good should from us goe, then come in greater store."[31] Here classical civility and Christian grace become one. For people of my generation and for older scholars like Edgar Wind or Thomas Roche, this epiphany of grace, even when located in a colonial landscape, was not seen as a grand gesture of poetic isolation, a futile act of cultural hypocrisy, but as a moment when we came to see Renaissance culture at its ideal.[32] "Colin's explanation of the vision of the dance," says Roche, "is the most self-conscious artistic act in Renaissance poetry." The poet in the persona of his character Colin, Roche continues, enters the poem to emphasize that grace is "the source of civilization" (1227). Grace as it manifests itself in civility, not least the civility of Spenser's own art, repairs the ruins of our first parents and transforms us into people who are truly human. These three graces, Euphrosyne, Aglaia, and Thalia, says Colin, "on men all gracious gifts bestow, / Which decke the body and adorne the mynde." Most important, they teach us how to negotiate difference:

> They teach us, how to each degree and kynde
> We should our selues demeane, to low, to hie;
> To friends, to foes, which skill men call Ciuility (FQ VI.x.23).

After thirty years of postcolonial critique, however, it is difficult to accept this idealism without wanting some kind of qualification. It now requires an act of imagination to see The Faerie Queene in quite the uninflected way Wind or Roche did. Because it is now so hard to forget colonial Ireland's suffering, we may feel that on Mount Acidale we are looking into the heart of darkness, but Spenser and his older interpreters clearly did not: they are staring into the heart of light. This incongruity or discrepant awareness is central to my argument about empire.

The immediate effects of Spenser's vision are for us, his postcolonial readers, profoundly ironic. Calidore returns to his duty, and grace most immediately manifests itself in the urbanity with which he deceives the brigands, the scarcely disguised Irish "runnagates" who have kidnapped Pastorella. After "gently waking them" and allaying all their fears, he slaughters them—"through dead carcasses he made his way" (*FQ* VI.xi.38, 47). Grace, so Spenser might argue, enables the less than competent Calidore to recover Pastorella and return the world to the moral balance or order civility promises. Grace, we might argue, does something quite different. It insulates Spenser against the incongruity of his own ferocious violence. It protects him against the irony or relativism that civility in the form of humanist education would teach. My point is that it is not so much Spenser's poetics that interrogate his politics as we, his critics, and that we do so in the way we do is a measure not of our superior virtue but of our historicism, not necessarily our "new historicism" but of the degree to which Spenser's early modern world is perceived as a discrete culture or foreign country. It is a measure of our historicism or cultural relativism that the lines that now haunt contemporary Spenser studies are not those of Mount Acidale but those from the *View* describing Munster's rebels as so many anatomies of death, their terrible suffering dismissed in a line as a fate that "they themselves had wrought" (102). But for Spenser, their suffering is as nothing compared to the vision of grace on Acidale, where change is no longer as "perilous" as Eudoxus and Irenius imagine (92) because it is aestheticized in the circulating dance of the graces and so made to signify the liberating permanence, immutability, the eternal stability of the world Spenser's culture promises him. The wide-ruling, ever-expanding argument of grace is as important as it is, especially when it is recreated in the sublime poetry of *The Faerie Queene,* because it enables Spenser to protect his way of being in the world against difference and mutability. Nowhere is this more clear than in the final cantos of the poem where the very real horror of change, death, decay, and difference is *aestheticized* by grace from the outset. In the very act of allegorizing mutability her threat is *anaesthetized*: as she enters the presence of the Gods, her words "marked well her grace" (*FQ* VII.vi.28) and her beauty, so Jove discovers, "could the greatest wrath turn to grace" (31). Jove's empire is saved before the debate has begun. For mutability personified is not real change but only change reassuringly imagined as a function of Nature's benign order.

Clearly, Jove's empire and maybe all empires have something to do with the longing for cultural permanence.

At the end of the British Empire things seem different, but only in this sense. It is not Protestant grace so much as its secularization in the nation's cultural memory, its aestheticization in narratives and cultural artifacts precisely like those of Spenser's poetry, that protects so many British people against difference and the impermanence of empire. In the late sixteenth century, at the beginning of the empire, cultural memory in the specific form of the nation's Protestant history is clearly a site of intense contention;[33] by the mid-twentieth century, however, at the end of the empire, cultural memory is dominated by the nation's progressive history, the unfolding story of popular liberties and parliamentary democracy. For so many British people what Herbert Butterfield called the "Whig interpretation" of history had become a fiction felt as fact. In order to make this clear, we need to return to Spenser's most illustrious descendant, Winston Churchill.

The End of the British Empire

Despite Spenser's own best efforts to associate himself with the Spencers of Althorp in *Prothalamion* (130–31) and *Colin Clout's Come Home Againe* (536–39), there was in fact no immediate blood relationship between him and that "house of ancient fame," nor consequently with their relatives, the Churchills.[34] But Spenser and the greatest of the Churchills, Winston Spencer-Churchill, are related in more substantial ways than those of genealogy. Between them they comprehend the British Empire. Not only do they mark out its beginning and end, but they allow us considerable insight into its longing for liberating permanence.

One of the most resonant images in the recent history of the West, especially as it has been cultivated, revived, and elaborated since September 2001, is that of Churchill refusing to appease the Nazis, staying the course, and leading Britain over the summer of 1940 in her lonely stand against Hitler's Germany. At that moment, so we are reminded, the West faced extinction, and only Churchill's indomitable will saved us. While Churchill's courage and intelligence are incontrovertible, his story has become a shaping fantasy of enormous power, and he himself has become a growth industry not only in Britain but even more so in the United States.[35] The British statesman who was best known before the advent of Hitler for his refusal to appease the democratic aspirations of Mahatma Gandhi and before that the naval ambitions of U.S. President Calvin Coolidge has somewhat ironically become an American icon—an exemplar of the grit the United States needs to show if its unique way of being in the world is to prevail. The rise of Churchill, it might be argued, is a surefire indication of the degree to which America, even now with a president as talented and enlightened as Barack Obama, has come to think of itself as an empire.

In his single most famous speech, the radio speech he delivered at the fall of France on June 18, 1940, Churchill talked of the end of the British Empire both in terms of its purpose and its final termination. While he imagined its purpose as the survival of what he called "Christian civilization," he projected its termination into a distant millenarian future. As he urged his fellow citizens to duty and resistance, he prophesied that "if the British Commonwealth and Empire should last a thousand years, men will still say, 'This was their finest hour.'"[36] In any event it only lasted another seven years, effectively disappearing in the summer of 1947 with the abandonment of Palestine and, more important, with the independence of India.[37] But in Churchill's romantic wartime imagination the essential meaning of the British millennium would be made manifest in this, its finest hour, an epiphany that would transcend time.[38] The speech, like much of Churchill's rhetoric, is carefully calibrated to enlist the prestige of Scripture without being explicitly religious, and in so doing it identifies itself with a genre of mystical English nationalism that flourished in the 1930s and 1940s and whose most authentic, genuinely religious expression was T. S. Eliot's *Four Quartets*. The complete version of Eliot's poem was published in 1944 just after the Normandy landings and within months of Laurence Olivier's *Henry V,* Michael Powell and Emeric Pressburger's wonderful *Canterbury Tale,* and C. S. Lewis's Clark lectures on Sidney and Spenser. For Lewis, Spenser represents the "ordered exuberance" of English culture.[39] Eliot would have agreed, for there in the *Four Quartets*, in that poem written in wartime London while Eliot listened to Churchill's speeches, England stands on Mount Acidale. At the beginning, in "Burnt Norton," we enter our first world and stare into the heart of light. At the end, in "Little Gidding," England stands at the still point of the turning world: "the communication / Of the dead is tongued with fire beyond the language of the living," Eliot explains. The dead are alive because England is the specific location of an eternal present. "Here the intersection of the timeless moment / Is England and nowhere."[40] If we were to look at Churchill's prophecy and Eliot's revelation through the skeptical eyes of a postcolonial critic or a contemporary anthropologist like Marshall Sahlins,[41] what we might see is the degree to which history has been reduced to a function of culture. That is, history has ceased to be a disinterested inquiry into the past, sensitive to discontinuity, inconstancy, and the frighteningly unpredictable lurches of contingency, but has become a function of a particular culture's determination to assimilate the past, aestheticize change, and maintain its identity.[42] What Churchill's rhetoric and Eliot's poetry have in common is the representation of the past not simply as cultural memory but also as their own culture's *very selective* memory.

In Eliot's highly influential 1919 essay "Tradition and the Individual Talent," the process of selection itself suggests how the aesthetic might be deployed to persuade the culture to believe more fully in its quest for permanence.[43] In that essay the past is represented not so much as a collection of fragments desperately shored against our ruin but as a resilient, ever-evolving structure of words, beliefs, and practices known as "tradition." There is nothing of Milton's violent, revolutionary contempt for tradition in Eliot's vision. It is not the peculiar amalgam of "unchewed notions and suppositions" that would sew up Milton's "womb of teeming truth,"[44] but an ideal order of great beauty only to be perceived by what Eliot calls the "historical sense." This historical sense is paradoxically but predictably intensely antihistoricist, that is, aggressively antipathetical to any sense of the past as a foreign country or genealogy of discrete cultures. The historical sense is the principle by whose possession writers select themselves as great or truly memorable. It "involves a perception not only of the pastness of the past," says Eliot, "but of its presence; the historical sense compels a man to write not merely with his own generation in his bones, but with the feeling that the whole of the literature of Europe from Homer and within it the whole of the literature of his own country has a simultaneous existence and composes a simultaneous order"(14). No poet, no artist, neither Spenser nor Milton, has his complete meaning outside this order. This, Eliot insists, is "a principle of aesthetic, not merely historical, criticism" (15). At this point it becomes clear that what Eliot means by aesthetic criticism is something more than the simple apprehension or evaluation of beauty; it is the perception of one's culture as a complete synchronic order idealized in such a way that change as in the dance of the graces only perfects that order. Culture is Europe or Western culture, and it is imagined, to use Northrop Frye's term, as a "secular scripture" in which the new only reveals more fully the universal truths of the old. From an anthropologist's perspective this constitutes a form of cultural solipsism of an extraordinarily high order but, most important, a form of solipsism whose political equivalent is empire.

In the same way that empire, from Jove's "high empire" in the Mutability Cantos to Hardt and Negri's new world order, from Harrington's *Oceana* to the neoconservative "Project for a New American Century," seeks to arrest mutability and represent itself as the once and future *telos*, so does Eliot's aesthetic tradition.[45] My point is that the end of empire imagined by Churchill and other imperial thinkers aspires to the same kind of absolute, "permanent and vital," cultural synchronicity imagined by Eliot and before any of them by Spenser. Michael Hardt and Antonio Negri put the idea this way: "Empire exhausts historical time, suspends history, and summons past and future with its own ethical order. In other words, Empire presents its order as permanent, eternal, and [morally] necessary."[46] Change is not change but the endless reproduction of novel simulacra of this final synchronic order. The Churchill whom neoconservatives like Niall Ferguson love to quote never really gives up on the empire but imagines it reproducing itself in the form of a great Anglo-American empire called "the English-speaking peoples,"[47] and the Bush administration, until its recent demise, routinely lectured academics on the way that not only the past but the future and indeed change itself was now government property: "We are an empire now," an anonymous Bush official said in 2004, "and when we act, we create our own reality. And while you are studying that reality—judiciously, as you will—we'll act again, creating new realities which you can study too, and that's how things will sort out."[48] The critical problem is this: by focusing on the fantasy of their absolute synchronicity, cultures at their most imperial erase the possibility of a plurality of ways of being in the world. The failure of early new historicism, certainly as it was articulated in classic essays like Stephen Greenblatt's wonderful "Invisible Bullets,", was that it took the claims of empire or what it called the "dominant ideology" at face value and refused to see its totalizing power as a cultural fiction.[49] As the Iraq War has most recently demonstrated, empires to the degree that they indulge their tendency to solipsism routinely overestimate their power and underestimate their fragility. For all their claims to unchanging synchronicity they are wracked with the fear of cultural mutability.

No one felt the fear of impermanence more powerfully than Spenser, but so at their darkest moments did Churchill and Eliot, and it seems significant that at these moments they both invoke not so much grace as the memory of Spenser as a metonym for cultural continuity. For Churchill, after World

War II, as he tries to re-create the British Empire in the history of the English-speaking peoples, he looks back for reassurance to Elizabethan England and Spenser's vision of Gloriana, a moment, he says, focusing on *The Faerie Queene,* when the English people first "awoke to consciousness of their greatness" (II:133). In this, he joins nationalist historians like Arthur Bryant and A. L. Rowse in the hope of a new Elizabethan age.[50] More pointedly, for Eliot, after World War I, as he gathers fragments to shore against the ruin of his culture, he dwells on Spenser's *Prothalamion.* In *The Waste Land* he sits down by the waters of the now polluted Thames and weeps, invoking the implicit resolve of Psalm 137—"By the rivers of Babylon there we sat down [and] wept when we remembered Zion...if I forget thee, O Jerusalem. . . ." The fear is that England is no longer England, but Babylon—"How shall we sing the Lord's song in a strange land?" The gracious answer is by remembering Zion in the specifically English form of Spenser's refrain: "Sweet Thames, run softly till I end my song" (*Waste Land* 183). The irony is that Eliot invokes the aesthetic resonances of Spenser's memory in almost exactly the same way that Spenser invokes the argument of grace. In *Prothalamion,* the poem Eliot remembers, the departed river nymphs return and sanctify the betrothal of the Somerset daughters with boundless grace, "endlesse Peace" and "blessed Plentie" (101–2). But most important, the betrothal erases the memory of decay and ushers in the prospect of imperial renewal. For out of Leicester House, the home of Spenser's former patron, Robert Dudley, Earl of Leicester, comes a new star, the patron of the betrothed, Robert Devereux, Earl of Essex, "Great Englands glory and Worlds wide wonder...Faire branch of Honor, flower of Cheualrie, / That fillest England with thy triumphes fame" (146–51). Because he comes like "Radiant *Hesper*" (164), it is difficult not to believe that it is morning again in England.

Conclusion

Let me conclude by returning to the imperial theorists with whom we began, Schumpeter and Armitage. For both these scholars the defining characteristic of empire is spatial expansion. For Schumpeter imperialism is "the objectless disposition on the part of a state to unlimited forcible expansion" and because expansion has no end but itself, empires tend "to transcend all bounds and limits to the point of exhaustion" (6). What I am suggesting is that the argument of grace as it manifests itself in the work of a great poet like Spenser and as it is reproduced in the cultural memory of so many people at the end of the British Empire indicates something different: that the key to understanding empire is not spatial but temporal; that the driving force at the heart of empire is a culture's longing for its own permanence, what I have been calling its absolute synchronicity; and that it articulates this longing in imaginations of ending history or transcending time on Mount Acidale, Arlo Hill, or indeed on Capitol Hill.

NOTES

INTRODUCTION

1   For recent efforts to study the relationship of religion to empire in the early modern world, see *Rereading the Black Legend: The Discourses of Religious and Racial Difference in the Renaissance Empires*, ed. Margaret R. Greer, Walter D. Mignolo, and Maureen Quilligan (Chicago: University of Chicago Press, 2007); A. R. Dilley, "Religion and the British Empire," in *The British Empire: Themes and Perspectives*, ed. Sarah Stockwell (Malden, Mass.: Blackwell, 2008); Carla Gardina Pestana, "Religion," in *The British Atlantic World, 1500–1800*, ed. David Armitage and Michael Braddick (New York: Palgrave Macmillan, 2002), 69–89; *Shaping the Stuart World, 1603–1714: The Atlantic Connection*, ed. Allan Macinnes and Arthur Williamson (Leiden, Netherlands: Brill, 2006), 117–46.

2   Daniel Goffman, *The Ottoman Empire and Early Modern Europe* (New York: Cambridge University Press, 2002); Karen Barkey, *Empire of Difference: The Ottomans in Comparative Perspective* (New York: Cambridge University Press, 2008); Virginia H. Aksan and Daniel Goffman, eds., *The Early Modern Ottomans: Remapping the Empire* (New York: Cambridge University Press, 2007); Bernard Lewis, *Cultures in Conflict: Christians, Muslims and Jews in the Age of Discovery* (New York: Oxford University Press, 1995).

3   Stephen Greenblatt, *Marvelous Possessions: The Wonder of the New World* (Chicago: University of Chicago Press, 1992); Anthony Pagden, *European Encounters with the New World: From Renaissance to Romanticism* (New Haven: Yale University Press, 1993); Tzvetan Todorov, *The Conquest of America: The Question of the Other*, trans. Richard Howard (New York: Harper & Row, 1984); Gordon Sayre, *"Les Sauvages Américains": Representations of Native Americans in French and English Colonial Literature* (Chapel Hill: University of North Carolina Press, 1997); Barbara Sebek and Stephen Deng, eds., *Global Traffic: Discourses and Practices in English Literature and Culture from 1550 to 1700* (New York: Palgrave Macmillan, 2008); Gerald M. MacLean, *Looking East: English Writing and the Ottoman Empire Before 1800* (New York: Palgrave Macmillan, 2007); Goran V. Stanivukovic, ed., *Remapping the Mediterranean World in Early Modern English Writings* (New York: Palgrave Macmillan, 2007); Barbara Fuchs, *Mimesis and Empire: The New World, Islam, and European Identities* (New York: Cambridge University Press, 2001); Jorge Cañizares-Esquerra, *How to Write the History of the New World: Histories, Epistemologies, and Identities in the Eighteenth-Century Atlantic World* (Stanford, Calif.: Stanford University Press, 2001).

4   J. H. Elliott, *Empires of the Atlantic World: Britain and Spain in America, 1492–1830* (New Haven: Yale University Press, 2006); Jorge Cañizares-Esguerra, *Puritan Conquistadors: Iberianizing the Atlantic, 1550–1700* (Stanford, Calif.: Stanford University Press, 2006); Robin Blackburn, *The Making of New World Slavery: From the Baroque to the Modern 1492–1800* (London: Verso, 1997); Hugh Thomas, *The Slave Trade: The Story of the Atlantic Slave Trade, 1440–1870* (New York: Simon and Schuster, 1997).

5   For examples of the combining of local and global perspectives in Atlantic history see Jon Sensbach, *Rebecca's Revival: Creating Black Christianity in the Atlantic World* (Cambridge, Mass.: Harvard University Press, 2006); Natalie Zemon Davis, *Women on the Margins: Three Seventeenth-Century Lives* (Cambridge, Mass.: Harvard University Press, 1997); Allan Greer, *Mohawk Saint: Catherine Tekakwitha and the Jesuits* (New York: Oxford University Press, 2005).

6   Arthur H. Williamson, "An Empire to End Empire: The Dynamic of Early Modern British Expansion," *Huntington Library Quarterly* 68 (2005): 227–56; C. R. Boxer, *The Church Militant and Iberian Expansion, 1440–1770* (Baltimore: Johns Hopkins University Press, 1978); Pauline Moffitt Watts, "Prophecy and Discovery: On the Spiritual Origins of Christopher Columbus's 'Enterprise of the Indies,'" *American Historical Review* 90 (1985): 73–102; Djelal Kadir, *Columbus and the Ends of the Earth: Europe's Prophetic Rhetoric as Conquering Ideology* (Berkeley: University of California Press, 1992); Geoffrey Parker, *The World Is Not Enough: The Imperial Vision of Philip II of Spain* (Waco, Tex.: Markham Press Fund, 2001); Kevin Sharpe, "Transplanting Revelation, Transferring Meaning: Reading the Apocalypse in Early Modern England, Scotland and New England," in *Shaping the Stuart World, 1603–1714*; C. R. Boxer, "Faith and Empire: The Cross and the Crown in Portuguese Expansion, Fifteenth-Eighteenth Centuries," *Terrae Incognitae* 8 (1976): 73–89; Richard W. Cogley, "The Fall of the Ottoman Empire and the Restoration of Israel in the 'Judeo-centric' Strand of Puritan Millenarianism," *Church History* 72 (2003): 304–32; .J. F. Maclear, "New England and the Fifth Monarchy: The Quest for the Millennium in Early American Puritanism," *William and Mary Quarterly*, 3d ser., 32 (1975): 223–60.

7   Benjamin Schmidt, *Innocence Abroad: The Dutch Imagination and the New World, 1570–1670* (Cambridge, U.K.: Cambridge University Press, 2001); John Canup, *Out of the Wilderness: The Emergence of an American Identity in Colonial New England* (Middletown, Conn.: Wesleyan University Press, 1990); Richard H. Popkin, "The Rise and Fall of the Jewish Indian Theory," in *Menasseh ben Israel and His World*, ed. Y. Kaplan, H. Méchoulan, and R. H. Popkin (Leiden, Netherlands: E. J. Brill, 1989); N. I. Matar, "Milton and the Idea of the Restoration of the Jews," *Studies in English Literature 1500–1900* 27 (1987): 109–24; James Holstun, "John Eliot's Empirical Millenarianism," *Representations* 4 (1983): 128–53; Gerald R. McDermott, "Jonathan Edwards and American Indians: The Devil Sucks Their Blood," *New England Quarterly* 72 (1999): 539–57; N. I. Matar, "The Idea of the Restoration of the Jews in English Protestant Thought, 1661–1701," *Harvard Theological Review* 78 (1985): 115–48; Paul Regan, "Calvinism and the Dutch Israel Thesis," in *Protestant History and Identity in Sixteenth-Century Europe*, vol. 2, *The Later Reformation*, ed. Bruce Gordon (Brookfield, Vt.: Scholar Press, 1996), 91–107; Avihu Zakai, *Exile and Kingdom: History and*

Apocalypse in the Puritan Migration to America (New York: Cambridge University Press, 1992); Graeme Murdock, "The Importance of Being Josiah: An Image of Calvinist Identity," *Sixteenth-Century Journal* 29 (1998): 1,043–59.

8   Alden Vaughan and Edward W. Clark, eds., *Puritans Among the Indians: Accounts of Captivity and Redemption, 1676–1724* (Cambridge, Mass.: Harvard University Press, 1981); Linda Colley, *Captives: Britain, Empire and the World, 1600–1850* (New Haven: Yale University Press, 2002); Lisa Voight, *Writing Captivity in the Early Modern Atlantic: Circulations of Knowledge and Authority in the Iberian and English Imperial Worlds* (Chapel Hill: University of North Carolina Press, 2009); Joe Snader, *Caught Between Worlds: British Captivity Narratives in Fact and Fiction* (Lexington: University Press of Kentucky, 2000); Richard Slotkin, *Regeneration Through Violence: The Mythology of the American Frontier, 1600–1860* (Middletown, Conn.: Wesleyan University Press, 1973); Ellen G. Friedman, *Spanish Captives in North Africa in the Early Modern Age* (Madison: University of Wisconsin Press, 1983); Alexander X. Byrd, *Captives and Voyagers: Black Migrants Across the Eighteenth-Century British Atlantic World* (Baton Rouge: Louisiana State University Press, 2008).

9   *The Jesuit Relations: Natives and Missionaries in Seventeenth-Century North America*, ed. Allan Greer (Boston: Bedford Press, 2000); for Iberian captive-martyrs, see *Diálogo de los mártires*, in Diego de Haedo, *Topographia e historia general de Argel* (Madrid, 1929 [orig. Valladolid], 1612).

10   Stephen Greenblatt, "Learning to Curse: Aspects of Linguistic Colonialism in the Sixteenth Century," in *First Images of America: The Impact of the New World on the Old*, 2 vols., ed. Fredi Chiappelli et al. (Berkeley: University of California Press, 1976), II: 561–80; Greenblatt, "Invisible Bullets: Renaissance Authority and Its Subversion," in *Shakespearean Negotiations: The Circulation of Social Energy in Renaissance England* (Berkeley: University of California Press, 1988), 21–65; Todorov, *Conquest of America*; Sean Hawkins, *Writing and Colonialism in Northern Ghana: The Encounter Between the LoDagaa and the "World on Paper"* (Toronto: University of Toronto Press, 2002); Sara Castro-Klaren, "Literacy, Conquest and Interpretation: Breaking New Ground on the Records of the Past," *Social History* 23 (May 1998): 133–45; *Writing Without Words: Alternative Literacies in Mesoamerica and the Andes*, ed. Elizabeth Hill Boone and Walter Mignolo (Durham, N.C.: Duke University Press, 1994); Thomas G. Kirsch, "Ways of Reading as Religious Power in Print Globalization," *American Ethnologist* 34 (2007): 509–20.

11   Patricia Seed, *Ceremonies of Possession in Europe's Conquest of the New World* (New York: Cambridge University Press, 1995); David Brading, *The First America: The Spanish Monarchy, Creole Patriots, and the Liberal State, 1492–1867* (New York: Cambridge University Press, 1991).

12   Kristina Bross, *Dry Bones and Indian Sermons: Praying Indians in Colonial America* (Ithaca, N.Y.: Cornell University Press, 2004); Laura J. Murray, "Joining Signs with Words: Missionaries, Metaphors, and the Massachusetts Language," *New England Quarterly* 74 (2001): 62–93.

13   David Tavarez, "Naming the Trinity: From Ideologies of Translation to Dialec-

tics of Reception in Colonial Nahua Texts, 1547–1771," *Colonial Latin American Review* 9 (2000): 21–47.

14   William Taylor provides a powerful critique of the conventional scholarly usage of the term *syncretism* to describe the flexible and eclectic mutations native and European spiritual practices underwent over the course of colonization in *Magistrates of the Sacred: Priest and Parishioners in Eighteenth-Century Mexico* (Stanford, Calif.: Stanford University Press, 1996), a caution echoed by Douglas Winiarski, "Native American Popular Religion in New England's Old Colony, 1670–1770," *Religion and American Culture* 15 (2005): 147–86.

15   Nancy M. Farriss, *Maya Society Under Colonial Rule: The Collective Enterprise of Survival* (Princeton, N.J.: Princeton University Press, 1984); Inga Clendinnen, *Ambivalent Conquests: Maya and Spaniard in Yucatan, 1517–1570* (New York: Cambridge University Press, 1987); Louise M. Burkhart, *The Slippery Earth: Nahua-Christian Moral Dialogue in Sixteenth-Century Mexico* (Tucson: University of Arizona Press, 1989); Sabine MacCormack, *Religion in the Andes: Vision and Imagination in Early Colonial Peru* (Princeton, N.J.: Princeton University Press, 1991); Fernando Cervantes, *The Devil in the New World: The Impact of Diabolism in New Spain* (New Haven: Yale University Press, 1994); Carolyn Dean, *Inka Bodies and the Body of Christ: Corpus Christi in Colonial Cuzco, Peru* (Durham, N.C.: Duke University Press, 1999); Nicholas Griffiths and Fernando Cervantes, eds., *Spiritual Encounters: Interactions Between Christianity and Native Religions in Colonial America* (Lincoln: University of Nebraska Press, 1999); Kenneth M. Morrison, *The Solidarity of Kin: Ethnohistory, Religious Studies, and the Algonkian-French Religious Encounter* (Albany: State University of New York Press, 2002); Allan Greer, "Conversion and Identity: Iroquois Christianity in Seventeenth-Century New France," in *Conversion: Old Worlds and New*, ed. Kenneth Mills and Anthony Grafton (Rochester, N.Y: University of Rochester Press, 2003): 175–98; Allan Greer and Jodi Bilinkoff, eds., *Colonial Saints: Discovering the Holy in the Americas* (New York: Routledge, 2003); David Tavarez, "The Passion According to the Wooden Drum: The Christian Appropriation of a Zapotec Ritual Genre in New Spain," *The Americas* 62 (2006): 413–44; Frank Shuffleton, "Indian Devils and Pilgrim Fathers: Squanto, Hobomok, and the English Conception of Indian Religion," *New England Quarterly* 49 (1976): 108–16.

16   Walter D. Mignolo, *The Darker Side of the Renaissance: Literacy, Territoriality and Colonization* (Ann Arbor: University of Michigan Press, 1995). See also the essays collected in *New World Encounters*, ed. Stephen Jay Greenblatt (Berkeley: University of California Press, 1993); Jose Rabasa, *Writing Violence on the Northern Frontier: The Historiography of Sixteenth-Century New Mexico and Florida, and the Legacy of Conquest* (Durham, N.C.: Duke Universitiy Press, 2000).

17   Jill Lepore, *The Name of War: King Philip's War and the Origins of American Identity* (New York: Knopf, 1998); Robert St. George, "'Heated' Speech and Literacy in Seventeenth-Century New England," in *Seventeenth-Century New England: A Conference Held by the Colonial Society of Massachusetts, June 18 and 19, 1982*, ed. David D. Hall and David G. Allen (Boston: Colonial Society of Massachusetts, 1984); Jane Kamensky, *Governing the Tongue: The Politics of Speech in Early New England* (New York: Oxford University Press, 1997).

18   Nicholas Griffiths, *The Cross and the Serpent: Religious Repression and Resurgence in Colonial Peru* (Norman: University of Oklahoma Press, 1996); Kenneth Mills, *Idolatry and Its Enemies: Colonial Andean Religion and Extirpation, 1640–1750* (Princeton, N.J.: Princeton University Press, 1997).

19   John Corrigan, "Amalek and the Rhetoric of Extermination," in *The First Prejudice*, ed. Chris Beneke and Christopher S. Grenda (Philadelphia: University of Pennsylvania Press, 2010); Cotton Mather, *A Discourse Delivered unto some part of the forces engaged in a just war of New England* (Boston, 1689), title page.

20   Luis Rivera, *A Violent Evangelism: The Political and Religious Conquest of the Americas* (Louisville: University of Kentucky Press, 1992).

21   Roland Greene, *Unrequited Conquests: Love and Empire in the Colonial Americas* (Chicago: University of Chicago Press, 1999).

CHAPTER I. THE POLEMICS OF POSSESSION

1   Eugenio Asensio, "La lengua compañera del imperio," *Revista de Filología Española* 43 (1960): 399–413; at 406.

2   Antonio de Nebrija, *Gramática de la lengua castellana* (1492), ed. Antonio Quillis (Madrid: Editora Nacional, 1980), 101–2. All English translations of Spanish texts are my own, unless otherwise credited.

3   Asensio, "La lengua compañera del imperio," 407.

4   Jesús P. Martínez, *Historia de España: Vol. II. Edades moderna y contemporánea*, 2nd ed. (Madrid: EPESA, 1963), 10.

5   This discussion follows portions of chapters 3 and 4 of my *The Polemics of Possession in Spanish American Narrative* (New Haven: Yale University Press, 2007). Its successive chapters examine the role of these ideas in the sixteenth- and seventeenth-century writing of Spanish conquest history, their presence in the transition from the writing of history to literature, and their resonances in Latin American literature today.

6   See a full discussion of the papal bulls' interpretation in Anthony Pagden, "Dispossessing the Barbarian: Rights and Property in Spanish America," in Pagden, *Spanish Imperialism and the Political Imagination* (New Haven: Yale University Press, 1990), 13–36; for quick reference see James S. Olson et al., eds., *Historical Dictionary of the Spanish Empire, 1402–1975* (New York: Greenwood Press, 1992), 469–71; for texts of the bulls see John H. Parry and Robert G. Keith, eds., *The Conquerors and the Conquered: Volume 1, New Iberian World: A Documentary History of the Discovery and Settlement of Latin America to the Early 17th Century* (New York: Times Books and Hector and Rose, 1984), 271–75.

7   Castile, Laws, statutes, etc. 1252–84 (Alfonso X), *Las siete partidas del sabio rey, don Alfonso el nono, nuevamente glosadas por el licenciado Gregorio López, del Consejo Real de Indias de Su Majestad* (1555) (Valladolid, Spain: Diego Fernández de Córdoba, 1587), vol. 1, fol. 795, fol. 83v [part. 2, tit. 23, law 2]. Las Casas and Sepúlveda likewise referenced these traditional definitions of the just war. See Bartolomé de las Casas, *Historia de las In-*

dias (1527–61), ed. Agustín Millares Carlo, introduction by Lewis Hanke, 3 vols. (Mexico City: Fondo de Cultura Económica, 1951), 1:134–35 [bk. 1, chap. 25]; and Juan Ginés de Sepúlveda, *Demócrates segundo o de las justas causas de la guerra contra los indios* (1545), ed. and trans. Ángel Losada (Madrid: Consejo Superior de Investigaciones Científicas, 1984), 16–17.

8   J. H. Elliott, *Imperial Spain, 1469–1716* (1963; repr. New York: New American Library, 1966), 156, 157.

9   See Adorno, *Polemics of Possession*, 54–55.

10   Paulino Castañeda Delgado, "La política española con los caribes durante el siglo XVI," in *Homenaje a D. Ciriaco Pérez-Bustamante*, vol. 2, introduction by Carlos Seco Serrano, 73–130 (Madrid: Instituto "Gonzalo Fernández de Oviedo," Consejo Superior de Investigaciones Científicas, 1970), at 81–85. Lewis Hanke, "Studies in the Theoretical Aspects of the Spanish Conquest of America," Ph.D. dissertation, Harvard University, 1935, Appendix VI, reproduces this "Carib questionnaire."

11   Elman R. Service, "Indian-European Relations in Colonial Latin America," *American Anthropologist* 57 (1955): 411–25, at 412–14.

12   Charles Gibson, *The Aztecs Under Spanish Rule: A History of the Indians of the Valley of Mexico, 1519–1810* (Stanford, Calif.: Stanford University Press, 1964), 58.

13   Ibid., 58.

14   There were two notable exceptions: the Dominican friars Fray Tomás Ortiz and Fray Domingo de Betanzos defamed the natives of the New World, claiming that they were incapable of receiving the Christian faith. See Adorno, *Polemics of Possession*, 106, 342, n. 23, for these sensational but quickly discredited cases.

15   Hanke, "Studies," 388–93 (see Adorno, *Polemics of Possession*, 341, n. 9); *Colección de documentos inéditos relativos al descubrimiento, conquista y organización de las antiguas posesiones españolas de Ultramar*, 25 vols. (Madrid, 1885–1932), 9: 268–280; 10: 38–43, 192–203.

16   Las Casas, *Historia*, 2: 441-42 [bk. 3, chap. 4].

17   "Las Casas and the papal bulls *Sublimis Deus* (1537) and *Veritas ipsa* (1537) specifically . . . declare that the Indians were *treated like* brute animals, and that the relationship was understood to be one of association, *not* identification" (Edmundo O'Gorman, "Sobre la naturaleza bestial del indio americano," *Filosofía y letras*, 1, no. 1 [1941]: 141–58; 1, no. 2 [1941]: 305–14, at 305).

18   Anthony Pagden, *The Fall of Natural Man: The American Indian and the Origins of Comparative Ethnology* (Cambridge: Cambridge University Press, 1982), 66.

19   Francisco de Vitoria, *Relectio de Indis o libertad de los indios* (1539), ed. and trans. Luciano Pereña and José María Pérez Prendes, Corpus Hispanorum de Pace 5 (Madrid: Consejo Superior de Investigaciones Científicas, 1967), 97, 13.

20   His seven legitimate titles of conquest were: the right of the Spanish to traverse and live in Indian territories, the right of the Spanish to announce the Gospel in Indian lands, the right to protect those Indians who converted to Christianity from their pagan princes, the right to impose a Christian prince, removing pagan rulers, the right to protect the innocent from human sacrifice and anthropophagy, the right to install Christian rule over

Indians who chose it freely, and the right to provide force to aid the Indians in wars against their Indian enemies (*Relectio de Indis*, 77–99).

21 Francisco de Vitoria, *De los indios, o del derecho de guerra de los españoles sobre los bárbaros (De indis, sive de iure belli hispanorum in barbaros, relectio posterior)* (1539), in *Obras de Francisco de Vitoria: Relecciones teológicas*, ed. and trans. Teófilo Urdánoz, Bibliotecas de Autores Cristianos 198 (Madrid: Editorial Católica, 1960), 811–58, at 823–26.

22 Ángel Losada, "Introducción," in Bartolomé de las Casas, *Apología* (1552–53), *Obras completas de Bartolomé de las Casas* 9, ed. and trans. Ángel Losada (Madrid: Alianza, 1988), 11–42, at 14–15. The royal order is printed in Vitoria, *Relectio*, 152–53.

23 Ángel Losada, "Juan Ginés de Sepúlveda y su 'Demócrates Secundus,'" in Sepúlveda, *Demócrates segundo*, vii–xxxii, at xiv–xv.

24 Pagden, *Fall of Natural Man*, 111.

25 Juan Ginés de Sepúlveda and Bartolomé de las Casas, *Apología de Juan Ginés de Sepúlveda contra Fray Bartolomé de las Casas y de Fray Bartolomé de las Casas contra Juan Ginés de Sepúlveda*, (1550, 1552–53), ed. and trans. Ángel Losada (Madrid: Editora Nacional, 1975), 79.

26 Las Casas, *Apología*, 627–29.

27 Juan Ginés de Sepúlveda, *De la compatibilidad entre la milicia y la religión* (1535), in *Tratados políticos de Juan Ginés de Sepúlveda*, ed. and trans. Ángel Losada (Madrid: Instituto de Estudios Políticos, 1963), 127–304.

28 Sepúlveda, *Demócrates segundo*, 21. He extends these hierarchical binary relationships to include "the lord over his servants, the magistrate over the citizens, the king over the peoples or individuals who are subject to his rule." While pointing out that each of these relationships is founded on its own distinctive juridical principles, he remarks that all have their origin in natural law and its single natural principle and dogma of the rule of perfection over imperfection.

29 O'Gorman, "Sobre la naturaleza bestial del indio americano," 306.

30 Sebastián de Covarrubias Horozco, *Tesoro de la Lengua Castellana o Española* (1611), ed. Martín de Riquer (Barcelona: S. A. Horta, 1943), 704.

31 Xavier Gómez Robledo, *Humanismo en México en el siglo XVI* (Mexico City: Editorial Jus, 1954), 232–33.

32 Sepúlveda, *Demócrates segundo*, 120.

33 Cited in Pagden, *Fall of Natural Man*, 115. *Aristotle's Politics*, trans. Benjamin Jowett, introduction by Max Lerner (New York: Modern Library, Random House, 1943), 1255b [bk. 1, chap. 6]: "Hence, where the relation of master and slave between them is natural they are friends and have a common interest, but where it rests merely on law and force the reverse is true."

34 Sepúlveda, *Demócrates segundo*, 21: "Thus in a single individual one can appreciate the masterly (*heril*) rule that the soul exercises over the body and the civil and royal (*civil y regio*) rule that the mind or reason exercises over the passions."

35 Sepúlveda, *Apología de Juan Ginés*, 79.

36 Pagden, *Fall of Natural Man*, 118.

37   Las Casas, *Historia*, 1:134 [bk. 1, chap. 25].

38   Bartolomé de las Casas, "Memorial de remedios para las Indias" (1516), in *Obras escogidas de Fray Bartolomé de las Casas*, ed. Juan Pérez de Tudela Bueso, vol. 5, Biblioteca de Autores Españoles 110 (Madrid: Atlas, 1958), 5–27, at 9, 17.

39   Las Casas, *Historia*, 3:275 [bk. 3, chap. 129].

40   For a fuller treatment of this topic see Adorno, *Polemics of Possession*, 64–69.

41   Kenneth J. Pennington, Jr., "Bartolomé de las Casas and the Tradition of Medieval Law," *Church History* 39, no. 2 (1970): 149–161, quotes on 157, 151.

42   José Alejandro Cárdenas Bunsen, "Escritura y derecho canónico en la obra de fray Bartolomé de las Casas," Ph.D. dissertation, Yale University, 2008.

43   Vitoria, *Relectio*, 31.

44   Sepúlveda, *Demócrates segundo*, 21: "Y enseñan que esta misma razón vale para los demás hombres en sus mutuas relaciones."

45   Las Casas, in Sepúlveda and Las Casas, *Apología de Juan Ginésde Sepúlveda contra Fray Bartolomé de las Casas y de Fray Bartolomé de las Casas contra Juan Ginés de Sepúlveda*, 1550, 1552-53, ed. and trans. Ángel Losada (Madrid: Editora Nacional, 1975), 139.

46   Ibid., 139.

47   Bartolomé de las Casas, *De unico vocationis modo* (1538–39), ed. Paulino Castañeda Delgado and Antonio García Moral, *Obras completas de Bartolomé de las Casas* 2 (Madrid: Alianza, 1990), 162–63, 573–75 [bk. 1, chap. 5, sec. 15].

48   Lewis Hanke's classic study (*The Spanish Struggle for Justice in the Conquest of America* [1949; repr. Boston: Little, Brown, 1965]) carries his examination of instances of this ideological struggle to the end of the sixteenth century.

49   Bernal Díaz del Castillo provides a vivid literary (and lived) example. See Adorno, *Polemics of Possession*, chaps. 6 and 7, esp. p. 103.

50   Las Casas had both works privately published in Seville a decade later. See *Entre los remedios*, 1542, and *Brevísima relación de la destruición de las Indias*, 1552, in Las Casas, *Obras escogidas*, 69–119, 131–81. For the New Laws, see Henry Raup Wagner, with Helen Rand Parish, *The Life and Writings of Bartolomé de las Casas* (Albuquerque: University of New Mexico Press, 1967), 108–20.

51   Losada, "Introducción," 18; Wagner and Parish, *Life and Writings of Bartolomé de las Casas*, 174–76.

52   Domingo de Soto, "Prólogo del maestro Soto," in Las Casas, "Aquí se contiene una disputa o controversia," in *Obras escogidas*, 295–308, at 295.

53   See Adorno, *Polemics of Possession*, 120–24; Wagner and Parish, *Life and Writings of Bartolomé de las Casas*, 170–82.

54   Losada, "Introducción," 30.

55   Sepúlveda, *Apología de Juan Ginés*, 78; Las Casas, *Apología de Juan Ginés*, 134.

56   Francisco López de Gómara,, *Historia general de las Indias* (1552), ed. Jorge Gurria Lacroix (Caracas: Biblioteca Ayacucho, 1979), 320 [chap. 214].

57   See Adorno, *Polemics of Possession*, 83–86; Wagner and Parish, *Life and Writings of Bartolomé de las Casas*, 213–20.

58   See Adorno, *Polemics of Possession*, 86–88.

59   See Cárdenas, "Escritura y derecho canónico," chap. 5.

CHAPTER 2. CRUELTY AND RELIGIOUS JUSTIFICATIONS FOR CONQUEST IN THE MID-SEVENTEENTH-CENTURY ENGLISH ATLANTIC

The author would like to thank Susan Juster and Linda Gregerson for the invitation to participate in the conference on Religion and Empire as well as for the further opportunity to explore aspects of a new project in this essay. Thanks are also due to Rolena Adorno, Linda Gregerson, Michael Meranze, and Sharon Salinger for insightful readings of an early draft.

1   For this wording see, for instance, The Third Charter of Virginia, March 12, 1611, printed in William Waller Hening, *The Statutes at Large; Being a Collection of all the Laws of Virginia, from the first session of the legislature, in the year 1619*, 23 vols. (Richmond, 1809–23), I: 99.

2   Rolena Adorno insightfully considers this debate in "The Polemics of Possession: Spain on America, Circa 1550," in this volume. Also see her *The Polemics of Possession in Spanish American Narrative* (New Haven: Yale University Press, 2007), esp. chap. 4.

3   These ideas and their application have been explored by numerous scholars. See especially Ken Macmillan, *Sovereignty and Possession in the English New World: The Legal Foundation of Empire, 1576–1640* (New York: Cambridge University Press, 2006); John C. Weaver, *The Great Land Rush and the Making of the Modern World, 1650–1900* (Montreal: McGill-Queen's University Press, 2003).

4   On anti-Catholicism see the classic essay by Peter Lake, "Anti-Popery: The Structure of a Prejudice," in *Conflict in Early Stuart England: Studies in Religion and Politics, 1603–1642*, ed. Richard Cust and Ann Hughes (New York: Longman, 1989), 72–106; more recently, Anthony Milton has noted the continued interplay with Catholics and their ideas even as antipopery functioned as a political ideology; see "A Qualified Intolerance: The Limits and Ambiguities of Early Stuart Anti-Catholicism," in *Catholicism and Anti-Catholicism in Early Modern English Texts*, Early Modern Literature in History, ed. Arthur F. Marotti (New York: St. Martin's Press, 1999), 86. Much has been written on the role of religion in Cromwell's career; for a general discussion see J. C. Davis, *Oliver Cromwell*, Reputations series (New York: Oxford University Press and Arnold, 2001), chap. 6; on Spain particularly see pp. 188, 189.

5   Geoffrey Parker, "The Etiquette of Atrocity: The Laws of War in Early Modern Europe," in *Success Is Never Final: Empire, War, and Faith in Early Modern Europe* (New York: Basic Books, 2002), 148. Mark Evans, "Moral Theory and the Idea of a Just War," in *Just War Theory: A Reappraisal*, ed. Evans (New York: Palgrave Macmillan, 2005), 4. For just-war theory in sixteenth-century England see Brian Lockey, "Conquest and English Legal Identity in Renaissance Ireland," *Journal of the History of Ideas* 65 (Oct. 2004): 544–48; and in Spain see Adorno, "The Polemics of Possession," chap. 1 in this volume.

6   For the foreign element's importance to this ideology see Milton, "A Qualified Intolerance," 103, 109.

7   Oliver Cromwell, "Speech at the Opening of Parliament, Wednesday, Sept. 17, 1656," in *Writings and Speeches of Oliver Cromwell*, 4 vols., ed. Wilbur Cortez Abbott (Cambridge, Mass.: Harvard University Press, 1937–47), IV: 262–63. On the Irish Rebellion see M. Perceval-Maxwell, *The Outbreak of the Irish Rebellion of 1641* (Montreal: McGill-Queen's University Press, 1994), esp. chap. 12; and the works of Kathleen M. Noonan, "'The cruel pressure of an enraged, barbarous people': Irish and English Identity in Seventeenth-Century Propaganda and Policy," *Historical Journal* 41 (March 1998): 151–77, "'Martyrs in Flames': Sir John Temple and the Conception of the Irish in English Martyrologies," *Albion* 36 (Summer 2004): 223–55.

8   Cromwell's commission to the five men leading the Western Design (as well as the commissions to Penn and Venables as commanders) is printed in Cromwell, *Writings and Speeches*, III: 530–34. For another justification see *A Declaration of His Highnes by the advice of his council; setting forth, on the behalf of this Commonwealth the Justice of their cause against Spain* (London, 1655), reprinted as *A Manifesto of the Lord Protector* (London, 1738) and in *Prose Works of John Milton*, ed. J. A. St. John, 5 vols. (London, 1848), II: 333–53.

9   John Morrill, "Postlude: Between War and Peace, 1651–1662," in *The Civil Wars: A Military History of England, Scotland, and Ireland, 1638–1660*, ed. John Kenyon and Jane Ohlmeyer (Oxford: Oxford University Press, 1998), 315.

10   S. A. G. Taylor, *The Western Design: An Account of Cromwell's Expedition to the Caribbean* (1965; repr. London: Solstice, 1969), 25.

11   For the English publications of Las Casas see William S. Maltby, *The Black Legend in England: The Development of Anti-Spanish Sentiment* (Durham, N.C.: Duke University Press, 1971).

12   *Brevísima relación de la destruición de las Indias*, 1552, in Las Casas, *Obras escogidas*, 69–119, 131–81. Bartolomé de las Casas, "Memorial de remedios para las Indias" (1516), in *Obras escogidas de Fray Bartolomé de las Casas*, Bartolomé de las Casas, ed. Juan Pérez de Tudela Bueso, vol. 5, Biblioteca de Autores Españoles 110 (Madrid: Atlas, 1958).

13   Bartolomé de las Casas, *The Tears of the Indians*, trans. J. Phillips (London, 1656), 3. I here quote from the English translation dating from the time of the attack on Jamaica.

14   Las Casas, *Tears of the Indians*, 8, 79, 127, 126.

15   *Seer cort Verhael vande destructie van d'Indien* ([Antwerp?], 1578). Benjamin Schmidt, *Innocence Abroad: The Dutch Imagination and the New World, 1570–1670* (New York: Cambridge University Press, 2001), 95. Other recent discussions of the Protestant publication history of Las Casas can be found in *Rereading the Black Legend: The Discourse of Religious and Racial Difference in the Renaissance Empires,* ed. Margaret R. Greer, Walter D. Mignolo, and Maureen Quilligan (Chicago: University of Chicago Press, 2007). See especially the essay "Rereading Theodore de Bry's Black Legend," by Patricia Gravatt on de Bry's illustrations (pp. 225–43).

16   The French edition was published in Antwerp (like the Dutch one), but the English edition appeared in London. An English translation of a pamphlet describing *The*

Spoyle of Antwerp appeared in 1576, authored by George Gascoigne. *A Larum for London, or the Siedge of Antwerpe* (1602) offered a play on the same subject.

17   Commission to General Venables, Dec. 4, 1654, in Cromwell, *Writings and Speeches*, III: 533.

18   *A Declaration of his Hignes, By the Advice of his council; Setting forth, On the behalf of this Commonwealth, the Justice of their Cause against Spain* (London, 1655; repr. Edinburgh, 1655), 4–5.

19   Phillips, dedicatory preface to Cromwell, in Las Casas, *Tears of the Indians*, A3–A3v; and preface, "To all true English-men," n.p. Thomas Campanella's treatise intended to guide the mighty Spanish king about how best to rule his vast empire advised avoiding cruelty—which the Spanish had become known for by 1600; Campanella attributed the depredations especially to poorly monitored lesser officers. An English edition appeared at this time too: *A Discourse Touching Spanish Monarchy*, trans. Edmund Chilmead (London, 1654), 59.

20   Phillips, preface, "To all true English-men," B4.

21   On the problem of English cruelty generally in this period see Barbara Donagan, "Atrocity, War Crimes, and Treason in the English Civil War," *American Historical Review* 99 (1994): 1137–66; and "Codes and Conduct in the English Civil War," *Past and Present* 118 (1988): 65–95. See also Philippe Rosenberg, "Thomas Tryon and the Seventeenth-Century Dimensions of Antislavery," *William and Mary Quarterly*, 3d ser., 61 (2004): 609–42. On the Pequots see Ronald Dale Karr, "Why should you be so Furious?: The Violence of the Pequot War," *Journal of American History* 85 (1998): 876–77. See also Samuel Clarke, *A Geographicall Description of all the Countries in the known World* (London, 1657), 186–90.

22   William Davenant, *The Cruelty of the Spaniards in Peru* (London, 1658), title page.

23   Davenant, *The Cruelty of the Spaniards in* Peru, 19, 20. Thomas Jackman would shortly opine that this policy as practiced by the English outstripped the cruelty of the Spanish; see his letter to Richard Baxter, May 6, 1659, Richard Baxter Collection, Letters, 59.6, 131, Dr. Williams' Library, London.

24   Davenant, *The Cruelty of the Spaniards in Peru*, 27. *The Siege of Rhodes* (1656) began at Rutland House but moved to the Cockpit; next Davenant put on *The Cruelty of the Spaniards*; later he offered *A History of Sir Francis Drake* (1660). All were on historical themes with music and "declamations"; they made a claim to recreate an ancient educational performance. See Mary Edmond, "Davenant, Sir William (1606–1668)," *Oxford Dictionary of National Biography* (Oxford: Oxford University Press, Sept. 2004; online edition May 2008, accessed [http://www.oxforddnb.com/view/article/7197, June 6, 2008]).

25   Cromwell, in his "Speech at the opening of Parliament," equated blood "unjustly shed" with Spanish efforts to block English trade in the Spanish colonies, 262. On Providence Island see Karen Ordahl Kupperman, *Providence Island, 1630–1641* (New York: Cambridge University Press, 1993).

26   John Callow, *The Formative Years of a Fallen King* (Phoenix Mill, U.K.: Sutton, 2000), 265. For Dutch usurpation of English territory in New Netherland see [Robert Codrington], *His Majesties Propriety and Dominion on the British Seas Asserted* (London,

1665), 174–75; E. Cliffe, comp., *An Abreviate of Hollands Deliverance by, and Ingratitude to the Crown of England and House of Nassau* (London, 1665), 40–42. According to Clarke's *Geographicall Description*, pp. 172–73, the Dutch had not even a foothold on the North American continent, and Virginia extended to New England.

27   "Grant of New Netherland, &c., to the Duke of York." For an earlier assertion of English claims to all the area, see Anonymous, "A brief narration of the English rights to the northern parts of America," [1656], in *A Collection of the State Papers of John Thurloe*, ed. Thomas Burch, 7 vols. (London, 1742), V: 81–83.

28   "Observations made by the Deputies of the High and Mighty Lords, States-General of the United Provinces, on the last Memorial presented by Sr. George Downing, Ambassador Extraordinary of the King of Great Britain," Feb. 9, 1665; and "Extract from the Register of the principal events which occurred in the Attack on and Reduction of New Netherland, Anno 1664," both in *Documents Relative to the Colonial History of the State of New York*, comp. John Romeyn Brodhead, trans. E. B. O'Callaghan, vol. II: *Holland Documents, VIII–XVI, 1657–1678* (Albany, 1858), 325, 411.

29   *A True Relation of the Uniust, Cruell, and Barbarous Proceedings against the English at Amboyna, in the East-Indies, by the Neatherlandish Gouernour, and Council there*, 3d ed. (London, 1665), preface, n.p.; almost the same wording—"they are not contented with the ordinary course of a fair Trade"—was used in *The Dutch Drawn to Life* (London, 1664), 143. See also Steven C. A. Pincus, *Protestantism and Patriotism: Ideologies and the Making of English Foreign Policy, 1650–1668*, Cambridge Studies in Early Modern British History (New York: Cambridge University Press, 1996), 260–61.

30   J.D., *A True and Compendious Narration or, second part of Amboyna* (London, 1665), 6, 8. See also Cliffe, *An Abreviate of Hollands Deliverance*, 51; and John Crouch, *Belgica Caracteristica, or, The Dutch character being news from Holland: a poem* (London, 1665), 5. For setting the natives on the English also see Steven C. A. Pincus, "Popery, Trade and Universal Monarchy: The Ideological Context of the Outbreak of the Second Anglo-Dutch War," *English Historical Review* 422 (1992): 9, 23.

31   Cliffe, *An Abreviate of Hollands Deliverance*, 49; N.R., *The Belgick Lyon Discovered* (London, 1665), broadside.

32   [Codrington?], *His Majesties Propriety and Dominion on the British Seas*, 121–24; published anonymously, the tract is also occasionally attributed to Robert Clavell, who signed the dedication; Crouch, *Belgica Caracteristica*, 7. For this point see also Charles Molloy, *Hollands Ingratitude, or, A Serious Expostulation with the Dutch; Shewing their Ingratitude to this Nation, and their inevitable Ruine, without a speedy Compliance and Submission to His Sacred Majesty of Britain* (London, 1666), 2–8; and [William Smith], *Ingratitude Reveng'd* (London, 1665).

33   For republicanism equated with ingratitude, see Molloy, *Hollands Ingratitude*, 7–8. The animosity to Dutch republicanism in royalist Restoration circles is discussed in Steven C. Pincus, "From Butterboxes to Wooden Shoes: The Shift in English Popular Sentiment from Anti-Dutch to Anti-French in the 1670s," *Historical Journal* 38 (1995): 338–39. For

ridiculing the achievement of reclaiming the land see [Andrew Marvell], *The Character of Holland* (London, 1665), 1.

34 The original edition of *A True Relation* (London, 1624) was published anonymously and has been variously attributed. It was clearly produced at the behest of the East India Company; for a discussion of the context for its initial publication see Anthony Milton, "Marketing a Massacre: Amboyna, the East India Company and the Public Sphere in Early Stuart England," in *The Politics of the Public Sphere in Early Modern England,* ed. Peter Lake and Steven Pincus, Politics, Culture and Society in Early Modern Britain (New York: Manchester University Press, 2007), 168–90. *A True Relation* went through two printings in 1624 and was reprinted under a version of the same title in 1632, 1651, 1665, and 1672. The text, or long excerpts from it, were also incorporated into numerous other publications, starting with Samuel Purchas, *Purchas his Pilgrimes* (London, 1625), "A Note Touching the Dutch" in the unpaginated preface, 1853–58. For the European activity in the Malukus from the native viewpoint (in which account the Amboyna incident receives no attention), see Leonard Y. Andaya, *The World of the Maluku: Eastern Indonesia in the Early Modern Period* (Honolulu: University of Hawaii Press, 1993).

35 John Dryden, "Amboyna, Or, The Cruelties of the Dutch to the English Merchants," in *The Works of John Dryden,* vol. 13: *Plays: Amboyna, The State of Innocence, and Aureng-Zebe,* ed. Vinton A. Dearing (Berkeley: University of California Press, 1994), 1–77. For analysis of the play in the context of emerging racial categories see Ayanna Thompson, *Performing Race and Torture on the Early Modern Stage,* Routledge Studies in Renaissance Literature and Culture (New York: Routledge, 2008), 99–119; for its role in the process of imagining the East see Shankar Raman, *Framing "India": The Colonial Imaginary in Early Modern Culture* (Stanford, Calif.: Stanford University Press, 2002), 189–236.

36 This account is taken from the 1665 edition of *A True Relation,* 4–23.

37 *A True Relation,* 24. For a discussion of this imagery see Carla Gardina Pestana, "Martyred by the Saints: Quaker Executions in Seventeenth-Century Massachusetts," in *Colonial Saints: Discovering the Holy in the Americas, 1500–1800,* ed. Allan Greer and Jodi Bilinkoff (New York: Routledge, 2003), 169–91. Martyrdom as a theme recurred throughout the history of European expansion, as a number of other essays in this collection make abundantly clear.

38 *A True Relation,* 25. See, for example, Matthew 27: 45, 51.

39 Daniel Baraz, *Medieval Cruelty: Changing Perceptions, Late Antiquity to the Early Modern Period,* Conjunctions of Religion and Power in the Medieval Past, ed. Barbara H. Rosenwein (Ithaca, N.Y.: Cornell University Press, 2003), 145, 157, 174.

40 On André see Sarah Knott, "Sensibility and the American War for Independence," *American Historical Review* 109 (2004): 19–40.

41 "Instructions . . . to the commissioners imployed by us to visite our Colony of ye Massachusetts," Apr. 23, 1664, in *Documents Relative to the Colonial History of the State of New York,* comp. John Romeyn Brodhead, vol. III: *London Documents, I–VIII, 1614–1692* (Albany, 1853), 51.

42 George Frederick Zook, *The Company of Royal Adventurers Trading into Africa* (Lancaster, Penn.: Press of New Era, 1919), 42–47, 61. For the rumored atrocities see *The Diary of Samuel Pepys*, vol. VI: *1665*, ed. Robert Latham and William Matthews (Berkeley: University of California Press, 1972), 42 (Feb. 23).

43 J. R. Jones, *The Anglo-Dutch Wars of the Seventeenth Century,* Modern Wars in Perspective (New York: Longman, 1996), 142.

44 The quirky pamphleteer Bethel Slingsby made this case at the time of the third Anglo-Dutch War. See his *Observations on the Letter written to Sir Thomas Osborn* (London, 1673), 4.

45 On the Restoration church see N. H. Keeble, *The Restoration: England in the 1660s,* History of Early Modern England (Malden, Mass.: Blackwell, 2002), 124–29.

46 Ridiculing diversity is [Marvell], *The Character of Holland,* 5; on liberty of conscience for the sake of trade see *The Dutch Drawn to Life,* 49; and on trade over religion see Molloy, *Hollands Ingratitude,* 1; and Crouch, *Belgica Caracteristica,* 5. Tony Claydon, *Europe and the Making of England, 1660–1760,* Cambridge Studies in Early Modern British History (New York: Cambridge University Press, 2007), 50, 144–48, explores the issue of irreligion, in particular.

47 Thompson, *Performing Race and Torture on the Early Modern Stage,* 101; this observation, since it is based on Restoration-era theater only, does not overlook Davenant's reference in *Cruelty of the Spaniards.*

CHAPTER 3. RELIGION AND NATIONAL DISTINCTION
IN THE EARLY MODERN ATLANTIC

1 Jorge Cañizares-Esguerra, *Puritan Conquistadors: Iberianizing the Atlantic, 1550–1700* (Stanford, Calif.: Stanford University Press, 2006), 30 and *passim.*

2 Ibid., 9.

3 J. H. Elliott, *Empires of the Atlantic World: Britain and Spain in America 1492–1830* (New Haven: Yale University Press, 2006), 11, 66. Elliott cites Christopher Carleill's proposed goal, in 1583, of "reducing the savage people to Christianity and civility."

4 Ibid., xv.

5 See, among others, Myra Jehlen, "History Before the Fact: or, Captain John Smith's Unfinished Symphony," *Critical Inquiry* 19 (1992–93): 677–92; and David Read, "Colonialism and Coherence: The Case of Captain John Smith's *General Historie of Virginia,*" *Modern Philology* 91 (1994): 428–48. On the retrospective inevitability of the nation-state see Etienne Balibar, "The Nation Form: History and Ideology," in Etienne Balibar and Immanuel Wallerstein, *Race, Nation, Class: Ambiguous Identities,* trans. Chris Turner (London: Verso, 1991); and Barbara Fuchs, "Imperium Studies: Theorizing Early Modern Expansion," in *Postcolonial Moves: Medieval Through Modern,* ed. Patricia Clare Ingham and Michelle R. Warren (New York: Palgrave, 2003).

6 "Rycharde Eden to the Reader," in *The First Three English Books on America,* ed.

Edward Arber (1895, reprinted New York: Kraus, 1971), 57. Subsequent citations are in the text by page number only.

7   See Andrew Hadfield's reading of the son of the Comogruan king as a critic of European colonial excess, in "Peter Martyr, Richard Eden and the New World: Reading, Experience, and Translation," *Connotations* 5:1 (1995–96): 1–22.

8   Ibid., 3 and ff. Later editions of Martyr's work highlighted the ambiguities that Eden deliberately ignored. Consider the assessment by none other than the indefatigable colonial promoter Richard Hakluyt, who edited the 1587 Paris edition, in a prefatory Latin epistle to Walter Ralegh: "In many passages [Martyr] praises the constancy of the Spaniards and their stubborn spirit, and with the warmest approbation he recounts their endurance in thirst, hunger, danger, toils, watches, and in their frequent troubles. But, at the same time, he also records their avarice, ambition, butchery, rapine, debauchery, their cruelty towards defenceless and harmless peoples" (*The Original Writings and Correspondence of the Two Richard Hakluyts*, vol. 2, ed. E. G. R. Taylor [London: Hakluyt Society, 1935], 356–69). For a discussion of this Protestant edition see Michael G. Brennan, "The Texts of Peter Martyr's *De orbe novo decades* (1504–1628): A Response to Andrew Hadfield," *Connotations* 6:2 (1996–97): 227–46, quote on 239.

9   Claire Jowitt, "Monsters and Strange Births: The Politics of Richard Eden—A Response to Andrew Hadfield," *Connotations* 6:1 (1996–97): 51–61, quote on 52.

10   Jeffrey Knapp, *An Empire Nowhere: England, America, and Literature from Utopia to The Tempest* (Berkeley: University of California Press, 1992).

11   Thomas More, *Utopia*, trans. and ed. Robert M. Adams, 2nd ed. (New York: Norton, 1992 [1975]), 31. Note that there is no mention here of evangelization. The Utopians' own colonialism is breezily described in almost physiological terms, as the necessary outlet for a growing body politic. Colonies expand and shrink in perfect accord with the size of the population (41).

12   Peter C. Herman, "Who's That in the Mirror? Thomas More's *Utopia* and the Problematic of the New World," in *Opening the Borders: Inclusivity in Early Modern Studies: Essays in Honor of James V. Mirollo*, ed. Peter C. Herman (Newark: University of Delaware Press, 1999), 109–32, quote on 117.

13   *Letters from a New World: Amerigo Vespucci's Discovery of America*, ed. Luciano Formisano, trans. David Jacobson (New York: Marsilio, 1992), 65.

14   Hadfield, "Peter Martyr, Richard Eden and the New World," 2–7.

15   Antonis Balasopoulos, "The Latter Part of the Commonwealth Forgets the Beginning: Empire and Utopian Economics in Early-Modern New World Discourse," *Gramma* 9 (2001): 31–53.

16   Ibid., 33.

17   David Read, *Temperate Conquests: Spenser and the Spanish New World* (Detroit: Wayne State University Press, 2000), 17.

18   Ibid., 13–14. The most notorious instance of such violence is perhaps the English massacre of hundreds of Spanish troops and Irish camp followers despite their unconditional surrender at Smerwick.

19   Read, *Temperate Conquests,* 56, 72.

20   Walter Ralegh, *The Discoverie of the Large, Rich, and Bewtiful Empyre of Guiana,* transcribed, annotated, and introduced by Neil L. Whitehead (Norman: University of Oklahoma Press, 1997), 121. Subsequent citations are in the text by page number only.

21   Francis Pretty, *The Famous Voyage of Sir Francis Drake into the South Sea, and Therehence About the Whole Globe of the Earth, Begun in the Year of Our Lord, 1577,* in Richard Hakluyt, *The Principal Navigations, Voyages, Traffiques and Discoveries of the English Nation* (Glasgow: Maclehose and Sons, 1904), 12 vols., XI: 123.

22   See Barbara Fuchs, "An English *Pícaro* in New Spain: Miles Philips and the Framing of National Identity," *Early Modernities, CR: The New Centennial Review* 2:1 (Spring 2002): 55–68; and Richard Helgerson, "'I Miles Philips': An Elizabethan Seaman Conscripted by History," *PMLA* 118:3 (2003): 573–80.

23   Helgerson, "'I Miles Philips,'" 576.

24   Ibid., 578.

25   Ibid., 577.

26   Miles Philips, "A Discourse Written by One Miles Philips, Englishman," in Hakluyt, *Principal Navigations,* vol. 9, 445–65, quote on 431–32.

CHAPTER 4. THE COMMONWEALTH OF THE WORD

I am greatly indebted to Julia Adams, David J. Baker, John Knott, Willy Maley, and Steven Mullaney for their suggestions and scrupulous critique; to Laura Stevens for sharing with me the fruits of her research; and to John Schietinger and Erica Fenby for research assistance. Earlier versions of this paper were delivered at the annual meetings of the MLA in Washington, D.C. (1996); at the conference on Archipelagic Identities 1485–1791 at Hertford College, Oxford (1999); to members of the English Department at the University of North Carolina, Greensboro; and to members of the Early Modern Colloquium at the University of Michigan. My thanks to the organizers of those events and to members of the audience.

This essay is reprinted, with permission, from *British Identities and English Renaissance Literature,* ed. Willy Maley and David J. Baker (Cambridge: Cambridge University Press, 2002).

1   The New England mission was still quite new, at least as a practical reality, when the Society was established in 1649. On the Massachusetts mainland John Eliot first preached to the Indians of Nonantum in the fall of 1646, his earlier attempts to interest them in Christian salvation having been met with flat rejection: "They gave no heed unto it, but were weary, and rather despised what I said." See Harold W. Van Lonkhuyzen,"A Reappraisal of the Praying Indians: Acculturation, Conversion, and Identity at Natick, Massachusetts, 1646–1730," *New England Quarterly* 63 (1990): 396–428, quote on 401. On Martha's Vineyard the Indian Hiacoomes converted to Christianity under the guidance

of Thomas Mayhew, Jr., as early as 1642, but his example was chiefly scorned by other Wampanoags until the "universal sicknes" of 1645–46. Henry Whitfield, *The Light Appearing More and More Towards the Perfect Day, Or, a Farther Discovery of the Present State of the Indians in New-England, Concerning the Progresse of the Gospel Amongst them: Manifested by Letters from such as Preacht to them there* (London, 1651), 111.

2 *An Act for the promoting and propagating the Gospel of Jesus Christ in New England [27 July, 1649]*, in *Acts and Ordinances of the Interregnum, 1642–1660*, ed. C. H. Firth and R. S. Rait, 3 vols. (London: Wyman and Sons, 1911), II: 197–200.

3 Ibid., 197, 198, 199, 200.

4 William Kellaway, *The New England Company 1649–1776: Missionary Society to the American Indians* (London: Longmans, Green, 1961), 30–36. Kellaway's precise calculation of donations to the Society between 1649 and 1660 is £15,910, 15s, 6 1/2d.

5 Since the Commissioners, as Kellaway observes in *The New England Company*, had originally been charged with protecting colonists *against* the Indians (as well as against the Dutch and French), there was at times some dissonance between their original and their newly augmented responsibilities (62–63).

6 When the New England Company was reauthorized under the restored Stuart monarchy (its new charter was sealed on February 7, 1661), it was also allowed to regain control over the properties and rents it had obtained during the interregnum. In the case of its most valuable properties, however, estates purchased from the Royalist Thomas Bedingfield, this reassertion of title involved years of litigation and disrupted income. See Kellaway, *New England Company*, 41–55.

7 Kellaway, *New England Company*, 87.

8 That is, since the versions produced by "the almost legendary figures of the early Church—Ulfilas, Mesrop, and Cyril and Methodius." See "Bible Translations," in the *Encyclopedia of North American Indians*, ed. Frederick E. Hoxie (Boston: Houghton Mifflin, 1996), 67–69.

9 Kellaway, *New England Company*, 122–46.

10 The eleven promotional pamphlets, in order of publication, are as follows: *New Englands First Fruits; in respect. First of the Conversion of some, Conviction of divers, Preparation of sundry of the Indians. 2. Of the progresse of Learning, in the Colledge at Cambridge in Massachusetts Bay. With Divers other speciall Matters concerning that Countrey . . .* (London, 1643); [John Wilson?], *The Day-breaking, if not the Sun-Rising of the Gospell With the Indians in New-England* (London, 1647); Thomas Shepard, *The Clear Sun-shine of the gospel breaking forth upon the Indians in New-England* (London, 1648); Edward Winslow, *The Glorious Progress of the Gospel, amongst the Indians in New England. Manifested by three Letters, under the Hand of that famous Instrument of the Lord Mr. John Eliot, And another from Thomas Mayhew jun: both Preachers of the Word, as well to the English as Indians in New England . . .* (London, 1649); Henry Whitfield, *The Light Appearing More and More Towards the Perfect Day. Or, a Farther Discovery of the Present State of the Indians in New-England, Concerning the Progresse of the Gospel Amongst them. Manifested by Letters from such as Preacht to them there* (London, 1651); Henry Whitfield, *Strength out of Weaknesse; Or a Glorious Manifesta-*

tion of the Further Progresse of the Gospel among the Indians in New-England. Held forth in Sundry Letters from divers Ministers and others to the Corporation established by Parliament for promoting the Gospel among the Heathen in New England; and to particular members thereof . . . (London, 1652); John Eliot and Thomas Mayhew, Jr., *Tears of Repentance: Or, a further Narrative of the Progress of the Gospel amongst the Indians in New-England: Setting forth, not only their present state and condition, but sundry confessions of sin by divers of the said Indians, wrought upon by the saving Power of the gospel; together with the manifestation of their faith and hope in Jesus Christ, and the work of grace upon their hearts* (London, 1653); John Eliot, *A Late and Further Manifestation of the Progress of the Gospel amongst the Indians in New-England. Declaring their constant Love and Zeal to the Truth: With a readinesse to give Accompt of their Faith and Hope; as of their desires in Church Communion to be Partakers of the Ordinances of Christ* . . . (London, 1655); John Eliot, *A further Accompt of the Progresse of the Gospel amongst the Indians in New-England and Of the means used effectually to advance the same,* with Abraham Peirson, *Some Helps for the Indians* (London, 1659); John Eliot, *A further Account of the progress of the Gospel Amongst the Indians in New-England. Being a Relation of the Confessions made by several Indians* (London, 1660); John Eliot, *A brief narrative of the progress of the Gospel amongst the Indians in New-England, in the year 1670* (London, 1671).

11   Whitfield, *The Light Appearing* (London, 1651), reprinted in *Tracts Relating to the Attempts to Convert to Christianity the Indians of New England: Collections of the Massachusetts Historical Society,* 3rd ser., 4 (1834): 100–147.

12   Stephen Greenblatt usefully estranges the notion in *Marvelous Possessions: The Wonder of the New World* (Chicago: University of Chicago Press, 1991), 120.

13   William Strachey, *The Historie of Travell into Virginia Britania* (1612), ed. Louis B. Wright and Virginia Freund (London: Hakluyt Society, 1953), 101.

14   Ibid.

15   Whitfield, *The Light Appearing,* 111.

16   This "second" connotation is, of course, the explanation given by Christ himself in the biblical verse that prompts John Eliot's Indian's question: "No man can serve two masters: for either he will hate the one, and love the other; or else he will hold to the one, and despise the other. Ye cannot serve God and mammon" (Matthew 6:24; King James version).

17   John Eliot, in Whitfield, *The Light Appearing,* 140, 141.

18   "How much," he continues, "those winds and shakings which carried many good men out of *Old* into *New England* have made way to the publishing of the name of Christ in those barbarous places." Ed[ward] Reynolds, introductory epistle "To the Christian Reader," in Eliot, *A Further Accompt,* A2r.

19   J. D., appendix to Winslow, *Glorious Progress,* E1r.

20   John Morrill, "The Stuarts," in *The Oxford Illustrated History of Britain,* ed. Kenneth O. Morgan (Oxford: Oxford University Press, 1984), 295; Lacey Baldwin Smith, *This Realm of England: 1399 to 1688,* 6th ed. (Lexington, Mass.: D. C. Heath, 1992), 254–55.

21   Kellaway, *New England Company,* 82. The authors of the *Dictionary of National*

Biography assert that Eliot was first ordained within the Anglican church; Kellaway (81–82) thinks this is improbable.

22 J. D., appendix to Winslow, *Glorious Progress*, E1r.

23 Joseph Caryl, preface to Whitfield, *The Light Appearing*, 100.

24 J. D., appendix to Winslow, *Glorious Progress*, D3v.

25 Richard W. Cogley, "John Eliot and the Origins of the American Indians," *Early American Literature* 21: 3 (Winter 1986–87): 210–25.

26 Kellaway, *New England Company*, 26.

27 J. D., appendix to Winslow, *Glorious Progress*, D3v.

28 Joseph Caryl, in John Eliot, *A Late and Further Manifestation of the Progress of the Gospel amongst the Indians in New-England. Declaring their constant Love and Zeal to the Truth: With a readinesse to give Accompt of their Faith and Hope; as of their desires in Church Communion to be Partakers of the Ordinances of Christ* . . . (London, 1655); reprinted in *Tracts Relating to the Attempts to Convert to Christianity the Indians of New England: Collections of the Massachusetts Historical Society*, 3rd ser., 4 (1834): 261–87, quote on 267.

29 John Eliot, in Winslow, *Glorious Progress*, C1v.

30 *Acts of the Commissioners of the United Colonies*, ed. David Pulsifer, 2 vols. (Records of the Colony of New Plymouth in New England, IX & X; Boston, 1859), I: 203–4. Cited in Kellaway, *New England Company*, 92.

31 [John Wilson?] *The Day-breaking, if not the Sun-Rising of the Gospell With the Indians in New-England* (London, 1647); reprinted in *Tracts Relating to the Attempts to Convert to Christianity the Indians of New England: Collections of the Massachusetts Historical Society*, 3rd ser., 4 (1834): 1–23, quote on 15.

32 Caryl, preface to Whitfield, *The Light Appearing*, 100.

33 For some of the better-balanced attempts to assess the motives and impact of the New England missionaries, see Robert James Naeher, "Dialogue in the Wilderness: John Eliot and the Indian Exploration of Puritanism as a Source of Meaning, Comfort, and Ethnic Survival," *New England Quarterly* 62 (1989): 346–68; James P. Ronda, "Generations of Faith: The Christian Indians of Martha's Vineyard," *William and Mary Quarterly*, 3rd ser., 38:3 (July 1981): 369–94, and "'We Are Well As We Are': An Indian Critique of Seventeenth-Century Christian Missions," *William and Mary Quarterly*, 3rd ser., 34:1 (Jan. 1977): 66–82; Neal Salisbury, "Red Puritans: The 'Praying Indians' of Massachusetts Bay and John Eliot," *William and Mary Quarterly*, 3rd ser., 31:1 (Jan. 1974): 27–54; Laura Marie Stevens, "'The Poor Indians': Native Americans in Eighteenth-Century Missionary Writings," Ph.D. dissertation, University of Michigan, 1998; and Van Lonkhuyzen, "A Reappraisal."

34 Strachey, *The Historie of Travell*, 19, 23, 28. Strachey takes the first part of his text from Proverbs 16.

35 Eliot, in Winslow, *Glorious Progess*, C4v.

36 Eliot, postscript to *A Further Accompt*, D4r.

37 Ibid., C2v, C2r–v.

38 Ibid., D2r.

39 Thomas Mayhew, in Whitfield, *The Light Appearing*, 116.

40   J. D., appendix to Winslow, *Glorious Progress*, E2r.

41   Whitfield, *The Light Appearing*, 146–47.

42   Eliot, in Whitfield, *The Light Appearing*, 130.

43   Cogley, "John Eliot," 213.

44   See, for instance, David Armitage, *The Ideological Origins of the British Empire* (Cambridge: Cambridge University Press, 2000); Julia Adams, *The Familial State: Ruling Families and Merchant Capitalism in Early Modern Europe* (Ithaca, N.Y.: Cornell University Press, 2005); and Philip Gorski, *The Disciplinary Revolution: Calvinism and the Rise of the State in Early Modern Europe* (Chicago: University of Chicago Press, 2003).

45   Eliot, in Winslow, *Glorious Progress*, C3r.

46   Ibid., C2r.

CHAPTER 5. CATHOLIC SAINTS IN SPAIN'S ATLANTIC EMPIRE

1   The Spanish word *mercedes* like the English *mercy* connoted "grant" but also "God's gift of grace." I would like to extend my thanks to Linda Gregerson, Susan Juster, Ann Twinam, and Jorge Cañizares-Esguerra for their careful reading of this chapter and for their insightful suggestions for its improvement.

2   For liturgy in Mexico City I rely on current-events chronicler Antonio de Robles who was particularly fastidious about the finer points of worship. Antonio de Robles, *Diario De Sucesos Notables (1665–1703)*, ed. Antonio Castro Leal, 3 vols. (Mexico City: Editorial Porrúa, 1946).

3   My work addresses these martyrs in Cornelius Conover, "A Saint in the Empire: Mexico City's San Felipe de Jesús, 1597–1820" (Ph.D. dissertation, University of Texas, Austin, 2008). The Discalced Franciscans embraced a strict ascetic life. Starting in the late fifteenth century, founding members expanded through southern Spain to Asia via New Spain. Antolín Abad Pérez and Cayetano Sánchez Fuertes, "La Descalcez Franciscana en España, Hispanoamérica y Extremo Oriente: Síntesis histórica, geográfica y bibliográfica," *Archivo Ibero-Americano*, 2nd ser., 59 (Sept.–Dec. 1999): 461–84.

4   September 4, 1628, Mexico City Council, *Actas Antiguas de Cabildo*, vol. 26 (Mexico City: Imprenta de "El Correo Español," 1907), 341.

5   Miguel Sánchez, *Sermon de San Felipe de Iesvs* (Mexico City: Iuan Ruiz, 1640), 14.

6   I focus particularly on Mexico City's public religion or the processions and masses where colonial institutions formally attended. For the symbolic content of the processions so beloved by the Spanish Baroque see Carolyn Dean, *Inka Bodies and the Body of Christ: Corpus Christi in Colonial Cuzco, Peru* (Durham, N.C.: Duke University Press, 1999); or Linda Curcio-Nagy, *The Great Festivals of Colonial Mexico City* (Albuquerque: University of New Mexico Press, 2004).

7   For several variations on this hypothesis see Antonio Rubial García, *La Santa Controvertida: Hagiografía y conciencia criolla alrededor de los venerables no canonizados de Nueva España* (Mexico City: Universidad Nacional Autónoma de México; Fonda de Cultura

Económica, 1999); David A. Brading, *Mexican Phoenix: Our Lady of Guadalupe* (Cambridge: Cambridge University Press, 2001); and Ronald J. Morgan, *Spanish American Saints and the Rhetoric of Identity, 1600–1810* (Tucson: University of Arizona Press, 2002).

8 For an introduction into the field of liturgy and devotion in medieval history see Adalbert de Vogüé, *The Rule of St. Benedict: A Doctrinal and Spiritual Commentary*, trans. J. P. Hasbrouck, Cistercian Studies 54 (Kalamazoo, Mich.: Cistercian Publications, 1983). For devotion in a time of reform see Eamon Duffy, *The Stripping of the Altars: Traditional Religion in England, c. 1400–c. 1580* (New Haven: Yale University Press, 1992), 11–376.

9 The most famous of these critics was Erasmus of Rotterdam as described in Marcel Bataillon, *Erasmo y España, estudios sobre la historia spiritual del siglo xvi*, trans. Antonio Alatorre (Mexico City: Fondo de Cultura Económica, 1982). For the reform in the cult of saints and the historiography addressing it see Simon Ditchfield, *Liturgy, Sanctity, and History in Tridentine Italy: Pietro Maria Campi and the Preservation of the Particular*, Cambridge Studies in Italian History and Culture (Cambridge: Cambridge University Press, 1995), 1–9.

10 This was the first Roman Catholic breviary, but there were two other rites that became standard use throughout the church: the first was the Roman-Frankish rite, and the second was the Roman-Franciscan abbreviated version. John Harper, *The Forms and Orders of Western Liturgy* (Oxford: Clarendon Paperbacks, 1991), 11–12.

11 Historians still debate in voluminous literature the ultimate effect of this era's reform efforts. For a solid account of Spain see Sara Nalle, *God in La Mancha: Religious Reform and the People of Cuenca, 1500–1650* (Baltimore: Johns Hopkins University Press, 1992).

12 The papacy, in general, emerged from the Catholic Reformation with many of its traditional prerogatives intact and even increased. John O'Malley, *Trent and All That* (Cambridge, Mass.: Harvard University Press, 2000), 119–43.

13 The feast of precept was known as a *festa fori*. The liturgical feasts, *festa chori*, carry only the obligation to attend Mass and hear the recitation of the Divine Office.

14 The pope could also move feast days. For example, Clement X transferred the date of the feast of the Guardian Angel from March 1 to October 2. Robles, *Diario*, vol. 1, 153.

15 Congregation of Rites, Rome, September 26, 1629, *De facultate dicendi Officium & Missam de tribus sanctus Martyribus PAULO Michi, IOANNE de Goto, & DIDACO Quizai e Societate IESU in Japonia pro Christi FIDE crucifixis* (Rome: Ex Typographia Reu, Camerae Apost, 1629); Real Academia de Historia de Madrid, Madrid (RAHM), Jesuitas, Tomos, vol. 62/43.

16 In 1628 Urban extended this right to both dioceses. Urban VIII, *Alias pro parte* (Rome, September 11, 1628), in Francisco Matritensi, *Bullarium Fratrum ordinis minorum sancti francisci*, vol. 2 (Madrid: Ex Typographia Emmanuelis Fernandez, 1744), 98–99.

17 February 15, 1629, Archivo Histórico de la Catedral de México (ACCM), *Actas*, vol. 8, fol. 216.

18 Gertrude (1256–1301) was a Benedictine and a mystic. Ann W. Astell, *Eating Beauty: The Eucharist and the Spiritual Arts of the Middle Ages* (Ithaca, N.Y.: Cornell Universi-

ty Press, 2006). Blessed Innocent XI declared a universal feast in honor of her in 1677. Twenty years later the city council asked Rome for a special prayer to her. See also June 15, 1696, Francisco del Barrio Lorenzot, "Compendio de los libros capitulares de la Muy Noble Insigne, y Muy Leal Ciudad de México," Archivo Histórico de la Ciudad de México (AHCM), vol. 436a, fols. 339v–40.

19   Historiography has tended to assert the opposite. For one very influential proponent of an activist papacy see Peter Burke, "How to Be a Counter-Reformation Saint," in *Religion and Society in Early Modern Europe, 1500–1800*, ed. K. von Greyerz (London: George Allen & Unwin, 1984), 45–55.

20   Urban VIII, *Salvatoris Domini nostri* in Joannes Bollandus and Godefridus Henschenius, *Acta sanctorum*, ed. Joanne Carnandet, vol. February, tom. 1 (Paris: V. Palme, 1863), 748–49.

21   The pope could favor causes already proposed, for example, those of Dominic, Francis, Clare, and Anthony of Padua. André Vauchez, *Sainthood in the Later Middle Ages* (Cambridge: Cambridge University Press, 1997), 73.

22   Andrés Saenz de la Peña, *Manual de los santos sacramentos* (Mexico City: Francisco Robledo, 1642), 121.

23   Jews and Muslims were similarly "united" in Catholicism or invited to leave Spain. Henry Kamen, *Spain's Road to Empire: The Making of a World Power, 1492–1763* (London: Allen Lane, 2002), 17–20.

24   During the seventeenth century, twenty Spanish were beatified (plus the Nagasaki martyrs for a total of forty-six) and fifteen canonized; five cults were confirmed. In the entire Catholic Church a grand total of seventy-five were beatified and twenty-five canonized, and another thirty-three saints had their cult confirmed in the seventeenth century. Philippe Jansen and Dominique Le Tourneau, "Causes of Canonization," in *The Papacy: An Encyclopedia*, ed. Philippe Levillain, vol. 1 (New York: Routledge, 2002), 271.

25   Some Spanish saints whose liturgical ranking was raised include Thomas de Villanueva, Raymond Peñafort, Diego de Alcalá, Peter de Alcántara, and Domingo de la Calzada. The following Spanish saints obtained a double office: Ignatius Loyola, Francis Xavier, Liberatea, Peter Nolasco, Ferdinand III, Julián, Rose of Lima, Raymond Nonnatus, Eulalia de Mérida, Peter Arbues, and Francis Borgia. Robles, *Diario,* and Gregorio Martín de Guijo, *Diario, 1648-1664,* ed. Manuel Romero de Terreros, 3 vols. (Mexico City: Editorial Porrúa, 1952).

26   August 8, 1677, Robles, *Diario*, vol. 1, 220. St. Gertrude, mentioned above, was already canonized. In making this calculation I set aside the Virgin Mary, St. Joseph, the Apostles, and church fathers.

27   May 30, 1603, Mexico City Council, *Actas*, vol. 15, 167.

28   Guijo, *Diario*, vol. 2, 9.

29   October 12, 1620, Mexico City Council, *Actas*, vol. 22, 222.

30   This celebration became an annual event attended by the highest religious and secular administrators. Guijo, *Diario*, vol. 1, 206–7; ACCM, *Actas*, vol. 11, fol. 241.

31   Guijo, *Diario*, vol. 1, 239.

32   November 10, 1656, ACCM, *Actas*, vol. 13, fols. 106–106v; and Guijo, *Diario*, vol. 2, 69.

33   This was celebrated at least in 1664, 1701, and 1703. Guijo, *Diario*, vol. 2, 238; Robles, *Diario*, vol. 3, 170–73, 298. King Philip and Pope Alexander VII reaffirmed its place in the Spanish liturgy. November 11, 1703, Robles, *Diario*, vol. 3, 298.

34   June 8, 1679, Robles, *Diario*, vol. 1, 263.

35   Mexico City Cathedral, "Cerem. pract. dela S. agr. Catred," Benson Latin American Collection, University of Texas, Austin (hereafter referred to as BLAC), G146, fol. 31v.

36   Guijo, *Diario*, vol. 2, 92–94. Felipe Próspero's death left Charles as the heir and eventual king.

37   Juan de Solórzano Pereira, *Política Indiana*, vol. 1 (1648: repr. Madrid: Ediciones Atlas, 1972), 87–88.

38   January 12, 1629, Mexico City Council, *Actas*, vol. 27, 40–41.

39   This was about what the city spent to receive a new archbishop. Ibid.

40   August 18, 1628, Barrio Lorenzot, "Compendio," vol. 436a, fol. 129.

41   Viceroys could also change the dates of events. Viceroy Juan Leyva de la Cerda postponed the festival of Hippolytus in 1661 because his granddaughter had died. August 16, 1661, Guijo, *Diario*, vol. 2, 157.

42   January 12, 1629, Mexico City Council, *Actas*, vol. 27, 40-41.

43   Marcelo de Ribadeneira, Ordo Fratrum Minorum, *Historia del Archipielago y otros Reynos* . . . (1601), Historical Conservation Society, 17 (Manila: MDB Printing, 1970), 435, 438, 446–47.

44   December 5 and 15, 1628, Barrio Lorenzot, "Compendio," vol. 436a, fols. 136v–137, 137–137v.

45   August 20, 1629, ibid., fol. 152.

46   Ibid., fols. 152, 152v, 158.

47   Francisco Javier Alegre, *Historia de la provincial de la Compañía de Jesus de Nueva España*, ed. Ernest J. Burrus and Félix Zubillaga, vol. 2 (Rome: Institutum Historicum S.J., 1956), 405.

48   January 11, 1630, Barrio Lorenzot, "Compendio," vol. 436a, fol. 161. In William Christian's classic study of central Castile in the late sixteenth century, 90 percent of the communal vows were aimed at protecting the town from natural disasters. Christian, *Local Religion in Sixteenth-Century Spain* (Princeton, N.J.: Princeton University Press, 1981), 32.

49   September 3, 1607, Mexico City Council, *Actas*, vol. 17, 91–92; and September 24, 1607, ibid., 103–4. In 1611 the council adopted St. Nicolas Tolentino for earthquakes; August 26, 1611, ibid., vol. 18, 155–56.

50   The city appealed specifically to Gregory Thaumaturgus on only three occasions: 1607, 1629, and 1645. September 3, 1607, Mexico City Council, *Actas*, vol. 17, 91–92; and September 24, 1607, ibid., 103–4; August 20, 1629, Barrio Lorenzot, "Compendio," vol. 436a, fol. 152; September 26, 1645, ACCM, *Actas*, vol. 10, fol. 462–462v. The city never used St. Nicolas; the standard reaction to an earthquake was a general prayer in the churches.

51   For a good summary of the cult of Remedies in Mexico City see Linda Curcio-

Nagy, "Native Icon to City Protectress to Royal Patroness: Ritual, Political Symbolism and the Virgin of Remedies," *The Americas* 52:3 (Jan. 1996): 367–91.

52   July 6, 1620, Mexico City Council, *Actas*, vol. 22, 170–82. The minutes do not include the rationale for this reprimand, nor indeed do they explain how it came to be ignored, since Teresa appeared later as a patron saint apparently without a subsequent city council vote. Mexico City adopted Isidor Labrador in 1638. January 22, 1638, Barrio Lorenzot, "Compendio," vol. 436a, fol. 217.

53   The Franciscans had Philip; the Jesuits had Francis Xavier; the Carmelites had Teresa of Ávila; the Augustinians had Nicolas; and the Cistercians had Isidor. Gregory and Hippolytus were celebrated in their own churches. Surprisingly, the Dominicans did not have a patron saint singled out in Mexico City.

54   February 19, 1659, Guijo, *Diario*, vol. 2, 115. With their institutional stability and well-established traditions, the orders constituted one of the most influential factors in forming the devotional culture of Mexico City and deserve a more detailed look than this chapter can afford.

55   Kenneth L. Woodward, *Making Saints: How the Catholic Church Determines Who Becomes a Saint, Who Doesn't, and Why* (New York: Simon and Schuster, 1990), 51.

56   José Antonio Pichardo, *Vida y martirio del protomártir Mexicano San Felipe de Jesús de las Casas, religioso del hábito y orden de San Francisco de Manila* (Guadalajara, Mexico: Francisco Loreto y Diéguez Sucr., 1934), 147.

57   January 18, 1636, Mexico City Council, *Actas*, vol. 30, 118.

58   Ibid.

59   January 18 and 21, 1636, ibid., 118, 123.

60   January 21, 1636, ibid., 123.

61   ACCM, *Actas*, vol. 9, fol. 330v.

62   October 19, 1640, ACCM, *Actas*, vol. 10, fol. 61.

63   [Dr. Rodrigo Ruíz de Zepeda Martínez], *Auto de fe de María Zarata* (Mexico City: Viuda de Bernardo Calderón, 1659).

64   Sponsorship for the Mexico City cathedral meant they hosted the office, decorated the church, and elected a cleric to give a sermon to the attending dignitaries. The archbishop said the office.

65   October 19 and 29, 1640, ACCM, *Actas*, vol. 10, fols. 61, 62v. This is one of a few instances where the Franciscans figured into Philip's cult. In 1704 an exasperated city council took the Franciscans out of the celebration altogether. February 4, 1704, Barrio Lorenzot, "Compendio," vol. 437a, fol. 18. No information suggests why their support was so faint in Mexico City.

66   October 19 and 29, 1640, ACCM, *Actas*, vol. 10, fols. 61, 62v.

67   January 22, 1641, and May 10, 1641, Mexico City Council, *Actas*, vols. 32–33, 174 and 209.

68   The majority of these disputes were resolved in the Mexico City community, but some of the suits did go to the king and pope for final resolution. In August 1703 a royal de-

cree and papal brief reprimanded the archbishop for failing to implement a previous decree giving the Discalced Franciscans preference. August 19, 1703, Robles, *Diario*, vol. 3, 282.

69 Mexico City Cathedral, "Cerem. pract. dela S. agr. Catred," G146, fol. 4.

70 Jacinto de la Serna, *Sermon predicado el la Santa Iglesia Cathedral de Mexico* (Mexico City: Viuda de Bernardo Calderon, 1652), iv.

71 Hiacinto de la Caxica, *Sermon predicado en la Santa Iglesia Cathedral Metropolitana de Mexico, a la fiesta del glorioso S. Felipe de Iesus, protomartir de las Indias, y patron de la muy noble Ciudad de México* (Mexico City: Bernardo Calderon, 1639), s/f.

72 Luis Vaca Salasar, *Sermon predicado en la Sancta Iglesia Cathedral Metropolitana de Mexico, á la fiesta del glorioso S. Felipe de Iesvs, protomartyr de la Indias, y patrón de la mvy noble y leal ciudad de México* (Mexico City: Iuan Ruys, 1638), 3.

73 Caxica, *Sermon*, s/f.

74 Sánchez, *Sermon de San Felipe de Iesvs*, 9v.

75 Vaca Salasar, *Sermon*, 12v.

76 Several publications on San Felipe predated the first dealing with Guadalupe, which was Miguel Sánchez, *Imagen de la virgen Maria Madre de Dios de Gvadalvpe, milagrosamente aparecida en la civdad de Mexico* (Mexico City: Bernardo Calderon, 1648).

77 Catholic heavyweights St. Joseph and St. Francis had a larger following. Among premodern saints Teresa de Ávila was perhaps the most prominent saint of the Spanish Baroque in Mexico City. She was a titular saint, patron saint, and frequently mentioned role model. Her church was rebuilt twice: in 1684 and 1701. Robles, *Diario*, vol. 2, 74; vol. 3, 165.

78 March 22, 1661, ACCM, *Actas*, vol. 14, fol. 8–8v.

79 Brading, *Mexican Phoenix*, 76–77; Stafford Poole, *Our Lady of Guadalupe: The Origins and Sources of a Mexican National Symbol, 1531–1797* (Tucson: University of Arizona Press, 1995), 128–43.

80 The historiography on St. Rose of Lima is extensive, but a good start might be Frank Graziano, *Wounds of Love: The Mystical Marriage of Saint Rose of Lima* (New York: Oxford University Press, 2004).

81 August 30, 1673, Robles, *Diario*, vol. 1, 132.

82 April 11, 1671, ibid., 109; April 7, 1671, ACCM, *Actas*, vol. 18, fols. 142–142v. Celebrations for the universal patron took place on August 30, 1673. Robles, *Diario*, vol. 1, 132.

83 September 4, 1672, Robles, *Diario*, vol. 1, 117.

84 Pedro del Castillo, *La estrella del occidente, la Rosa de Lima* (Mexico City: Bartholome de Gama, 1670).

85 May 18, 1674, ACCM, *Actas*, vol. 19, fol. 101v.

86 February 4, 1678, ibid., vol. 20, fol. 68.

87 Letter to Mexico City Cathedral chapter, Rome, July 11, 1676, BLAC, G50, fols. 379–80.

88 Br. Don Alonso de Gomez Rui Gomez Robles to Mexico City cathedral chapter, Mexico City, August 8, 1699, BLAC, G64, fol. 101v.

89   Charles II, Madrid, May 25, 1689, "Real cedula sobre la festividad de San Felipe de Jesus en Mexico," Archivo de la Curia Provincial Franciscana Santo Evangelio, Convento de Santa Barbara (Puebla), caja 182, s/f.

90   Ibid.

91   Mexico City Cathedral, "Cerem. pract. dela S. agr. Catred," BLAC, G146, fol. 30.

CHAPTER 6. A WANDERING JESUIT IN EUROPE AND AMERICA

1   In the absence of a systematic overview of Jesuit missions in the Americas, see Nicholas P. Cushner, *Why Have You Come Here? The Jesuits and the First Evangelization of Native America* (New York: Oxford University Press, 2006).

2   José de Acosta, *The Natural and Moral History of the Indies*, ed. Jane E. Mangan (Durham, N.C.: Duke University Press, 2002); Joseph-François Lafitau, *Customs of the American Indians Compared with the Customs of Primitive Times*, ed. and trans. William N. Fenton and Elizabeth L. Moore, 2 vols. (Toronto: Champlain Society, 1974); Margaret Hodgen, *Early Anthropology in the Sixteenth and Seventeenth Centuries* (Philadelphia: University of Pennsylvania Press, 1964), chaps. 8 and 11; Anthony Pagden, *The Fall of Natural Man: The American Indian and the Origins of Comparative Ethnology* (Cambridge: Cambridge University Press 1982); Sabine MacCormack, "Limits of Understanding: Perceptions of Greco-Roman and Amerindian Paganism in Early Modern Europe," in *America in European Consciousness, 1493–1750*, ed. Karen Kupperman (Chapel Hill: University of North Carolina Press, 1995).

3   See Jonathan Spence, *The Memory Palace of Matteo Ricci* (New York: Penguin, 1984); Liam Brockey, *Journey to the East: The Jesuit Mission to China, 1579–1724* (Cambridge, Mass.: Harvard University Press, 2007); Ines Zupanov, *Disputed Mission: Jesuit Experiments and Brahmanical Knowledge in Seventeenth-Century India* (New York: Oxford University Press. 1999).

4   See Allan Greer and Kenneth Mills, "A Catholic Atlantic," in *The Atlantic in Global History, 1500–2000*, ed. Jorge Cañizares-Esguerra and Erik R. Seeman (Upper Saddle River, N.J.: Prentice Hall, 2006), 3–19.

5   Elsewhere I have already made a similar point about another Jesuit, Claude Chauchetière: see Allan Greer, *Mohawk Saint: Catherine Tekakwitha and the Jesuits* (New York: Oxford University Press, 2005), esp. 59–88.

6   I have been unable to locate the original document in Chaumonot's hand, but various copies, manuscript and published, are available. The best-known edition of the autobiography was published in France in 1869: Auguste Carayon, ed., *Le père Chaumonot de la compagnie de Jésus: autobiographie et pièces inédites* (Poitiers: Henri Oudin, 1869). However, this book appears to have been copied from an earlier American edition: [J. M. Shea, ed.], *La vie du R. P. Pierre Joseph Marie Chaumonot, de la compagnie de Jésus, missionnaire dans la Nouvelle France* (New York: Cramoissy, 1858). The 1858 edition was recently republished together with an English translation: *Pierre-Joseph-Marie Chaumonot, S.J.: Autobiography*

and Supplement, trans. William Lonc (Midland, Ontario: Steve Catlin, 2002). The Jesuits of Quebec copied a condensed version of the autobiography to send to France shortly after Chaumonot's death in 1693: Archives du séminaire de Québec, lettres R, numéro 4, "Lettre circulaire contenant un abrégé de la vie et de la mort du père Chaumonot, décédé au collège de Québec le 21 février 1693." For a modern account of Chaumonot's life, viewed from a religious perspective, see René Latourelle, *Pierre-Joseph-Marie Chaumonot: Compagnon des martyrs canadiens* (Saint-Laurent, Quebec: Bellarmin, 1998).

7   See Archivum Romanum Societatis Iesus, Rome, provincia Romana 57, cat. trienn. 1636–1639; 173, ingressus novitiorum, 1631–1675.

8   Musée de Ste.-Colombe, parish registers, baptism of Pierre Chaumonot, son of Clément Chaumonot and of Jehanne, his wife, March 9, 1611.

9   Carayon, *Le père Chaumonot,* 2–3. "Je me déterminai donc à courir en vagabond par le monde, plutôt que de m'exposer à la confusion que méritoit ma friponnerie."

10   This was a region where a hundred years later a more famous teenage runaway named Jean-Jacques Rousseau would take his apprenticeship in vagabondage. The experiences of the two boys, as well as the picaresque style in which each recounted them in their respective memoirs, display remarkable parallels. See Jean-Jacques Rousseau, *Les Confessions* (Paris: Gallimard, 1959); Leo Damrosch, *Jean-Jacques Rousseau, Restless Genius* (New York: Houghton Mifflin, 2005), 43–68.

11   Carayon, *Le père Chaumonot,* 11. "J'étois pieds nuds, ayant été obligé de jetter mes souliers, qui étant rompus me blessoient. Ma chemise pourrie et mes habits déchirés étoient plains de vermine, ma tête mesm que je ne peignois point se remplit d'une si horrible galle qu'il s'y forma du pus et des vers avec une exteme puanteur."

12   Ibid., 24. "Tous jeunes hommes d'une naissance distinguée." "Je me sentois souvent caressé de Notre Seigneur, comme l'enfant l'est de sa mère, qui pour l'endormir plus doucement lui fait sucer le lait de son sein maternel."

13   The *Jesuit Relations* were reports from the Canadian missions published annually in France from 1632 to 1673. See Allan Greer, ed., *The Jesuit Relations: Natives and Missionaries in Seventeenth-Century North America* (Boston: Bedford, 2000), 1–19.

14   Carayon, *Le père Chaumonot,* 29. "Pour instruire et pour convertir ces nations barbares."

15   Archivum Romanum Societatis Iesus, fondo gesuitico, vol. 741, f. 40, Calmonotto to Vitelleschi, Sept. 16, 1637. Thanks to Giovanni Pizzorusso for locating and translating this *indipeta* from the original Italian. Cf., Giovanni Pizzorusso, "Le choix indifférent: Mentalités et attentes des jésuites aspirants missionnaires dans l'Amérique française au XVIIe siècle," *Mélanges de l'école française de Rome—Italie et Méditerranée* 109 (1997): 881–94.

16   Karin Velez, personal communication.

17   Carayon, *Le père Chaumonot,* 32. "Je vis en songe, une personne que je pris pour ma mère; mais son visage noirâtre et bazané m'étonna . . . qui vouloit me servir de mère."

18   Note that images of the Virgin with a dark complexion were found in various locations in early modern Europe. See Monique Scheer, "From Majesty to Mystery: Change in the Meanings of Black Madonnas from the Sixteenth to Nineteenth Centuries," *American Historical Review* 107 (Dec. 2002): 1412–40.

19   Musée de Ste-Coulombe, parish registers, death of Jeanne Le Roux, May 2, 1640. (His father, Clément Chaumonot, died Jan. 12, 1648.)

20   Reuben Thwaites, ed., *The Jesuit Relations and Allied Documents*, 73 vols. (Cleveland, Ohio: Burrows Brothers, 1896–1900), 15: 198–201, Chaumonot to Mutio Vitalleschi, Sept. 7, 1639; François Du Creux, *The History of Canada or New France*, trans. Percy J. Robinson, ed. James B. Conacher, 2 vols. (Toronto: Champlain Society, 1951), 272–73. For more on the religious women of early New France see Elizabeth Rapley, *The Dévotes: Women and Church in Seventeenth-Century France* (Montreal: McGill-Queen's University Press, 1990); Leslie Choquette, "'Ces Amazones du Grand Dieu': Women and Mission in Seventeenth-Century Canada," *French Historical Studies* 17 (1992): 628–55; Dominique Deslandres, "Les femmes missionnaires de la Nouvelle-France," in *La religion de ma mère: les femmes et la transmission de la foi*, ed. Jean Delumeau (Paris: Le Cerf, 1992), 74–84; Natalie Z. Davis, *Women on the Margins: Three Seventeenth-Century Lives* (Cambridge, Mass.: Harvard University Press, 1995), 63–139.

21   See Eric J. Leed, *The Mind of the Traveller from Gilgamesh to Global Tourism* (New York: Basic Books, 1991).

22   Carayon, *Le père Chaumonot*, 38–39. "Comme cette contagion n'attaquoit pas les François, on nous prenoit pour des sorciers qui causions ce mal, et lesquels on chassoit de la plupart des cabanes."

23   Ibid., 46.

24   Ibid., 40. "La plus difficile de toutes celles de l'Amérique Septentrionale"; "J'avois tant de répugnance à faire ces visites qu'à chaque fois que j'entrois dans les cabanes, il me sembloit que j'allois au supplice: tant j'appréhendois les railleries qu'il m'y falloit souffrir."

25   Ibid., 46–47. "Il plut à Dieu de donner à mon travail tant de bénédiction, qu'il n'y a dans le Huron ni tour ni subtilité ni manière de s'énoncer dont je n'aie eu la connoissance."

26   This treatise, written jointly with Brébeuf, has not survived. Victor Egon Hanzeli, *Missionary Linguistics in New France: A Study of Seventeenth- and Eighteenth-Century Descriptions of American Indian Languages* (The Hague and Paris: Mouton, 1969), 22.

27   Thwaites, *Jesuit Relations*, 18: 14–35, Chaumonot to Ph. Nappi, May 26, 1640.

28   Lucien Campeau, ed., *Monumenta Novae Franciae,* 9 vols. (Rome: Monumenta Historica Societatis Jesu, 1967–2003), 7: 404, editor's footnote.

29   Ibid., 7:581, 616–19.

30   Bruce G. Trigger, *The Children of Aataentsic: A History of the Huron People to 1660* (Montreal: McGill-Queen's University Press, 1976), 725–88.

31   Jean Dequen, "Relation de 1655 et 1656," in Campeau, *Monumenta*, 8: 842. "[Il] possède la langue, le coeur et l'esprit des sauvages."

32   Ibid., 855–59.

33   Carayon, *Le père Chaumonot*, 55–56, "qu'elles voulurent m'en remercier dans un grand festin qui se fit dans leur bourg." This experience prompted him to reflect on the favorable disposition of women, both European and Iroquois, toward Christian piety: "It is not only in Europe that women are more inclined to sweetness and piety than men." "Ce

n'est pas seulement en Europe que les personnes du sexe sont plus portées à la douceur et à la piété que les hommes."

34 Relation of 1655–56, Campeau, *Monumenta*, 8: 869–76. On the midwinter ceremony of *Onnonhouarori* see Dean Snow, *The Iroquois* (Oxford: Blackwell, 1994), 7; and Bruce Elliott Johansen and Barbara Alice Mann, eds., *Encyclopedia of the Haudenosaunee (Iroquois Confederacy)* (Westport, Conn.: Greenwood, 2000), 52–53, 203.

35 Gordon M. Sayre, *Les Sauvages Américaines: Representations of Native Americans in French and English Colonial Literature* (Chapel Hill: University of North Carolina Press, 1997).

36 Davis, *Women on the Margins*, 107–22.

37 See Allan Greer, "Colonial Saints: Gender, Race and Hagiography in New France," *William and Mary Quarterly*, 3rd ser., 57 (April 2000): 323–48.

38 Relation of 1651–52, Campeau, *Monumenta*, 8: 292–96. "Ah quelle perte! . . . Quoyque vous ayez esté tesmoins occulaires de ses vertus, lorsque nous demeurions ensemble chez luy, en mesme cabane, à mesme feu et à mesme table, ou plustost à mesme pot ou à mesme chaudière, puisque les tables ne sont pas en usage en ce pays-là."

39 Archives des colonies, C11A, vol 2, 263–69 (National Archives Canada microfilm copy). This document has been reproduced, with commentary: "[Mémoire concernant la nation iroquoise], Pierre-Joseph-Marie Chaumonot, 1666," *Recherches amérindiennes au Québec* 26 (1996): 5–10. "La Nation Iroquoise est composé de neuf familles qui font deux Bandes dont l'une est de quatre familles et l'autre de cinq"; "La première bande Gueyniotiteshesgué qui veut dire les quatres familles." This document can be viewed at the Archives and Library Canada website: http://data2.archives.ca/e/e032/e000778101.jpg.

40 Ibid. "Quand ils vont en guerre et qu'ils veulent informer des partis, ceux qui pourroient passer sur leurs routes; ils depeignent lanimal de la famille dont ils sont avec une hache qu'il tient de la patte droite."

41 Carayon, *Le père Chaumonot*, 58–59. "Pour moi il y avoit quatorze ans et plus que j'avois de très ardents désirs et presque continuels que la divine Marie eut grande quantité d'enfans spirituels et adoptifs pour la consoler des douleurs que lui avoit causé la perte de son Jésus." On the confraternity of the Holy Family see Marie-Aimée Cliche, *Les pratiques de dévotion en Nouvelle-France: Comportements populaires et encadrement ecclésial dans le gouvernement de Québec* (Quebec: Presses de l'Université Laval, 1988), 158–70.

42 Carayon, *Le père Chaumonot*, 88–89. "Comme il possédoit en perfection les langues sauvages, nommément le Huron et l'Onnontagué, il a presque toujours eu le principal soin des missions où il s'est trouvé et la principale partie des biens qui s'y sont faits. Il a formé plusieurs de nos missionnaires. Tous ceux Memes des Notres qui apprendront jamais le Huron l'apprendront à la faveur des préceptes, des racines, des discours et de plusieurs autres beaux ouvrages qu'il nous a laissés en cette langue. Les sauvages eux-mêmes avouoient qu'il la parloit mieux qu'eux, qui se piquoient la plupart de bien parler, et qui parlent en effet avec beaucoup de pureté, d'éloquence et de facilité." Some of Chaumonot's writings on language have survived, including a French-Huron dictionary and vocabulary housed at the John Carter Brown Library, Codex Ind 12.

43 The history of the early modern world is rife with stories of cross-cultural identity shifts. In addition to the Jesuit cases of Matteo Ricci and Roberto di Nobili, mentioned above, consider the cases of Pierre-Esprit Radisson, successively French-Canadian settler, Mohawk warrior, and English gentleman, as well as Eunice Williams and Mary Jemison, both New England settlers captured in war who were assimilated into the culture of their Iroquois captors. Martin Fournier, *Pierre-Esprit Radisson, aventurier et commerçant* (Sillery, Quebec: Septentrion, 2001); John Demos, *The Unredeemed Captive: A Family Story from Early America* (New York: Random House, 1994); James E. Seaver, *A Narrative of the Life of Mrs. Mary Jemison* (Syracuse, N.Y.: Syracuse University Press, 1990).

CHAPTER 7. FROM LONDON TO NONANTUM

1 Eliot's description is included in Edward Winslow, *The Glorious Progress of the Gospel Amongst the Indians in New England* (London, 1649), Early English Books Online, Purdue University Libraries (July 29, 2009), http://eebo.chadwyck.com,B3v.

2 For discussions of the deathbed confession genre see Erik R. Seeman, *Pious Persuasions: Laity and Clergy in Eighteenth-Century New England* (Baltimore: Johns Hopkins University Press, 1999); and Kristina Bross, "Dying Saints, Vanishing Savages," chap. 7, in *Dry Bones and Indian Sermons: Praying Indians in Colonial America* (Ithaca, N.Y.: Cornell University Press, 2004).

3 She goes unnamed in the mission literature, but Eliot tells us that she is the wife of Wampooas, whose life receives somewhat more attention in his writing. See Thomas Shepard, *Clear Sun-shine of the Gospel* (London, 1648), Early English Books Online, Purdue University Libraries, http://eebo.chadwyck.com, 6–7. See Linda Gregerson's "The Commonwealth of the Word," chapter 4 in this volume, for an account of the connections the Indian mission made between Old and New England. A very short list of studies of the seventeenth-century New England mission includes Elise Brenner, "To Pray or to Be Prey: That Is the Question: Strategies for Cultural Autonomy of Massachusetts Praying Town Indians," *Ethnohistory* 27:2 (1980): 135–52; Richard W. Cogley, *John Eliot's Mission to the Indians Before King Philip's War* (Cambridge, Mass.: Harvard University Press, 1999); Dane Morrison, *A Praying People: Massachusetts Acculturation and the Failure of the Puritan Mission, 1600–1690* (New York: Peter Lang, 1995); Kenneth M. Morrison, "'That Art of Coyning Christians': John Eliot and the Praying Indians of Massachusetts," *Ethnohistory* 21:1 (1974): 77–92; Robert James Naeher, "Dialogue in the Wilderness: John Eliot and the Indian Exploration of Puritanism as a Source of Meaning, Comfort, and Ethnic Survival," *New England Quarterly* 62:3 (1989): 346–68; David J. Silverman, *Faith and Boundaries: Colonists, Christianity, and Community Among the Wampanoag Indians of Martha's Vineyard, 1600–1871* (New York: Cambridge University Press, 2005); Neal Salisbury, "Red Puritans," *William and Mary Quarterly*, 3rd ser., 31 (Jan. 1974): 27–54.

4 I borrow the phrase "Indian place" from Jean O'Brien's study of the praying town

of Natick, in *Dispossession by Degrees: Indian Land and Identity in Natick, Massachusetts, 1650–1790* (Lincoln: University of Nebraska Press, 2003).

5 For accounts of the New England mission and Eliot's role see Bross, *Dry Bones and Indian Sermons*; Cogley, *John Eliot's Mission*; and William Kellaway, *The New England Company, 1649–1776* (New York, Barnes & Noble, 1962).

6 Also in *Glorious Progress*, Thomas Mayhew, ministering on Martha's Vineyard, tells a counter-story of a "bad death" brought about because of powwowing. A man he calls Saul, who when taken sick first consulted with Mayhew, seemed to be persuaded by his prayers but later "sought againe unto Witches." Mayhew sent word to Saul that because of his backsliding he would follow the example of Ahaziah, "who because he had the knowledge of the great God, and sought unto an inferiour God; God was angry with him, and killed him . . . and so it shortly came to passe" (B2v).

7 Shepard, *The cleare Sun-shine of the Gospel.*

8 Winslow, *Glorious Progress*, B3r.

9 Eliot also describes the project in another letter included in *Glorious Progress*, addressed to a recipient in London (likely Winslow himself). Although he mentions the expense in that letter as well, he leaves out any mention of New England establishing a "Common-weal": "a place must be found . . . some what remote from the English, where they must have the word constantly taught, and government constantly exercised, means of good subsistence provided, incouragements from the industrious, meanes of instructing them in Letters, Trades, and Labours, as building, fishing, Flax and Hemp dressing, planting Orchards, etc. Such a project in a fit place would draw many that are well minded together: but I feare it will be too chargeable" (B4r).

10 For a discussion of the New England mission's links to the metropole, and especially of Parliament's support of the mission, see Gregerson, "Commonwealth of the Word," in this volume.

11 The House of Commons passed in short order an act making it treasonous to declare a successor to King Charles (Jan. 30, 1649), an act establishing a counsel of state for the Commonwealth (Feb. 13, 1649), and an act abolishing the "Kingly office" in March, stating that "it is and hath been found by experience, that the Office of a King in this Nation and Ireland, and to have the power thereof in any single person, is unnecessary, burthensom and dangerous to the liberty, safety and publique interest of the people." The act to support New England's missions was passed July 27, 1649. These acts are collected in C. H. Firth and R. S. Rait, eds., *Acts and Ordinances of the Interregnum, 1642–1660* (London, 1911), available through *British History Online*, University of London and History of Parliament Trust (2009), http://www.british-history.ac.uk/Default.aspx (accessed July 16, 2009).

12 Of course, several of the men who presided over the trial and execution of Charles I were hung, drawn, and quartered as traitors.

13 On the regicides in New England see Mark Sargent, "Thomas Hutchinson, Ezra Stiles, and the Legend of the Regicides," *William and Mary Quarterly* 49:3 (1992): 431–448;

and Lemuel Welles, *The History of the Regicides in New England* (New York, Grafton Press, 1927).

14   Eliot would go on to become an ardent millennialist and subscribe to the theory that Indians are members of the lost tribes of Israel, but, as I argue in *Dry Bones and Indian Sermons*, his fellow colonists were not as eager to embrace these theories. Eliot's most aggressive print articulation of his views, which included clear antimonarchical sentiments, was published in 1659, just before the Restoration. Eliot recanted his views at that point, and the book was burned.

15   A. Zakai, "Thomas Brightman and the English Apocalyptic Tradition," in *Menasseh ben Israel and His World*, ed. Y. Kaplan, H. Mechoulan, and R. H. Popkin (Leiden: E. J. Brill, 1989), 35. On Brightman see also David Katz, *Philo-Semitism and the Readmission of the Jews to England, 1603–1655* (Oxford: Clarendon Press, 1982), 92.

16   Thomas Thorowgood, *Jewes in America* (London, 1649).

17   Winslow, *Glorious Progress*, A3v. On millennial beliefs in this period see Katz, *Philo-Semitism*; "Transformations of Millennial Thought in America," introduction to *Millennial Thought in America: Historical and Intellectual Contexts, 1630–1860*, ed. Bernd Engler, Joerg O. Ficthe, and Oliver Scheiding (Trier, Germany: Wissenschaftlicher Verglad Trier, 2002), 9–37; and J. F. Maclear, "New England and the Fifth Monarchy: The Quest for the Millennium in Early American Puritanism," *William and Mary Quarterly*, 3rd ser., 32, no. 2 (April 1975): 223–60.

18   Caspar Sebelius, *Of the Conversion of five thousand and nine hundred East-Indians, in the isle Formosa, neere China, to the profession of the true God, in Jesus Christ* (London, 1650).

19   In one of the only recent analyses of this tract Laura Stevens argues that it presents Dutch and English missions "as parallel projects, moving in opposite directions around the earth to fulfill a shared goal." See Stevens, *The Poor Indians: British Missionaries, Native Americans, and Colonial Sensibility* (Philadelphia: University of Pennsylvania Press, 2004), 76. While it is true that Jessey was personally and professionally connected to Dutch theologians and presents a clear ecumenical vision here, one that linked all Protestants everywhere in a common task of global evangelism, his readers may not have matched his hopeful view of the Dutch; the tract suggests that even Jessey saw England as first among Protestant equals. For Jessey's biographical details see *National Biography* entry and David Katz's work. On Jessey's contributions to Eliot's mission in New England, see Cogley, *John Eliot's Mission*, 213. Jessey also kept up close relations with a variety of pro–New England men. See Francis Bremer, *Congregational Communion* (Boston: Northeastern University Press, 1994), 102, 190.

20   Note that Jessey felt it necessary to gloss "Sinim," suggesting that he expected his readers would know the geographic location of "North" and "West"—England and America, perhaps?

21   Bross, *Dry Bones and Indian Sermons*, 61–80.

22   Histories of the world in this period lumped New England, Virginia, Florida, and the Caribbean under the term "West Indies." So does Edward Philips's dictionary, *The New

World of English Words (London, 1658), but publications specific to New England or to the English cause in the Americas make a distinction between New England and the West Indies—and the New England colonists themselves insisted on the division.

23   "Leaving Me and Then Loving Many," from *Poems Written by A. Cowley* (London, 1656), Early English Books Online, Purdue University Libraries, http://eebo.chadwyck. com: lines 15–16.

24   On Cromwellian-era foreign policy see Carla Pestana, *The English Atlantic in an Age of Revolution, 1640–1661* (Cambridge, Mass.: Harvard University Press, 2007); and C. A. Pincus, *Protestantism and Patriotism: Ideologies and the Making of English Foreign Policy, 1650–1668* (Cambridge: Cambridge University Press, 1996).

25   Many in New England agreed with this assessment—or fought against it. See Andrew Delbanco, *The Puritan Ordeal* (Cambridge, Mass.: Harvard University Press, 1989), and Theodore Bozeman, *To Live Ancient Lives: The Primitivist Dimension in Puritanism* (Chapel Hill: University of North Carolina Press, 1988) on colonial self-perception in the 1630s and 1640s, as well as the crisis of identity experienced during the English Civil Wars.

26   *To all persons whom these may concern, in the several townes, and plantations of the United Colonies in New-England* (London, 1656). On Cromwell's recruitment of New Englanders see Karen Kupperman, "Errand to the Indies: Puritan Colonization from Providence Island Through the Western Design," *William and Mary Quarterly,* 3d ser., 45, no. 1 (1988): 70–99.

27   Although Jessey does not summarize Dury's appendix, he does recommend it to his readers.

28   On New England's use of the Western Design in mission tracts see Bross, *Dry Bones and Indian Sermons,* 1–27.

29   For a discussion of Shepard's skepticism (especially as compared with Eliot's beliefs) see Bross, *Dry Bones and Indian Sermons,* 13, 31–32.

30   Cogley, *John Eliot's Mission,* 207.

31   Murray Tolmi, *The Triumph of the Saints: The Separate Churches of London, 1616–1649* (London: Cambridge University Press, 1977: ix), quote in of in Zakai, "Thomas Brightman."

32   See David Katz, "Menasseh ben Israel's Christian Connection: Henry Jessey and the Jews," in *Menasseh ben Israel and His World,* 117–38.

33   Jessey's account of Wight's speeches galvanized believers throughout the seventeenth century. *Exceeding Riches* (see note 46) was immensely popular, going through seven editions before 1670 and reappearing in abridged editions in the late 1700s. See Carola Scott-Luckens, "Propaganda or Marks of Grace? The Impact of the Reported Ordeals of Sarah Wight in Revolutionary London, 1647–52," *Women's Writing* 9:2 (2002): 215–32. During Wight's three-month ordeal, Jessey ministered to her. There he would have met other important religious women, such as Lady Mayerne, the woman who transmitted the Dutch missionary Robert Junius's book describing his work on Formosa to Jessey. Also notable is the visit of Hannah Allen, who subsequently had her hand in publishing and distributing

not only *Exceeding Riches* but also *Of the Conversion* and several of the Eliot tracts. See Maureen Bell, "Hannah Allen and the Development of a Puritan Publishing Business, 1646–51," *Publishing History* 26 (1989): 5–66.

34   *Exceeding Riches of Grace Advanced by the Spirit of Grace in an Empty Nothing Creature* (London, 1647), Early English Books Online, Purdue University Libraries (July 29, 2009), http://eebo.chadwyck.com, 158.

35   I argue elsewhere that the treatment of praying Indian women generally in the original New England mission tracts was meant to assure English readers that native women proselytized by New Englanders are safely orthodox. Bross, *Dry Bones and Indian Sermons*, 107–9; 135–37.

36   For accounts of basket making in this period see *A Key into the Language of Woodsplint Baskets*, ed. Ann McMullen and Russell G. Handsman (Washington, Conn.: American Indian Archaeological Institute, 1987); and Laurel Thatcher Ulrich, *The Age of Homespun: Objects and Stories in the Creation of an American Myth* (New York: Alfred A. Knopf, 2001).

37   Daniel Gookin, *Historical Account of the Doings and Sufferings of the Christian Indians in New England in the Years 1675, 1676, 1677*, in *Transactions and Collections of the American Antiquarian Society* 2:6 (1836; repr. New York: Arno, 1972), 151.

38   "The Cultural Work of a Mohegan Painted Basket," in *Early Native Literacies in New England*, ed. Kristina Bross and Hilary Wyss (Amherst: University of Massachusetts Press, 2008), 84. We can even see in the print archive the recognition by colonists of that power, albeit only in a limited way. John Eliot recounts an attempt to "read" a basket within a Christian missionary context, despite the fact that he is functionally illiterate when it comes to traditional signification practices. In response to a question about whether God could understand converts who prayed in their native language, Eliot reports, "wee bid them looke upon that *Indian* Basket that was before them, there was black and white straws, and many other things they made it of, now though others did not know what those things were who made not the Basket, yet he that made it must needs tell all things in it" (*The Day-breaking, if not the sun-rising of the Gospell with the Indians in New-England* [London, 1647], Early English Books Online, Purdue University Libraries, http://eebo. chadwyck.com), 5. It is important to note that this basket and its design are understood as Indian, and a uniquely Indian meaning is assumed by Eliot, but this meaning is elided as he "translates" the text of the basket into a parable for potential converts.

39   As I read the significance of the woman's basket making, I am extending arguments made about later Mohegan baskets to a woman in an earlier time and different place, but I think such speculation is possible because praying-town residents were drawn from several tribes and probably their baskets did not have a unique style, at least not as the movement came together. See Fitzgerald, "The Cultural Work of a Mohegan Painted Basket" in *Early Native Literacies in New England*, ed. Kristina Bross and Hilary E. Wyss (Amherst: University of Masschuestts Press (2008): 52–56; Ulrich, *The Age of Homespun*; and McMullen and Handsman, eds., *A Key into the Language of Woodsplint Baskets*, especially the essay by Ann McMullen, "Looking for People in Woodsplint Basketry Decoration," 102–23.

40 See especially Morrison, *Praying People.*

41 Eliot's emphasis on the "here" of Nonantum, I am suggesting, is also the woman's emphasis. Though they have different reasons, both colonial actors (Eliot and the woman) are interested in establishing Nonantum as a place of significance.

42 See Kathleen Bragdon, *Indians of Southern New England, 1500–1650* (Norman: University of Oklahoma Press, 1996), chaps. 3 and 6; and chap. 3 in her later book by a similar name, *Indians of Southern New England, 1650–1775* (Norman: University of Oklahoma Press, 2009).

43 See Bragdon, *Indians of Southern New England, 1500–1650*, chap. 2. In the charge to her daughters that Eliot records, the woman worries that her daughters will be importuned by their grandmother in addition to their grandfather and uncles. Moreover, the woman must have understood by this time that the English would allow only men as authorities among the praying Indians. My speculation is not meant to establish some kind of utopian, feminist consciousness on her part but rather to suggest alternatives to Eliot's interpretation of her speech.

CHAPTER 8. DREAMS CLASH

1 Jean de Brébeuf, *Relation of 1636*, in R. G. Thwaites, ed., *The Jesuit Relations and Allied Documents: Travels and Explorations of the Jesuit Missionaries in New France, 1610–1791*, 73 vols. (Cleveland: Burrows, 1891–1901), 10: 169–71. (This collection is revised and completed by Lucien Campeau, ed., *Monumenta Novae Franciae* [Rome-Québec: Monumenta Historia Societatis Iesu–Presses de l'Université Laval, 1967–89], 9 vols. to this date.)

2 Joseph-François Lafitau, *Moeurs des sauvages amériquains comparées aux moeurs des premiers temps* (Paris: Saugrain l'Aîné, 1724). In this book Lafitau attempts to show that the Iroquois customs are not very different from those of the societies of antiquity; he writes, "Tout le fonds de la Religion ancienne des Sauvages de l'Amérique est le même que celui des Barbares, qui occupèrent en premier lieu la Grèce, & qui se répandirent dans l'Asie, le même que celui des Peuples qui suivirent Bacchus dans ses expéditions militaires, le même enfin qui servit ensuite de fondement à toute la Mythologie payenne, & aux fables des Grecs" (vol. 2, 104; see also 223 and sq). And "L'âme des Sauvages est bien plus indépendante de leur corps, que n'est la notre, & prend bien plus de liberté; elle s'en sépare, quand elle juge à propos, pour prendre l'essor, & aller faire des excursions, où bon lui semble, sans qu'elle en perde la direction, & qu'elle cesse de l'animer. Les grands voyages ne luy coûtent rien; elle se transporte dans les airs; elle passe les mers; elle pénètre dans les lieux les plus inaccessibles, & les mieux fermés, rien ne l'arrête, parce qu'elle est esprit" (vol. 2, 73–74). That is : "The entire basis of the former religion of the American Indians, as well as that of the barbarians who first occupied Greece, spreading later into Asia, is the same as that of the followers of Bacchus in his military expeditions and as that which served afterwards as the basis of all pagan mythology and of the Greek myths" (*Customs of the American Indians*

compared with the Customs of Primitive times by Father François Lafitau, ed. and trans. William N. Fenton and Elizabeth Moore [Toronto: Champlain Society, 1974], vol. 1, 95) and "The soul of the Indians is much more independent of their bodies than ours is and takes much more liberty. It leaves the body whenever it deems it proper to do so to take flight and go to make excursions wherever it seems desirable without losing [the power of] direction [of the body] or ceasing to animate it. Long journeys are not difficult for it. It transports itself into the air, passes over the seas and penetrates into the most inaccessible and tightly closed places. Nothing stops it because it is a spirit" (idem, vol. 1, 231).

3   The most famous treatise on the interpretation of dreams since antiquity is Artemidore's *Onirocritique*, A.D. 150, followed by of Girolamo Cardano's *Treaty of Dreams*, in 1563; see Jean-Yves Boriaud, *La clef des songes: Onirocritique* (Paris: Arléa, 1998), 7–10. Jean-Yves Boriaud has recently translated Girolamo Cardano's *Somniorum synesiorum libri quatuor: Les quatre livres des Songes de Synesios* (Florence: Olschki, 2008). See Aurélia Gaillard, "Songes et enchantements à la fin de l'âge classique," in Nathalie Dauvois and Jean-Philippe Grosperrin, *Songes et songeurs, XIII–XVIIIe siècles* (Québec: Presses de l'université Laval, 2003), 170–86.

4   Yannick Ripa, *Histoire du rêve: Regards sur l'imaginaire des Français au XIXe siècle* (Paris: Oliver Orban, 1988), 18–20, 28, 32–43, 48–51; Florence Dumora, *L'oeuvre nocturne: Songe et representation au XVIIe siècle* (Paris: Champion, 2005), 82 et seq.

5   Simon Légasse, "Songes-rêves," in *Dictionnaire de spiritualité ascétique et mystique*, vol. 14 (Paris: Beauchesne, 1988), col. 1054–60.

6   A semantic shock that could maybe reflect the passage from "Renaissance *songe*," as Dumora writes: "le *songe* de la Renaissance, constitué d'images, soumis à l'interprétation, et témoignant éventuellement d'une transcendance (le songe divin ou angélique) ou d'une sympathie (en tant que lien du microcosme et du macrocosme, ou bien dans les sphères médicales et rationnelles, du corps et de l'âme) au *rêve* mécanique de la fin des Lumières, fait de traces mnésiques, pensée vaine et restes automatiques de la psyché et des motions diurnes." That is "the visionary dream of the Renaissance, made up of images, subject to interpretation and bearing witness to a transcendence (the divine or angelic dream) or to a sympathy (such as a link between the micro-cosmos and macro-cosmos, or, in the medical and rationalistic spheres, between body and soul) to the mechanical dream of the end of the Enlightenment, made up of remembered traces, vain thought and automatic reminders of the psyche and the actions of the day." Dumora, *L'oeuvre nocturne*, 10, 96–124; see also "Faire l'histoire du rêve," in Dauvois and Grosperrin, *Songes et songeurs*, 15–32. Dumora refers to a book I could not find: Jean-Luc Gautier, dir., *"Rêver en France au XVIIe siècle,"* Revue des Sciences Humaines, Université de Lille III, 1988.

7   Pierre Adnès, "Visions," in *Dictionnaire de spiritualité ascétique* (hereafter *DSAM*), vol. 16, col. 950–1,022. Actually, as referred to by Adnès: from Luis de la Puente (in *Guia espiritual*, 1609) to Francis Suarez (*De angelis*, before 1617) and Maximilian Sandaeus (*Pro theologia mystica clavis*, 1640), among others, the Jesuit authors were very preoccupied with visions, apparitions, and dreams. Toward the end of the seventeenth century Madame Guyon writes, "c'est la manière dont Dieu sert et se communique aux âmes de foi pour

leur donner des significations de l'avenir en choses qui les concernent, . . . Ces songes mystérieux se trouvent en quantité d'endroits de l'Écriture sainte." That is: "it is the way God uses to communicate Himself to the souls of faith in order to foretell the future using things which concern them . . . These mysterious dreams are in many places in the Holy Scriptures." *La vie de Madame Guyon écrite par elle-même,* quoted by Yvan Loskoutoff, "Les récits de songe de Jeanne Guyon à Fénélon," in Dauvois and Grosperrin, *Songes et songeurs,* 155–70, quote on 156.

8 Dominique Deslandres, *Croire et faire croire: Les missions françaises au XVIIe siècle* (Paris: Fayard, 2003).

9 See Louise Dechêne, *Habitants et marchands de Montréal au XVIIe siècle* (Montreal: Plon, 1974); Denys Delâge, *Le pays renversé: Amérindiens et Européens en Amérique du nord-est, 1600–1664* (Montreal: Boréal, 1985); William J. Eccles, *France in America* (Markham, Ontario: Fitzhenry & Whiteside, 1990); Jacques Mathieu, *La Nouvelle France: Les Français en Amerique du nord, XVIe–XVIIIe siècle* (Quebec: Presses de l'université Laval, 1991); Bruce G. Trigger, *The Children of Aataentsic: A History of the Huron People to 1660* (Montreal: McGill-Queen's University Press, 1976); Marcel Trudel, *Histoire de la Nouvelle France III, la seigneurie des Cent Associés, 1627–1663,* vol. 1, *Les événements* (Montreal: Fides, 1979); Norman Doiron, "Songes sauvages: De l'interprétation jésuite des songes amérindiens au XVIIe siècle," *L'Esprit créateur* 30:3 (Autumn 1990), 59–66.

10 Antoine Boschet, *Le Parfait missionnaire ou la vie du R. P. Julien Maunoir, de la Compagnie de Jésus missionnaire en Bretagne* (Paris: J. Anison, 1697; 2nd ed., Lyon: Périsse, 1834): 211–14 seq; Charles de Genève, in Felix Tisserand, ed., *Les Trophées sacrés* (Lausanne, Switzerland: Société d'histoire de la Suisse romande, 1976), 1: 328. See also Serge Gruzinski, "Délires et visions chez les Indiens du Mexique," in *Mélanges de l'École française de Rome* 86 (1974/2): 446–80, and *La Colonisation de l'imaginaire* (Paris: Gallimard, 1988); Jean-Michel Sallmann, ed., *Visions indiennes, vision baroques: les métissages de l'inconscient* (Paris: Presses universitaires de France 1992); C. S. Watkins, *Sin, Penance and Purgatory in the Anglo-Norman Realm: The Evidence of Visions and Ghost Stories,* with Christopher Hill, ed., *Past and Present Society* (Oxford; Charlesworth Group, 2002), 4–33.

11 "Un laboureur, nommé Yves le Goff, de la paroisse de Castre de l'évêché de Quimper, alla trouver le Père Maunoir au Collège de Quimper, en 1655, pour le consulter sur de fréquentes apparitions que lui faisoit la Sainte Vierge et pour savoir ce qu'il en jugeoit. [Le père Maunoir] lui enjoignit, la prochaine fois que cette dame, qu'il prenoit pour la Sainte Vierge, lui apparoîtroit, de lui présenter à adorer la croix qu'il portoit sur lui." Boschet, *Le Parfait missionnaire,* 214. That is: "A farmer named Yves Le Goff of the parish of Castres in the Bishopric of Quimper came to Father Maunoir in the College of Quimper in 1655 to consult him on frequent apparitions of the Virgin Mary and to ask the father's judgment of it. Father Maunoir ordered him to show the cross he was wearing to this lady he believed to be the Holy Virgin next time she would appear and to ask her to worship it." Thanks to Jessica Coiteux for showing me this quote.

12 Adnès, "Révélations privées," in *DSAM,* vol. 13, col. 482–92, here col. 482.

13 Dumora, *L'oeuvre nocturne,* 93–97, see esp. 94, n. 3

14   Simon Légasse, "Songes-rêves," *DSAM*, vol. 15, col. 1,059. See also J. Gagey and P. Adnes, *Phénomènes extraordinaires, Phénomènes mystiques: Stigmates-Transverberation* (Paris: Beauchesne, 1993), 10 et seq.

15   Henri Bremond, *Histoire littéraire du sentiment religieux en France*, ed. François Trémolières, 5 vols. (Grenoble: Éditions Jérôme Million, 2006), http://www.abbaye-saint-benoit.ch/histoiredusentimentreligieux/index.htm. See also Alice Brown, *Religious Dreams and Their Interpretation in Some Thinkers of the Seventeenth Century*, Ph.D. dissertation, Warburg Institute, University of London, 1975.

16   For example, on the one hand, theologians like Jean Gerson in *De probatione spirituum*, (1415, in Opera, Paris, 1601, vol. 1) asked for prudence in the evaluation of the authenticity of dreams and revelations, and, on the other hand, Juan de Torquemada took on the defense of holy women in *Defensorium super revelationes S. Birgittae* (Mansi, vol. 30, 698–814), as quoted by Adnes, *DSAM*, vol. 13, col. 483–84; see also col. 486–87. See also Jacques Le Brun, "Rêves de religieuses: Le désir, la mort et le temps," *Revue des sciences humaines* 211 (July–Sept. 1988), 27–47. Also from the same, "Jérôme Cardan et l'interprétation des songes," in Jacques Le Brun, *La jouissance et le trouble: Recherches sur la littérature chrétienne de l'âge classique* (Geneva: Droz, 2004), 108–36.

17   Jérôme Lalemant, in Thwaites, *Jesuit Relations*, 22: 227.

18   The quote begins with "The dream is the oracle that all these poor Peoples consult and listen to, the Prophet which predicts to them future events, the Cassandra which warns them of misfortunes that threaten them, the usual Physician in their sicknesses, the Esculapius and Galen of the whole Country,—the most absolute master they have." Jean de Brébeuf, in Thwaites, *Jesuit Relations*, 10 : 169–71.

19   Paul Le Jeune, in Thwaites, *Jesuit Relations*, 5: 159–61.

20   Charles Lalemant, in Thwaites, *Jesuit Relations*, 4: 219.

21   Ibid.

22   Samuel de Champlain, *Relation du voyage en Canada*, in Campeau, *Monumenta Novae Franciae*, 2: 367.

23   For example, Paul Le Jeune, in Campeau, *Monumenta Novae Franciae*, 4: 92–93.

24   "To shine on those who sit in darkness and in death's shadow" (Luke 1: 79) in Jean de Brébeuf, in Thwaites, *Jesuit Relations*, 1636, 10 : 147.

25   Paul Le Jeune, in Thwaites, *Jesuit Relations*, 18: 201.

26   Paul Ragueneau, in Thwaites, *Jesuit Relations*, 30: 25.

27   Bruce G. Trigger, *The Children of Aataentsic: A History of the Huron People to 1660* (Montreal: McGill-Queen's University Press, 1975), 722–23.

28   Paul Ragueneau, in Thwaites, *Jesuit Relations*, 30: 27.

29   Ibid., 29-31.

30   François Le Mercier, in Campeau, *Monumenta Novae Franciae*, vol. 3: 754; Barthélémy Vimont, in ibid., vol. 5: 450–51; Jérôme Lalemant, ibid., vol. 5: 528; and Jérôme Lalemant, in Campeau, *Monumenta Novae Franciae*, vol. 6: 202–3.

31   Paul Le Jeune, in Thwaites, *Jesuit Relations*, vol. 5: 131. See also in Thwaites, *Jesuit Relations*, 22: 103.

32 Le Jeune, in Thwaites, *Jesuit Relations,* 8: 261–63.

33 Ibid., 6: 181–83.

34 Ibid., 7: 169.

35 Brébeuf, in Thwaites, *Jesuit Relations,* 8: 227. See also Le Jeune, ibid., 263.

36 Deslandres, *Croire et faire croire,* 325, n. 19, for the numerous references to this.

37 Pierre Biard, in Thwaites, *Jesuit Relations,* 3: 133; Le Jeune, ibid., 15: 81, 125, 133; Lalemant, in Thwaites, *Jesuit Relations,* 19: 245–49.

38 Lalemant, in Thwaites, *Jesuit Relations,* 19: 245, 259.

39 "Celui [le néophyte] qui a eu la vision, ne se peut empêcher de prêcher à ses Compatriotes ce qu'il a veu. Cette vision est de notre Seigneur qui lui a apparu, et qui, après lui avoir montré ses plaies sacrées, lui a fait voir la gloire des Bien-heureux, et les peines des Damnez, avec la juste raison qu'il a de châtier les Hommes, qui ne font pas un bon usage du bienfait de la Rédemption." That is: "The neophyte who had the vision, cannot stop himself from preaching to his fellow countrymen about what he has seen. This vision is of our Lord who appeared before him, and who, after having showed him his sacred wounds, made him see the glory of the Blessed, and the punishments of the damned, and that it is right to punish the people who do not take up the Redemption offered them." Marie de l'Incarnation, *Correspondance,* ed. dom Guy-Marie Oury, Solesmes: Abbaye de Saint Pierre, 1971, *Letter to Her Son* (1645) : 260–61. See also the same process at work during exorcism in Thwaites, *Jesuit Relations,* 27: 136; 50: 48; 14: 138–40; 19: 194–96; 26: 188–290; 27: 184–88; 30: 102–4; 31: 62–68, 74–76; 34: 174–76, 184–86; 38: 94–96; 46: 30–32; 48: 186–88, 196–98; 41: 110–12 ; and 42: 234–36.

40 Le Jeune, in Thwaites, *Jesuit Relations,* 15: 133.

41 *Episteme* can be defined as the field knowledge proper to a group at a certain period of time. Michel Foucault, *Les mots et les choses* (Paris: Gallimard, 1966), 13.

42 Marie de l'Incarnation, *Letter to Her Son,* 379–80.

43 Brébeuf, in Thwaites, *Jesuit Relations,* 10: 169.

44 Le Jeune, in Thwaites, *Jesuit Relations,* 14: 139–41. See also Brébeuf, in Thwaites, *Jesuit Relations,* 13: 149–51; François Le Mercier, ibid., 15: 73.

45 François Le Mercier, in Thwaites, *Jesuit Relations,* 15: 73.

46 Lalemant, in Thwaites, *Jesuit Relations,* 26: 263.

47 Le Jeune, in Thwaites, *Jesuit Relations,* 11: 179.

CHAPTER 9. "FOR EACH AND EVERY HOUSE TO WISH FOR PEACE"

1 Christoph Saur (The Elder), *High German American Almanac 1754 (Hoch-Deutsch Americanische Calender)* (Germantown, Pa.: Saur, 1753). The *Almanac* is unpaginated throughout its long print run. All quotes reference the year as given on each issue's title page (not the year of publication).

"Neukommer: Die Teutschen werden bald halb englisch, und sagen Hau di thu?
Einwohner: Was heißt das?

Neukommer: Ich weiß selber nicht recht, und mögte es lieber erst wissen.

Einwohner: Als die ersten Einwohner nach Pensylvanien kamen, und funden kein Hauß, kein Pferdt, keine Kuh, keine Frucht, keine Mühl, keine Butter, kein Saltz, und kein Brod, da gings manchen hart. Wann dan gottseelige Freundte zusamen kamen, aus liebe, um zu sehen ob einer dem andern etwas dienen oder helffen könte, so war die erste Anrede: *Hau di thu?* (wie geht dirs) Und wan der andere nicht klagen wolte, so antwortete er: *Indifferent! Das ist:* Leidlich, oder mittelmäsig. Da sie dan das andere Jahr Indianisch-Korn gebaut hatten, und mancher eine Tagreise sein Korn in die Mühl tragen müste, und wieder heim kam, so kamen wohl die Nachbars-Weiber, und jede hätte gern ein wenig Mehl gehabt vor ihr klein Kind (Dan die älteren mogten ihr Korn gekocht essen) so war des Manns kleine Buschel Mehl bald all; und konte aus Liebe zu seinen Nachbars Kindern abermahl eine Last auf die Schulter nehmen und zur Mühl gehen. Begnete ihm alsdan ein guter Freund, und fragte: *Hau dost thi* oder *Hau di thu?* So antwortete er: *Pretty well,* das ist: *Annehmlich wohl.* Da aber hernach selbige und solche Leute in grosem uberfluß gelebt, oder noch leben, so reithen sie mit gebutzten Pferden neben einander vorbey, der eine sagt *Hau di thu?* Und der andere sagt auch: *Hau di thu.* Damit weiß keiner wie es dem andern geht, und ist nun zur Gewohnheit worden.

Neukommer: Was mögen doch wohl die alten Vätter vor einen Gruß gehabt haben wan sie zusamen kamen, oder einander begegnet sind?

Einwohner: Die Juden sagen heutiges Tages noch *Schoulum Legum:* [Ich wünsch dir den Frieden.] Und Christus grüßte seine Jünger mit diesen Worten: Friede sey mit euch Luc. 24, 36. und sagte zu seinen Jüngern: Wan ihr in ein Hauß komt, so sprecht zu erst: *Friede sey in diesem Hauß* Luc. 10, 5.

Neukommer: Mich wundert, daß diese Anrede so sehr abgekommen, mich deucht es sey noch auf den heutigen tag in einem jeden Hauß nöthig den Frieden zu wünschen."

2 Citing Marianne Wokeck and Farley Grubb, Peter Silver writes, "A minimum of seventy thousand German-speakers arrived in Philadelphia during the fifty years before the Revolution, with a full half that total flooding in—as immigration surged to levels ten times those recorded only twenty-five years before—in one five-year span (1749–54) at mid-century, after which the outbreak of the Seven Years' War had the effect of turning off a tap." Peter Silver, *Our Savage Neighbors: How Indian War Transformed Early America* (New York: W. W. Norton, 2008), 6; Marianne Wokeck, "The Flow and Composition of German Immigration to Philadelphia, 1727–1775," *Pennsylvania Magazine for History and Biography* 105 (1981): 259–78; Farley Grubb, "German Immigration to Pennsylvania, 1709 to 1820," *Journal of Interdisciplinary History* 20 (1990): 417–36. German speakers were estimated to have made up between a third and a half of Pennsylvania's population in 1755. The most comprehensive account of German migration and Pennsylvania demography is provided by Marianne Wokeck, *Trade in Strangers: The Beginnings of Mass Migration to North America* (University Park: Pennsylvania State University Press, 1999), 45–46. See also Aaron Spencer Fogleman's discussion of Germans' settlement patterns in Pennsylvania in *Hopeful Journeys: German Immigration, Settlement, and Political Culture in Colonial America, 1717–1775* (Philadelphia: University of Pennsylvania Press, 1996), 69–99.

3　Jan Stievermann, "A 'Plain, Rejected Little Flock': The Politics of Martyrological Self-Fashioning Among Pennsylvania's German Peace Churches, 1739-65," *William and Mary Quarterly* 66, no. 2 (April 2009): 287–324.

4　Fogleman estimates that "radical pietists accounted for less than 10 percent of the entire German-speaking immigration" (*Hopeful Journeys,* 102–3). Radicals and sectarians made up a far higher percentage of the relatively small number of German migrants to Pennsylvania between 1682 and the 1720s (Wokeck, *Trade in Strangers,* 47–48).

5　Silver, *Our Savage Neighbors.*

6　Pennsylvania governor Robert Hunter Morris and the Assembly officially declared war against the Delawares in April 1756. Jane Merritt provides a map and chronology of Delaware attacks on European settlements in *At the Crossroads: Indian and Empires on a Mid-Atlantic Frontier, 1700–1763* (Chapel Hill: University of North Carolina Press, 2003), 184. For an atmospheric account of the attacks at Penn's Creek, see James Merrell, *Into the American Woods: Negotiators on the Pennsylvania Frontier* (New York: W. W. Norton, 1994), 225–30.

7　Earlier colonial historians often readily accepted Proprietary accounts of the Assembly's "failure" to defend the colony, more or less explicitly also repeating charges that Quakers were unfit to govern. Sally Schwartz provides a refreshingly nonpartisan account of the conflict over defense appropriations and property taxes in the 1750s in *"A Mixed Multitude": The Struggle for Toleration in Colonial Pennsylvania* (New York: New York University Press, 1987), 208–20.

8　Jack D. Marietta discusses American Quakers' troubled negotiation of George Fox and other Quaker patriarchs' injunction, "To the earthly we give the earthly things: that is, to Caesar we give unto him his things, and to God we give Him his things;" Marietta, "Conscience, the Quaker Community, and the French and Indian War," *Pennsylvania Magazine for History and Biography* 94 (Jan. 1971): 3–27, quote on 4. Marietta assesses that Quaker politicians' pacifist "code was nevertheless deficient, the understanding of the satisfied brethren was superficial, and a potential dilemma, at least, did exist for the church in Pennsylvania" since as early as 1692. See also Hermann Wellenreuther, "Conscience, the Quaker Community, and the French and Indian War," *Pennsylvania Magazine for History and Biography* 94 (Jan. 1971), 141–44.

9　Fogleman treats the Moravian challenge and the complex ways Moravian devotional practices threatened colonial society's gender norms in *Jesus Is Female: Moravians and the Challenge of Radical Religion in Early America* (Philadelphia: University of Pennsylvania Press, 2007), 73–104. As Fogleman also illuminates, Moravian ecumenicism threw down a challenge both to other "sectarians" and to the established churches.

10　Merritt provides an overview of land claims up to the Walking Purchase of 1737, a land grab soon known among Delaware as "Ye Walking Run" (*At the Crossroads,* 19–49). It must also be noted that colonial elites too were uneasy about "the lower sort" of European settlers who moved into already disputed territory. Merritt explains, "In many ways, the elite leadership preferred that Indians under the control of the Iroquois live on their frontiers rather than 'the lower sort of People who are exceedingly loose and ungovernable.'" The 1737 Walking Purchase already indicated the squeeze placed on Delawares by the Six Nations–colonial Pennsylvanian alliance. A subsequent enormous land purchase in 1749 had occurred, again in cooperation with the Iroquois. But Delawares, Merritt writes, "were particularly incensed by the Albany Purchase [of 1754 which included established Indian communities in the Ohio Valley] because they had been neither consulted nor invited to attend the conference" (*At the Crossroads*, 171–73). Nonetheless, three years later the Delaware leader Teedyuscung reported that the Walk was "not the principal cause that made us Strike our Brethren, the English, yet it has caused the stroke to come harder than it otherwise would have come" (quoted in *Conscience in Crisis: Mennonites and Other Peace Churches in America, 1739–1789—Interpretation and Documents*, ed. Richard K. MacMaster, Samuel L. Horst, and Robert F. Ulle [Scottdale, Pa.: Herald Press, 1979], 72).

11   A concise biography of Smith is available at "Penn in the Eighteenth Century: William Smith (1727–1803)," University of Pennsylvania, Philadelphia, http://www.archives. upenn.edu/people/1700s/smith_wm.html. Peter Silver correctly calls Smith "incendiary" (*Our Savage Neighbors*, 77).

12   I quote from the London 1756 edition. Sally Schwartz emphasizes that Smith's pamphlet (*A Brief State of the Province of Pennsylvania*), with language that may have been "too Violent," in the words of Proprietor Thomas Penn, was also "the catalyst for serious thought about restricting participation in provincial affairs" (*Mixed Multitude*, 215). Marietta makes a similar point, emphasizing Smith's pamphlet as spin, a blatant ploy to divert attention from the real issues. Smith, Marietta elaborates, perceived that a false issue might be raised from the impasse between Assembly and Governor that could capture the attention of persons not normally hostile toward Friends or the Pennsylvania Assembly but who were anxious for the defense of the British dominions. If such persons could be persuaded that the Quakers, composing a majority of the Assembly, had refused to appropriate defense funds because it violated their Quaker pacifism, Smith could then suggest that British authorities should remove all Friends from the Assembly in order to defend Pennsylvania. The superficial cogency and merit of this false explanation might even eclipse the constitutional debate so that the Proprietor's role in the fiscal impasse might never be noticed ("The Quaker Community," 7). Smith himself referred to his pamphlet as "a Clap of Thunder," and as Silver rightly emphasizes, there were "nowhere near enough copies to meet demand" (*Our Savage Neighbors*, 194).

13   Crypto-Catholicism had been a charge sometimes leveled against Quakers in Restoration England. The so-called French Prophets were also known as the Inspirés or the "Congénies Quakers," since as Maurice Jackson notes, many members of this group originally came from this French town before migrating variously to Holland, to London, or to Pennsylvania (Maurice Jackson, *Let This Voice Be Heard: Anthony Benezet, Father of Atlantic Abolitionism* [Philadelphia: University of Pennsylvania Press, 2009], 4).

14   In the fall of 1755 a raid at Shamokin mobilized even the pacifist German Moravians; the Mennonites too took up arms. So did many Quakers (see Silver, *Our Savage Neighbors*).

15   Saur's broadside was entitled *Eine Zu dieser Zeit höchstnöthige Warnung und Erin-nerung an die freye Einwohner der Provintz Pensylvanien von Einem, dem die Wohlfahrt des Landes angelegen und darauf bedacht ist* (A Sorely Needed Warning and Reminder to the Free Inhabitants of the Province of Pennsylvania from Someone Concerned and Anxious about the Welfare of this Land) (Germantown, Pa., 1755).

16   That same year Benjamin Franklin too famously called Germans "boors" and, like Smith, worried that they would soon outnumber English speakers in the colony. His essay *Observations Concerning the Increase of Mankind* asked, "Why should Pennsylvania, founded by the English, become a *Colony of Aliens*, who will shortly be so numerous as to Germanize us instead of our Anglifying them, and will never adopt our Language or Customs, any more than they can acquire our Complexion" (quoted in Liam Riordan, "'The Complexion of My Country': The German as 'Other' in Colonial Pennsylvania," in *Germans and Indians: Fantasies, Encounters, Projections,* ed. Colin G. Calloway, Gerd Gemünden, and Susanne Zantop (Lincoln: University of Nebraska Press, 2002), 97–120, quote on 99.

17   At roughly the same time, Smith was busy proposing his scheme for the "German Charity Schools." Saur's marked lack of enthusiasm for the project, despite Conrad Weiser's initial support, and the project's eventual failure, after Saur published strongly against it, is hardly surprising. On the schools see J. Bell Whitefield, Jr., "Benjamin Franklin and the German Charity Schools," *Proceedings of the American Philosophical Society* 99:6 (1955): 381–87; and Samuel Edwin Weber, *The Charity School Movement in Colonial Pennsylvania 1754–1763: A History of the Educational Struggles Between the Colonial Authorities and the German Inhabitants of Pennsylvania* (Philadelphia: William J. Campbell, 1905).

18   An article in Saur's newspaper, the *Pennsylvanische Berichte,* of September 16, 1755, had explicitly recommended that Germans vote for Quaker candidates. Curiously, their resignation a few months later did not give any Saur media cause to lament. Another article in the *Berichte* opined that those Quakers who resigned "know that they are only a hindrance in the house, when during this time of war they must undertake or legislate things that are contrary to their consciences; they should and will leave it to those who are capable of serving during wartime" (Schwartz, *Mixed Multitude,* 221; for a broad account of these elections see 211–21). For a summary of the election's aftermath in the American Quaker community see Marietta, "Quaker Community," 3.

19   See Merritt, *At the Crossroads.* And Christopher Beneke explains, "Had the so-called Quaker Party sponsored only Quaker candidates for election in 1756, its prospects would have been dismal. But its leaders did something entirely unorthodox that year: running like-minded Anglicans, Presbyterians, Dutch Reformed and Swiss-Mennonites in the place of those Quakers who chose not to run. The strategy worked. Even as the deep divisions among Quakers persisted, and even as the number of Friends in the Assembly declined from twenty-seven before July 1756 to just twelve by October of that same year, the Quaker Party managed to maintain its political muscle. From this point onward it was represented in the Assembly by men of several denominations" (*Beyond Toleration: The Religious Origins of American Pluralism* [New York: Oxford University Press, 2006], 93).

20   Merritt, *At the Crossroads*, 201.

21   Silver, *Our Savage Neighbors*, 100.

22   The literature on the Paxton Boys is voluminous. See especially Merritt, *At the Crossroads*, 283–94; and Krista Camenzind, "Violence, Race, and the Paxton Boys," in *Friends and Enemies in Penn's Woods: Indians, Colonists, and the Racial Construction of Pennsylvania*, ed. William A. Pencak and Daniel K. Richter (University Park: Pennsylvania State University Press, 2004), 201–20. On the vilification of Quakers see especially Silver, *Our Savage Neighbors*, 202–12.

23   One version of this cartoon is available at http://www.hsp.org/default. aspx?id=325.

24   Reprinted in MacMaster et al., *Conscience in Crisis*, doc. 55, 136, and reprinted in translation, doc. 57, 137–39.

25   Silver's delineation of the "anti-Indian sublime" is helpful to understand the efficacy of the propaganda in which it was articulated. Yet the efficacy of the rhetoric, what Silver calls its "inevitability," should not blind us to the seriousness with which many parties took up peace talks.

26   Silver, *Our Savage Neighbors*, 30.

27   Like Voltaire's *Candide*, Woolman insisted that his contemporaries must remember how sugar was produced. Consequently, Geoffrey Plank stated that Woolman "refused cakes and sweetened tea." The reformer's critique grew to encompass all areas of Atlantic trade and commerce. After roughly 1757, Plank explains, "Woolman's politics became at once more intimate and more globally diffuse, and he adopted ever more measures to minimize his own participation in an economic and social system that he believed deeply unjust and unjustifiable. As [Woolman] aged he became increasingly fastidious. While continuing to protest against slavery, he developed a comprehensive critique of the Atlantic economy, associating transatlantic commerce with warfare, economic inequality, godlessness, intemperance and cruelty to animals. By the end of his life he believed that the clothes he wore, his manner of speaking, the gifts he accepted and refused, the way he traveled, where he slept, the food he ate and his choice of spoons were freighted with moral significance" ("The First Person in Antislavery Literature: John Woolman, His Clothes and His Journal," *Slavery and Abolition* 30:1 [March 2009]: 67–91, quote on 70).

28   Stievermann, "A 'Plain, rejected little flock.'"

29   Other readings of the dialogue include Fogleman's *Hopeful Journeys* (97–99) and Bethany Wiggin, "Forecasting Loss: Christoph Saur's Pennsylvania German *Calender* (1751–1757)," in *Enduring Loss in Early Modern Germany*, ed. Lynne Tatlock (Amsterdam: Brill, 2010): 397–414.

30   All yearly references to the *Almanac* are to the year for which it was written, not to the year of publication.

31   Silver, *Our Savage Neighbors*, 19–20. In his review of Frank Lambert's *Inventing the "Great Awakening,"* Joseph Conforti provides a synopsis of arguments, including his own, over the usefulness of the term "Great Awakening" and debates over its invention.

32   Merritt, *At the Crossroads*, 89–128.

33 Jon F. Sensbach. *Rebecca's Revival: Creating Black Christianity in the Atlantic World* (Cambridge, Mass.: Harvard University Press, 2005).

34 No doubt the use of Penn's name for diplomatic purposes would have provided Penn comfort. A series of sentences collected in Penn's florilegium, the *Fruits of Solitude*, from 1682, elaborated upon the power of true F/friends to institute an "immortal" "friendship and society." Even after death, friends' memory joins them in eternal bonds where "they see face to face; and their converse is free, as well as pure." Under the heading "Union of Friends," Penn cannily anticipated the function that his own name was to provide colonists and Indians throughout the first half of the eighteenth century: "127. They that love beyond the world cannot be separated by it./ 128. Death cannot kill what never dies./ 129. Nor can spirits ever be divided, that love and live in the same divine principle, the root and record, of their friendship./ 130. If absence be not death, neither is theirs./ 131. Death is but crossing the world, as friends do the seas; they live in one another still./ 132. For they must needs be present that love and live in that which is omnipresent./ 133. In this divine glass, they see face to face; and their converse is free, as well as pure./ 134. This is the comfort of friends, that though they may be said to die, yet their friendship and society are, in the best sense, ever present, because immortal" (155–56).

35 Merrell, *American Woods*, 122, 221.

36 Merritt, *At the Crossroads*, 205.

37 Merrell, *American Woods*, 240.

38 Merrell, "Council Speeches," 820.

39 Silver, *Our Savage Neighbors*, 101.

40 Saur was certainly not deaf to colonists' accounts of their sufferings. The previous year Saur had the Flemings' harrowing tale of captivity translated and published.

41 James H. Merrell, "'I desire all that I have said . . . may be taken down aright': Revisiting Teedyuscung's 1756 Treaty Council Speeches," *William and Mary Quarterly* 63:4 (Oct. 2006), 777–826, quote on 788. Merrell provides an illuminating account of the confused events in Easton on November 12, 1756. Emphasizing the "maddening" nature of the written records of the 1756 treaty councils, he explains, "At one delicate moment in the negotiations, Peters [official scribe for the Governor and Penn family protegé] so lost control that he abruptly announced he would write no more. On November 12 Governor William Denny—a novice at Indian affairs who had recently replaced Robert Hunter Morris—asked Teedyuscung, despite strenuous objections from Peters, what had set the Delaware people on the warpath. . . . With his patrons [the Penns] under attacks, some observers claimed, Peters tried everything to put a stop to the proceedings. 'Being or pretending to be in the Utmost Confusion, so that he could not take the Minutes,' he 'threw down his Pen' as the Delaware spoke and declared that it was time to break for dinner" (802).

42 Merrell has supplied a wealth of materials, documenting the bewildering range in transcripts of the treaties and available on the *William and Mary Quarterly* Web site, http://oieahc.wm.edu/wmq/Oct06/merrell_final.pdf.

43 Merritt, *At the Crossroads*, 229.

44   On Franklin's "misguided" gambit to royalize Pennsylvania and make it a Crown colony, see Silver, *Our Savage Neighbors*, 215–19.

45   Franklin had notoriously called the Germans "boors," a term whose significance was endlessly debated by colonial media. See also note 16 above.

46   For a somewhat different view of this election among the German pacifist community, see Jan Stievermann, "A 'Plain, Rejected Little Flock.'" See also Fogleman, *Hopeful Journeys*, 142–48.

47   The *Almanac* condemned owning slaves in several issues, a sin it represented as particularly American and particularly incomprehensible when committed by Germans.

CHAPTER 10. RECONFIGURING MARTYRDOM IN THE COLONIAL CONTEXT

1   The Spanish mystic and founder of the Reformed Carmelites, Teresa de Jesus, also known as Teresa of Ávila (1515–82), published her *Vida* in 1562 and was canonized in 1622. On Teresa see especially Gillian T. W. Ahlgren, *Teresa of Avila and the Politics of Sanctity* (Ithaca, N.Y.: Cornell University Press, 1996); and Alison Weber, *Teresa of Avila and the Rhetoric of Femininity* (Princeton, N.J.: Princeton University Press, 1990).

2   This is my translation of the French text Marie would have read, which runs "nous nous mettions luy et moy ensemble à lire la legende des saincts, et comme je voyois les martyres, que les saincts enduroient pour l'amour de Dieu: il sembloit qu'ils achetoient à très-bon marché la iouyssance de Dieu, et je desirois grandement de mourir ainsi, non pour l'amour que je pensasse et cogneusse luy porter: mais pour ioüir si tost des grands biens, que je lisois, qu'il y avoit au ciel. Je me mettois avec ce mien frere, pour traicter ensemble, quel moyen il y auroit pour parvenir, et faisions complot, de nous en aller au païs des Mores en demandant l'aumosne afin qu'y estant ils nous decapitassent, et me sembloit que si nous eussions trouvé quelque moyen, que Dieu nous donnoit le courage: mais le plus grand empeschement qu'il nous sembloit que nous avions, c'estoit seulement de ce que nous avions nos parens." *La vie de la Mere Terese de Jesus.* Par I.D.B.P et L.P.C.D.B (Paris: Guillaume de la Noüe, 1601), 4. This edition was in large part a biography of Teresa written by Ribera, but it also incorporates excerpts from the autobiography itself. For a reading of Teresa that makes sense of this troubled publication history, see Nicholas D. Paige's *Being Interior: Autobiography and the Contradictions of Modernity in Seventeenth-Century France* (Philadelphia: University of Pennsylvania Press, 2001), 67–71. On Teresa in seventeenth-century France see also Alphonse Vermeylen, *Sainte Thérèse au XVIIe siècle, 1600–1660* (Louvain, France: Publications Universitaires de Louvain, 1958).

3   My translation again from *La vie de la Mere Teresa de Jesus* (hereafter referred to as *Vie*): "quand nous vismes, qu'il estoit impossible d'y aller en lieu où l'on nous fist mourir pour l'amour de Dieu, proposions d'estre hermites, et en un jardin qu'il y avoit en nôtre maison, nous taschions et procurions le mieux que nous pouvions de faire des hermitages en ramassant et agençant quelques petites pierres ensemble" (5).

4   George Eliot, *Middlemarch* (Harmondsworth: Penguin, 1979), 25, 26.

5   For many years scholarship on Marie suffered from an overly hagiographical and nationalistic approach. In recent years, however, the scholarship on Marie has opened up to larger narratives, focusing mainly on her publication history in relation to a larger discussion about women and writing as well as on an account of the place of women and in particular women mystics in relation to specific religious affiliations. For a publishing history of Marie's work see especially Elizabeth Goldsmith, *Publishing Women's Life Stories in France, 1647–1720* (Burlington, Vt.: Ashgate, 2001), 12–41. For other accounts of Marie's life and work see Dominique Deslandres, "In the Shadow of the Cloister: Representations of Female Holiness in New France," in *Colonial Saints: Discovering the Holy in the Americas*, ed. Allan Greer and Jodi Bilinkoff (New York: Routledge, 2003), 129–52; Deslandres, "Marie de l'Incarnation et la femme amérindienne," *Recherches Amérindiennes au Québec* 13:4 (1983): 277–85; Marie-Florine Bruneau, *Women Mystics Confront the Modern World: Marie de l'Incarnation and Madame Guyon* (Albany: State University of New York Press, 1998); Anya Mali, *Mystic in the New World: Marie de l'Incarnation (1599–1672)* (Leiden: Brill, 1996); Natalie Zemon Davis, *Women on the Margins: Three Seventeenth-Century Lives* (Cambridge, Mass.: Harvard University Press, 1995), 63–139; Françoise Deroy-Pineau, *Marie de l'Incarnation: Marie Guyart femme d'affaires, mystique, mère de la Nouvelle France* (Paris: Laffont, 1989). For a trenchant psychoanalytic reading of Marie's work, see Mitchell Greenberg, *Baroque Bodies: Psychoanalysis and the Culture of French Absolutism* (Ithaca: Cornell University Press, 2001), 160–208; for a reading of Marie's delicate positioning on the border between France and the New World, see Carla Zecher, "Life on the French-Canadian Hyphen: Nation and Narration in the Correspondence of Marie de l'Incarnation" *Quebec Studies,* 26 (Fall 1998–Winter 1999): 38–51.

6   Claude Martin, ed., *Vie de la vénérable mère Marie de l'Incarnation* (Paris: L. Billaine, 1677), n.p. All translations from Marie's writings are my own.

7   Goldsmith, *Publishing Women's Life Stories in France*, 14.

8   Julia Boss, "Writing a Relic: The Uses of Hagiography in New France," in *Colonial Saints,* 211–33 (214).

9   Brad Gregory, *Salvation at Stake: Christian Martyrdom in Early Modern Europe* (Cambridge, Mass.: Harvard University Press, 1999), 251.

10   On the Bollandists see Michel De Certeau, "A Variant: Hagio-Graphical Edification," in *The Writing of History*, trans. Tom Conley (New York: Columbia University Press, 1988), 269–83.

11   On this insistence on the visible see Frank Lestringant, "Témoignage et martyre: Donner à voir, donner à croire (XVIe–XVIIIe siècle)," *Revue des sciences humaines* 269:1 (2003): 111–34.

12   Bruneau, *Women Mystics*, 80.

13   On missionary deaths in Japan, see Marie-Christine Gomez-Géraud, "Le théâtre des premiers martyrs japonais: la leçon de théologie," *Revue des sciences humaines* 269:1 (2003): 175–87, special issue, ed. Frank Lestringant and Pierre-François Moreau.

14   Paul Perron, "Isaac Jogues: From Martyrdom to Sainthood," in *Colonial Saints*, 153–68, quote on 156.

15   On Protestant martyrologies see Frank Lestringant, *Lumière des martyrs: essai sur le martyre au siècles des Réformes* (Paris: Honoré Champion, 2004); Gregory, *Salvation at Stake*.

16   Jacques Le Brun, "Mutations de la notion de martyre au XVIIe siècle d'après les biographies spirituelles féminines," *Sainteté et martyre dans les religions du livre*, ed. Jacques Marx (Brussels: Editions de l'Université de Bruxelles, 1989), 77–90, quote on 80.

17   Marie de l'Incarnation, *Ecrits spirituels et historiques*, ed. Albert Jamet, vol. 1 (Paris: Desclée de Brouwer, 1929), 209 (hereafter referred to as *Ecrits*). This edition includes extracts from both Marie's writings and her son's commentaries.

18   *Ecrits*, I, 224.

19   Published by Claude Barbin (Paris, 1669); see also modern edition by Frédéric Deloffre (Paris, Gallimard, 1990).

20   *Vie*, 128, 135.

21   *Vie*, 118.

22   Guy Oury, ed., *Correspondance* (Solesmes, France: Presses Universitaires de Laval/ Abbaye Saint-Pierre, 1971), 81.

23   *Ecrits,* II, 354 (taken from the *Relation* of 1653).

24   *Correspondance*, 132–33.

25   On the enclosure and the impossibility of martyrdom see Deslandres, "In the Shadow of the Cloister," 138; and Davis, *Women on the Margins*, 74. On religious women in Canada see Elizabeth Rapley, *The Dévotes: Women and Church in Seventeenth-Century France* (Montreal: McGill-Queen's University Press, 1990).

26   Quoted in Deslandres, "In the Shadow of the Cloister," 136.

27   For a reading of the Jesuit *Relation*'s substantial accounts of Jogues see Paul Perron, "Isaac Jogues: From Martyrdom to Sainthood," in *Colonial Saints*, 153–68.

28   See, for example, Nancy Armstrong and Leonard Tennenhouse, *The Imaginary Puritan: Literature, Intellectual Labor, and the Origins of Personal Life* (Berkeley: University of California Press, 1992), 196–216; Tara Fitzpatrick, "The Figure of Captivity: The Cultural Work of the Puritan Captivity Narrative," *American Literary History* 3:1 (Spring 1991): 1–26; and Richard Slotkin, *Regeneration Through Violence: The Mythology of the American Frontier 1600–1860* (Middletown, Conn.: Wesleyan University Press, 1973), 94–115.

29   *Correspondance*, 207, 218, 219, 324.

30   On threes and repetition see Sigmund Freud, "The Theme of the Three Caskets," in *The Standard Edition of the Complete Psychological Works of Sigmund Freud*, vol. 12, ed. James Strachey (London: Hogarth Press, 1958), 291–301.

31   *Correspondance*, 365.

32   Cited in Henri Raymond Casgrain, *Histoire de la mère Marie de l'Incarnation première supérieure des Ursulines* (Quebec City: G.E. Desbarats, 1864), 367.

33   Ibid., 324.

34   Ibid., 323.

35   Of course, in describing these deaths in such a way I am presenting things from the point of view of European missionaries. Within Amerindian culture there was also a highly developed and ritualized tradition of suffering and honor. A scholar with a deeper knowledge of this domain would be able to suggest more about each culture's understanding of the other's discourses on death and to point to ways in which indigenous peoples understood the missionaries' movements; I regret that this more complex task falls beyond the scope of this essay. For an account of such complex relations to violence that refrain from accounting for Indian practices only in relation to European paradigms, see, for example, Daniel K. Richter and James H. Merrell, eds., *Beyond the Covenant Chain: The Iroquois and Their Neighbors in Indian North America, 1600–1800* (Syracuse, N.Y.: Syracuse University Press, 1987); and Bruce Trigger, *The Children of Aataentsic: A History of the Huron People to 1660* (Montreal: McGill-Queen's University Press, 1976).

36   *Correspondance*, 390, 397.

37   In a letter of 1649 accounting for the death of Antoine Daniel, Marie describes how the slain body is destroyed after death, "consumé au pied de l'Autel avec l'Autel même" (C364). Shortly after, she reports, another Jesuit asks the ghost of Daniel how God permitted such an undignified treatment of his body.

38   *Correspondance*, 801.

39   From a letter to her son of 1668: "Depuis le commencement du Carême dernier jusqu'à l'Ascension j'ay écrit un gros livre Algonquin de l'histoire sacrée et de choses saintes, avec un Dictionaire et un Catéchisme Hiroquois, qui est un trésor. L'année dernière j'écrivis un gros Dictionnaire Algonquin à l'alphabet François; j'en ai un autre à l'alphabet Sauvage. Je vous dis cela pour vous faire voir que la bonté divine me donne les forces dans ma foiblesse" (*Correspondance*, 801). [Since the beginning of Lent to the Ascension I wrote a big book about sacred history and holy things in Algonquin, with an Iroquois dictionary and catechism, which is a treasure. Last year I wrote a big Algonquin-to-French dictionary; I have another one for the savages' alphabet. I tell you that to show you that the divine goodness gives me strength in my weakness.]

40   "To illustrate that "the life which one conducts in the company of the barbarians is a continual martyrdom," the Jesuit Jacques Bruyas described the daily martyrdom of the senses by enumerating how one's sight was affected by the smoke in the cabins; one's hearing by the natives' "importuning cries," one's sense of smell by the stench of natives' oiled hair and bodies; one's sense of touch by the cruel cold of Quebec; and one's sense of taste by the "insipid food which is fit for dogs." Quoted by Anya Mali, "Strange Encounters: Missionary Activity and Mystical Thought in Seventeenth-Century New France," *History of European Ideas* 22:2 (1996): 67–92, quote on 79.

41   Anya Mali shows how the *Jesuit Relations* also return repeatedly to the tension between ideas of salvation as a one-off brought about by baptism and the more difficult sustenance of a life in faith thereafter. "Strange Encounters," 70.

42   Boss, "Writing a Relic," 211–33.

43   Ibid., 229, 215.

44   *Vie*, preface, n.p.

45   *Ecrits*, I, 269.

46   *Ecrits*, I, 275.

47   *Correspondance*, 836, 837.

48   *Ecrits*, I, 266.

49   Annette Kolodny, *The Land Before Her: Fantasy and Experience of the American Frontiers, 1630–1680* (Chapel Hill: University of North Carolina Press, 1984), xiii–xiv.

50   Emily R. Wilson, *Mocked with Death: Tragic Overliving from Sophocles to Milton* (Baltimore: Johns Hopkins University Press, 2004).

CHAPTER II. BOOK OF SUFFERING, SUFFERING BOOK

1   The author would like to thank the archivists who have assisted greatly in completing this essay with their knowledge about the *Martyrs' Mirror* and in obtaining the reproductions and permissions: Joel Alderfer at the Mennonite Heritage Center in Harleysville, Pennsylvania; Jeff Bach at the Young Center for Anabaptist and Pietist Studies, Elizabethtown College, Pennsylvania; Amos Hoover at the Muddy Creek Library in Ephrata, Pennsylvania; Dana Lamparello at the Historical Society of Pennsylvania in Philadelphia; and Hunt Schenkel at the Schwenkfelder Library and Heritage Center in Pennsburg, Pennsylvania. He also thanks the two anonymous readers for their helpful comments on an earlier version of the chapter.

Quoted in Richard K. MacMaster, Samuel L. Horst, and Robert F. Ulle, *Conscience in Crisis: Mennonites and Other Peace Churches in America, 1739–1789, Interpretation and Documents*, Studies in Anabaptist and Mennonite History 20 (Scottdale, Pa.: Herald Press, 1979), 121–22.

2   Thieleman J. van Braght, *Het Bloedigh Tooneel der Doops-Gesinde, en Weereloose Christenen* . . . (Dordrecht, Netherlands: Jacob Braat, 1660); and Van Braght and Jan Luyken (illustrations), *Het Bloedig Tooneel, of Martelaers Spiegel der Doops-Gesinde of Weereloose Christenen* . . . (Amsterdam: J. vander Deyster, H. vanden Berg, Jan Blom, S. Swart, S. Wybrands, and A. Ossaan, 1685). For the most recent English-language edition see *The Bloody Theater or Martyrs Mirror of the Defenseless Christians* . . . , trans. Joseph F. Sohm, 8th ed. (Scottdale, Pa.: Herald Press, 1968). See also Sarah Covington, "Paratextual Stategies in Thieleman van Braght's *Martyr's Mirror*," *Book History* 9 (2006): 1–29; James W. Lowry, *The* Martyrs' Mirror *Made Plain* (Aylmer, Ontario: Pathway, 1997); Lowry, "*Martyrs' Mirror* Picture Albums and Abridgments: A Surprising Find," *Pennsylvania Mennonite Heritage* 25:4 (2002): 2–8; John S. Oyer and Robert S. Kreider, *Mirror of the Martyrs* (Intercourse, Pa.: Good Books, 2003); Gerald Studer, "A History of the Martyrs' Mirror," *Mennonite Quarterly Review* 22 (1948): 163–79; and A. Orley Swartzentruber, "The Piety and Theology of the Anabaptist Martyrs in Van Braght's *Martyrs' Mirror*," *Mennonite Quarterly Review* 28 (1954): 5–26, 128–42.

3   Jan Thieleman van Braght, *Der blutige Schau-Platz oder Martyrer-Spiegel der Tauffs gesinnten oder Wehrlosen-Christen* . . . , trans. Johann Peter Miller (Ephrata, Pa.: Brüder-

schafft, 1748–49). On the Ephrata *Martyrs' Mirror* see Daniel R. Heatwole, *The Ephrata Martyrs' Mirror: Past and Present* (Scottdale, Pa.: Mennonite Publishing House, [n.d.]); Julia Kasdorf, "'Work and Hope': Tradition and Translation of an Anabaptist Adam," *Mennonite Quarterly Review* 69 (1995): 178–204; David Luthy, "The Ephrata *Martyrs' Mirror*: Shot from Patriots' Muskets." *Pennsylvania Mennonite Heritage* 9:1 (1986): 2–5; Samuel Whitaker Pennypacker, "A Noteworthy Book," *Pennsylvania Magazine of History and Biography* 5 (1881): 276–89; Julius Friedrich Sachse, *The German Sectarians of Pennsylvania, 1708–1742: A Critical and Legendary History of the Ephrata Cloister and the Dunkers* (New York: AMS, 1971); and Sachse, *The German Sectarians of Pennsylvania, 1742–1800: A Critical and Legendary History of the Ephrata Cloister and the Dunkers* (New York: AMS, 1971).

4   Thomas S. Freeman and Thomas F. Mayer, *Martyrs and Martyrdom in England, c. 1400–1700* (Woodbridge, U.K.: Boydell Press, 2007); Susannah Brietz Monta, *Martyrdom and Literature in Early Modern England* (Cambridge: Cambridge University Press, 2005); John R. Knott *Discourses of Martyrdom in English Literature, 1563–1694* (Cambridge: Cambridge University Press, 1993); Friedericke Pannewick, *Martyrdom in Literature: Visions of Death and Meaningful Suffering in Europe and the Middle East from Antiquity to Modernity* (Wiesbaden: Eichert, 2004). On the history of Anabaptist martyr-book traditions see Peter Burschel, *Sterben und Unsterblichkeit: Zur Kultur des Martyrium in der frühen Neuzeit* (Munich: R. Oldenbourg Verlag, 2004); Brad S. Gregory, *Salvation at Stake: Christian Martyrdom in Early Modern Europe* (Cambridge, Mass.: Harvard University Press, 1999), especially the chapter "*Nachfolge Christi*: Anabaptists and Martyrdom" (197–249). For the most recent work interpreting the Pennsylvania *Martyrs' Mirror* as a means for German "Peace Sects" to forge a common identity and resist the militarization of Pennsylvania's Indian policies, see Jan Stievermann, "A 'plain, rejected little flock'": The Politics of Martyrological Self-Fashioning Among Pennsylvania's German Peace Churches, 1739–65," *William and Mary Quarterly* 66:2 (Apr. 2009): 287–324.

5   MacMaster, Horst, and Ulle, *Conscience in Crisis*; Stephen J. Stein, *Communities of Dissent: A History of Alternative Religions in America* (Oxford: Oxford University Press, 2003), 31–48.

6   "Martyrs," *The Mennonite Encyclopedia*, vol. 3 (Scottdale, Pa.: Mennonite Publishing House, 1990).

7   Ethelbert Stauffer, "The Anabaptist Theology of Martyrdom," trans. and ed. Robert Friedmann, *Mennonite Quarterly Review* 19 (1945): 179–214; Cornelius J. Dyck, trans. and ed., *Spiritual Life in Anabaptism* (Scottdale, Pa.: Herald, 1995), and "The Suffering Church in Anabaptism," *Mennonite Quarterly Review* 59 (1985): 5–23; Alan F. Kreider, "'The Servant Is Not Greater Than His Master': The Anabaptists and the Suffering Church," *Mennonite Quarterly Review* 58 (1984): 5–29.

8   Quoted in James W. Lowry, *The* Martyrs' Mirror *Made Plain* (Aylmer, Ontario: Pathway Publishers, 2000), 9.

9   Gregory, *Salvation at Stake*, 227, 228.

10   Ibid., 197–249; and Burschel, *Sterben und Unsterblichkeit*, 159–96. See also Hans de Ries, *Historie der Martelaren* . . . (Harlem: Daniel Keyser, 1615); and de Ries, *Martelaers*

Spiegel der Werelosen Christen: t'zedert Ao. 1524 (Harlem: Hans Passchiers van Wesbusch, 1631).

11   Beulah Stauffer Hostetler, "The Place of Confessions in the Mennonite Church (MC)," *Pennsylvania Mennonite Heritage* 12:2 (1989): 1–6.

12   *The Christian Confession of the Faith of the Harmless Christians, in the Netherlands Known by the Name of Mennonists* (Amsterdam, 1712).

13   *An Appendix to the Confession of Faith of the Christians, Called, Mennonites . . .* (Philadelphia: Andrew Bradford, 1727); *The Christian Confession of the Faith of the Harmless Christians, in the Netherlands, Known by the Name of Mennonists* (Amsterdam, Philadelphia: Andrew Bradford, 1727).

14   MacMaster, Horst, and Ulle, *Conscience in Crisis,* 25–59.

15   Robert L. Davidson, *War Comes to Quaker Pennsylvania, 1682–1756* (New York: Columbia University Press, 1957).

16   Alan Tully, "Englishmen and Germans: National-Group Contact in Colonial Pennsylvania, 1700–1755," *Pennsylvania History* 45 (1978): 237–56.

17   Leaders of the Mennonite Congregations in Pennsylvania, "To all the ministers and elders of the nonresistant Mennonite congregations of God in Amsterdam and Haarlem, October 19, 1745." In MacMaster, Horst, and Ulle, *Conscience in Crisis,* 84–86.

18   Ibid.

19   Mennonites, *Ausbund, das ist: Etliche schöne christliche Lieder. . .* (Germantown, Pa.: Christoph Saur, 1742).

20   Quoted in MacMaster, Horst, and Ulle, *Conscience in Crisis,* 84–86.

21   Thomas R. Brendle and Milton Rubincam, *William Rittenhouse and Moses Dissinger: Two Eminent Pennsylvania Germans* (Scottdale, Pa.: Herald Press, 1959). On Christoph Saur and his son, Christoph II, see Donald F. Durnbaugh, "Christopher Sauer, Pennsylvania-German Printer: His Youth in Germany and Later Relationships with Europe," *Pennsylvania Magazine of History and Biography* 82 (1958): 316–40; Ralph Frasca, "'To Rescue the Germans Out of Sauer's Hands': Benjamin Franklin's German-Language Printing Partnerships," *Pennsylvania Magazine of History and Biography* 121 (1997): 329–50; Stephen L. Longenecker, *The Christoph Sauers: Courageous Printers Who Defended Religious Freedom in Early America* (Elgin, Ill.: Brethren Press, 1981); Anna Kathryn Oller, "Christoph Saur, Colonial Printer: A Study of the Publications of the Press, 1738–1758," Ph.D. dissertation, University of Michigan, Ann Arbor, 1963.

22   MacMaster, Horst, and Ulle, *Conscience in Crisis,* 88; John C. Wenger, *History of the Mennonites of the Franconia Conference* (Telford, Pa.: Franconia Mennonite Historical Society, 1937), 319.

23   Whitfield J. Bell, Jr., *Patriot-Improvers: Biographical Sketches of Members of the American Philosophical Society* (Philadelphia: American Philosophical Society, 1999), 82–91.

24   Conrad Beissel, *A Dissertation on Man's Fall,* trans. Peter Miller (Ephrata, Pa.: Typis Societatis, 1765). See also Jeff Bach, *Voices of the Turtledove: The Sacred World of Ephrata* (University Park: Pennsylvania State University Press, 2003), 33–35; E. Gordon Alderfer,

The Ephrata Commune: An Early American Counterculture (Pittsburgh, Pa.: University of Pittsburgh Press, 1985).

25   Harold S. Bender, *Two Centuries of American Mennonite Literature: A Bibliography of Mennonitica Americana, 1727–1928* (Goshen, Pa.: Mennonite Historical Society, 1929).

26   Brother Lamech and Brother Agrippa (Jacob Gass and Peter Miller), *Chronicon Ephratense; a History of the Community of Seventh Day Baptists at Ephrata, Lancaster County, Pennsylvania, by "Lamech and Agrippa,"* trans. J. Max Hark (Lancaster, Pa.: Zahm, 1889), 210; Lamech and Agrippa, *Chronicon Ephratense . . .* (Ephrata, Pa.: [Brüderschaft], 1786).

27   Lamech and Agrippa, *Chronicon Ephratense,* 214.

28   Ibid., 213.

29   In the *Chronicon,* Miller stated that "the edition consisted of 1,300 copies" (p. 212), but he mentioned to the visiting Swedish minister Israel Acrelius that it was 1,200 copies; see *Ephrata as Seen by Contemporaries,* ed. Felix Reichmann and Eugene E. Doll (Allentown: Schlechter's, 1952), 60.

30   Van Braght (Miller trans.), *Martyrer-Spiegel,* 4. All translations mine unless otherwise noted.

31   The afterword and endorsement are titled "Kurtze Nachrede einiger Mitglieder der Gemeinde der Mennonisten / als welche die Hochdeutsche Uebersetzung gegen der Holländischen genau überlesen / und darauf die vor dem Register angeführte Druckfehler zur Bekanntmachung haben zugesandt" [A brief afterword by several members of the congregation of Mennonites, who have diligently read the high-German translation from the Dutch and submitted the printing errors listed in the index for publication] (s.p.).

32   Dielman Kolb and Heinrich Funck, "Kurtze Nachrede," in Van Braght (Miller trans.), *Martyrer-Spiegel,* s.p.

33   Ibid.

34   Ibid.

35   Pennypacker, "A Noteworthy Book," 276–89.

36   I thank archivists Amos Hoover (Muddy Creek Farm Library) and Joel Alderfer (Mennonite Heritage Center) for discussing this question and showing me a wide selection of *Martyrs' Mirror* association copies.

37   Conrad Beissel, *A Dissertation on Man's Fall,* trans. Peter Miller [Prior Jaebez] (Ephrata, Pa.: Typis Societatis, 1765).

38   Van Braght (trans. Miller), *Martyrer-Spiegel* (Ephrata, Pa.: Brüderschafft, 1748–49), No. 1, *Martyrs' Mirror* Editions, Lancaster Mennonite Historical Society, Lancaster, Pa.

39   On Decker see the brief biography in "Wer ist wer in Bayreuth?" www.barnick. de/bt/wer/index.htm, August 26, 2008. On Martin Engelbrecht see Friedrich Schott, *Der Augsburger Kupferstecher und Kunstverleger Martin Engelbrecht und seine Nachfolger: Ein Beitrag zur Geschichte des Augsburger Kunst—u. Buchhandels von 1719 bis 1896* (Augsburg, Germany: Schlossersche Buch- und Kunsthandlung, 1924).

40   The plates included in this particular Ephrata *Martyrs' Mirror* copy are Jesus, John the Baptist, James the Greater, Philip, James the Lesser, Peter, Paul, Andrew, Bartholomew, Matthew, Simon, Judas Thaddeus, Matthias, and John the Evangelist. The motto under-

neath this engraving depicting Jesus is "Ich bin der Weg u. die Warheit und das Leben. / Ego sum Via, Veritas, et Vita" [I am the way, the truth, and the life]. The scene on the left depicts the crucifixion—the ultimate martyrdom—and the scene on the right Christ's ascension into heaven.

41   Cynda L. Benson, *Early American Illuminated Manuscripts from the Ephrata Cloister*, Exhibition Smith College Museum of Art and State Museum of Pennsylvania, 1995 (Chicopee, Mass.: AM Lithography, 1995).

42   Don Yoder, "A Fraktur Primer," *Folklife Annual: A Publication of the American Folklife Center at the Library of Congress* 1988: 100–111.

43   Lamech and Agrippa, *Chronicon Ephratense*, 213–14, n. 2.

44   David Luthy, "The Ephrata Martyrs' Mirror: Shot from Patriots' Muskets," *Pennsylvania Mennonite Heritage* 9.1 (1986): 2–5.

45   Joseph von Gundy (Luthy trans.), "Hand-Written Folio Page in the Von Gundy 1748–49 Märtyrer Spiegel," in "The Ephrata *Martyrs' Mirror*: Shot from Patriots' Musket," by David Luthy, *Pennsylvania Mennonite Heritage* 9:1 (1986): 5; emphasis added.

46   Luthy, "The Ephrata Martyrs' Mirror," 3.

47   Von Gundy (Luthy trans.), "Hand-Written Folio Page," 5; emphasis added.

CHAPTER 12. ICONOCLASM WITHOUT ICONS?

1   David D. Hall, *Worlds of Wonder, Days of Judgment: Popular Religious Belief in Early New England* (New York: Knopf, 1989), 4–5.

2   Charles Vesey's Petition, 1714, vol. 9, no. 6, New York Papers, p. 191; Society for the Propagation of the Gospel in Foreign Parts, Letter Books, Series "A," 1702–37 (hereafter SPG Records). The desecration of Trinity Church was reported in the *Boston News-Letter*, March 22–29, 1714, and picked up by the press in London; "A Proclamation," *Daily Courant*, May 22, 1714.

3   Eamon Duffy, *The Stripping of the Altars: Traditional Religion in England, 1400–1580* (New Haven: Yale University Press, 1992), 480.

4   Quoted in Clifford Davidson, "The Anti-Visual Prejudice," in *Iconoclasm vs. Art and Drama*, ed. Clifford Davidson and Ann Elijenholm Nichols (Kalamazoo, Mich.: Cistercian Publications, 1989), 33–46, quote on 41.

5   Michael O'Connell, *The Idolatrous Eye: Iconoclasm and Theater in Early-Modern England* (New York: Oxford University Press, 2000); Julie Spraggon, *Puritan Iconoclasm During the English Civil War* (Woodbridge, U.K.: Boydell Press, 2003); Lee Palmer Wandel, *Voracious Idols and Violent Hands: Iconoclasm in Reformation Zurich, Strasbourg, and Basel* (New York: Cambridge University Press, 1995); Phyllis Mack Crew, *Calvinist Preaching and Iconoclasm in the Netherlands, 1544–1569* (New York: Cambridge University Press, 1978).

6   James Simpson, *Burning to Read: English Fundamentalism and Its Reformation Opponents* (Cambridge, Mass.: Harvard University Press, 2007), 21.

7   Paul Seaver, *Wallington's World: A Puritan Artisan in Seventeenth-Century London* (Stanford, Calif.: Stanford University Press, 1985).

8   Clifford Davidson, "'The Devil's Guts': Allegations of Superstition and Fraud in Religious Drama and Art During the Reformation," in Davidson and Nichols, *Iconoclasm vs. Art and Drama*, 92–144, quote on 103.

9   John Weever, *Ancient Funerall Monuments within the United Monarchies of Great Britaine, Ireland, and the Ilands Adjacent with the dissolved Monastaries therein contained* (London, 1631), 50.

10   *The Journal of William Dowsing: Iconoclasm in East Anglia During the English Civil War*, ed. Trevor Cooper (Woodbridge, U.K.: Boydell Press, 2001), 165, 210, 234.

11   George Juirson to Secretary, SPG Records, vol. 3, no. CLXVIII, August 4, 1708, p. 467.

12   Ann Kibbey, *The Interpretation of Material Shapes in Puritanism: A Study of Rhetoric, Prejudice, and Violence* (New York: Cambridge University Press, 1986), 43.

13   Samuel Mather, *A Testimony from the Scripture Against Idolatry and Superstition, in Two Sermons* (Cambridge, Mass., 1672), 7, 26, 35.

14   *Winthrop's Journal, "History of New England," 1630–1649*, 2 vols., ed. James Kendall Hosmer (New York: Barnes & Noble, 1946 [1908]), I:137, 151, 182.

15   William Bradford tells the story of Thomas Morton and his "idle or idol maypole"; *Of Plymouth Plantation, 1620–1647*, ed. Samuel Eliot Morrison (New York: Modern Library, 1967), 206. See also *Winthrop's Journal*, I: 53.

16   Kenneth Silverman, *The Life and Times of Cotton Mather* (New York: Harper & Row, 1985), 62–63.

17   Edward Randolph to the Bishop of London, "From the common gaol in Algiers," October 25, 1689, Colonial Office Papers, National Archives, London (hereafter CO Papers), 5/855, no. 42.

18   C.D., *New England's Faction Discovered; Or, A Brief and True Account of their Persecution of the Church of England* (London, 1690), 259. While Mather dismissed the charge, arguing that "all the mischief done is the breaking of a few Quarels of glass by idle Boys," the historian Charles Andrews concludes that the charge of desecration "had a basis in fact." Charles M. Andrews, ed., *Narratives of the Insurrections, 1675–1690* (New York: C. Scribner's Sons, 1915), 259.

19   Thomas Maule, *New-England Persecutors Mauled with their own Weapons: Giving some account of the bloody laws made at Boston against the Kings subjects that dissented from their way of worship* (New York, 1697), 51.

20   Abstract of a letter from Samuel Myles, Minister at Boston, December 12, 1690, CO Papers 5/855, no. 127.

21   Jacob Leisler to William and Mary, New York, August 20, 1689, CO Papers 5/1081, no. 50. David William Voorhees explores the anti-Catholic roots of Leisler's rebellion in his article, "The 'Fervent Zeale' of Jacob Leisler," *William and Mary Quarterly* 51 (July 1994): 447–72.

22   *A Journal of the Proceedings in the Late Expedition to Port-Royal* (Boston, 1690), 6. The firing of the church at Port Royal is also described in the letter of Lt. Governor Usher to the Council of Trade and Plantations, June 28, 1708, CO Papers 5/864, no. 225, enclosure 3.

23   Owen Stanwood, "Creating the Common Enemy: Catholics, Indians, and the Politics of Fear in Imperial North America, 1678–1700," Ph.D. dissertation, Northwestern University, 2005, p. 186.

24   Ibid., 185.

25   Quoted in ibid., 32.

26   Thomas Cobbet to Increase Mather, February 19, 1683, *Massachusetts Historical Society* Collections, Boston, 4th ser., 8 (1868), 296–97.

27   Mather described the Canadians as half-breeds, "Half Indianized French and Half Frenchified Indians" who combined the worst vices of both groups. *Decennium Luctuosum: An history of remarkable occurrences, in the long war, which New-England hath had with the Indian salvages, from the year, 1688. To the year 1698* (Boston, 1699), 46. For two recent discussions of the phenomenon of Puritan captives converting to Catholicism, see Ann Little, *Abraham in Arms: War and Gender in Colonial New England* (Ithaca, N.Y.: Cornell University Press, 2007); and William Foster, *The Captors' Narrative: Catholic Women and Their Puritan Men on the Early American Frontier* (Ithaca, N.Y.: Cornell University Press, 2003).

28   Cotton Mather, *Souldiers counselled and comforted: A discourse delivered unto some part of the forces engaged in the just war of New-England against the northern & eastern Indians* (Boston, 1689), 32–33.

29   Mather, *Decennium Luctuosum*, passim.

30   Cotton Mather, *Observable Things: The History of Ten Years Rolled away under the great Calamities of War, with Indian Salvages* (Boston, 1699), 224.

31   Samuel Penhallow, *History of the Wars of New-England with the Eastern Indians* (Boston, 1726), 37.

32   Mather, *Souldiers Counselled*, 28.

33   Edward G. Gray, *New World Babel: Languages and Nations in Early America* (Princeton, N.J.: Princeton University Press, 1999), 80. See also Kenneth Mills, *Idolatry and Its Enemies: Colonial Andean Religion and Extirpation, 1640–1750* (Princeton, N.J.: Princeton University Press, 1997); and Margaret J. Leahey, "Iconic Discourse: The Language of Images in Seventeenth-Century New France," in *The Language Encounter in the Americas, 1492–1800*, ed. Edward G. Gray and Norman Fiering (New York: Berghahn Books, 2000).

34   [Nathaniel Saltonstall], *A New and Further Narrative of the State of New-England, Being a Continued Account of the Bloudy Indian-War* (London, 1676), 6–7.

35   My analysis builds on the insight of Ann Kibbey (in *Interpretation of Material Shapes*) that violence against Antinomians, Indians, and witches constituted a form of iconoclasm in Puritan thought. Kibbey's focus is on the formal rhetorical homologies linking various *figura* in the sermons of John Cotton, whereas my analysis moves beyond formal semiotics to encompass the broader cultural milieu in which Old World acts of iconoclasm and New World Indian warfare took place.

36   Anon., *The Case for all Crucifixes, images, &c. made with hands, and for religious use, in the case of Cheapside-Crosse, is discussed whether their militia, the setting of them in a posture of defence, be according to law, Printed in the Climactericall Yeer of Crosses and Cross-men* (London, 1643), 11, 14.

37   Mack Crew, *Calvinist Preaching and Iconoclasm*, 12, 25–26.

38   Weever, *Ancient Funerall Monuments*, 51, 55.

39   Anon., *The Dolefull Lamentation of Cheap-Side Crosse; Or Old England Sick of the Staggers* (London, 1641); Anon., *The Downfall of Dagon, or, The taking downe of Cheap-side Crosse this second of May, 1643* (London, 1642); Anon., *A Vindication of Cheapside Crosse against the Roundheads* (London, 1643). See also Anon., *The Remarkable Funeral of Cheap-side Crosse in London* (London, 1642); Richard Overton, *Articles of High Treason Exhibited against Cheap-side Crosse: With the Last Will and Testament of the Said Crosse* (London, 1642); Samuel Loveday, *An Answer to the Lamentation of Cheap-side Crosse: Together with the Reasons why so many doe desire the downfall of it, and all such Popish Reliques* (London, 1643).

40   Increase Mather, *A Relation of the Troubles which have Hapned in New-England, by Reason of the Indians there: From the year 1614 to the year 1675* (Boston, 1677), 46. For a discussion of Anglo-Indian treatment of corpses in war see Andrew Lipman, "'A meanes to knit them together': The Exchange of Body Parts in the Pequot War," *William and Mary Quarterly* 65 (Jan. 2008), 3–28; Eric Seeman, "'Not One of His Bones Should Be Buried': Corpses and Cross-Cultural Religious Violence," paper presented at "Religion and Violence in Early America," Yale University School of Graduate Studies and the Omohundro Institute of Early American History and Culture, New Haven, April 2008.

41   Robert Blair St. George, *Conversing by Signs: Poetics of Implication in Colonial New England Culture* (Chapel Hill: Universisty of North Carolina Press, 1998), 3.

42   Mather, *Observable Things*, 211.

43   George Bishop, *New England Judged, Not by Man's, but the Spirit of the Lord: And the Summe sealed up of New-England's Persecutions* (London, 1661), 119, 171.

44   Clayton Colman Hall, ed., *Narratives of Early Maryland 1633–1684* (Bowie, Md.: Heritage Books, 1998), 16, 349.

45   *Extracts from the Annual Letters of the English Province of the Society of Jesus, 1640, 1655 and 1656*, in ibid., 134, 141–42.

46   SPG Records, vol. 3, no. 184, 529.

47   Ibid., vol. 9, no. 13, 20 Apr. 1714, 116.

48   Ibid., vol. 6, no. 153, 6 Nov. 1711.

49   On the "Anglican Renaissance" in the South see Thomas J. Little, "The Origins of Southern Evangelicalism: Revivalism in South Carolina, 1700–1740," *Church History* 75 (Dec. 2006), 768–808.

50   SPG Records, vol. 10, no. 9, Robert Maule to Secretary, January 23, 1714, 79; and vol. 11, Gideon Johnston to Secretary, December 19, 1715.

51   Charles Woodmason, "A Report on Religion in the South" (1765), in *The Carolina Backcountry on the Eve of the Revolution: The Journal and Other Writings of Charles Woodma-*

son, Anglican Itinerant, ed. Richard J. Hooker (Chapel Hill: University of North Carolina Press, 1953), 70–81.

52   SPG Records, vol. 7, no. 2, July 7, 1711.

53   *Carolina Backcountry on the Eve of the Revolution,* 46, n. 40.

54   The classic work on the theme of pollution in anthropology is Mary Douglass, *Purity and Danger: An Analysis of the Concepts of Pollution and Taboo* (New York: Routledge, 2002; orig. pub. 1966)

55   David Ramsay, *History of South Carolina from Its First Settlement in 1670 to the Year 1808* (Charleston, S.C.: D. Longworth, 1809), 87. See also Steven J. Oatis, *A Colonial Complex: South Carolina's Frontiers in the Era of the Yamassee War, 1680–1730* (Lincoln: University of Nebraska Press, 2004), 50–51.

56   *An Account of what the Army Did, under the Command of Col. [James] Moore, in His Expedition last Winter, Against the Spaniards and Spanish Indians: In a Letter, from the said Col. Moore to the Governor of Carolina. Printed in the Boston News, May 1, 1704,* (New York, 1836), 574–75.

57   Quoted in Mark F. Boyd, Hale G. Smith, and John W. Griffin, eds., *Here They Once Stood: The Tragic End of the Apalachee Missions* (Gainesville: University of Florida Press, 1951), 35–38.

58   Jon Sensbach, "Religion and the Early South in an Age of Atlantic Empire," *Journal of Southern History* 73 (Aug. 2007), 631–43; and especially his "Seventeen Stations of the Cross: Reassessing the Destruction of the Florida Missions," paper presented at "Religion and Violence in Early America," 2008.

59   Nathaniel Osborne to secretary, May 28, 1715, SPG Letterbook, vol. 10, 99.

60   Dr. Hewit, *An Historical Account of the Rise and Progress of the Colonies of South Carolina and Georgia* (London, 1779), in *Historical Collections of South Carolina; Embracing Many Rare and Valuable Pamphlets and Other Documents,* ed. B. R. Carroll, 2 vols. (New York: Harper & Bros., 1836), vol. 1, 197.

61   Oatis, *Colonial Complex,* 95.

62   Ramsay, *History of South Carolina from Its First Settlement,* 89–90, 92.

63   Joseph Boone and Richard Beresford, agents for the Commons House of Assembly in South Carolina to the Council of Trade and Plantations, December 5, 1716, enclosure i, Committee of the Assembly of Carolina, CO Papers, 5/1265, nos. 44, 44 i–v.

64   Oatis, *Colonial Complex,* 1.

65   Le Jau to Secretary, May 10, 1715, SPG Records, vol. 10, 114.

66   John Archdale, *A New Description of that Fertile and Pleasant Province of Carolina: with a Brief Account of its Discovery, Settling, and the Government Thereof to this Time* (London, 1707), 306.

67   John Lawson, *A New Voyage to Carolina: Containing the Exact Description and Natural History of that Country: Together with the Present State thereof: And a Journal of a Thousand Miles, Travel'd thro' several Nations of Indians* (London, 1709), 200–201.

68   Quoted in Joseph Casino, "Anti-Popery in Colonial Pennsylvania," *Pennsylvania Magazine of History and Biography* 105 (1981): 279–309; quote on 283, n. 8.

69   Brendan McConville, *The King's Three Faces: The Rise and Fall of Royal America, 1688–1776* (Chapel Hill: University of North Carolina Press, 2006), 296, 306.

FINAL REFLECTIONS

1   A version of this essay was first delivered at the International Spenser Conference, "Spenser's Civilizations," in Toronto in May 2006. I am grateful to all those who responded to the paper on that occasion, including Joseph Campana, Linda Gregerson, Marshall Grossman, Tom Herron, Willy Maley, Richard McCabe, James Nohrnberg, and Bart Van Es. The essay was published in *Spenser Studies* 22 (2007): 5–26. It is here revised and republished with permission.

2   Winston Churchill, *My Early Life* (1930; repr. London: Eland, 2000), 119.

3   For his late Victorian contemporaries young Churchill's Gibbonian style excited widespread admiration, but for the bitterly disillusioned Evelyn Waugh writing in the 1950s, it was merely "sham-Augustan" (*Men at Arms* [1952; repr. Harmondsworth, U.K.: Penguin, 1975), 176.

4   Quoted in John Charmley, *Churchill: The End of Glory: A Political Biography* (Toronto: Macfarlane Walter & Ross, 1993), 431.

5   Joseph Schumpeter, *Imperialism [and] Social Classes: Two Essays* (1919; 1927), trans. Heinz Norden (New York: Meridian, 1972).

6   David Armitage, *The Ideological Origins of the British Empire* (Cambridge: Cambridge University Press, 2000).

7   Quentin Skinner, *Liberty Before Liberalism* (Cambridge: Cambridge University Press, 1998), 105.

8   Paul Kennedy, *The Rise and Fall of British Naval Mastery* (Harmondsworth, U.K.: Penguin, 1976), 24.

9   See Paul Stevens, "Heterogenizing Imagination: Globalization, *The Merchant of Venice*, and the Work of Literary Criticism," *New Literary History* 36:3 (2005): 425–37.

10   The Bible is quoted from the 1611 Authorized Version.

11   The letter was probably written by Ignatius, Bishop of Antioch, around A.D. 110–17; see, for instance, *The Cambridge Companion to the Bible*, ed. Howard Clark Kee et al. (Cambridge: Cambridge University Press, 1997), 565–67.

12   Edmund Spenser, *The Faerie Queene*, ed. Thomas P. Roche (1978; repr. Harmondsworth, U.K.: Penguin, 1987), Letter of the Authors, 17.

13   Richard A. McCabe, *Spenser's Monstrous Regiment: Elizabethan Ireland and the Poetics of Difference* (Oxford: Oxford University Press, 2002), 4. Hereafter cited in the text. See also Ciaran Brady, "Spenser's Irish Crisis: Humanism and Experience in the 1590s," *Past & Present* III (1986):17-49, and Paul Stevens, "Spenser and Milton on Ireland: Civility, Exclusion, and the Politics of Wisdom," *ARIEL* 26:4 (1995):151–67.

14   Thomas Herron, "Guyon's Angel," paper presented at "Spenser's Civilizations," International Spenser Society Conference, University of Toronto, May 2006.

15   Obviously, the doctrine of election was double-edged and could lead to despair, but it is extraordinary how little of the temptation to doubt one's own election enters public arguments for imperial or colonial expansion.

16   John Bradley, response to "Archeologies of Spenser," presented at "Spenser's Civilizations," International Spenser Society Conference, University of Toronto, May 2006.

17   Ian Paisley, "A Prime Text for a Prime Minister" (December 15, 1985), quoted in Steve Bruce, *God Save Ulster: The Religion and Politics of Paisleyism* (Oxford: Clarendon, 1986), 269–70. Over thirty years of violence has had an impact on Paisley, but even after the compromises of old age and becoming Northern Ireland's First Minister in 2007, Paisley's views on Protestant exceptionalism remain largely unchanged. Consider his embarrassment at having inadvertently taken part in an ecumenical service, as reported in *Times online,* Jan. 21, 2008

18   The *View* is quoted from Edmund Spenser, *A View of the State of Ireland* (1633), ed. Andrew Hadfield and Willy Maley (Oxford: Blackwell, 1997). Hereafter cited in the text.

19   See Stevens, "Spenser and Milton on Ireland."

20   Milton is quoted from *John Milton: Complete Poems and Prose*, ed. Merritt Y. Hughes (Indianapolis: Odyssey, 1957).

21   *FQ* V.Proem, 10.

22   Linda Gregerson, *The Reformation of the Subject: Spenser, Milton, and the English Protestant Epic* (Cambridge: Cambridge University Press, 1995), 236.

23   John Rolfe, letter to Sir Thomas Dale, in Ralph Hamor, *A True Discourse of the Present Estate of Virginia* (London, 1615).

24   Samuel Purchas, "Virginias Verger" (1625), in *Hakluytus Posthumus, or Purchas his Pilgrimes*, 20 vols. (1906; repr. New York: AMS, 1965).

25   Oliver Cromwell, *A Declaration of His Highness, by the Advice of His Council . . . against Spain* (1655), in *The Works of John Milton*, ed. Frank Allen Patterson et al., 18 vols. (New York: Columbia University Press, 1931–38), XIII: 509–63.

26   The classic account is H. F. Russell-Smith, *Harrington and His Oceana: A Study of a 17th-Century Utopia and Its Influence in America* (Cambridge: Cambridge University Press, 1914). See also J. G. A. Pocock, ed., *The Political Works of James Harrington* (Cambridge: Cambridge University Press, 1977), esp. 128–52; James Holstun, *A Rational Millennium: Puritan Utopias of Seventeenth-Century England and America* (Oxford: Oxford University Press, 1987); and David Norbrook, *Writing the English Republic: Poetry, Rhetoric and Politics, 1627–1660* (Cambridge: Cambridge University Press, 1999), esp. 357–78.

27   Pocock, *Political Works of James Harrington,* 19.

28   *Oceana* is quoted from Pocock's edition, on p. 332. I am indebted to Philip Loosemore for drawing my attention to this passage.

29   While Armitage, *Ideological Origins* (137–39), shows no interest in the religious quality of Harrington's republican vision, Norbrook, *Writing the English Republic* (357–78), somewhat more surprisingly, shows little or no interest in the overtly imperial quality of what he calls English republicanism's "most important text" (357).

30   Vaughan is quoted from *The Works of Henry Vaughan*, ed. L. C. Martin, 2nd ed. (Oxford: Clarendon, 1957).

31   *FQ* VI.x.24.

32   See, for instance, Edgar Wind, *Pagan Mysteries in the Renaissance,* rev. ed. (New York: Norton, 1958).

33   Building on the work of scholars like Richard Helgerson, especially in *Forms of Nationhood: The Elizabethan Writing of England* (Chicago: University of Chicago Press, 1992), there is now a wealth of imaginative scholarship on Spenser and the construction of English national history: see, for example, David Galbraith, *Archtectonics of Imitation in Spenser, Daniel, and Drayton* (Toronto: University of Toronto Press, 2000); Andrew Escobedo, *Nationalism and Historical Loss in Renaissance England* (Ithaca, N.Y.: Cornell Universtiy Press, 2004); Philip Schwyzer, *Literature, Nationalism, and Memory in Early Modern England and Wales* (Cambridge: Cambridge University Press, 2004); and Bart Van Es, *Spenser's Forms of History* (Oxford: Oxford University Press, 2002).

34   See, for instance, Richard Rambuss, "Spenser's Life and Career," in *The Cambridge Companion to Spenser Studies,* ed. Andrew Hadfield (Cambridge: Cambridge University Press, 2001), 14–16. Spenser's shorter poems are quoted from *The Yale Edition of the Shorter Poems of Edmund Spenser,* ed. William Oram et al. (New Haven: Yale University Press, 1989).

35   For a perceptive overview of this phenomenon see Geoffrey Wheatcroft, "A Man So Various: The Misappropriated Winston Churchill," *Harper's* magazine (May 2006): 86–94.

36   Quoted from Roy Jenkins, *Churchill* (London: Macmillan, 2001), 621.

37   As Willy Maley reminds me, in strict Harringtonian terms the empire lingers on in the sovereign state of the United Kingdom of Great Britain and Northern Ireland: both Marpesia and the northern part of Panopea are still subject to Oceana.

38   On Churchill's romanticism see Paul Stevens, "Churchill's Military Romanticism," *Queen's Quarterly* 113:1 (2006): 70–85.

39   C. S. Lewis, *English Literature in the Sixteenth Century, Excluding Drama* (Oxford: Clarendon, 1954), 393.

40   Eliot's poetry is quoted from T. S. Eliot, *The Complete Poems and Plays, 1909–1950* (New York: Harcourt, Brace, 1971). "Little Gidding," 50–53.

41   See Marshall Sahlins, *Apologies to Thucydides: Understanding History as Culture and Vice Versa* (Chicago: University of Chicago Press, 2004).

42   This is what John Considine, following David Lowenthal, calls "heritage": see his brilliant book, *Dictionaries in Early Modern Europe: Lexicography and the Making of Heritage* (Oxford: Oxford University Press, 2008), esp. 5, 8–9, 285.

43   T. S. Eliot, "Tradition and the Individual Talent" (1919), in *Selected Essays* (1932; repr. London: Faber, 1969), 13–22. Hereafter cited in the text.

44   John Milton, "The Doctrine and Discipline of Divorce" (1643), in Hughes, *Complete Poems,* 697.

45   On the Project for a New American Century, see its "Statement of Principles," June 3, 1997, www.newamericancentury.org/statementofprinciples.htm, and "Rebuilding America's Defenses," Sept. 2000, www.newamericancentury.org/RebuildingAmericasDefenses.pdf.

46   Michael Hardt and Antonio Negri, *Empire* (Cambridge, Mass.: Harvard University Press, 2000), 11.

47   Winston S. Churchill, *A History of the English-Speaking Peoples,* 4 vols. (1956; repr. New York: Dodd, Mead, 1966). Hereafter cited in the text. See also Niall Ferguson, *Empire: The Rise and Demise of the British World Order and the Lessons for Global Power* (New York: Basic, 2002); and David Reynolds, *In Command of History: Churchill Fighting and Writing the Second World War* (London: Penguin, 2004).

48   Anonymous Bush administration official quoted in Ron Suskind, "Faith, Certainty, and the Presidency of George W. Bush," *New York Times* (Oct. 17, 2004).

49   Stephen Greenblatt, "Invisible Bullets: Renaissance Authority and Its Subversion," *Glyph* 8 (1981): 40–61. See especially Jonathan Dollimore's critique in *Political Shakespeare: New Essays in Cultural Materialism,* ed. Jonathan Dollimore and Alan Sinfield (Manchester, U.K.: University of Manchester Press, 1985), 11–13. See also Paul Stevens, "Pretending to Be Real: Stephen Greenblatt and the Legacy of Popular Existentialism," *New Literary History* 33:3 (2002): 491–519.

50   Rowse was one of the team of historians who worked on Churchill's *History of the English-Speaking Peoples.* See Reynolds, *In Command of History,* 509.

CONTRIBUTORS

Rolena Adorno is the Reuben Post Halleck Professor of Spanish and Chair of the Department of Spanish and Portuguese at Yale University. Her most recent books are *De Guancane a Macondo: Estudios de literatura hispanoamericana* (2008) and *The Polemics of Possession in Spanish American Narrative* (2007), which in 2008 was awarded the Katherine Singer Kovacs Prize from the Modern Language Association. She is a member of the American Academy of Arts and Sciences.

Kristina Bross is Associate Professor of English and American Studies at Purdue University. Her publications include *Dry Bones and Indian Sermons: Praying Indians in Colonial America* (2004) and *Early Native Literacies: A Documentary and Critical Anthology* (2008), coedited with Hilary Wyss. She is currently working on an edition of Pequot War narratives with Kevin McBride and a study of New England's reception of Oliver Cromwell's "Western Design."

Cornelius Conover is Visiting Assistant Professor of Atlantic History at Augustana College, South Dakota. His current research focuses on Catholicism and imperialism in the Spanish Empire with particular attention to colonial Mexico City.

Dominique Deslandres is Professor of History at the Université de Montréal. Her most recent publications include *Croire et faire croire: Les missions françaises au XVIIe siècle* (2003) and *Les Sulpiciens de Montréal: Une histoire de pouvoir et de discrétion 1657–2007* (2007, coauthored with John A. Dickinson and Ollivier Hubert). She is currently working on a biography of the mystic Marie Guyart de l'Incarnation, part of a larger project on the history of gender in the French religious world from the sixteenth through the eighteenth century.

Patrick Erben is Assistant Professor in the Department of English and Philosophy at the University of West Georgia. His book, *A Harmony of the Spirits: Multilingualism, Translation, and the Language of Spiritual Community in Early Pennsylvania,* is forthcoming with the Omohundro Institute of Early American History and Culture and the University of North Carolina Press. He is currently working on a selective edition of the writings of Francis Daniel Pastorius to be published by Pennsylvania State University Press.

Barbara Fuchs is Professor of Spanish and English at the University of California at Los Angeles. Her most recent book is *Exotic Nation: Maurophilia and the Construction of Early Modern Spain* (2009). With Aaron Ilika, she has recently published an edition and translation of Cervantes's *The Bagnios of Algiers* and *The Great Sultana* (2009). She is an editor for the forthcoming *Norton Anthology of World Literature* and is also working on the disavowal of Spanish influences in early modern English literature.

Allan Greer is Professor of History and Canada Research Chair in Colonial North America at McGill University. Among his publications are *Mohawk Saint: Catherine Tekakwitha and the Jesuits* (2005) and *The People of New France* (1997). He is currently at work on two projects: an overview of the history of New France and a comparative study of the clash of indigenous and European forms of land tenure in New Spain, New France, and New England.

Linda Gregerson is the Caroline Walker Bynum Distinguished University Professor of English at the University of Michigan. She is the author of *The Reformation of the Subject: Spenser, Milton, and the English Protestant Epic* (1995) and *Negative Capability: Contemporary American Poetry* (2001) as well as four books of poetry. She is currently at work on *Commonwealth of the Word,* a study of imagined collectivity in the works of John Eliot, John Milton, and William Shakespeare.

Katherine Ibbett is Lecturer in French at University College London and has recently published *The Style of the State in French Theater, 1630–1660* (2009). She is currently working on a book-length project about compassion in early modern France.

Susan Juster is Professor of History and Associate Dean for Social Sciences, College of Literature, Science, and the Arts, University of Michigan. She is the author most recently of *Doomsayers: Anglo-American Prophecy in the Age of Revolution* (2003) and is currently working on a cultural history of religious violence in British North America in the seventeenth and eighteenth centuries.

Carla Gardina Pestana is W. E. Smith Professor of History at Miami University, Ohio. Her most recent publications include *English Atlantic in an Age of Revolution, 1640–1661* (2004) and *Protestant Empire: Religion and the Making of the British Atlantic World* (2009). She is currently working on two projects: a history of the English invasion of Jamaica and a study of the heightened imperial conflicts of the 1660s, especially in the Caribbean.

Paul Stevens is Professor and Canada Research Chair in Early Modern Literature and Culture at the University of Toronto. During 2007–8 he was President of the Milton Society of America and Visiting Fellow at All Souls College, Oxford. His most recent publications include *Milton in America* (special issue of *University of Toronto Quarterly* 77:3 [2008]) and *Early Modern Nationalism and Milton's England* (2008), which he coedited with David Loewenstein. He is about to complete the manuscript of a new book called *Milton Imagining England, 1620–45.*

Bethany Wiggin is Assistant Professor of German in the Department of Germanic Languages and Literatures, University of Pennsylvania. She is the author of *Novel Translations: The European Novel and the German Book, 1680–1730* (2010) and is currently working on a project exploring early modern globalism and the vagaries of cultural translation through the planetary circulation of slave narratives.

INDEX

Acosta, José de, 106
Acrelius, Israel, 201
Acta Sanctorum, 178
Acts and Monuments. See Foxe, John
Adams, John, 235–36
African: conversion of slaves, 46; enslaved people, 30–31, 46, 160, 164, 171; slave trade, 171; slavery in the New World, 21, 234
Algonquian Indians, 10, 72, 79, 83, 149–50; alliance with the French, 225; anonymous woman convert, 4, 11, 123–25, 130–31, 137–41; and the Bible (*see* Eliot, John); Christian communities of, 72; conversion of, 79, 83, 124; and the English, 72; and the Jesuits, 12; and John Eliot (*see* Eliot, John). *See also* basket weaving
Amboyna, 50–57
American Revolution, 193, 211–12, 215, 236, 240
Anabaptists, 231, 235; coherence between biblical martyrdom and persecution of, 195; Dutch, 193, 198; and martyr books, 198; and martyrdom, 192–96, 211, 213; movement of, 191, 195; as part of tradition of radical Protestantism, 205. *See also* Mennonites
Anglican, 157–58, 161, 217, 221–24, 230–33, 236–37; Church, 223; destruction of symbols of, 236
Anglicanism, 232
Apalachicola Indians, 233
Armitage, David, 14, 239–42, 246–47, 255; *The Ideological Origins of the British Empire*, 239–42
Augustine, 32; and role of images in religious worship, 218

Aztec: destruction of pictographic texts of, 226; federation, 9; Spanish plunder of riches of, 63

Baraz, Daniel, 52
basket weaving, 12, 123; Mohegan, 140; as signing practice for native women, 140; traditional, 141; and use as means of entering colonial economic system, 139–40
Bear Nation, 185
Beissel, Conrad, 199–200
Benezet, Anthony, 159; *Observations of the Enslaving, Importing and Purchasing of Negroes*, 171
Bible, 1, 8, 72, 130, 164–66, 195, 232; Abraham, 189, 246; Acts, 247; Berleburg, 199; Book of Daniel, 77; Book of Revelation, 77, 129, 203; destruction of during wars, 226, 233, 237; Epistle to the Ephesians, 243–45; Exodus, 5; Genesis, 73, 81, 246–47; Job, 243; John, 27, 243, 249; Matthew, 33, 81, 205–7, 243, 245; Mosaic law, 243; Paul, 243; Psalms, 81; Second Coming, 5, 129; Sodom and Gomorrah, 243, 246; Thessalonians, 197; Thomas, 207
biblical translation, 72–73, 80; Algonquian (*see* Eliot, John); German (*see* Saur, Christoph); Indian (*see* Eliot, John); Irish, 72–73; Scots Gaelic, 73; vernacular, 1, 7
Blackburn, Robin, 4
Black Legend, 21, 41, 55, 69
Boehme, Jacob, 199
bookbinding, 200
Book of Common Prayer, 221–23, 232
Book of Martyrs. See Foxe, John
Boss, Julia, 178, 187

ACKNOWLEDGMENTS

This volume took shape over two stimulating days in October 2007, when twenty scholars of the early modern Atlantic world gathered at the University of Michigan for a conference on "Religion and Empire," sponsored by the university's Atlantic Studies Initiative. Ten months earlier, a group of intrepid graduate students from History, English, Comparative Literature, and MEMS (Medieval and Early Modern Studies) had gathered for the first session of an interdisciplinary course by the same name. For the two of us who taught that course, friends and fellow-travelers in the field of early modern religious studies, the seminar was a chance to explore together the role of texts and cultural practice in the reformation of western Christendom and in the competitive emergence of New World empires, driven as they were by confessional rivalries and divides. As our students gamely plowed through the epic poetry of John Milton and Edmund Spenser (a challenge for the historians in the room) and the historiography of the European Reformation (less daunting, perhaps, but still a test for the literary scholars) over fourteen vigorous weeks, we were encouraged by their example to continue our collective inquiry by means of a conference. Our first thanks, then, go to our students: Patrick Tonks, Susanna Linsley, Kealani Cook, Katie Wills, Gavin Hollis, Nilanjana Majumdar. Their probing questions, their openness to (and occasional skepticisms about) authentic interdisciplinary exchange, their devotion to early modern studies have made us better teachers and scholars. They also did much of the leg work for our conference: transporting the visiting scholars to and from the airport, chairing sessions, providing a knowledgeable and intent audience for our speakers. Our special thanks go to Suzi Linsley, organizer extraordinaire, without whose energy and good humor the conference would never have gotten off the ground. At the eleventh hour, Cordelia Zukerman stepped in and helped us pull together the index; her cheerful assistance and calm professionalism were much appreciated in the final days of preparing the volume for publication.

At the University of Michigan, a number of programs, departments, and colleagues provided invaluable assistance, both material and intellectual. Our home departments allowed us to team-teach a relatively small graduate course, a real luxury in these days of heightened scrutiny over enrollments and budgets. Our colleagues helped in so many ways: suggesting possible contributors and conference speakers, calling our attention to emergent work in the field, finding time in their busy schedules to attend the conference panels, reading portions of this book in manuscript, and generally providing one of the most vibrant and rich environments for pursuing multidisciplinary work on the early modern era to be found anywhere in the country. Special thanks go to Steven Mullaney, Valerie Kivelson, George Hoffman, Mary Kelley, Jonathan Sheehan, Jeremy Mumford, and above all, to Carroll Smith-Rosenberg and David Hancock, directors of the Atlantic Studies Initiative (ASI). When Carroll arrived in Ann Arbor in 1996, little did we know that our intellectual lives were about to be transformed. ASI was her creation, the vehicle for her formidable powers of community-building and her unstinting generosity. David, with characteristic grace and acumen, has sustained and augmented the House That Carroll Built—the series of workshops, seminars, conferences, and informal conversations devoted to the study of the circum-Atlantic world. We are truly fortunate to be teaching at an institution where such leadership, and such forms of inquiry, are so bountifully sustained.

In an era of rapidly constricting publishing opportunities, we are particularly grateful to Peter Agree and the University of Pennsylvania Press for their support. Essay collections are always a gamble for academic presses: we would like to thank Peter for sharing our sense of intellectual urgency in this project and for guiding it so deftly through the review and editing process. Sue and Peter have now worked together on four projects, and she will remain forever grateful for the day twenty years ago that he walked into her office on the campus of the University of California, Santa Barbara, and asked about her first book. This project, like all previous collaborations with Peter, has been a model of the kind of intellectual companionship between author and editor so cherished in the academic community.

Our thanks, finally, to four people who will live to see the Atlantic world change quite beyond our powers to imagine it. To our children: Jane and Matt, Emma and Megan.